MOVED BY COMPASSION

Exploring the Core of Orthodox Christian Spiritual Life

T0339064

Moved by Compassion

Exploring the Core of
Orthodox Christian Spiritual Life

John D. Jones

ST VLADIMIR'S SEMINARY PRESS
YONKERS, NEW YORK
2022

Library of Congress Cataloging-in-Publication Data

Names: Jones, John D., author.
Title: Moved by compassion : exploring the core of Orthodox Christian spiritual life / John D. Jones.
Description: Yonkers, New York : St Vladimir's Seminary Press, 2022. | Includes bibliographical references and index. | Summary: "Though compassion is central to a Christian understanding of God's love for us and the love we ought to have for one another, English translations of Scripture and the Fathers tend to be imprecise, so that eusplanchnia, oiktirmos, eleos, philanthōpia, and sympatheia can all be easily confused. This text is not a historical study of compassion in the Orthodox Christian tradition, nor does it give a purely theoretical or "scholarly" approach to this topic. It is not a guidebook for how to show compassion to others in particular situations. Rather, Moved by Compassion aims to develop a framework, theological and philosophical, in which to explore the dynamics of being moved by compassion and the vital role it plays in Orthodox Christian spiritual life and everyday life generally in order to provide a response to the question "why should we care about being compassionate?" The book draws extensively not only on Scripture and the patristic tradition, but also especially on the hymns of the Church. The author clearly demonstrates the meaning, centrality, and importance of compassion"-- Provided by publisher.
Identifiers: LCCN 2022043686 (print) | LCCN 2022043687 (ebook) | ISBN 9780881417111 (paperback) | ISBN 9780881417128 (kindle edition)
Subjects: LCSH: Compassion--Religious aspects--Christianity. | Christian life.
Classification: LCC BV4647.S9 J65 2022 (print) | LCC BV4647.S9 (ebook) | DDC 241/.4--dc23/eng/20221108
LC record available at https://lccn.loc.gov/2022043686
LC ebook record available at https://lccn.loc.gov/2022043687

COPYRIGHT © 2022 BY
ST VLADIMIR'S SEMINARY PRESS
575 Scarsdale Road, Yonkers, NY 10707
1-800-204-2665
www.svspress.com

ISBN 978-088141-711-1 (paper)
ISBN 978-088141-712-8 (electronic)

The views of the authors of St Vladimir's Seminary Press books
do not necessarily reflect those of the seminary.

PRINTED IN CANADA

To the memory of our son Gabriel
—kind and gentle at heart—
and to everyone who graced his life
with their love and compassion.
~ May his memory be eternal ~

Numbering of the Psalms

Septuagint	Masoretic Text	Septuagint	Masoretic Text
1–8	1–8	115	116.10–19
9	9–10	116–145	117–146
10–112	11–113	146	147.1–11
113	114–115	147	147.12–20
114	116.1–9	148–150	148–150

Table of Contents

List of Abbreviations

ANF   Roberts, Alexander, and James Donaldson, eds. *The Ante-Nicene Fathers: Translations of the Writings of the Fathers down to A.D. 325.* 10 vols. Michigan: Eerdmans, 1998 [repr.]. Online edition: Christian Classics Ethereal Library, <https://www.ccel.org/fathers.html>.

Divine Liturgy, Chrysostom   St Tikhon's Seminary Press. *The Divine Liturgy According to St John Chrysostom with Appendices.* Second Edition. South Canaan, Pennsylvania: St Tikhon's Seminary Press, 1977.

FM   Mary, Mother and Kallistos Ware, trans. *The Festal Menaion.* South Canaan, PA: St Tikhon's Seminary Press, 1998.

FOC 107   Gregory of Nazianzus [Gregory the Theologian]. *Select Orations.* Translated by Martha Vinson. Fathers of the Church Series, vol. 107. Washington: Catholic University of America Press, 2003.

Great Book of Needs   *The Great Book of Needs: Expanded and Supplemented,* 4 vols. South Canaan, Pennsylvania: St Tikhon's Seminary Press, 1999–2002.

Great Octoechos   Eastern Orthodox Church. *The Great Octoechos.* 4 vols. West Roxbury, MA: Sophia Press, 2013.

LT   Mary, Mother and Kallistos Ware, trans. *The Lenten Triodion.* South Canaan, PA: St Tikhon's Seminary Press, 2002.

LT Supp.   Mary, Mother and Kallistos Ware, trans. *The Lenten Triodion: Supplementary Texts.* South Canaan, PA: St Tikhon's Seminary Press, 2007.

mod.   Translation modified.

Menaion, month   Holy Transfiguration Monastery. *The Menaion.* 12 vols. Boston: Holy Transfiguration Monastery, 2005.

NPNF[1] = series 1
NPNF[2] = series 2   Schaff, Philip, and Henry Wace, eds. *A Select Library of Nicene and Post-Nicene Fathers of the Christian Church.* 28 vols. in 2 series. Grand Rapids, MI: Eerdmans, 1997 [repr.]. Online edition: Christian Classics Ethereal Library, <https://www.ccel.org/fathers.html>.

Octoechos	Lambertsen, Isaac, trans. *The Octoechos: The Hymns of the Cycle of the Eight Tones for Sundays and Weekdays.* 4 vols. Liberty, TN: St John of Kronstadt Press, 1999.
Pentecostarion	Holy Transfiguration Monastery. *The Pentecostarion.* Boston: Holy Transfiguration Monastery, 2014.
PG	Migne, J.-P. Patrologiae Cursus Completus, seu bibliotheca universalis. Series Graeca. 161 vols. Paris: Migne, 1857.
Philokalia (English)*	Nikodimos of the Holy Mountain and Markarios of Corinth, comp. *The Philokalia: The Complete Text.* Translated and edited by G. E. H. Palmer, Philip Sherrard, and Kallistos Ware. 4 vols. London: Faber and Faber, 1983–98.
Philokalia (Greek)*	Nikodimos of the Holy Mountain and Makarios of Corinth, comp. *Philokalia tōn hierōn nēptikōn.* 5 vols. Athens: Astir Publishing Co, 1957–63.
PL	Migne, J.-P. Patrologiae Cursus Completus seu bibliotheca universalis. Series Latina. 220 vols. Paris: Migne, 1844.
PPS	Popular Patristics Series. 63 vols., ongoing series. Crestwood and Yonkers, NY: St Vladimir's Seminary Press, 1982–.
Service Books	St Tikhon's Seminary Press. *Service Books of the Orthodox Church.* South Canaan, PA: St Tikhon's Seminary Press, 2010.
Testaments (English)*	Hollander, H. W., and M. de Jong. *The Testaments of the Twelve Patriarchs: A Commentary* [*Testamenta XII Patriarcharum*]. Leiden: E. J. Brill, 1985.
Testaments (Greek)*	Charles, Robert Henry. *The Greek Versions of the Testaments of the Twelve Patriarchs.* London: Adam and Charles Black, 1908.

*Citations of these works in both languages will have the following form with the English edition first and the Greek edition second: (*Philokalia* vol.: p.; Greek vol.: p.) and (*Testaments* p.; Greek p.)

NOTE: Online sources are cited for the lives of the compassionate saints mentioned in Chapter 4, but if anyone would like printed sources, the works by Lawrence Farley and Hieromonk Makarios of Simonos Petra may be consulted (publication details are found in the Bibliography).

Prologue

I have been interested in the nature and role of compassion in human life for many years. The proximate origin of this current project dates back several years to work I did on an Orthodox Christian (or, Eastern Orthodox) approach to poverty.[1] I was interested in how poverty was conceptualized and not just the social or ethical questions about how we ought to respond to poverty. Much of my earlier work on poverty dealt with the stigma of poverty and the tragic way it exacerbates the significant social disaffiliation that often plagues those who are poor in the ordinary social and economic sense. This social disaffiliation, of course, is one of the effects of stigmatization and denigration generally.

In reading St John Chrysostom and St Gregory the Theologian (Gregory Nazianzen), I was struck by their significant concern that people who were poor or seriously afflicted in other ways (e.g., by leprosy) were denigrated and stigmatized by others, as well as how that stigmatization resulted in significant social marginalization and dehumanization. This was particularly clear in St Gregory's Oration 14, *On the Love of the Poor*. In reading both Fathers, it was also evident that their rebuke of those who lacked compassion and stigmatized others was not just about their general lack of assistance to such people, but about the very ways in which they viewed or objectified them. Even if such people might give alms or some form of assistance to others, the spiritual and moral value of that assistance was eliminated by their denigration of people.

Over time, this provided a very important anchor and stimulus for the present work: compassion is not just about how we treat people through actions but, in a prior sense, about how we view and understand them. Stigmatization and denigration undermine a basic feature of compassion; namely, in compassion, as many patristic texts make clear, we do not judge, despise, or denigrate others but fully affirm them in their humanity as made in the image and the likeness of God. Moreover, stigmatization and denigration are deeply visceral and affective, and not merely cognitive, in nature. They involve a disordered and toxic heart and not

[1]John D. Jones, "Confronting Poverty and Stigmatization: An Eastern Orthodox Perspective," *Philosophy and Theology* 18.1 (2007): 169–94.

only a confused mind. I will argue that compassion for others, which is rooted in the heart, is a powerful corrective for stigmatization and other toxic passions, and that it is far more potent than mere cognitive appeals to reason alone. This is also one of the basic reasons I have worked to distinguish compassion from pity. Among other differences between them, pity, especially as we understand that term today, is perfectly compatible with judging and denigrating people; compassion is not.

Along with many patristic and other Orthodox Christian writings that exhort us about the crucial importance of being compassionate—and, more importantly, the remarkable witness to compassion in the personal lives and collective actions of many Orthodox Christians—one text attributed to St John of Damascus is particularly striking. It comes at the close of the work on *Virtues and Vices*, in which, after indicating what it means to be created in the image of God, he concludes:

> Every human is said to be made in the likeness of God as regards his posses-
> sion of the principle of virtue and as regards his imitation of God through
> virtuous and godlike actions. Such actions consist in being disposed with
> *philanthrōpia* (love of humanity or kindness) towards one's fellow humans;
> in being compassionate, merciful, and loving towards one's fellow servant;
> and in manifesting compassion or tender affection and sympathy to all.[2]

Since all human beings are created in the image of God, the capacity for compassion belongs to all human beings by nature. In the Orthodox Christian tradition, aspiring to the likeness of God is something that we seek through our cooperation with God's grace. It refers to our growth in the perfection and flourishing of our life in Christ, of becoming living icons of Christ. We often think of compassion as an emotion that wells up at times in people in response to various situations. For St John of Damascus, however, compassion is a virtue—an abiding disposition or character trait that is essential to our lives. This provided a second stimulus and a primary guiding question for the present study: in what sense is compassion a virtue or a persistent disposition and orientation towards others that responds to suffering, affliction, and vulnerability?

---

[2]John of Damascus, *On the Virtues and Vices* (*Philokalia* 2:341; Greek 2:238). Attributed to St John of Damascus by St Nikodimos, one of the compilers of the *Philokalia*, the actual author is unknown. Versions of the work appear in the writings attributed to the early patristic authors such as St Athanasius of Alexandria and St Ephrem the Syrian. But as the editors of the English edition of the *Philokalia* note, "it is a concise and clear summary of standard ascetic teaching" (*Philokalia* 2:333).

The third stimulus for this project has been my own lived experience as an Orthodox Christian and priest participating in the worship services of the Church. In serving the Divine Liturgy, for example, I have found myself constantly drawn to the multiple references in the liturgical prayers in which we commemorate God's compassion, mercy, and *philanthrōpia* as well as when we pray that he will impart them in the Liturgy—most especially at the consecration and subsequent distribution of the Gifts of bread and wine as the holy Body and Blood of Christ. In addition to these references, there are, as you will see in Chapter 4, pervasive references in the hymns of the Church to the compassion of Christ, the Theotokos, and the saints. They provide a remarkably robust commemoration of divine and human compassion throughout the entire church year. Given that our engagement with others is often referred to as a "liturgy after the Liturgy,"[3] it became important for me to draw on and explore the rich treasury of service texts and hymns that celebrate compassion.

Much to my surprise, I could find no sustained examination of the role of compassion in the Orthodox Christian tradition. The work by Demetrios Constantelos and others has provided a sustained discussion of the role of *philanthrōpia* in this tradition. I have listed some of his principal works in the bibliography. But while the realities of *philanthrōpia*—as the Orthodox Christian tradition understands it—and compassion are very close, they are related, it seems to me, somewhat like the different timbres, registers, and voices of a choir.

The Greek terms used to express compassion in the Greek patristic and Byzantine tradition are different from *philanthrōpia*, and they have a rich history reaching back into the Septuagint text of the Old Testament, the Synoptic Gospels, and other writings around the time of Christ (e.g., *The Testaments of the Twelve Patriarchs*). I have drawn on those texts in exploring the meaning of compassion in ways that I have not seen in discussions about *philanthrōpia*.

The present study is in one sense very personal. It reflects my own efforts as an Orthodox Christian and priest and also as a philosopher to make sense of the role of compassion in the spiritual life of Orthodox Christians and in human life generally, and to understand it. As you will see, philosophical and theological concerns are interwoven with pastoral and moral concerns. My principal aim, however, is profoundly "practical": why should we care about being compassionate as human beings and also as Orthodox Christians? The phrase, "being moved

[3] See Ion Bria, *The Liturgy after the Liturgy: Mission and Witness from an Orthodox Perspective* (Geneva: WCC Publications, 1996). Fr Bria notes that this idea dates back to the mid-1970s (p. 19).

by compassion," translates a Greek verb, *splanchnizomai*, that is uniquely applied to Christ in the Synoptic Gospels and that Christ uses to characterize several people in his parables (e.g., the father in the parable of the prodigal son and the Samaritan in the parable of the good Samaritan). What does compassion, being moved by compassion, have to do with the task of becoming a living icon of Christ?

In this work, I do not intend to offer a historical study of compassion in the Orthodox Christian tradition of the sort that is reflected in the remarkable scholarship of Demetrios Constantelos. I am not attempting to develop a purely theoretical or "scholarly" approach to this topic. I am not attempting to offer a guidebook for how to show compassion to others in particular situations. Rather, my work aims to develop a framework, theological and philosophical, in which to explore the dynamics of being moved by compassion and the vital role it plays in Orthodox Christian spiritual life and everyday life generally in order to provide a response to the question, "Why should we care about being compassionate?" I will expand on what this framework involves in Chapter 1.

I have tried to cite many relevant patristic texts as well as prayers and hymns from Orthodox services. Given their importance and beauty, I have made a special effort to "document" them in extended quotations. I have done this especially for the hymns since they are not likely to be known apart from the context of the worship services in which they occur. Yet the material I have cited barely scratches the surface of extant patristic and Orthodox Christian writings, prayers, and hymns regarding compassion.

Orthodox Christians have no monopoly on compassion. After all, as I noted above, patristic authors regularly refer to a capacity for natural compassion or a compassion that we have by nature. Dialogue with other Christian and non-Christian religious traditions on the role of compassion in human life would be extremely useful for everyone. So too would dialogue with those who explore the reality of compassion outside the context of any religious tradition. But those projects well exceed the scope of this work.

As you venture forth in reading this work, keep in mind this text by St Gregory the Theologian (Gregory Nazianzus):

> Contemplation [especially prayer and worship] is a beautiful thing, as is action: the one because it rises above this world and advances towards the Holy of Holies and conducts our mind upward to what is akin to it, the other

because it welcomes Christ and serves Him and confirms the power of love through good works. . . . We must regard charity [or, love] as the first and greatest of the commandments . . . its most vital part is love of the poor, compassion, and sympathy for our fellow humans. Of all things, nothing so serves God as mercy because no other thing is more proper to God.[4]

---

[4]Gregory of Nazianzus, *Oration* 14.4–5 (FOC 107:41–2; PG 35:864). Compassion, as we will see in Chapter 6, is not limited to mercy alone, but extends also to seeking justice for people.

Acknowledgments

I would like to thank my wife, Presbytera Eileen, for her ongoing support, conversations, and suggestions about my work. We are, of course, to be moved by compassion and not just think about it. I am most thankful to the members of my family for all of the ways in which they have worked to express compassion, in thought and in action, in their lives. I am also most grateful to St Vladimir's Seminary Press and their staff for accepting this book and bringing it to publication. My colleague and friend, Rev. Bogdan Bucur, has also been a very valuable support.

As this is the first book-length study of compassion in the Orthodox Christian tradition, it took a good deal of time and extensive computer work to identify, digitize, and search a wide range of relevant sources in Greek and Latin and also in English and other modern languages. I was very fortunate in this endeavor to work with several research assistants while I was active in the philosophy department at Marquette University: Catlyn Origitano, Jennifer Sorensen, Daniel Adsett, Shaila Wadhwani, Rory O'Donnell, and Jeffrey Smeland. My thanks to all of them.

As I mention in the Prologue, executing this project has involved interweaving my professional work as a philosopher and my pastoral work as a priest. One of my great enjoyments has been to fruitfully integrate my work as a scholar with teaching. The Marquette Philosophy Department provided more than a few opportunities to relate this project to teaching at the graduate and undergraduate level. The community of Holy Theophany Church in Walworth, WI, an OCA mission at which I am priest-in-charge, has been very supportive with the many ways I have linked the themes of this book to preaching and to working with them. So too, with the community and Very Rev. Thomas Mueller at Saints Cyril and Methodius Church in Milwaukee, which I attended for many years as a parishioner, deacon, and associate priest.

Finally, I want to thank two friends and fellow clergy, Protodeacon George Potym, who serves with me at Holy Theophany Church, and Rev. David Moga (Rector, St Nicholas Antiochian Church, Cedarburg, WI) who have been very supportive, patient, and helpful with many conversations about the subject matter of this book.

CHAPTER I

Introduction

" The Lord God, compassionate, merciful, long suffering, and most merciful."[1] Thus God proclaims his name and reveals himself to Moses on Mount Sinai. In this theophany, God reveals his glory and goodness to Moses to show that he will not forsake or abandon the Israelites. Compassion and mercy, after all, are not fleeting "feelings" for God. They are not simply attributes of some divine essence or "abstract" being. They are fundamental "characteristics" or, in the Orthodox Christian tradition, energies (*energeiai*)[2] of a profoundly personal God, and they express the way he engages with creation.

Experience of God's compassion and mercy pervade Orthodox Christian theology, worship, and life. It is through mercy that God creates beings from nothing.[3] It is because of compassion that God promises to remain with the Israelites despite the frequency with which they forsake him.[4] This same compassionate God promises to offer salvation to all people.[5] It is out of compassion that the Son of God becomes incarnate in human form. His Incarnation, life, crucifixion, death, and Resurrection are expressed in the divine compassion of the good Samaritan.[6]

Compassion, however, does not belong solely to God. God expects us to be compassionate towards others, reflecting the compassion he shows to us.

---

[1] Ex 34.6. I use the Septuagint for translations of the Old Testament since this is the version of the Old Testament that has been used in the Orthodox Christian tradition since the beginning of Christianity. The Hebrew text for this verse begins with "The Lord, the Lord, God..." "Compassionate" translates *rachuwm* (Hebrew) and *oiktirmōn* (Greek); "merciful" translates *channun* (Hebrew) and *eleēmōn* (Greek). See Chapter 1, pp. 90–91 for a brief discussion of the significance of the difference between the Hebrew and Greek variants of this verse.

[2] The notion of divine energies (*energeiai*) plays a distinctive role in the Greek patristic and Byzantine understanding of God. See Appendix 2, pp. 265–68, for a very brief discussion of this notion. Also, see Chapter 5, below for a relevant text from St Gregory of Nyssa.

[3] "We give thanks unto you, O King invisible ... who ... in the greatness of your mercy (*eleos*) brought all things from non-existence into being...." (Head-bowing prayer, Liturgy of St John Chrysostom [*Service Books*, 77]. I will discuss this idea in some detail in Chapter 5, pp. 207–209.

[4] Cf. Neh 9.6–31. See Chapter 3, pp. 95–96 for the text.

[5] Is 49.6, 8–13. See Chapter 3, p. 97 for the text.

[6] Christ, according to various patristic authors, is the good Samaritan (Lk 10.25–37). John W. Welch, "The Good Samaritan: A Type and Shadow of the Plan of Salvation," *BYU Studies* 38.2 (1999): 79–80 provides a good discussion of the patristic identification of Christ with the good Samaritan.

Thus says the Lord Almighty: render just [or, "righteous"] judgment, and show mercy and compassion (Heb. *racham*, Gr. *oiktirmōn*) every one with his brother. Oppress not the widow, or the fatherless, or the stranger, or the poor; and let not one of you remember in his heart the injury of his brother.[7]

Created in the image and according to the likeness of God, we are fundamentally dependent upon God and interdependent with each other and, one should add, with the natural world as well. The essentially social, interdependent nature of humanity reflects the eternal *koinōnia*, or fellowship, of the persons of the Trinity.[8] In being compassionate—better, in living compassionately—we reflect the compassion and mercy of God the Father, the Son, and the Holy Spirit towards all creation. As our Lord says: "Be merciful (*oiktirmones* or 'compassionate') just as your Father also is merciful (*oiktirmōn* or 'compassionate')."[9] We are to be neighbors to each other as our Lord shows us in the parable of the good Samaritan.[10] Indeed, our love for one another is to express and be modeled on the love that Christ has shown to us: "I give you a new commandment—love one another as I have loved you."[11]

As compassion and mercy belong fundamentally to God in his relation to creation, they belong—whether we recognize it or not—fundamentally to us. The psalmist tells us that God crowns us with mercy and compassion.[12] In creating us in his image and according to his likeness, God shares his own compassion and mercy by investing us by nature with the power and freedom to actualize compassion and mercy in the world around us.[13] Orthodox Christians often make a distinction between image and likeness. Being made in the image of God is what pertains to us as humans by nature—that is, our rationality and our freedom.

---

[7]Zech 7.9–10. I will typically supply a transliterated version of relevant Greek and/or Hebrew words in quotations or the body of the text within parentheses. This will allow the reader to get a sense of these terms. This is important because in dictionaries and translations, there is simply no one-to-one mapping of English terms with corresponding Greek or Hebrew terms. In Appendix 1, I have provided information that the reader can use to explore the meanings of these terms.

[8]Cf. Kallistos Ware, "The Mystery of the Human Person," *Sobornost (incorporating Eastern Churches Review)* new series 3.1 (1981): 62–69.

[9]Lk 6.36. The Greek *oiktirmōn* is often translated as "merciful" in this text although "compassionate" is the common translation of the term in the Septuagint. There are a number of English translations of this phrase that use "compassion" rather than "merciful," cf. <https://biblehub.com/luke/6–36.htm>, April 20, 2020. A thought question for the reader: Are compassion and mercy the same thing for God? Are they for us?

[10]Lk 10.25–37.

[11]Jn 13.34.

[12]Ps 102(103).4. I will list the Septuagint (LXX) psalm number first and the Hebrew number in parentheses.

[13]See Chapter 5, pp. 226–27.

What pertains to us in this sense is never completely lost as a result of sin. On the other hand, being made according to the likeness of God is something that we attain by God's grace together with our cooperation or synergy.[14] Becoming like God is a process that we call salvation or deification. The virtue of being compassionate is one of the key traits that are to be cultivated by those who strive to attain a likeness to God.

A disposition (*diathesis*) is a settled state or condition of a person. Virtues are dispositions. As a virtue, compassion is a settled disposition and not simply an occasional emotion or feeling. If someone performs acts of compassion (*eleēmosynē*) only occasionally or for an improper reason such as vanity, that person would not be called merciful or compassionate (*eleēmōn* or *oiktirmōn*). Compassion is a virtue when, like every other virtue, it is a stable character trait or disposition that is manifested persistently.[15] Noting that we are created in the image of God in relation to the "dignity of [our] intellect and soul," St John of Damascus provides this brief account of what it means to be created in the likeness of God:

> Every human is said to be made in the likeness of God as regards his possession of the principle of virtue and as regards his imitation of God through virtuous and godlike actions. Such actions consist in being disposed with *philanthrōpia*[16] towards one's fellow humans, in being compassionate (*oikteirein*), merciful (*eleein*), and loving (*agapan*) towards one's fellow servant, and in manifesting compassion (*eusplanchnia*) and sympathy (*sympatheia*) to all.[17]

This text from St John reflects pervasive references and exhortations to compassion throughout the Orthodox Christian tradition. Celebration of the Trinity's and Christ's[18] compassion and mercy, as well as that of the Theotokos and

---

[14] "Synergy" translates the Greek word *synergeia* that refers to the cooperation (i.e., working together) of humans with God especially in terms of actions: faith without works is dead (cf. Jas 2.17). See Michael Prokurat, et al., *Historical Dictionary of the Orthodox Church* (Lanham, MD: Scarecrow Press, 1996), 321; John Meyendorff, *Byzantine Theology* (New York: Fordham University Press, 1987), 139; Georges Florovsky, *The Byzantine Ascetic and Spiritual Fathers*, trans. Raymond Miller (Vaduz, Liechtenstein: Büchervertriebsanstalt, 1987), 38, 49–50, and 52–3.

[15] John of Damascus, *On the Virtues and Vices* (*Philokalia* 2:339–40; Greek 2:236–7).

[16] In the Byzantine tradition, *philanthrōpia*, and *agapē* are virtually identified. Demetrios J. Constantelos, *Byzantine Philanthropy and Social Welfare* (New Brunswick, NJ: Rutgers University Press, 1968), 3.

[17] John of Damascus, *On the Virtues and Vices* (cf. *Philokalia* 2:341; Greek 2:238).

[18] Christ, of course, is the incarnate Son of God, the second Person of the Trinity: the God-man who is both one in essence (*homoousios*) with the Father and Holy Spirit and one in essence (*homoousios*) with human beings

many saints, abound in various hymns and prayers. "Lord have mercy" (*Kyrie eleēson*) is perhaps the most frequently offered prayer in the Orthodox Church. There are more than 3,400 references to mercy (*eleos*[19]) in the service texts for the Church, e.g., the various liturgies, other sacramental services (e.g., Baptism, Marriage, and so forth.), the *Octoechos, Menaion, Triodion*, and the *Pentecostarion*.[20] Moreover, evocations of compassion (*oiktirmos* and *splanchnon/eusplanchnia*), philanthropy/love of man/humanity/kindness (*philanthrōpia*), sympathy (*sympatheia*) also abound in these texts. There are about 1,300 references to *oiktirmos*, about 1,600 references to *splanchnon/eusplanchnia*, approximately 400 references to *sympatheia*, and more than 1,900 references to *philanthrōpia*. These multiple references complement the more than 1,300 references to *agapē*. There are also a few references to hospitality (*philoxenia*).

References to compassion abound in other Orthodox Christian writings. Oddly, however, so far as I can tell, there is no sustained work that focuses specifically on the nature and role of compassion in the Orthodox Christian tradition. There are numerous references to compassion in works of Orthodox scholars, but they often involve a simple mention of compassion without any more extensive study of what is meant by compassion. I am not aware of any modern scholarship that develops an Orthodox Christian understanding of compassion as found in the lives of Orthodox Christians or with reference to compassion in Scripture or in the many hymns of the Church. Fr Boris Bobrinskoy's work, *The Compassion of the Father*,[21] is the only book that specifically addresses divine compassion in any extensive manner. There is also a very perceptive although brief discussion about

---

(Fourth Ecumenical Council, of Chalcedon, AD 451). Citations to Christ's compassion refer to the distinctive compassion the Son of God shows as the incarnate Christ. Citations to the compassion of God and Christ, or of the Trinity and Christ are intended to remind the reader of the compassion or mercy of the Trinity itself (e.g., in creating the world, etc.), and the distinctive compassion of Christ (e.g., in healing people or in assuming the cross for our sake).

[19] I include all of the related parts of speech for this term and the following terms.

[20] The List of Abbreviations at the beginning of this book shows the editions of these works that I am using. See Chapter 4, pp. 126–28 for further information about these service books. The Greek texts that I have primarily consulted for these service books can be found at "Greek Liturgical Texts of the Orthodox Church," <https://glt.goarch.org/>, April 20, 2020. This site is hosted by the Greek Orthodox Archdiocese of America. The data I provided has been obtained by searching texts from this site together with other digitized versions of Orthodox Christian services in Greek.

[21] Boris Bobrinskoy, *The Compassion of the Father*, trans. Anthony P. Gythiel (Crestwood, NY: St Vladimir's Seminary Press, 2003). Although he offers no focused discussion on compassion itself, Fr Bobrinskoy weaves a rich tapestry of ways in which compassion animates God—the Trinity—and Christ, and should also animate us. I will cite many of them in footnotes throughout the text.

the nature of compassion and God's impassibility in Paul L. Gavrilyuk's work, *The Suffering of the Impassible God.*[22]

There are also several works that focus on the notion of *philanthrōpia.*[23] In the Orthodox Christian tradition, *philanthrōpia* comes to be a decisive characterization of God's love for us and a norm for our love for others. At times, this term is even translated as compassion or "social compassion."[24] The term itself is borrowed from the classical Greek tradition. It plays virtually no explicit or foundational role in the Old and New Testament. The meanings that *philanthrōpia* acquire that identify it with some understanding of Christian compassion need to be linked, in my view, with the terms and corresponding concepts that are used to express compassion in the Old and New Testament and in early writings such as the *Testament of Zebulun* in the *Testaments of the Twelve Patriarchs.*[25] Unfortunately, none of the modern studies of the meaning of *philanthrōpia* in the Orthodox Christian tradition, which I have seen, seeks to interpret the expressions of compassion in these ancient works. For the most part the meaning of compassion, if the term is mentioned at all, seems to be assumed to have a straightforward definition so that authors and translators do not clearly specify its meaning or clarify the relation of compassion to things such as pity, empathy, and so forth.

Tasks and Goals

Let me briefly set forth the basic tasks and goals for this project. I will explore the nature and fundamental role of compassion in Orthodox Christian theology, tradition, and spiritual life. Theology here does not refer simply to academic concepts and theories. Rather, it is essentially connected with our own lived

[22]Paul L. Gavrilyuk, *The Suffering of the Impassible God* (Oxford: Oxford University Press, 2006), 8–12.

[23]Demetrios J. Constantelos, Poverty, Society and Philanthropy in the Late Mediaeval Greek World (New Rochelle, NY: A. D. Caratzas, 1992); Demetrios J. Constantelos, *Byzantine Philanthropy and Social Welfare* (New Brunswick, NJ: Rutgers University Press, 1968); and Danilo Krstić, *On Divine Philanthropy: from Plato to John Chrysostom* (Los Angeles: Sebastian Press, 2012).

[24]Matthew J. Pereira, ed., *Philanthropy and Social Compassion in Eastern Orthodox Tradition* (New York: Theotokos Press, 2010), 93. Constantelos, "Origins of Christian Orthodox Diakonia: Christian Orthodox Philanthropy in Church History," *Greek Orthodox Theological Review* 52.1–4 (2007): 15, cites the Pseudo-Clementine's (3rd century) definition of *philanthrōpia* that is remarkably similar—as we will see in Chapter 6, p. 243—to the nature of compassion as a neighborliness to everyone without judgment: "The greatness of *philanthrōpia* lies in the fact that it means love *(storgē)* towards any one, whatever one may be as a person, including physical appearance . . . *philanthrōpia* loves and benefits every person because every person is a human being *(anthrōpos)* apart from its [*sic*] personal beliefs . . . every person is a neighbor to every other person."

[25]See Chapter 5, pp. 175–76 for the extensive use I will make of this work in unpacking the meaning of compassion.

experience of God's presence and how we respond to that presence in our lives, especially in and through prayer and worship. Spiritual life means the entirety of our lives as animated by the Holy Spirit, which includes the manifestation of compassion and mercy both individually and corporately or collectively[26] in the lives of laity, clergy, and monastics.

This project has several fundamental goals. Within the Orthodox Christian tradition, I aim to show that:

- The compassion of the Trinity and Christ fundamentally shapes their presence to creation, while, in striving for a likeness to divine compassion, human compassion is not simply an emotion but should be developed as a fundamental virtuous disposition or character trait.

- Compassion does not involve merely how we act towards others. It constitutes a fundamental way of "seeing" or viewing and experiencing all people through holistically affirming them in their humanity and, thus, in their uniqueness as persons. Our compassion is based on a capacity for compassion that all of us have by nature as human beings. But in the Orthodox Christian tradition, we are to realize this virtue in terms of our own created human vocation—a lifelong process of repentance—to develop as living icons of Christ. In other words, the cultivation and manifestation of a settled compassionate disposition is integral to attaining to the likeness of Christ.

- Compassion is rooted in the heart as the holistic center of our existence. Moreover, compassion plays a vital role in resisting and helping us overcome an array of toxic passions that poison our hearts and undermine our relationships with others and also with God. I will focus especially on those passions and attitudes that lead us to stigmatize, denigrate, and marginalize others. In connection with this goal, I will also show that there

---

[26]For the vital importance of collective expressions of compassion and *philanthrōpia* in the life of the Church, see Demetrios Constantelos, "Origins of Christian Orthodox Diakonia," 19–27; Philip LeMasters, "Philanthropia in Liturgy and Life: The Anaphora of Basil the Great and Eastern Orthodox Social Ethics," *St Vladimir's Theological Quarterly* 59.2 (2015): 187–211; and John D. Jones, "The Church as Neighbor: Corporately and Compassionately Engaged," *In Communion* 66 (Winter 2013): 13–24, <http://incommunion. org/2013/04/26/the-church-as-neighbor/>, April 20, 2020. See also the other works listed in the bibliography by Constantelos and also by Timothy S. Miller, *The Birth of the Hospital in the Byzantine Empire* and *The Orphans of Byzantium: Child Welfare in the Christian Empire* (Washington: Catholic University of America Press, 2003), for numerous historical examples of the collective work of the Church during the patristic and Byzantine periods.

are fundamental ways in which compassion is different from pity as it is understood in contemporary discourse.

- Compassion is integral to our responsibility to face the world and live for others. Our understanding of compassion should be grounded in our experience of the compassion that the Trinity and Christ impart to us and, in response to which and through the grace of the Holy Spirit, we are called to manifest our compassion to the world. If our Christian experience of compassion is centered in our worship of the Trinity and Christ, especially in the Divine Liturgy, our manifestation of compassion in the world, both individually and collectively, is fittingly characterized as an integral part of our own liturgy after the Liturgy.[27]

- Compassion is not simply a matter of interpersonal "charity" or mercy but is fully compatible with individual and collective efforts to promote justice and especially social justice in the sense of working to establish inclusive and fair social structures and institutions that are free from the denigration and marginalization of people that so often mar human social life.

- In light of the above, a study of compassion is vital to any Orthodox Christian anthropology and theology.

Establishing a Framework for Examining Compassion in the Orthodox Christian Tradition

As I indicated in the Prologue, I am not attempting to develop a purely theoretical or "scholarly" approach to this topic. I am not aiming to develop some sort of guidelines or specific directives for how we should manifest compassion in our lives in particular situations. Rather, I hope to develop a framework in which compassion is understood, experienced, and lived out in Orthodox Christian spiritual and everyday life. A framework refers to the basic beliefs, concepts, and values that underpin our understanding of reality; the ways by which we know, experience, understand, and interpret some aspect of reality; and the basic normative principles that guide human action in its moral and spiritual dimension. A framework in this broad sense is sometimes referred to as the worldview within which we think about, experience, and act in the world.

[27]Cf. Bobrinskoy, *Compassion*, 30, 109, and 115–16; Ion Bria, "The Liturgy after the Liturgy," *International Review of Missions* 67.265 (1978): 86–90; Philip LeMasters, "Philanthropia in Liturgy and Life," 187–211.

People and cultures adopt a wide range of worldviews. For example, people who adopt a completely materialistic worldview have certain core beliefs about the basic makeup of reality: e.g., whatever exists is material; humans are basically bodies with minds that are identified with the brain; and so forth. This sort of worldview also adopts certain criteria for knowing reality: all of our knowledge of reality, including moral norms and principles, has to be derived from sensory experience. This sort of worldview obviously differs from, and is in fundamental ways incompatible with a worldview that allows for the existence of both material and non-material things, or that allows for forms of knowing and experiencing the world that function independently of sense experience.[28]

In a religious world view, there might be a belief in a divine reality that transcends and creates everything else who, if personal, may reveal things to us that must be apprehended through faith and not only through reason or sense experience. Knowledge will be based on faith in a divine revelation and not on sense experience and reason alone. In developing a framework for thinking about, experiencing, and manifesting compassion in the Orthodox Christian tradition, I aim to set forth the framework, the basic elements of the Orthodox Christian "worldview," in which the understanding and manifestation of compassion are embedded. This framework has several components.

a) Any framework or worldview has certain basic concepts and ideas. Elaborating this part of a framework involves conceptual and descriptive analysis. For this project, these concepts include compassion, mercy, sympathy, being an icon of Christ, and so forth. Developing this aspect of the framework involves a good deal of what philosophers commonly regard as conceptual analysis: clarifying the basic meanings of terms and the concepts to which they refer, comparing and contrasting them, sorting out "grey areas" about what a term denotes, and developing descriptions, as it were, of what is implied by them.[29] Much of this aspect of the framework will be developed in Chapter 2, as well as in Chapters 5 and 6. I will discuss in greater detail how I am employing philosophical analysis in the next section on methodology.

b) The framework is theological in an "intellectual" or "academic" sense. In order to provide a broader theological context for developing the nature and role of compassion, I will lay out the basic Orthodox Christian teachings and

---

[28]Many Western philosophers, such as Plato, Plotinus, Descartes, and Hegel, developed such worldviews.

[29]Cf. John Wilson, *Thinking with Concepts* (Cambridge: Cambridge University Press, 1963) for an excellent discussion and presentation of the "nuts and bolts" of conceptual analysis.

doctrines about God—the Trinity—and Christ as well as the created status of human beings as made according to the image and likeness of God. This aspect of the framework is developed in the sections in Chapter 3 on compassion in the Old and New Testament, and in the opening section of Chapter 5. Some of my comments in Chapter 4, which introduce the feasts of the Christ and the Theotokos, also make use of this approach. In the Orthodox Christian tradition, however, this "intellectual" approach rests on our experience of God and Christ.

c) Hence, the framework is also theological in an experiential sense. Theology in the Orthodox Christian tradition is primarily experiential (e.g., the encounter with the personal presence of the Trinity and Christ in prayer and in worship) and not initially based in a theological or philosophical metaphysics or anthropology.

> Orthodoxy is first of all, an orthodoxy of life. . . . Orthodoxy is before all else, not a doctrine, not an external organization, not an external norm of behavior but a spiritual life, a spiritual experience and a spiritual path. . . . Orthodoxy is primarily liturgical; [the liturgies] themselves give a foreshadowing of transfigured life.[30]

The Orthodox Christian focus for our experience, life, and understanding is on divine and human relationships and community structured by sharing or fellowship (*koinōnia*). Theology is "practiced" and grounded in worship, prayer, being engaged in the ongoing task of repentance, and so forth. I will develop this aspect of the framework by drawing attention to the manifestation of God's compassion within the Divine Liturgy, which is the center of Orthodox Christian experience and life. I will also develop this aspect of the framework in Chapter 4 by setting out the brief selection of the hymns of the Church that celebrate the compassion of Christ, the Theotokos, selected saints, and the exhortations and injunctions in those hymns that remind us of our responsibility to be compassionate. This component of the framework also involves how we experience compassion, not just conceptually or rationally, but in a holistic manner that is centered in the heart as the Orthodox Christian tradition understands it.

In the Orthodox Christian tradition, these two aspects of theology are interconnected. The more rational reflections about theological issues should be

---

[30]Nicholas Berdyaev, "The Truth of Orthodoxy," trans. by Alvian Smirensky, *The Wheel* 8 (2017): 47–48, <https://static1.squarespace.com/static/54d0df1ee4b036ef1e44b144/t/58efc8a6db29d67bb267dc42/149 2109479567/Berdyaev.pdf>, April 20, 2020. Originally printed in *Vestnik Russkogo Zapadno-Evropeiskogo Ekzarkhata* 11 (July 1952): 4–10.

grounded in and reflect what was revealed to and experienced by the apostles and manifest within the holy tradition of the Church; our lived experience of Orthodox worship services; a practical or "pastoral" engagement with Scripture, patristic texts, and other writings; our own spiritual life of prayer, repentance, and so forth. An example of this interconnection can be found in my reflection at the end of Chapter 3 on how divine compassion and our response of being compassionate play a crucial role in the gospel texts for the Sundays that precede the beginning of Great Lent. While these texts could be read "independently," their regular place in the liturgical cycle of the Sunday Divine Liturgies that prepare us for Great Lent provides the context for the reflection I will offer.

d) The scaffolding to the framework that I will develop in Chapters 2–4 provides the basis for developing in some detail the balance of the framework in Chapters 5 and 6: an articulation of the nature and role of compassion in Orthodox Christian spiritual life. As the reader will see, these chapters interweave the philosophical and theological approaches throughout.

Methodology

I have had longstanding interest personally and as a philosopher in the reality of compassion. My participation in the rich liturgical tradition of the Orthodox Church that pervasively and profoundly celebrates compassion, as well as reading an array of patristic authors, such as Saints John Chrysostom and Gregory the Theologian, ignited an interest in exploring compassion in Orthodox Christian spiritual life. Yet after perusing a wide array of literature, both Orthodox Christian and otherwise, I discovered that the more I read, the more perplexed I became about the nature and meaning of compassion, because there is simply no consensus about the meaning of compassion and related terms such as pity, sympathy, and so forth. Moreover, none of the key terms that I want to discuss is used in any consistent manner in the translations of Scripture, or of patristic or liturgical texts.

For example, the relevant Hebrew and Greek terms and the corresponding English terms that express what we call "compassion," "sympathy," "pity," and so forth have a range of meanings. I will explore some of them in Chapter 2. Yet there seems to be no clear agreement among English scholars and translators about the meanings, similarities, and differences for the English terms. English translators rarely make clear what they mean by the English terms they use to translate Greek and Hebrew terms. From a conceptual point of view, this literature was as confusing and perplexing as the literature I read many years ago when I worked on the topics of poverty and human needs.[31] It became extremely clear to me that until I tried to develop some relatively stable definitions and analyses of terms such as compassion, pity, empathy, and so forth, within contemporary English, I simply could not carry out the present project in any way that would be helpful to me or to anyone else.

a) The first part of my methodology or strategy for this project was to bring some conceptual clarification to the key English terms that I was going to use. This is especially important since contemporary meanings of terms such as compassion and pity are not completely the same as those used in earlier periods. I have carried out this strategy primarily in Chapter 2 by sorting out meanings of these terms in a preliminary way by doing the kind of conceptual analysis commonly employed in philosophy.

b) The second part of the method was to identify and provide a preliminary interpretation of major scriptural and liturgical texts that provided a context for thinking about and experiencing compassion. I have executed this part of the method throughout the book but especially in Chapters 3 and 4. While the many liturgical and scriptural texts that I cite provide key clues or indicators for understanding the nature and role of compassion in the Orthodox Christian tradition, I have made no sustained effort in these chapters to develop that understanding. However, I will draw on those clues and indicators in the analysis of compassion in Chapters 5 and 6.

c) Finally, drawing on the work in Chapters 2–4, I will proceed to carry out the sustained analysis of the nature and role of compassion in Chapters 5 and 6. As the reader will see, my discussion in these chapters presupposes and builds upon earlier chapters.

In addition to drawing on a wide range of sources from the Orthodox Christian tradition, I will also draw on a wide range of contemporary sources from various disciplines to assist with my analysis and often to provide contemporary examples of various issues that I discuss: for example, the nature of stigmatization, compassion in relation to the criminal justice system, bullying, justice, and so forth.

---

[31]Cf. John D. Jones, *Poverty and the Human Condition* (New York: Edwin Mellen Press, 1990), 44–53; "Assessing Human Needs," *Philosophy and Theology* 5.1 (fall 1990): 55 and 64; "How Basic Are Basic Needs?" *Journal for Peace and Justice Studies* 8.1 (1997): 37–56.

Organization of the Book

The chapter organization of the book follows from the methodology or strategy that I am employing. In Chapter 2, I will attend to the language we use to talk about compassion and at least sketch some similarities and differences between compassion and various phenomena such as empathy, sympathy, pity, mercy, and justice. I will also discuss the notions of *splanchna* ("bowels" or viscera) and *kardia* (heart) since compassion in the Orthodox Christian tradition is related in a basic way to the "bowels" or viscera as well as to the heart. This chapter basically sets forth the conceptual dimension of the framework I am developing for this project.

As the celebration of and participation in the Eucharist is at the center of Orthodox Christian religious experience and life, I will devote Chapter 3 to some of the key texts of the Divine (i.e., Eucharistic) Liturgies that emphasize the manner in which God's compassion is enacted in the Liturgy. This will provide the background for discussing the nature of God's compassion as manifest in the Old Testament and, through Christ, in the New Testament. I will then focus on a set of gospel texts that are read before Great Lent to provide a discussion of the fundamental role of compassion in Christian life and repentance: what is often called the "liturgy after the Liturgy."

In Chapter 4, I will display and discuss references to compassion in an array of hymns of the Church. These hymns, many of which are quite ancient, express the lived theology or experience of compassion in the Church. In Chapter 5, I will develop the nature and role of compassion in human life in a more systematic manner. The focus of this chapter will be to elucidate the nature of compassion as a disposition and a virtue. Finally, in Chapter 6, I will offer some observations about the relation between compassion and justice and the possible limits to compassionate action in confronting people who do harmful things.

At the beginning of each chapter, I will provide an overview of its contents. At the end of Chapters 2–4, I will provide a Summary and Looking Forward section that will highlight key indicators about compassion within those chapters and that will be used for the more systematic analysis of compassion in Chapters 5 and 6.

CHAPTER 2

Sketching the Lay of the Land
for Exploring Compassion

We experience compassion primarily through the ways in which people treat one another and in the ways that God relates to us. However, we express this reality in words—indeed an array of words that are more or less closely related: "compassion," "pity," "sympathy," "mercy," "empathy," and so forth. We find a similar array of terms in Greek and also in Hebrew. We can, of course, inquire about the meaning(s) of these various terms. We can wonder how to translate various terms in one language such as Hebrew into another language such as Greek or English. Yet every translation involves some level of interpretation. Hence, the question of how to translate a certain phrase from one language into another already raises the question of how the translator "hears" or understands words in the original language (e.g., Hebrew) and in the target language (e.g., Greek or English).

For example, the Hebrew word *racham* and the related adjective *rachuwm* are translated in the Greek Septuagint variously by *oiktirmos*, *eleos*, and their related parts of speech. The same Greek terms are also often used to translate *chanan*. *Oiktirmos* is used about sixty percent of the time to translate *racham*; *eleos* about forty percent of the time. However, *eleos* is used about eighty percent of the time to translate *chanan*. *Oiktirmos* is usually translated in English by "compassion" or "pity," *eleos* by "mercy," even though "pity" and "compassion" are common English translations of the various forms of this word as it appears in classical Greek texts. One need only consult various English translations of the Septuagint to see varying translation choices. For the most part, however, the New American Standard Bible (NASB) translation of the Hebrew (Masoretic) text of the Old Testament (abbreviated MT) renders *racham* and its related terms by "compassion." The Septuagint, then, effectively seems to blur the difference between distinct terms *chanan* and *racham* by using *oiktirmos* and *eleos* for both. Does this matter? Are the English terms "compassion," "mercy," and "pity" virtual synonyms of each other as is suggested in a number of glossaries and dictionaries? Or are there differences in meaning among them to which we should attend?

As I indicated in Chapter 1, clarifying what we mean by "compassion," "pity," or "sympathy" is extremely important if we are to develop a framework for understanding compassion in the Orthodox Christian tradition. We have to carry out this clarification with respect to how we understand terms in our own English language. So, this chapter will be devoted to what philosophers commonly call conceptual analysis: exploring the meanings of various terms and trying to specify similarities and differences between them as they bear on the project for this book.

I am not concerned simply with exploring various dictionary definitions. Rather, the analysis in this chapter involves trying to clarify for ourselves as far as possible the nature of and relation among several things—the realities signified by words—while trying as far as possible to avoid blurring boundaries between them. This is fundamentally a practical and moral issue concerning how we live in the world and relate to others. It is not simply a conceptual issue.

Let me expand on this issue a bit since in my experience more than a few people think that philosophers' (and anyone else's) concern with conceptual analysis is a mere "head trip" that is basically irrelevant for daily life. But consider Socrates. In various Platonic dialogues, Socrates spends a good deal of time exploring possible definitions of terms such as "virtue," "knowledge," and "piety."[1] While he is very much concerned with carefully defining terms, what we would likely call "conceptual analysis," it is abundantly clear that he does this for the practical task of living. After all, as he says, we cannot very well understand whether justice or virtue are valuable in human life until we have some clear understanding of what we mean by those terms.[2]

For example, we might be very much concerned to direct our energies to being compassionate to those in need.[3] But what might we mean by compassionate treatment of others? Is that the same as pitying others? If not, why? Can compassionate treatment of people who are in need, e.g., those who are poor, be reduced to "almsgiving" from a distance or patronage forms of charity that maintain social distances between those who are "respectable" and those who are poor? Do we have to make ourselves needy, e.g., poor, to be compassionate towards those who

---

[1] See Plato's *Meno*, *Theaetatus*, and *Euthyphro* respectively.

[2] Plato, *Republic* 1, 354C.

[3] Perhaps even more so than is the case with compassion, sorting out what "human needs" are involves a conceptual quagmire. Cf. John D. Jones, "Assessing Human Needs," 55–64; "How Basic are Basic Needs?" 37–56; and Katrin Lederer, ed., *Human Needs: A Contribution to the Current Debate* (Cambridge, MA: Oelgeschlager, Gunn, and Hain, Inc., 1980).

are poor? Is that what compassion involves when we say that in being compassionate, we suffer with others? Does compassion for others require empathy for them? Does compassion for others involve simply providing others with whatever they might need or desire? Can compassion for others involve a kind of "tough love" for others?

The practical import of a careful and precise thinking about concepts is not just a philosophical, secular concern. We see this same importance in the precision of conceptual and logical analysis that has been involved in the formulation of key dogmas of the Orthodox Christian Church. Of course, at the core of Orthodox Christian faith there is a profound stress on the utter unknowability of God's nature.[4] So too, there is a fundamental paradoxical character to the Incarnation that none of us can wrap our minds around. Liturgical worship and prayer open us to the divine revelation of a mystery to which we respond most fundamentally with silence and wonder—a spiritual awareness that goes beyond all concepts and images.

Yet we bring this mystery into language such as the language of Scripture, parables, hymns, and devotional poetry. Moreover, there is also the language of dogma that is found in the Symbol of Faith: the Nicene-Constantinopolitan Creed (AD 381). One essential part of that creed declares that the Son of God is *homoousios* (one in being or essence) with the Father. The formulation of that dogma involved an extraordinary labor of conceptual analysis and argumentation in clarifying and making precise the differences and relation between *ousia* (being or essence), *hypostasis* (person), and *energeia* (energy). This was done to provide a dogmatic definition of the divinity of the Son of God in order to shield the Orthodox Christian faith from the wide range of what were determined to be heretical attacks on it. Fr Georges Florovsky's observation about the nature of dogma is worth noting:

> Dogma is the testimony of thought about what has been seen and revealed . . . and this testimony is expressed in concepts and definitions. Dogma is an "intellectual vision" . . . a "logical icon" of Divine Reality. And at the same time, a dogma is a definition—that is why its logical form is so important for dogma, that "inner word," which acquires force in its external expression. This is why the external aspect of dogma—its wording—is so essential.[5]

[4] See Appendix 2 for some texts that illustrate this.

[5] Georges Florovsky, "Revelation, Philosophy and Theology," in *Creation and Redemption,* trans. Richard Haugh (Belmont, MA: Nordland Publishing Co., 1976), 29.

Our recitation of the Symbol of Faith is not simply an intellectual exercise that we recite before the anaphora (eucharistic) prayer. Rather, our recitation and acceptance of that creed affirms core beliefs about our faith as set forth by the Church that are vital if we are to honestly partake of the eucharistic Gifts of the Body and Blood of our Lord.

As the title of this chapter indicates, I will spend most of the chapter sketching out conceptual relations between compassion, sympathy, empathy, pity, mercy, and justice. I will wait until Chapter 5 to develop the robust understanding of compassion as I believe it is found in the Orthodox Christian tradition. I will do that after we have looked at the expression of compassion in the Divine Liturgy, Scripture, and the hymns of the Church. Throughout this chapter, however, I will focus on common definitions of compassion as an emotion or affective state. The more robust Orthodox Christian understanding of compassion as a cultivated virtuous disposition or abiding character trait will be postponed until Chapter 5.

I will spend a significant section of this chapter exploring what I believe are fundamental differences between compassion and pity as we understand the term "pity" today. I want to do this because in modern dictionaries as well as dictionaries of Greek or Hebrew terms "compassion" and "pity" seem more or less synonymous. As the reader will see, however, there are significant differences between them in our own contemporary English that are crucial to highlight for this project. To bring out these differences, I will draw on some sources from outside the Orthodox Christian tradition. In particular, I will use Bishop Joseph Buter's very perceptive contrast between compassion and pity to provide a point of departure for my analysis. Also, I will make extensive use of Stefan Zweig's novel *Beware of Pity* to draw out what I believe are central features of pity in our modern sense, which simply do not belong to the notion of compassion.

Zweig's novel, in my estimation, is a simply brilliant literary presentation of the features of pity that I am trying to isolate. There is nothing comparable in any patristic texts.[6] One of my basic concerns has been that English translators rarely make clear what they mean by terms such as "pity," "compassion," or "sympathy" when they translate texts. The great advantage to Zweig's novel is that he is quite clear what term he uses for pity (*Mitleid*) and how he understands this term.[7] The English translation nearly always respects the consistency of his terminology.

---

[6]While there may be something in Russian literature (e.g., Dostoevsky), I do not read Russian and will not work with English translations without having some ability to look at the original text.

[7]There is one key text, however, where *Mitleid* takes on different meanings. See below, Chapter 2 (pp. 53–5), for a discussion of this text.

Hence, the novel provides an excellent source for the sort of conceptual analysis I am doing.

For the last section of this chapter, I am going to switch gears a bit and look at the relation between compassion, the "bowels" (*splanchna*), and the heart (*kardia*). In particular, the Greek term *splanchna* has a metaphorical or transferred meaning referring to the seat of our emotions. The chief issue for this section is how we might render that term in English since as the reader will see, the traditional English rendering of the Greek with "bowels" makes use of a meaning of that English term that we now regard as archaic and misleading for a translation of *splanchna*. While *kardia* is uniformly translated in English as "heart," it is important for this project to have a sense of what this means in the Orthodox Christian tradition.

In the final section of the chapter, Summary and Looking Forward, I will provide a brief review of this chapter and point out several indicators about compassion in this chapter that will be developed in Chapters 5 and 6. Let me turn, then, to developing the conceptual map for this project.

Compassion and Sympathy

Consider these three texts:

1) O God: You are holy, almighty, all-powerful, good, fearful, merciful, and *most sympathetic* (*sympathēs malista*) to your creatures. You made man from earth after your own image and likeness. You gave him the joy of paradise; and when he transgressed your commandment, and fell away, you did not disregard nor desert him, O Good One ... but sent your only-begotten Son Himself, our Lord Jesus Christ, into the world, that he by his coming might renew and restore your image.[8]

2) You alone know the weakness of mankind's nature, yet in *sympathy* (*sympatheia*) you took up its form. ...[9]

3) But remember the former days, when, after being enlightened, you endured a great conflict of sufferings, partly by being made a public spectacle

[8]Anaphora Prayer, *Divine Liturgy of St James the Holy Apostle and Brother of the Lord* (ANF 7.544 mod.). My italics.

[9]Octoechos, Tone 1, Sunday, Matins, Canon 3, Ode 3, Irmos; *The Octoechos or the Book of Eight Tones* (Otego, NY: Archdiocese of Canada, 2005), 18 (modified). The translation in this text has "compassion" for *sympatheia* although "sympathy" is a common translation of the term in Greek-English dictionaries.

through reproaches and tribulations, and partly by becoming companions with those who were so treated. For you *showed sympathy* (*synepathēsate*) to the prisoners[10] and joyfully accepted the seizure of your property, knowing that you have for yourself a better possession and a lasting one.[11]

The English word "sympathy" in these texts is a literal translation of the Greek word *sympatheia*. "Showed sympathy" or "sympathizes" translate the corresponding verb *sympatheō*. "Sympathy" typically means to share in someone's feelings or to express one's own feelings of commiseration, condolence, or support for someone in light of a certain loss, affliction, or difficulty. Sympathy, of course, is different from empathy—at least if the latter term means to be able to put oneself into the position of how another person experiences something. It is hard, of course, to see how people could sympathize with anyone if they did not have some sense of what it means to suffer some sort of loss or distress. Sympathy, however, at least as we typically understand the term, certainly does not require that someone understand in any specific or detailed way what another person is enduring, e.g., the violation of rape and its aftermath.

Sympathy, as a kind of fellow-feeling for people, also need not lead to any sort of action on their behalf to relieve their distress or even to comfort them. But besides referring to a kind of fellow-feeling with others, the Greek term *sympatheia* can also have a sense of being moved to actively assist them and even bear with or suffer with them—that is, to establish a fellowship with them in order to assist them. *Sympatheia* in this more robust sense begins to resemble compassion.

Our English term "compassion" is derived from the Latin *compassio*, which is one of the Latin terms that is used to translate the Greek term *sympatheia*. *Compassio* is a literal translation of *sympatheia*.[12] It can have the weak sense of a kind of fellow-feeling for others. It can, however, have a more basic meaning of "suffering

---

[10]The Greek text at this point has two versions: *tois desmiois synepathēsate* ("sympathized with the prisoners") and *tois desmiois mou synepathēsate* ("sympathized with me in my bonds [or, "chains"]"). The latter reading is found in a number of Greek editions of the New Testament—e.g., the Textus Receptus of Stephanus (1550), the Textus Receptus of Scrivener (1894), the Byzantine Majority Text, Ecumenical Patriarch of Constantinople (1904)—as well as English translations of the New Testament, e.g., The King James Version (KJV) and NKJV. However, both Bruce Metzger, *A Textual Commentary on the Greek New Testament,* 2nd ed. (New York: American Bible Society, 2002), 600–01, and Frederic Gardiner, ed. and trans., *Chrysostom's Commentary on the Epistle to the Hebrews* (NPNF[1] 14:461, n. 1337) argue that the first version is the oldest. I am using the first version since that is the text that Chrysostom uses and to which I allude below.

[11]Heb 10.32–34 NASB, my italics.

[12]*Compassio* is called a calque or loan translation of *sympatheia*.

with" someone in the sense of sharing in and even bearing someone's burdens or suffering.[13] Tertullian, who seems to be the first to use *compassio*, employs the term to describe not merely fellow-feeling but the way in which the soul's *compassio* with the body—its suffering with the body—belongs to the soul so that the body and soul suffer together (*compati*). His reason is that through this compassion or co-suffering, the soul will be glorified together with the body when the body is resurrected from the dead.[14]

Sympatheia as compassion points to an affective response to the suffering or distress of others in order to act on their behalf for their sake and not simply one's own. It is perhaps not surprising that in the two liturgical texts I cited, "compassion" can be and, in fact, is used to translate *sympatheia*. When we use "compassion" in place of the English term "sympathy," we likely "hear" these texts in a different manner. Consider the first text above:

1) O God: you are holy, almighty, all-powerful, good, fearful, merciful, and most *compassionate* to your creatures. You made man from earth after your own image and likeness. You gave give him the joy of paradise; and when he transgressed your commandment, and fell away, you did not disregard nor desert him, O Good One . . .

"Compassionate" in this text makes reference to one of the principal characteristics of God's compassion for the Israelites in the Old Testament: that he is committed to them as a people through his actions on their behalf and that he will not forsake or abandon them.[15] The same is true of the compassion that "drives" the Incarnation of the Son of God: after the Resurrection, he tells the disciples, "I am with you always, even to the end of the age."[16]

Replacing "sympathy" with "compassion" in the second text, we have:

2) You alone know the weakness of mankind's nature, yet in *compassion*, you took up its form. . . .

While the English term "sympathy" in our contemporary usage suggests perhaps only certain "feelings" that God has for us, "compassion" emphasizes the action

---

[13]See Chapter 4, hymns H-48 and H-49, TBD, for examples of *sympatheia* used as compassion.

[14]Tertullian, *De resurrectione carnis* 40, ed. and trans. Ernest Evans (London: SPCK, 1960), 112, lines 45–55, <http://www.tertullian.org/articles/evans_res/evans_res_03latin.htm> and <http://www.tertullian.org/articles/evans_res/evans_res_04english.htm>, April 20, 2020. Evans translates *compassio* as "suffering together."

[15]See Chapter 3, pp. 90–94.

[16]Mt 28.20.

that flows from his knowledge or awareness of our weakness. Translating *sympatheia* by "compassion" draws out the fundamental impetus to action that belongs to God's *sympatheia* for us in a way that our English "sympathy" does not. It is not surprising, then, that the second translation I cited for this verse used "compassion" to render *sympatheia*. As we will see in Chapter 4, the hymns of the Church throughout the liturgical year constantly describe the Incarnation of the Son of God as an action expressive of and resulting from God's compassion for the world.[17]

While the third text above taken from Hebrews 10 is often translated as shown, the context makes clear that Paul is not simply commenting on the fact that someone expressed sympathy to the prisoners, in the sense that this person felt sorry for them or was "touched by the feeling"[18] of their sufferings. Rather, this person established an association or fellowship with the prisoners, suffered in prison with them, and interacted with them on their behalf. That is, he showed compassion to the prisoners. So, replacing "sympathy" with "compassion," we have:

> But remember the former days, when, after being enlightened, you endured
> a great conflict of sufferings, partly by being made a public spectacle through
> reproaches and tribulations, and partly by becoming sharers with those who
> were so treated. For, you had *compassion*[19] on the prisoners and accepted joy-
> fully the seizure of your property . . .

St John Chrysostom makes a point of noting that St Paul refers to this person as encouraging or "comforting" the prisoners. St Paul, as Chrysostom notes, did not report this person as saying to the prisoners that they should bear his afflictions or share them with him. Rather, St Paul says to this person: "you had compassion on the prisoners." The focus of this person's "sympathy" was entirely on the prisoners and not himself. This compassion, according to St John, takes the form of a consolation (*paraklēsis*). But this is an active consolation and not merely an inactive form of offering condolences. For St John Chrysostom, the person to whom St Paul is writing stands with the prisoners as a noble athlete who, rather than needing consolation or encouragement, is able to offer that to the others.[20]

---

[17] See Chapter 4, pp. 132–55.

[18] The KJV uses this phrase to translate *sympatheō* at Hebrews 4.15.

[19] The KJV and NKJV versions use "compassion" rather than "sympathy" at this point as does the Douay-Rheims English translation of the Vulgate. The Douay-Rheims translation is not surprising since the Vulgate uses *compati esse*, a form of the verb *compatior*, from which *compassio* is derived.

[20] John Chrysostom, *Homilies on Hebrews* 21 (NPNF[1] 14:461; PG 63:149).

One final thought: Sympathy, as understood in English, and compassion are not quite the same since, as I have noted, sympathy for others need not prompt one to any sort of action on their behalf. Compassion prompts people to action. If sympathy, however, need not move one to compassion, it is not clear that compassion for others requires sympathy for them. I might have no sympathy[21] for someone who is injured as the result of reckless and negligent behavior, e.g., someone who falls through the ice on a lake despite being repeatedly warned not to go out on the ice because it is too thin. In this case, sympathy may not be extended if we believe that the person brought the misfortune on himself. Yet I can perfectly well be moved by compassion to render assistance to him even at risk to myself.

Compassion and Empathy

The term "empathy" was coined around 1908 to translate the German word *Einfühlung*.[22] There is no specific corresponding Greek term in the Septuagint, New Testament, or Orthodox Christian service texts. The term is not found in any traditional English translations of patristic texts.[23] Empathy can have various meanings. It seems to have a general sense of being able to share in the experiences or feelings of another person in a way that one somehow experiences and, in some manner, understands those feelings or experiences. My empathy with you certainly does not mean that I experience your pain as you do since that would require me to participate in or to have your actual experience of pain and suffering. Empathy, however, does seem to involve or require that I can somehow "put myself in someone else's shoes"—that I can somehow "understand" or imagine what another person is going through. People who empathize with those who are suffering typically can express themselves by saying something such as "I understand"—cognitively and affectively—"what you are going through."

---

[21]"Pity" in Aristotle's sense. See below, p. 47.

[22]Karsten Stueber, "Empathy," *The Stanford Encyclopedia of Philosophy* (Spring 2018 Edition), Edward N. Zalta (ed.), <https://plato.stanford.edu/archives/spr2018/entries/empathy/>, April 20, 2020.

[23]The term is not found in the *Ante Nicene Fathers* and *Nicene and Post-Nicene Fathers* series since those series predate the origin of the term. It is not found in the broad collection of English translations of classical Greek and Latin texts contained on the Perseus website, <http://www.perseus.tufts.edu/hopper/collection>. So far as I can tell, it is not used in translations found in the digitized versions of the *Loeb Classical Library* series (Harvard) or the *Fathers of the Church* series (Catholic University Press of America). Both digitized series allow for word searches. "Empathy" also does not appear in any of the English translations of Orthodox service texts that I am using for this book.

There are, however, abundant examples where we can be moved by compassion for someone without in fact understanding what they are going through or thinking that we can or even should somehow put ourselves in the other person's place. If I have never experienced a close relative's murder, can I really comfort someone whose child has been murdered by telling them, "I understand what you are going through"? Indeed, if I have never experienced the death of a child but perhaps have lost a family member or close friend, can I simply assume that I really understand what someone is undergoing who has experienced the death, violent or otherwise, of a child?[24] Can I really claim to imagine in any robust sense what such a person is going through?

Can someone who is completely comfortable with the match between their gender identity and their body really claim to understand, feel, or put themselves in the place of someone who is struggling, and may often be suffering or in distress, in trying to deal with their own gender dysphoria? Can those of us who have never really been poor for a protracted period claim to understand in a lived sense what it means to be chronically poor?

For a final example, discrimination on the basis of race, sex, or disability is not necessarily the same for everyone in a particular group. Rather, there is what philosophers call intersectionality; namely, an individual may belong to distinct groups in which the members of each group are subjected to unjust discrimination. "This overlapping membership can generate experiences of discrimination that are very different from those of persons who belong to just one, or the other, of the groups."[25]

Even if I have been poor for a protracted period but live in the United States and am white and healthy, I cannot assume that my experiences simply replicate the experiences of people who are poor and disabled and/or black. Thus, I can never really say with any comprehensiveness to them that "I understand what you are going through." A partial empathy with others is possible in these circumstances but not necessarily any full-blown or comprehensive empathy.

[24]"The death of a child is a fire in the mind—a fire that burns a long time, for no other loss is so difficult to accept; no other loss feels so utterly un-natural. It is a loss beyond comprehension." Lynna Y. Littleton, *Maternal, Neonatal, and Women's Health Nursing* (New York: Delmar/Thompson Learning, 2002), 1257. Quotation from an anonymous maternity nurse.

[25]Andrew Altman, "Discrimination," *The Stanford Encyclopedia of Philosophy* (Winter 2016 Edition), ed. Edward N. Zalta, <https://plato.stanford.edu/archives/win2016/entries/discrimination>, April 20, 2020. The term "intersectionality" was introduced by Kimberlē Crenshaw, "Demarginalizing the Intersection of Race and Sex: A Black Feminist Critique of Antidiscrimination Doctrine, Feminist Theory and Antiracist Politics," *The University of Chicago Legal Forum* 140 (1989): 139–67.

The empathetic understanding of another person's experience is not just a general sort of understanding: I have suffered in some sense; therefore, I can understand what others go through when they suffer. Suffering is not suffering *simpliciter*. Rather, as the examples above suggest, human suffering is often "particularized": the source of suffering, as well as the particular history of someone who suffers, can profoundly affect the experience, quality, and meaning of the suffering for that person.

In the Orthodox Christian tradition, we affirm the humanity of all people in light of a common humanity we share as made in the image and according to the likeness of God—as living icons of Christ. But in our common humanity, we each exist as unique persons. To affirm people's humanity, then, is to affirm their uniqueness as persons: e.g., their own personal history, experiences, limitations, talents, the particular gifts they have been given by God, and so forth. Each person, in his or her uniqueness, is different from others. So far as these differences shape their experiences, their feelings, and in particular the ways in which they might suffer, we must always be careful not to simply assume that we understand what others are going through.

The inability to understand what other persons are going through, to be able to "put myself in their shoes," or see things from their perspective, does not preclude a compassionate response to people. At times, the most, and perhaps the only, compassionate response we can have to people in acute distress is simply to be present with them in silence—a compassionate co-presence in which there is nothing to say. We can bear with them or even assist them without at all thinking or feeling that we can put ourselves in their shoes or see things from their perspective.

In supporting others, moreover, it is truly crucial to listen to them and allow them to speak for themselves. A compassionate response to others opens up the possibility of listening to them express their own experiences and the meaning they see in them. Compassion for others in this sense is linked with a humility in the face of another person's experience that empathy may preclude. If I think I can empathize with your experience so that I think I know what you are going through, I may not believe that it is really necessary to listen to you or for you to have a voice.

I do not mean to suggest that compassion and empathy are incompatible. Someone who has been wrongfully convicted of a felony may very well have empathy for a victim of this injustice and also be moved by compassion for that person. A compassionate engagement with people in which I truly take the time to listen to their own experience may allow for some greater understanding of their situation.

Empathy for the suffering of others might certainly arise if I live through and share their suffering. This is suggested by St Paul when he writes of Christ, "we do not have a High Priest who cannot sympathize with our weaknesses (*mē dynamenon sympathēsai*), but was in all points tempted as we are, yet without sin."[26] Sympathy here certainly does not mean simply that he "is touched with the feeling of our infirmities."[27] Rather, Christ is able to sympathize with, and suffer with us, in our weakness because he lived through and, thus, understood what we go through in our weakness and affliction. This ability to sympathize with someone in this sense does fit a legitimate sense of empathy. In the case of Christ, however, this is an empathy that results from the compassion that leads to his Incarnation, in which he chose to experience the weakness and affliction of our human condition. It was not a precondition for it. In any event, the main point I want to make is that compassion cannot simply be identified with empathy or require it.[28]

Compassion and Pity

Pity and compassion both have the sense of an affective awareness of the distress or affliction to which another person is subjected that can lead to action to relieve the distress. While this impetus to action belongs virtually by definition to compassion, it does not for pity. We can pity people, at least as we commonly use the term today, without being moved in any way to assist them. Privileged persons, for example, might pity very poor persons in the sense of feeling sorry for them while simultaneously regarding them as some sort of inferior beings whom they have no intention of helping. Compassion, on the other hand, at least involves some volitional impetus to act to relieve someone's distress.[29]

---

[26]Heb 4.15. NKJV.

[27]KJV.

[28]See the very perceptive article by Paul Bloom, "Against Empathy," *Boston Review*, September 10, 2014, <http://bostonreview.net/forum/paul-bloom-against-empathy>, April 20, 2020. He develops his position in much more detail in *Against Empathy: The Case for Rational Compassion* (New York: Harper Collins, 2016). On the other hand, see the brief discussion of "empathetic remembering" in Susan Holman, *God Knows There's Need: Christian Responses to Poverty* (Oxford: Oxford University Press, 2009), 7–8. For a somewhat different perspective see Kristen Monroe, *Heart of Altruism: Perceptions of a Shared Humanity* (Princeton: Princeton University Press, 1996), 202–4. Much recent research on mirroring neurons has suggested that they are the basis of our empathetic awareness of others. For a critical review of that theory, see Claus Lamm and Jasminka Majdandžić, "The Role of Shared Neural Activations, Mirror Neurons, and Morality in Empathy—A Critical Comment," *Neuroscience Research* 90 (2015): 15–24.

[29]That impetus might be thwarted: I might be moved by compassion to rescue someone who is drowning yet realize that there is nothing I can do to effect a rescue, although I certainly can and should pray for them.

If we look at how the terms "pity" and "compassion" are used and what they signify, we have to acknowledge a great deal of flexibility: at times, the terms seem synonymous; at times, different. At times, both are linked with sympathy or empathy; at other times, both are distinguished from them. They can both bear a very close relationship to the notion of mercy, or they can be differentiated from it. Different people hear and understand these terms in different ways.[30] These terms are heard and understood differently—they carry different nuances of meaning—in different periods.

My concern at present is not to settle upon one definitive meaning for these terms but, rather, to note that we often use compassion to signify certain things that may but need not belong to pity and vice versa. In contemporary English, moreover, pity can carry a pejorative meaning of condescension that does not belong to compassion. For example, health care providers and facilities commonly talk about providing compassionate health care as a basic component of how patients and families are to be treated. But no one today would likely say that health care providers should provide pitying or pity-based health care.

The use and meaning of these English terms have changed over time. For example, an older, and now archaic, meaning of "pitiful" is "full of pity." Corresponding adjectives are merciful or compassionate. Brenton translates God's description of himself in Exodus 34.6 as: "pitiful (*racham, oiktirmōn*) and merciful." The translations of the Church Fathers in the *Ante Nicene Fathers* and the *Nicene and Post-Nicene Fathers* series regularly use pitiful in the "active" sense, as does Brenton, and also in the "passive" sense. Indeed, one contemporary translation of St Gregory of Nyssa's homily on the fifth beatitude renders the Greek as "Blessed are the pitiful (*eleēmones*), for they shall be pitied (*eleēthēsontai*)."[31] While the "active" sense of this term might have been understood in a past era, it is an archaic meaning that is virtually lost in any modern sense where "pitiful" is restricted to a passive meaning of being lamentable or an object of pity. You might seek out care in a hospital that claimed to provide compassionate treatment and perhaps even merciful treatment. You would likely avoid one that boasted about its pitiful heath care even if you took pitiful to mean "full of pity."

---

[30]For one exceptional analysis of empathy, sympathy, and compassion and ways in which they can be related and differentiated see Peter Rosan, "The Varieties of Ethical Experience: Empathy, Sympathy, and Compassion," *Phänomenologische Forschungen* 1 (2014): 155–89.

[31]Mt 5.7. H. R. Drobner and A. Viciano, eds, *Gregory of Nyssa: Homilies on the Beatitudes: An English Version with Commentary and Supporting Studies, Proceedings of the Eighth International Colloquium on Gregory of Nyssa (Paderborn, 14–18 Sept. 1998)* (Leiden: Brill, 2000), 57.

The Apostolic Bible Polyglot version of the Septuagint occasionally replaces Brenton's "pitiful" with "pitying."[32] But the more common practice is simply to use "compassionate" rather than "pitiful."[33] Or, we could replace "pitiful" with "filled with pity"[34] or "full of pity"[35] if we insist on using the term "pity." We might say that God is filled with pity and merciful. We should be filled with pity for our neighbors. But then we are back to the ambiguous meanings that pity can have in relation to compassion. Someone, including God, could be filled with pity for others simply "by feeling sorry for them" or by looking down on people's situation in a condescending manner. Is being filled with pity for those less fortunate than ourselves the same as being filled with compassion for or being compassionate to those less fortunate than ourselves?

At the beginning of the chapter, I briefly discussed this text: "O God: you are holy, almighty, all-powerful, good, fearful, merciful, and most *sympathetic* to your creatures." Given a robust meaning of *sympatheia*, the text is usually translated in English as "O God: you are holy, almighty, all-powerful, good, fearful, merciful, *and most compassionate* towards your creatures." Suppose, we write: "O God: you are holy, almighty, all-powerful, good, fearful, merciful, and most pitiful towards [or, filled with pity for] your creatures." Do we in our present age hear and understand this text in the same way with these different translations?

I raise this issue because the group of English terms: sympathy, empathy, mercy, pity, compassion have a variety of different senses. They are used and/ or heard in ways that a particular meaning might not be clear to the reader. To repeat an earlier point, in exploring the meaning of compassion in the Orthodox Christian tradition, we cannot simply express the meaning of terms in Hebrew or Greek that we might translate as "compassion," "mercy," or "pity" without first being clear how we ourselves as translators, dictionary compilers, scholars, or readers understand the English terms that we seek to use to unpack the meaning of the Hebrew and Greek terms.

One of my central concerns is to make some analytical distinctions between pity and compassion, which are in turn essential to understanding compassion in the Orthodox Christian tradition. I hope the reader attends to these distinctions

[32] Cf. Ex 34.6, Neh 9.31, and Ps 112(111).20. The Apostolic Bible Polyglot can be accessed at, <https://study-bible.info/version/ABP_Strongs>, April 20, 2020.

[33] Cf. Ex 34.6 and Ps 112(111).20.

[34] Mk 1.41: "Jesus was filled with pity" (Good News Translation).

[35] "Be full of pity (*oiktirmones*) like your father is full of pity (*oiktirmōn*)" (Lk 6.36), Françoise Mirguet, *An Early History of Compassion: Emotion and Imagination in Hellenistic Judaism* (Cambridge: Cambridge University Press, 2017), 229.

as we progress through this volume until we reach Chapter 5, where I will attempt to unpack the nature and meaning of compassion in a detailed manner. From the outset, I want to emphasize that the distinctions I will make between compassion and pity are not intended to be mapped onto the ways in which Greek terms and their English translations might be used in patristic texts or in texts from classical Greek.

For example, Aristotle defines pity (*eleos*) in this way:

> Pity (*eleos*) may be defined as a pain arising from an apparent evil, destructive or painful, befalling a person who does not deserve it, when we might expect such evil to befall ourselves or some of our friends, and, when, moreover, it seems near. Plainly the man who is to pity (*eleēsein*) must be such as to think himself or his friends liable to suffer some evil, an evil of such a sort as has been defined, or of a like or comparable sort.[36]

St Basil the Great seems to follow suit: He describes *eleos* as

> an emotion (*pathos*) experienced toward those who have been degraded beyond what they deserve, expressed in those who are sympathetically disposed (*sympathōs diatithemenōn*). We pity (*eleoumen*) one who has fallen from great wealth into the ultimate poverty . . . and one who gloried in bodily beauty and the prime of life and then was ruined by most disgraceful passions. And therefore since we too were glorying once upon a time in the life of paradise, yet have become inglorious and lowly because of our banishment, "our God shows us mercy" (*eleos, racham,* or "compassion")[37] as he looks upon what we have become from what we once were.[38]

While St Basil might assume that *eleos* is a type of pain in the face of another's misfortune, he does not refer to our liability to that same misfortune as does Aristotle, nor does he assume that there must be a kind of social or filial equality between one who suffers misfortune and the one who pities him as does Aristotle. At the end of his definition of *eleos*, Basil effectively abandons Aristotle's

---

[36] Aristotle, *Rhetoric* 2.8.2, 1385B; *The Rhetoric of Aristotle*, trans. Richard C. Lebb (Cambridge: Cambridge University Press, 1909), 89. Of course, *eleos* and its cognates can be translated as "mercy," "merciful," and so forth, which is the standard translation in Orthodox Christian service texts.

[37] Ps 114(116).5.

[38] Basil, *Homiliae in Psalmos* 22.3 (PG 29:489B). The text is Paul Blowers' translation in Paul Blowers, "Pity, Empathy, and the Tragic Spectacle of Human Suffering: Exploring the Emotional Culture of Compassion in Late Ancient Christianity" (2009 Presidential Address for the North America Patristics Society), *Journal of Early Christian Studies* 18.1 (2010): 7 and n. 20.

claim that *eleos* is felt only for one who does not deserve the misfortune, since it certainly cannot be said that we do not deserve the misfortune that befalls the human race and each of us personally as a result of sin.[39]

St Basil also allows that we show *eleos* "to one who gloried in bodily beauty and the prime of life and then was ruined by most disgraceful passions." If the passions of people were the cause of their being ruined, it is hard to see why they do not deserve being ruined. The person showing pity (*eleos*) in Aristotle's sense might have reservations about this. But the person showing compassion in the non-judgmental sense that pertains to Christian compassion would have no such reservation. Moreover, in the psalm verse that Basil cites "Our God shows us mercy," the Hebrew refers to God's *racham* or compassion that is extended to us even though we do not deserve it but more likely deserve punishment.

St Basil is using a notion of *eleos* that seems to slide towards compassion. Of course, *eleos* and *oiktirmos* are often translated by both "pity," and "compassion," as well as "mercy." Regardless of the historical or exegetical issues about how to translate these terms, I think that it is simply not helpful for us to identify "pity" and "compassion" in our own contemporary discussion of these texts or in trying to understand how Christian compassion fundamentally diverges from the sort of egoistic traits that often belong to the notion of pity, e.g., in Aristotle[40] and later in Hobbes.[41]

Let me begin by noting some basic definitions of "compassion" and "pity" in various English dictionaries. The Merriam Webster Dictionary defines the noun "pity" as: "sympathetic sorrow for one suffering, distressed, or unhappy."[42] In contrast, "compassion" is defined as "sympathetic consciousness of others' distress together with a desire to alleviate it."[43] It appears, then, that while both pity and compassion refer to a particular feeling or affective state, compassion also includes action based on or motivated by that affective state. On the other hand, the Oxford English Dictionary provides another definition of pity that blurs this distinction: "Pity" is "tenderness and concern aroused by

---

[39] Blowers, "NAPS Presidential Address," 7.

[40] Ibid., 7 and n. 20. Unfortunately, Blowers makes no reference to the language of compassion in the Old or the New Testament in his article.

[41] For Hobbes, see below, pp. 50–51.

[42] Merriam-Webster, "Pity," *Merriam-Webster*. <www.merriam-webster.com/dictionary/pity>, April 20, 2020.

[43] Merriam-Webster, "Compassion," *Merriam-Webster*, <https://www.merriam-webster.com/dictionary/compassion>, April 20, 2020.

the suffering, distress, or misfortune of another, and prompting a desire for its relief; compassion."[44]

It appears then that in common English and American usage, pity and compassion are related in two different ways. First, "pity" and "compassion" are basically synonymous as a particular feeling or affective state that leads one to act to assist another. Second, by way of contrast, pity refers solely to an affective state, while compassion refers to an affective state and to the action that may follow from it. Yet none of these definitions focuses on certain key issues that will allow us to distinguish pity from compassion in a way that will delineate the sense of compassion I think we find in Scripture and the Orthodox Christian tradition.

I want to note three distinctions to demarcate compassion from pity:

1) Suppose pity and compassion both involve actions to relieve another person's distress based upon an emotional or affective awareness of the distress. For whose sake does the person relieve the distress? I suggest that pity has a basically egoistic orientation—namely, one acts to relieve another's distress primarily or exclusively for one's own sake. That is, one is really interested in relieving one's own distress in the face of another person's distress. Compassion, on the other hand, is fundamentally directed towards acting on behalf of and for the sake of another person. [45]

2) In contrast to compassion, pity can be condescending in a pejorative sense. That is, pity is perfectly compatible with viewing others in terms of an array of invidious distinctions that marginalize them. Pity, thus, is perfectly compatible in the context of the prejudiced distinctions by which various groups are marginalized and denigrated in society. The characterization of pity by the Center for Compassion and Altruist Research and Education illustrates this aspect of pity: "Pity is sorrowfully noting another person's suffering, but regarding them as outgroup, weak and/or inferior and hence, undeserving of any wish to alleviate, or efforts towards alleviating suffering."[46]

---

[44] Oxford English Dictionary, "Pity" def 2.b, <http://www.oed.com/view/Entry/144814?rskey=1DsY7L &result=1&isAdvanced=false#eid>, April 20, 2020.

[45] This does not mean that compassionate actions must be entirely and exclusively other directed. See Chapter 5, pp. 212–3.

[46] Stanford Medicine, "Pity," The Center for Compassion and Altruism Research and Education, <http://ccare.stanford.edu/research/wiki/compassion-definitions/pity/>, April 20, 2020.

This definition is perhaps too strong since the pity I am describing is perfectly compatible with paternalistic or patronage forms of assistance that are still based on, or at least support, marginalizing social differences between those who offer assistance and those who receive it. Compassion, by way of contrast, is fundamentally non-judgmental or non-accusatory in nature. Compassion always involves the full affirmation of each person's humanity, and thus, his or her uniqueness as a person whether that affirmation is embedded in a religious or non-religious context.

3) Compassion and pity both involve an awareness of the distress, affliction, or vulnerability of another person. What distinguishes the two, however, is the way in which people deal with their *own* vulnerability to distress in encountering the distress and vulnerability of another. People who solely feel pity for others can "push them away" as defective or "dirty"—physically, psychologically, and socially—to avoid contact with them and establishing a genuine fellowship or community with them. As we will see, this pity arises out of a fear of one's own vulnerability. In being moved by compassion for others, however, we engage with them in a neighborly way in light of accepting our shared humanity or dignity but also our weakness and vulnerability.

The Self-Interested Character of Pity

Let me develop in a bit more detail the egoistic orientation of pity in contrast to compassion. Thomas Hobbes, for example, defines pity as "imagination or fiction of future calamity to ourselves, proceeding from the sense of another man's calamity."[47] In his sermon on compassion, Bishop Joseph Butler claims that Hobbes essentially links this notion of pity with fear for self.[48] Butler, on the other hand, argues that compassion, as we ordinarily understand it, is something quite different from pity, since when we talk about a compassionate feeling or affection, we

---

[47] Thomas Hobbes, *Human Nature of the Fundamental Elements of Policy* 9.10 (London: Printed for Matthew Gilliflower, Henry Rogers, and Tho. Fox, 1684), 52.

[48] Hobbes' definition implies that "fear and compassion would be the same idea, and a fearful and a compassionate man the same character; which every one immediately sees are totally different." Joseph Butler, *Sermon Five on Compassion*, in Joseph Butler, *Fifteen Sermons Preached at Rolls Chapel: to which is added Six Sermons Preached on Publick Occasions* (London: Printed for J. and P. Knapton, 1749), 83, updated to modern spelling. Regarding Hobbes, see Richard Bourke, *Empire and Revolution: The Political Life of Edmund Burke* (Princeton: Princeton University Press, 2015), 128.

always refer to a sorrow or concern for the misery of someone else and not simply for ourselves. So, in his sermon on compassion, Butler observes:

> There are often three distinct perceptions or inward feelings upon sight of persons in distress: real sorrow and concern for the misery of our fellow-creatures; some degree of satisfaction from a consciousness of our freedom from that misery; and, as the mind passes on from one thing to another, it is not unnatural from such an occasion to reflect upon our own liableness to the same or other calamities. The two last frequently accompany the first, but it is the first only which is properly compassion, of which the distressed are the objects, and which directly carries us with calmness and thought to their assistance.[49]

Butler takes note of the egoistic or self-interested intentionality that is properly absent from compassion but often present in pity. For Hobbes, the concern for the other, such as it may be, is counterbalanced or framed by a concern for oneself that the passion evokes. The emotion of pity in this sense does not amount to a sorrow or concern for another primarily for the sake of the other. It is fundamentally a kind of pain someone feels in the face of the distress of another person—a pain that needs to be relieved. But relieved for whose sake?—for the sake of the one who feels that pain or pity.

We see an excellent example of this self-interested pity in Stefan Zweig's portrayal of Lt Anton Hofmiller in his novel *Beware of Pity*.[50] The novel consists of Lt Hofmiller's first-person narrative, related to a stranger who wants to acknowledge him as a hero because of his military exploits. The lieutenant counters by recounting his relationship with a young paralyzed woman Edith and her family in order to show that his courage in war was the inversion of his weakness when he was a young man.[51]

Lt Hofmiller's first encounter with Edith ends in disaster when he asks her to dance with him at a social event, unaware that she is paralyzed and unable to walk.[52] She responds with disconsolate sobbing that so unnerves him that he

---

[49]Ibid., 85, updated to modern spelling.

[50]Stefan Zweig, *Beware of Pity*, trans. Phyllis and Trevor Blewitt (New York: New York Times edition, 2006). The German title, *Ungeduld des Herzens*, is literally and more properly translated as *The Impatience of the Heart*. The novel is about a young cavalry officer, Lt Hofmiller, just prior to the Austro-Hungarian war, and his interactions with a young crippled woman, Edith, and her family. The English title refers to the pity (*Mitleid*) that overcomes Lt Hofmiller, 56–8.

[51]Zweig, xxxiii–xxxiv.

[52]Ibid., 11–12.

leaves the party.[53] Eventually, he is invited back to visit with Edith and her family.[54] Afterwards, he is overcome with a kind of maudlin, sentimental[55] pity for the "pathetic creature" and "helpless invalid."[56] He is also delighted with the fact that he has been useful to someone for the first time in his life.[57]

In his recollection of this experience, his description of his encounter with Edith's physical disability and his own emotional reaction to it focuses primarily on how he has been affected by her suffering. He has never encountered such feelings of pity before. His own pity is sentimental in the sense that his maudlin descriptions of Edith's condition serve primarily to heighten his own sense of the distress he feels in response to her condition and her suffering generally.[58] He subsequently notes that his pity is accompanied by an "unknown and unsuspected zone of tenderness," which is dangerous because "it is never possible for a relationship between a healthy person and an invalid, a free person and a prisoner, to hang fire forever."[59] In Hofmiller's eyes, the healthy person is reduced to the role of care giver and the invalid to the role of patient and recipient.[60]

Despite all of his attempts to extricate himself from the relation with Edith and her family or set limits to his interactions with them, he becomes addicted to his pity for them.[61] Throughout the novel, he is basically unable to set appropriate limits on his interaction with Edith and her family because he is moved to pity in interacting with them and he relents to unreflective "assistance" out of pity. This is well illustrated in a long conversation between Edith's father and Hofmiller. Since Edith is refusing any further treatment for her illness because of her unrequited love for Hofmiller, she has become so distraught that the father pleads with Hofmiller and insists on his responsibility to marry Edith as the only way to prevent Edith from committing suicide. Despite being on guard for having been manipulated by the father and professing more than once during the conversation

[53]Ibid., 12.
[54]Ibid., 23–30.
[55]Ibid., 34.
[56]Ibid., 45.
[57]Ibid., 40.
[58]Ibid., 33–35.
[59]Ibid., 44.
[60]Ibid., 45.
[61]After discovering that he lied about why he did not come out to visit (64–66), Edith is bluntly critical of the fact that he always comes out of pity rather than simply not visiting and being honest about it (67). In fact, she attacks him for simply "playing the good Samaritan" through his dissembling efforts to avoid her condition when he interacts with her (66–67, cf. 193–94). Her caustic reference to Hofmiller as the "good Samaritan" is, of course, quite different from what Jesus intended to convey in the parable of the good Samaritan.

that he cannot marry Edith, at the end of the conversation when the father is utterly disconsolate, he gives in to his pity for the father and Edith and promises to marry Edith "when she is cured."[62]

Hofmiller is thrilled by the power he has to make people happy.[63] After he has become engaged to Edith, he even likens himself to God because his pity and munificence has this remarkable power to make other people happy.[64] This exhilaration, however, is short lived. On his way home, he bemoans his engagement.[65] When he returns to town, he discovers that his military comrades have learned that he is engaged to Edith. They grill him on this, and to put an end to their inquisition, he denies the engagement.[66] Unable to face her and ask for forgiveness, he manages to be sent away from Vienna to another assignment.[67] He relies on her physician, Dr Condor, to deliver his message of repentance.[68] However, she finds out about his actions before Dr Condor can speak with her and she commits suicide.[69]

Lt Hofmiller suffers a great deal in his response to Edith's disability and the profound neediness of her family. Nevertheless, the ego-directed focus of his suffering means that he is not really suffering with or for them. At one point in the novel, Dr Condor makes this point by chastising Hofmiller for his self-interested pity.

> Pity (*Mitleid*)—that's all right! But there are two kinds of pity. One, the weak and sentimental kind, which is really no more than the heart's impatience to be rid as quickly as possible of the painful emotion aroused by the sight of another's unhappiness, that pity (*Mitleid*) which is not compassion (*Mitleiden*), but only an instinctive desire to fortify one's own soul against the sufferings (*Leidens*) of another; and the other, the only kind that counts, the unsentimental but creative kind (*Mitleid*), which knows what it is about and is determined to hold out, in patience and forbearance, to the very limit of its strength and even beyond [namely, *Mit-leiden,* or compassion]. It is only when one goes on to the end, to the extreme, bitter end, only when one has

[62]Ibid., 290–99.
[63]Ibid., 40, 159.
[64]Ibid., 306.
[65]Ibid., 311.
[66]Ibid., 319.
[67]Ibid., 334.
[68]Ibid., 338–39.
[69]Ibid., 348–39.

an inexhaustible fund of patience, that one can help one's fellows. Only when one is prepared to sacrifice oneself in doing so—and then only![70]

This is a particularly famous passage in Zweig's novel. But the standard English translation and, frankly, the German are a bit vague about the use of *Mitleid*. I want to spend a moment discussing this matter to point out something important for the sharp distinction I think Zweig is making between pity and compassion, which I am trying to stress.

Let me begin with a slightly different translation of this passage:

Mitleid ["response to suffering"]—that's all right! But there are two kinds of *Mitleid* ["response(s) to suffering"]. One, the weak and sentimental kind [*Mitleid* translated as "pity" throughout the novel], which is really no more than the heart's impatience to be rid as quickly as possible of the painful emotion aroused by the sight of another's unhappiness, that *Mitleid* [pity] which is not at all compassion [*Mit-leiden*][71] but only an instinctive desire to fortify one's own soul against the sufferings [*Leidens*] of another; and the other, the only kind that counts, the unsentimental but creative *Mitleid* [response to suffering], which knows what it is about and is determined to hold out, in patience and forbearance [namely, *Mit-leiden,* or compassion]. . . .

Zweig makes it very clear that compassion (*Mit-leiden*) is not a kind of pity (*Mitleid*). Rather, both pity and compassion are two kinds of *Mitleid*, which in this generic sense is probably better understood as "a response to suffering"[72] in English rather than "pity."

So, we have two kinds of *Mitleid* (taken as "a response to suffering"):

1) The weak sentimental kind, which is called *Mitleid*, or "pity" in English.

2) The creative unsentimental kind that knows what it is about, which is called *Mit-leiden*, or "compassion" in English.

Zweig's term *Mit-leiden* ("compassion") literally means to bear, to endure, or to suffer (*leiden*) with (*mit*) someone. Like *Mitleid*, *Mitleiden* carries the sense of

---

[70]Zweig, 176.

[71]The standard English translation misses the sharp contrast Zweig makes between pity (the first sense of *Mitleid*) and compassion (the second sense of *Mitleid*): pity "is not at all compassion" (*gar nicht Mit-leiden ist*).

[72]The German equivalent might be *Reaktion auf Leiben*. Cf. Robert Scholz, *Übergang zur Vaterschaft: Persönliche Nische, Belastung und protektive Faktoren* (Hamburg: Diplomica Verlag, 2002), 27.

both "pity" and "compassion." So, Zweig inserts the hyphen, "-", between *Mit* and *leiden* to emphasize that this second kind of *Mitleid* has a fundamentally different intentionality from the first kind; namely, to suffer with someone for that other person's sake rather than be egoistically driven as is the case with pity.

In any event, someone who experiences or is moved by the first kind of *Mitleid*—namely pity—focuses on the pain or discomfort caused by pain. The suffering and affliction of the other person is primarily an occasion for this pain mixed with a sentimental passion to render assistance in the observer. Someone who responds to suffering with pity, suffers as it were alongside the person who suffers but not with or for that person. Moreover, the assistance provided to the other person is valued primarily for the happiness it brings to the person who shows pity.

Hofmiller unwittingly displays this egoistic focus of his pity when Edith takes him aback by asking why he really visits her and her family, and he responds that he is simply happier with her at her house than anywhere else and, in the bargain, feels more important.[73]

I will develop the contrast between a self-interested pity and an other-directed compassion in Chapter 5. By way of anticipation, compassion (*Mit-leiden*)—the second sense or kind of *Mitleid* ("response to suffering"), which Dr Condor mentions—can be linked with the Christian understanding of compassion as fundamentally involving self-sacrificial love. In the context of the Orthodox Christian tradition, we might reframe Zweig's characterization of compassion—"which knows what it is about and is determined to hold out, in patience and forbearance, to the very limit of its strength and even beyond"—along with Butler's observation that compassion leads us with "calmness and thought" to assist others—by saying that a true com-passion (a co-suffering love) requires and flows out of a dis-passion (*apatheia*), by which we are freed from the self-aggrandizing passions that separate us from God and from others.[74]

For now, however, I want to note how self-interested motives for helping others with what I regard as pity and not compassion are present throughout the patristic tradition. A number of the Church Fathers—especially in the fourth and fifth centuries—developed elaborate and often lugubrious portraits of people—e.g., who were poor, sick (e.g., those suffering from leprosy), or suffered from disabilities—to create an experience of pain and sorrow in their listeners. In many cases, these audiences consisted of very wealthy and privileged people who, like

[73]Zweig, 193–94.
[74]See Chapter 5, pp. 203–5 for a brief discussion about dispassion.

the rich man in the parable of the rich man and Lazarus,[75] were simply indifferent to the suffering of those around them. The portraits painted by these Church
Fathers were designed to shame the hearers for their indifference and lack of pity
or compassion and move them to provide assistance.[76]

> Why then does no pity (*oiktos*, or compassion?) for what you see come to
> you?[77] You see human beings scattered about like cattle in search of food:
> tattered rags—these are his clothes; a cane in his hands ... bound with some
> sort of thongs to the palms; a torn leather sack ... is the entire source of his
> life's provisions.[78]

At times, however, the motives presented for rendering assistance to people
seem self-serving: the failure to render assistance will end in eternal judgment
and damnation. Or, assistance is to be given to the poor—not really to alleviate
their poverty or because one is concerned about them—but because the poor or
others in need, being grateful, will pray for their benefactors or carry their alms
to heaven. Or, one might give assistance to people to gain a kind of redemptive
almsgiving: one's past sins can be "wiped away" by God through one's current
generosity. Appeals couched in these sorts of motivations or intentions can dis-
tract people from developing a robust sense of compassion. They can amount to
rewards to motivate people who are too weak to value a virtue such as compassion
as "beautiful in itself."[79] If they are not qualified,[80] these appeals have the flavor of
simply trying to dislodge people, who are utterly indifferent to or merely manipulative of others in their suffering, in order at least to awaken in them some sense
of pain or sorrow at the suffering of others that might move them to act primarily
for their own self-advantage—namely, what I am calling pity.

[75]Lk 16.19–31.

[76]For some examples, see St Gregory the Theologian, who offers this dramatic description of lepers whom
he observes are stigmatized since "we avoid at all costs—the inhumanity of it!—hardly abiding the thought that
in fact we breathe the same air as they," *Oration* 14.10 (FOC 107.45–6; PG 35:870B); John Chrysostom, *Eight
Sermons on the Book of Genesis*, Sermon 5, trans. Robert C. Hill (Brookline, MA: Holy Cross Orthodox Press,
2004), 92; Michael De Vinne, "The Advocacy of Empty Bellies: Episcopal Representation of the Poor in the
Late Roman Empire" (Ph.D. Diss., Stanford University, 1995), 5–47, provides numerous episcopal examples of
these descriptions combined with the severe criticism of the ways in which these people were neglected and
ostracized.

[77]"Pity," even in the sense that I am using it, involves some awareness of another person's suffering or distress.
St Gregory is addressing those who were utterly indifferent or blind to the suffering of others.

[78]Gregory of Nyssa, *On the Love of the Poor* 2 (PG 46:477A), cited in De Vinne, "Advocacy of Empty
Bellies," 5–6, his translation.

[79]See John Chrysostom, *Homilies on John* 77 (NPNF[1] 14:284–85; PG 59:418). See Chapter 5, pp. 215–6.

[80]See Chapter 5, pp. 217–25 for an extended discussion of this issue.

These sorts of appeals, however, often sit side-by-side with other appeals designed to move such people to respect the equality of honor (*homotimia*) and primary equality of rights (*prōtē isonomia*) that all people have in light of our common nature as made in the image of God.[81] So, St Gregory the Theologian writes about lepers who have been ostracized and rejected from the city:

> [They are] our brothers in God, whether you like it or not; whose share in nature is the same as ours; who are formed of the same clay from the time of our first creation, knit together with bones and sinews just as we are, clothed with skin and flesh like everyone else … or rather, more importantly, who have the same portion of the image of God just as we do.[82]

When these appeals are accompanied with the expectation that people should work to alleviate the suffering of others without depending upon or even thinking about a reward as the justification for the assistance, we come closer to what might be regarded as compassion. Moreover, this appeal to our equality of honor and equality of right undercuts the disaffiliation and marginalization of those who suffer. It stresses a common humanity that binds all of us together as unique persons created in the image of Christ. It rejects the disdainful and condescending character that can pertain to pity. Let me now turn to discuss what that aspect of pity involves.

Pity, Disdain, Condescension, and Stigmatization

The pity that Hofmiller shows to Edith is framed by reducing her to an object of pity: She is a "helpless cripple,"[83] "helpless invalid,"[84] and "a suffering, helpless, unsuspecting creature."[85] For him, until, indeed if, she happens to be fully cured,

---

[81] St Gregory the Theologian uses both terms to refer to the intrinsic character of human beings that requires they be treated with a fundamental respect. For *homotimos*, see *Oratio* 19.13 (PG 35:1060A): "Rather than simply save us by his word alone with which he created everything, he gave us *sympatheia* (compassion) and *homotimia* (equality of honor)." See also *Oratio* 18.20 (PG 35:1008C) where he refers to the "equality of honor of nature" (*homotimou physeōs*) that is due to those who are poor. For *prōtē isonomia* (first equality) see *Oratio* 14.26 (PG 35:892B) where he refers to the primary equality of rights that we had in virtue of our creation, which has been abused since the fall. For good discussions see: Tasos Michopoulos, "*Mimisometha Nomon Theou*: Gregory the Theologian's Ontology of Compassion," *Greek Orthodox Theological Review* 39 (1994): 2 and Susan Holman, "The Entitled Poor: Human Rights Language in the Cappadocians," *Pro Ecclesia* 9.4 (2000): 483–84.

[82] Gregory the Theologian, *Oration* 14.14 (FOC 107.48–9; PG 35:876).

[83] Zweig, 18.

[84] Ibid., 45.

[85] Ibid., 321. Edith is certainly aware of how her inability to move freely renders her helpless in certain ways (220). But Hofmiller transforms her physical helplessness into what he construes as a stigmatizing global

she is confined to this identity: he will not agree to marry her until she is cured. He gives a clear idea of what this means, when he contrasts his description of her "normal" older sister Ilona with Edith:

> The one was completely different from the other: Ilona, already a woman, full-blooded, well-developed, voluptuous, healthy; beside her, Edith, half child, half young woman, about seventeen or eighteen, still appeared somehow immature. Curious contrast: one would have liked to dance with the one, to kiss her; the other, one wanted to spoil as an invalid, to pet and make a fuss of, to protect and, above all, to soothe.[86]

Here we see the "petting zoo" side of Lt Hofmiller's pity. But the fear-driven, hostile, brutal rejection of Edith that frames his pity is just around the corner. For the lieutenant, Edith has what we might call a spoiled identity: she is "the crippled one." Everything she does, or thinks, or feels is contaminated and ineluctably framed by the fact that she is crippled. He is, in essence, stigmatizing Edith for her disability. Edward Jones and Amerigo Farina provide this pointed description of "the dramatic essence of the stigmatizing process":

> a label marking the deviant status is applied and this marking process typically has devastating consequences for emotions, thought, and behavior. . . . The deviant person [is taken to be] flawed, blemished, discredited, spoiled, or stigmatized. In the classic case, the mark or sign of deviance initiates a drastic inference process that engulfs impressions of the deviant target person and sets up barriers to interaction and intimacy.[87]

Except for rare occasions, Edith has no reality for Hofmiller except as "the crippled girl." Edith herself becomes aware of this when she asks him what it is about her that leads him to visit her. When he responds that he comes because she is lonely, she immediately senses that "the only reason you come trotting out here every day [is] simply to play the Good Samaritan to a 'poor, sick child'—that's

---

helplessness and defectiveness: she is unable to love. He is by no means alone in this sort of transformation. For an interesting review of how this transformation is expressed and resisted in a range of contemporary TV programs, comic strips, and other visual and printed media, see "Disabled Means Helpless," TVTropes, <https:// tvtropes.org/pmwiki/pmwiki.php/Main/DisabledMeansHelpless>, April 20, 2020. For a general discussion of the portrayal of disability in the media, see Tracy Worrell, *Disability in the Media: Examining Stigma and Identity* (Lanham, MD: Lexington Books, 2018).

[86]Zweig, 25–26.

[87]Edward Jones and Amerigo Farina, et al., Social Stigma: *The Psychology of Marked Relationships* (San Francisco: W. H. Freeman and Co., 1984), 4.

what you all call me, I expect, when I'm not there—I know, I know. It's only out of pity that you come." He comes, she says, because she is a cripple.[88]

The tragic consequence of his stigmatization of Edith is that he cannot possibly imagine that a "cripple" like Edith would or could love him. When she expresses her own attraction and love for him by passionately kissing him, he is repulsed. His own description of his response to that kiss shows exactly how his pity for her has been offered to her as someone he construes to be a defective human being.

> I was appalled. I felt like one who, stooping innocently over a flower, is stung by an adder. If the hypersensitive creature had struck me, reviled me, spat at me, I should have been less disconcerted, for in view of her uncertain temper I was prepared for anything but this one thing—that she, an invalid, a poor, afflicted cripple, should be able to love, should desire to be loved ... [and] ... should have the temerity (I cannot express it otherwise) to love, to desire, with the conscious and sensual love of a real woman.[89]

Hofmiller goes on to add: "Never had I, even in my wildest dreams, imagined that invalids, cripples, the immature, the prematurely aged, the despised and rejected, the pariahs among human beings, dared to love."[90] One of the main reasons Hofmiller bemoans his engagement to her is the reaction people will have to Edith.[91] I bring this up because it is all too easy for us to talk about showing mercy or relieving the distress of those who are poor, or homeless, or strangers, or prisoners, and so forth. Yet, we live in a world in which people subjected to these conditions are often despised, marginalized, and otherwise pushed to the fringes of society. When personal biases and discriminatory attitudes are embedded in and supported by the social world, it is all too easy to view people subjected to such conditions as more or less permanently inferior beings to whom we might render aid but whom we can never really engage as fellow humans. In this way, we reduce people to these stigmatized conditions and define them, and marginalize them, by these conditions.

[88]Zweig, 195.

[89]Ibid., 205.

[90]Ibid., 205. When Dr Condor asks Lt Hofmiller whether Edith's deformity inspires a certain repugnance and disgust in him, he vigorously denies it claiming that her helplessness and defenselessness had attracted him to her (263). Yet in his panic-driven ruminations while going home from his engagement, Hofmiller cannot get the "revolting" "tap-tap" of Edith's crutches out of his mind (311) while bemoaning that "one can't marry a woman like that, she's not a real woman" (312).

[91]Ibid., 313–14.

We may not radically stigmatize them to deny them any sort of assistance. We may bestow various forms of assistance on them, usually at a distance, social as well as physical; yet we are never really interested in interacting with them as fellow humans. We show at best a sort of condescending pity towards them. For example, personal and community-based Christian "outreach" programs can fall prey to this sort of condescending pity if those involved in them do not critically and self-consciously work to eliminate the subtle and often not so subtle biases and prejudices that can infect how people can view those to whom "charity" is dispensed.

The sort of deprecating, condescending pity that Hofmiller shows is fundamentally different from compassion. Preeminently directed to the welfare of others, compassion, as I will argue in Chapter 5, always responds to the other as fully possessed of human dignity, to use a modern phrase or, as I noted above, in sharing in the "equality of honor" (*homotimos*) or "primary equality of rights" (*prōtē isonomia*) that belongs to each of us in light of our common humanity: that we are unique persons made in the image and according to the likeness of God. Compassion for others fundamentally refuses to let others be viewed as "objects of pity" who are reduced to the conditions that afflict and distress them. I will discuss the non-judgmental and non-accusatory nature of compassion in detail in Chapter 5.

For now, however, here is a remarkable text from St Macarius about the non-judgmental character of compassion that holistically affirms people in stark contrast to the denigrating pity Lt Hofmiller shows to Edith.

> Christians [and presumably everyone] ... ought not to pass judgment of any kind on anyone. ... But they should look upon all persons with a single mind and a pure eye,[92] so that it may be for such a person almost a natural and fixed attitude never to despise or judge or abhor anyone or to divide people according to categories.[93]

This second distinction between pity and compassion is, it seems to me, particularly important and less noticed than it should be. The difference goes not so much to the actions that people perform as the basic ways in which others are "viewed" and understood. To repeat: Compassion always affirms the full

[92]Note: the mind and the intellect are in the heart and not divorced from the heart! Judgment here is not just cognitive but affective as well.

[93]Pseudo-Macarius, *Homily* 15.8, in *The Fifty Spiritual Homilies*, trans. George Maloney (Mahwah, NJ: Paulist Press, 1992), 111 (PG 34:581).

humanity of others and, thus, the possibility of genuine community with them as unique persons. However, what pity gives with one hand—assistance—can be taken away with the other hand by retaining the invidious distinctions by which those who render assistance objectify, marginalize, and dominate those to whom assistance is given.

As an aside: provided that this sort of condescending pity is free of outright denigration and stigmatization, it might be regarded as a type of flawed compassion. This would occur if someone is interested in helping other people for their sake and yet, unwittingly or not, accepts depictions of those persons that view them as inferior in ways that block developing any sense of genuine respect for and community with them.

Compassion, Pity, and Vulnerability

The third difference between pity and compassion concerns how we come to terms with our own vulnerability in the face of others who suffer. I suggest that in directing pity to persons or groups who are stigmatized, marginalized, or viewed as inferior, we aim to create a distance between ourselves and others as a way of coping with our own vulnerability—to death, affliction, and whatever it is about ourselves that we fear—that leads us to stigmatize a condition. After all, stigmas reflect underlying anxiety about and rejection of conditions that are stigmatized.[94] Hence, pitying responses to others who are stigmatized can aim to limit our exposure to the vulnerability and affliction that others actually experience.[95] To illustrate this, Franz Fanon relates this encounter with a child while he was taking a walk. After the child had said to its mother: "Look, a Negro," the child finally blurts out, "Mama, see the Negro! I'm frightened!" For Fanon, the blackness of his body was the source of this fear: In being stigmatized by the child—who obviously learned this from white adults—he writes:

> I was responsible at the same time for my body, for my race, for my ancestors. I discovered my blackness, my ethnic characteristics; and I was battered down

[94]Jones, *Social Stigma*, 82–89; Michelle R. Hebel, Jennifer Tickle, and Todd F. Heatherton, "Awkward Moments in Interactions between Nonstigmatized and Stigmatized Individuals," ed. Todd Heatherton, R. Kleck, et al., *The Social Psychology of Stigma* (New York: Guilford Press, 2000), 285–86.

[95]For an extensive discussion of stigmatization in relation to a wide range of diseases and disabilities, see Patrick W. Corrigan, ed., *The Stigma of Disease and Disability: Understanding Causes and Overcoming Injustices* (Washington: American Psychological Association, 2014).

by tom-toms, cannibalism, intellectual deficiency, fetishism. . . . And above all else, above all: "Sho' good eatin'."[96]

Sartre's classic description of the anti-Semite pinpoints the fear that grips people and societies insofar as they engage in denigration and stigmatization: "The anti-Semite is . . . a man who is afraid. Not of the Jews, to be sure, but of himself, of his consciousness, of his liberty . . . of society, and of the world—of everything that is except the Jews." Sartre adds that anti-Semitism is not merely an opinion but a form of cowardice and a way of "choosing [oneself] as a person." If there were no Jews, he would denigrate other groups (e.g., blacks). Projecting his fears onto Jews through stigmatization, and thus marginalizing them, is simply a way for him to "stifle his anxieties at their inception by persuading himself that his place in the world has been marked out in advance, that it awaits him, and that tradition has given him the right to occupy it. Anti-Semitism is, in short, fear of the human condition."[97]

Sartre provides a decisive characterization of the fears and anxieties that drive stigmatization. Compassion, however, involves coming to terms with our human condition and the fundamental vulnerability and weakness of our own life, and indeed, all human life. We see this preeminently in the compassion Christ shows in his Incarnation, in which he willingly takes on human vulnerability and weakness. Compassion, accordingly, allows for a genuine solidarity or neighborliness with those who suffer and are vulnerable precisely because one no longer denies the vulnerability that pervades one's life and no longer denigrates those who are perceived as threats. I will discuss this in Chapter 5 in the section dealing with vulnerability.[98] I want to add that issues of vulnerability do not simply concern physical or emotional vulnerability, e.g., to illness or death. Pity can undermine neighborliness when those who are socially privileged keep themselves at a distance—socially and symbolically—from those whom they marginalize or denigrate.[99]

[96] Franz Fanon, *Black Skin, White Masks*, trans. Charles Lamm Markmann (London: Archway Press: 1986), 111–12.

[97] Jean-Paul Sartre, *Anti-Semite and Jew: An Exploration of the Etiology of Hate,* trans. George Becker (New York: Schocken Books, 1948), 53–54. In composing this work immediately after World War II, Sartre made a concerted attempt to examine the dynamics of anti-Semitism. For an excellent discussion of the context, strengths, and limitations of Sartre's analysis, see the preface to the 1995 edition of the novel by Michael Walzer (New York: Schocken Books, 1995), v–xvi.

[98] See Chapter 5, pp. 205–10.

[99] See the excellent discussion on the point in Steven Tudor, *Compassion and Remorse: Acknowledging the Suffering Other* (Leuven: Peeters Publishers, 2001), 105–7. By way of contrast, the Orthodox and Western

Compassion and Mercy

In various theological dictionaries and lexicons, "compassion" and "mercy" at times appear not just as related to one another but as near synonyms. More accurately, no effort is really made to define or distinguish the terms. In the Greek text of the Septuagint, as I noted earlier, *eleos* and *oiktirmos* seem to be interchanged with each other especially in translating the Hebrew term *racham*. While *eleos* is often translated as mercy in English versions of the Septuagint, *eleos* is often just as easily translated as pity, e.g., when discussing Aristotle's notion of *eleos* in the *Rhetoric*. Compassion and mercy are indeed often related to each other, but they have different meanings and emphases.

When we refer to someone as compassionate or merciful, we can refer both to merciful or compassionate actions as well as to inner mental—in a very broad sense—states or dispositions. If I refer to someone as compassionate, I would typically mean that he or she experiences some emotion or affective state that involves a sympathetic awareness of another person's distressed or afflicted condition that moves them as far as possible to render assistance to the person (compassionate action). Mercy seems to have an "internal" and an "external" sense like compassion. In the external sense, I can describe certain actions as merciful. Mercy, or merciful action, has two basic senses. On the one hand, mercy can have the sense of "forgiveness shown towards someone whom it is within one's power to punish or harm."[100] Thus a judge might treat a convicted defendant mercifully by imposing a more lenient sentence than is mandated. A judge might act in this way out of pity or out of compassion. On the other hand, mercy has a second, broader sense of kind, favorable, or benevolent treatment of someone independently of any calculation or determination of what a person might deserve. I can extend mercy to a sick person by tending to their wounds as did the good Samaritan, who took care of the man lying by the side of the road.[101] It is in this sense that we refer to "acts of mercy" or "acts of compassion" as more comprehensive translations of *eleēmosynē* than "alms." But this sort of mercy also can proceed out of pity or compassion if we do not specify the intention that belongs to such actions.

Christian examples of kissing lepers (e.g., Saints Basil the Great, Martin of Tours, and Francis of Assisi) profoundly counter this disaffiliating tendency. See Timothy Miller and John Nesbitt, *Walking Corpses: Leprosy in Byzantium and the Medieval West* (New York: Cornell University Press, 2014), 43–44.

[100] "Mercy: Definition of Mercy in English by Oxford Dictionaries," Oxford Dictionaries, <en.oxforddictionaries.com/definition/mercy definition 1>, April 20, 2020.

[101] Lk 10.37.

In addition to merciful actions, mercy might appear to refer to some sort of "mental or affective state." As far as I can tell, however, there is no emotion or affective state called "mercy."[102] We might think that someone who is compassionate has feelings of compassion. Yet it seems quite odd to say that "I feel mercy" in the sense that I can say that "I feel compassion" or "I feel pity." In the latter cases, I can identify some "feeling" or affective state that I can refer to as compassion and/or pity. But what emotional or affective state would I have in mind if I said "I feel mercy"? Suppose I am merciful to someone in the sense of sparing him some punishment or harm that he is due as a matter of justice. I might do this in response to emotions or affective states of compassion, pity, or kindness. But any ostensible emotion or feeling of mercy, which prompts the action, would simply seem to be one of those other feelings or affective states. So too, if I treat someone mercifully by being kind to him or rendering aid to him, the underlying emotion or affective state would seem to be that of compassion, pity, sympathy, and so forth. Aquinas for example, characterizes *misericordia* (mercy) as a "*compassio* (sympathy/compassion) for someone's distress that results in an action to assist someone."[103]

If so, merciful actions and mercy can stem both from pity and compassion unless pity simply involves feeling sorry for someone in a way that does not lead to action. Works of mercy (*eleēmosynē*) can reflect the tenor of the compassion or pity from which they spring. In the novel *Beware of Pity*, for example, Edith more than once caustically accuses Lt Hofmiller of being a good Samaritan,[104] who is moved solely by pity and self-interest and who treats her in a demeaning way because he views her as nothing more than a helpless cripple who is at best a child. On the other hand, in Jesus' parable of the good Samaritan, the Samaritan "moved by compassion" (*splanchnizomai*) is the only one in the parable who shows mercy (*eleos*) to the man who had been assaulted—a Jew,[105] whom Samaritans typically despised and who typically despised Samaritans. The mercy the Samaritan shows to the Jew out of compassion cuts through the denigrating ways in which Samaritans and Jews typically viewed each other, so that the Samaritan was a true neighbor to the Jew.

Moreover, while compassion may and often does give rise to merciful actions in either sense of mercy (judicial mercy or works of mercy), compassion is not

---

[102] Aaron Ben-Zeév, *The Subtlety of Emotions* (Cambridge, MA: MIT Press, 2000), 334.
[103] Thomas Aquinas, *Summa Theologiae* 2.2ae.30.1.res. Aquinas follows Augustine, *De Civitate Dei* 9.5.
[104] Zweig, 66, 187, and 195.
[105] The parable does not actually indicate the man is a Jew, but he is usually taken to be one.

limited to such actions. For example, one might be moved by compassion to render assistance of some sort (medical, food, water, and so forth) to those who live in a refugee camp. Providing such assistance might be described as acts of mercy in the sense of being kind or benevolent to others. However, I might also offer compassionate assistance by rendering them aid that I believe they deserve and to which they are entitled. My compassion for them might lead me to pursue justice for them.[106] This observation leads to the next section of this chapter.

Compassion and Justice

At first glance, justice and compassion appear to be rather disparate notions. Justice—at least human justice—typically refers to what is due to someone morally or legally as a duty or obligation. Hence, it does not seem to depend on particular feelings or affective stances towards individuals that someone might have. A trial judge, who operates within the rule of law in the United States, might find a particular defendant loathsome and believe that the defendant actually committed the crime of which he or she is charged. Nevertheless, the judge may be obligated to dismiss the charges if a confession made by the defendant was obtained illegally and violates procedural justice. A trial judge might be exceptionally sympathetic or compassionate towards the plight of a person found guilty of a crime. But the judge may lack any legal basis for discretion to act on that compassion if there are mandatory sentencing guidelines. As an officer of the court, the judge has an obligation in this case to comply with procedural justice in these cases even if that means that a factually guilty person goes free or a legally guilty[107] person receives an inordinately harsh sentence.

Treating people justly often requires following certain rules or at least using some sort of rational deliberation to uphold the requirements of justice. However, in being moved by compassion (or pity), one seems to allow oneself to be moved by a certain affective stance that either sets aside what justice requires, or that prompts one to go beyond the demands of justice. In this case, being moved by compassion (or pity) seems to result in treating people mercifully rather than justly. Helping people out of compassion (or pity) seems to be basically different from responding to someone because of a particular moral or legal obligation.

---

[106] In addition to the next section, see Chapter 6, pp. 241–47 for further discussion.

[107] "Factual guilt" means the person in fact did what he is accused of doing. "Legal guilt" means that the person has been found guilty only as the result of a criminal trial, confession, plea bargain, or some other legal process that is accepted by the court. The two kinds of guilt do not always coincide with each other in every criminal proceeding.

This view, however, might be a bit too premature. While justice may require that people act in certain ways independently of whether they have sympathy, empathy, or compassion towards people, being moved by compassion to act on behalf of people is clearly compatible with treating people justly. Indeed, it can involve treating people justly by working to ensure that conditions of justice exist. For example, one could be moved by compassion to assist people in refugee camps by working to eliminate unjust conditions of supply distribution, e.g., when certain groups or individuals receive excess supplies relative to others based upon some discriminatory criteria. Or, one could be moved by compassion to assist refugees by working with them to create infrastructures that would facilitate the efficient and just distribution of goods. In these sorts of situations, compassion does not lead to mercy in the sense of doing something beyond or even in opposition to justice. Compassion cannot be reduced simply to treating people in a non-obligatory kindly and benevolent manner. In a similar vein, Chrysostom writes to those who were obsessed with determining whether people merited assistance: "So then if you see any one in affliction, be not curious to enquire further. His being in affliction involves a just claim on your aid (*to dikaiōma tēs boēthieas*)."[108]

Moreover, compassion can play an important role in helping people to realize that other people are suffering or afflicted precisely because they are unjustly denigrated and stigmatized. Our history is littered with far too many examples of degradation, marginalization, exploitation, or oppression of some groups by those who justify such treatment since they believe the members of these marginalized groups are ostensibly not fully human or are "defective" in ways that justify depriving them of full moral or legal status. We are remarkably adept at creating "out groups" whose differential treatment is ostensibly justified because of their alleged danger to society, depravity, or lack of full humanity. These justifications can even be proffered in (pseudo-)rational terms, e.g., the use of Social Darwinism to support eugenics and racism.[109]

The "abstract" rational or even theological appeal to a common humanity with inalienable rights, inherent dignity, or equality of honor by no means effectively counters unjust discrimination and oppression. The "cognitive" basis of discrimination may not rest merely on conceptual mistakes (e.g., in stereotyping)

---

[108]John Chrysostom, *Homilies on Hebrews* 10 (NPNF[1] 14:602; PG 63:88).

[109]Carolyn Burdett, "Post Darwin: Social Darwinism, Degeneration, Eugenics," *Discovering Literature: Romantics & Victorians* (15 May 2014), <https://www.bl.uk/romantics-and-victorians/articles/post-darwin-social-darwinism-degeneration-eugenics>, April 20, 2020.

but on stigmatization in a full-blown sense or the condescending pity as exemplified by Lt Hofmiller. Stigmatization in particular is driven by a fundamentally affective component of rejection and/or denigration that typically resists simple appeals to reason and in fact may be supported by the rationalizations of those who stigmatize others.

We have a clear example of this when we consider the words people use to denigrate and stigmatize people. The reader can easily think of an entire array of offensive terms that are used to denigrate people because of race, gender, disability, sexual orientation, religious affiliation, and so forth. These terms, such as "nigger," used in reference to black people, have a visceral meaning of rejection and disaffiliation built into them. They are uttered with a toxic edge that adds a strident meaning of hatred and fear to the term. People who use these terms are often unresponsive to rational discussion about those whom they stigmatize since the source of the stigmatization is not simply conceptual confusion but a deep-seated hatred and fear, as Sartre observed. We typically make no effort to rehabilitate these terms in civil discourse given the toxic meanings that are built into them.[110]

Put simply: discrimination and prejudicial treatment of people and groups, especially when they rest on stigmatization, lead to an objectification of people who are "reduced" to whatever characteristics are construed as the basis of their defectiveness. They fundamentally undercut any genuine just treatment of people and groups and effectively preclude and often reject genuine communion and solidarity between members of dominant and marginalized groups. Compassion, as I will argue later, can "cut through," protest against, and reject the visceral emotions and passions that individuals and social groups use to objectify, diminish, and degrade people. This is because compassion consists in an affective, nonjudgmental acceptance of others as fellow human beings that, at a visceral "level," counters the visceral rejection or denigration of others.[111] In this fundamental sense, compassion does not simply render mercy to people but it serves to do them justice. But more on this in Chapter 6.

---

[110]On the other hand, the context in which such terms are used, e.g., black people who use this term to refer to other black people, may affect the visceral, degrading meaning that otherwise attaches to it. Cf. Keith Allan, "Contextual Determinants on the Meaning of the N Word" *SpringerPlus* 5, article number 1141 (2016), <https://doi.org/10.1186/s40064-016-2813-1>, April 20, 2020.

[111]See Chapter 5, pp. 197–200.

Compassion, the Bowels or Viscera, and the Heart

We often refer to a "compassionate heart" or a "merciful heart."[112] These phrases are of particular significance in the Orthodox Christian faith given by St Isaac the Syrian's profound description of a merciful heart:

> And what is a merciful heart? . . . The burning of the heart for creation, man, fowls and animals, demons and whatever exists; so that by the recollection and sight of them the eyes shed tears on account of the force of mercy which moves the heart by great compassion. Then the heart becomes small and is not able to bear hearing or examining injury or any insignificant suffering of anything in the creation. . . . [E]ven in behalf of those who do harm to it, at all times he offers prayers with tears that they may be guarded and strength-ened . . . on account of his great compassion which is poured out in his heart without measure, after the example of God.[113]

We do not just talk about the human heart, but we also talk about God's heart or the heart of God. So, the Romanian Orthodox Theologian Dumitru Stăniloae writes:

> The intoxication of the love of God, experienced at the height of pure prayer, fills me with the impulse to love all people, to accept all in my heart, who are found in the heart of God, to feel that I am with all in the interior of the same "home" of God, which is the Church.[114]

In a somewhat different register, we also talk about the bowels of mercy (*splanchna eleous*) or the bowels of compassion (*splanchna oiktirou/oiktirmōn*). The scriptural basis for the first phrase is Luke 1.78, "Through the bowels of mercy (*splanchna eleous*) of our God, with which the Dayspring from on high has visited us." The second phrase occurs in Colossians 3.12 where adopting the bowels of compassion [*splanchna oiktirmōn*] is among the things St Paul exhorts us to do as sons of God or as putting on Christ.[115]

[112]Cf. Bobrinskoy, *Compassion*, 65–66.

[113]Isaac of Nineveh [Isaac the Syrian], *Mystic Treatises* 74; *Mystic Treatises of Isaac of Nineveh: Translated from Bedjan's Syriac Text with an Introduction and Registers*, trans. A. J. Wensinck (Amsterdam: De Akadamie: 1923), 341. Cf. *Homily* 71, in *The Ascetical Homilies of St Isaac the Syrian* [*Orationes ascetici*], 2nd rev. ed., trans. Holy Transfiguration Monastery (Boston: Holy Transfiguration Monastery, 2011), 491, which is translated from the Greek text (with reference to the Syriac).

[114]*Orthodox Spirituality: A Practical Guide for the Faithful and a Definitive Manual for the Scholar,* trans. Archimandrite Jerome and Otilia Kloos (Waymart, PA: St Tikhon's Seminary Press: 2003), 326.

[115]See Chapter 3, pp. 99–100 for further discussion of this text.

We are more likely today to link compassion and mercy with the heart (*kardia*) rather than the bowels (*splanchna*), whatever that might mean. But just the opposite is the case in Orthodox Christian service texts and Greek patristic and Byzantine writings. For example, in the principal service texts of the Church,[116] the phrase *splanchna eleous* occurs more than eighty times. The phrase *splanchna oiktirmōn* occurs more than thirty times. There is only one occurrence of the phrase *eleēmōn kardia* ("merciful heart"). The same disparity in use of these phrases occurs in the extensive collection of Greek texts in the *Thesaurus Linguae Graecae*.

However, simply because compassion and mercy in these Greek texts are connected far more directly with the bowels (*splanchna*) than with the heart does not mean that compassion and mercy are not connected with the heart. The seminal text by St Isaac the Syrian on the merciful heart makes this clear. So too:

> The invocation of the name of God is inseparable from the mystery of the heart, for there the Name is engraved, the presence of the beloved is lived. We can speak of the heart of God, of the heart of the Father, of His bowels of mercy. In the heart of the Father, the Name of the Son resides, just as in the heart of the Son the Name of the Father resides.[117]

This brief reflection raises the immediate questions: What is meant by *splanchnon/splanchna*? How can we effectively translate this term in contemporary English to convey its meaning? What is meant by heart (*kardia*), especially in the Orthodox Christian tradition? How might both heart and *splanchna* be related to compassion?

In classical Greek, the term *splanchnon*, most often used in the plural as *splanchna*, referred in the physiological sense to the internal organs especially used in a sacrifice (e.g., the heart, kidneys, lungs) and in a broader sense to any part of the "innards"—basically the internal organs that are found in the abdominal and thoracic cavities of the body. In a transferred or metaphorical sense, *splanchna* refers to the seat of the emotions, ranging from more aggressive emotions in classical Greek culture to mercy and compassion in the Judeo-Christian tradition.[118]

We find one mapping, by no means complete, of various affective and mental traits onto various organs in *The Testaments of the Twelve Patriarchs*: "For God

---

[116]See Chapter 4 for an overview of these texts.

[117]Bobrinskoy, *Compassion*, 104.

[118]John Thayer, *A Greek-English Lexicon of the New Testament: Being Grimm's Wilke's Clavis Novi Testamenti* (New York: Harper and Brothers, 1889), 584–5

made all things good, in order: the five senses in the head ... then the heart for understanding (*phronēsis*) ..., the liver for wrath, the gall for bitterness, the spleen for laughter, and the kidneys for knavery."[119] While there is no specific mapping of compassion (*eusplanchnia*) onto a particular organ, the term *eusplanchnos* in a medical sense literally means healthy or good *splanchna*. It certainly can carry the transferred sense of healthy or well-ordered *splanchna*; namely, in a Christian context, those that manifest compassion or mercy.

In either case, since the English term "bowels" generally refers to the intestines or entrails, it does not capture the broad sense of the internal organs signified by *splanchna*. Samuel Johnson's English Dictionary from 1768 defines bowels as "intestines; vessels or organs within the body."[120] However, the second meaning—"vessels or organs within the body"—is basically lost in later English. To use "bowels" in the usual meaning of intestines would not capture the second physiological meaning that Johnson gave to "bowels."

This narrow meaning of "bowels" has an important consequence for capturing in English the transferred or metaphorical meaning of *splanchna* as the "seat of the emotions." In many traditional English translations of *splanchna eleous* or *splanchna oiktirmou/oiktirmōn* we often find "bowels of mercy" or "bowels of compassion." For example, in the Darby translation of the Bible, published in the nineteenth century, we find: "Through the bowels of mercy (*splanchna eleous*) of our God" (Lk 1.78) and "put on.... bowels of compassion (*splanchna oiktirmou*)" (Col. 3.12). It is not likely that anyone understood this literally to mean "intestines of mercy" or "intestines of compassion." More modern translations, often use phrases like "tender mercy/mercies"[121] or "compassion."

While these latter translations capture a basic sense of the Greek, they miss the important point in the literal translation of the Greek, which indicates the "place" of mercy and of compassion: mercy and compassion belong to or are located in the *splanchna*. Moreover, while compassionate action expresses tenderness; compassion, as I note below, involves an awareness of suffering or distress which can be, and often is, acute. In any event, if "bowels" does not work for conveying this transferred sense, how might we translate it? The phrase "inward parts" is an older expression in English that captured the broad meaning of *splanchna* and also a cluster of Hebrew terms. The term "innards" carries the broad physiological

---

[119] *Testament of Naphtali* 2.8 (*Testaments* 301; Greek 147–48).
[120] Samuel Johnson, *A Dictionary of the English Language*, 3rd ed. (Dublin: W. G. Jones, 1768), 41.
[121] The KJV uses "tender mercy" at Luke 1.78.

meaning of *splanchna*. The term "gut" seems to refer to the entrails in the physiological sense but has the broad transferred sense of *splanchna* as the seat of our emotions.

The term, however, in English that is perhaps closest in meaning to *splanchna* is "viscera," the *viscera nobilia*; namely, the organs of the chest such as heart, lungs, liver, spleen etc.[122] The English term "viscera" has the same meaning as the Latin term *viscera*. In the Vulgate translation of Luke 1.78 and Colossians 3.12, *viscera misericordiae* is used to translate the Greek phrases above. In other words, "viscera" can serve to capture both the physiological and the transferred or metaphorical meanings of *splanchna*. The phrases "viscera of mercy" or "viscera of compassion" are used at times in English, and they quite closely follow the literal sense of *splanchna eleous*. But the equivalent phrases that I will use at times for this project are "visceral mercy" and "visceral compassion."

These phrases are particularly helpful in capturing the meaning of one of the principal Greek terms to express compassion, especially in the Synoptic Gospels. The verb is *splanchnizomai* which means a "movement as to the *splanchna*."[123] One theological dictionary has a general definition of the verb as "a movement as to the bowels."[124] But the term "bowels" in any modern literal sense as "intestines" is too narrow. Rather, one who is moved by compassion in this sense experiences a deep visceral, affective awareness of the suffering of someone that leads him to act on behalf of this person. Moreover, this compassionate awareness of others often involves distress, sadness, grief, and even tears for the person who is moved by compassion. This awareness may, but need not be, "gut-wrenching."

Standard translations of this verb in Greek-English dictionaries and in translations of the verb in English versions of the Bible by "has compassion," "feels compassion," or even "moved with compassion" miss the sense of the verb *splanchnizomai* that compassion is the source or that out of which someone is moved towards another person to act on his behalf. In modern English, at least, I may be moved with love to care for you; or, I may be moved with anger to correct you. That is, my love or my anger is that by means of which, taken in an instrumental sense, I am caring for you or correcting you. But that is simply not the same as saying that I am moved by love to care for you or I am moved by anger to correct you. Moved by love or anger means that I am moved out of love or anger—that

[122]James Hastings, *Dictionary of the Apostolic Church* (New York: Charles Scribner's Sons, 1918) 2:240.
[123]See Chapter 3, pp. 103–105 for its reference to Christ.
[124]Thayer, *Greek English Lexicon*, 584.

is, my love or my anger is the source of my movement towards you to care for you or correct you. Of course, in being moved out of love to care for you, I can also be moved with love to care for you. The same distinction between "with" and "by" applies to translating *splanchnizomai*, which is why I will use "moved by compassion" for translating it. In any event, to be moved by compassion is to be moved in a deeply visceral manner.

But we have to be careful of the term "viscera," since we often construe visceral emotions to be negative and crude or simply irrational. Yet, while the ancient Greeks may have linked the viscera with toxic emotions and passions, the Hellenic-Hebrew and Greek tradition capture a visceral dimension to mercy and compassion by situating them in the *splanchna*. Moreover, while we often tend to compartmentalize ourselves by opposing the heart and the embodied source of our emotions (*splanchna*) with the mind and reason, the Orthodox Christian tradition adopts a far more holistic and integrated view of our being. To see that, I will turn very briefly to the notion of heart (*kardia*) in the Orthodox Christian tradition.

The heart (Hebrew *lev*, Greek *kardia*) can, of course, refer to the physical organ (e.g., 2 Sam 18.14). But in both the Old and the New Testament, "heart" has the transferred meaning of the holistic center—physical, mental, and spiritual—of the human person as the "seat and center of spiritual life." Prayer of the heart, for example, is a prayer of the whole person: body, soul or mind, and spirit. The heart is where we encounter the Holy Spirit. But the heart is also the battleground of good and evil.[125] In the Orthodox tradition, then, the heart is not simply the seat of irrational emotions in contrast to the mind. Rather, emotions (affectivity), mind (*nous* or intellect),[126] and spirit are united in the heart. [127] There is, then, some overlap in meaning between *kardia* (heart) and *splanchna* (viscera).

[125]Ware, "How Do We Enter the Heart and What Do We Find When We Enter," in *Merton & Hesychasm: The Prayer of the Heart and the Eastern Church*, ed. Bernadette Dieker and Jonathan Montaldo, Fons Vitae Merton Series (Louisville, KY: Fons Vitae, 2003), 8.

[126]The Greek term *nous* is often translated both as "mind" and as "intellect." The former term has the broad sense of referring to our mental life and capacities. However, the Greek term *nous* has a narrower sense: the capacity to intuitively or directly know certain realities. In the Greek philosophical tradition, these realities are basically fundamental immaterial principles that can be rationally known (e.g., the Forms for Plato). In the Orthodox Christian tradition, *nous* is understood as a spiritual intellect that "understands divine truth [and other divine realities] by means of immediate experience, intuition, or 'simple cognition'" (*Philokalia* 1:362). I will use both "mind" and "intellect" throughout the book since the distinction between them in English is not critical for this project.

[127]See below, Chapter 5, pp. 181–85. Cf. Archimandrite Zacharias, *The Hidden Man of the Heart: The Cultivation of the Heart in Orthodox Christian Anthropology*, ed. Christopher Veniamin (Waymart, PA: Mount Thabor Publishing, 2008), 12–13.

Both designate the seat of human affectivity, although *splanchna* (viscera) does not quite seem to connote the depth of spiritual reality as does *kardia* (heart). Moreover, *splanchna* in some contexts acquires the sense of heart in the Christian tradition. For example, the term is translated that way in some newer English translations of the New Testament.[128]

In light of this more modern choice to translate *splanchna* as "heart," it is perhaps not surprising that some newer translations of Colossians 3.12 render *splanchna oiktirmou* as "heart of compassion" or "heart of mercy."[129] If we recall that we are to put on a heart of mercy because we are God's elect, or because we are to put on Christ, then this is a particularly apt translation, as long as we bear in mind the holistic nature of the heart as rooted in and animated by the grace of the Holy Spirit, the center and ground of our experience of God's presence and compassion for us. So animated, we are able to experience God's—Christ's—compassion in our lives and respond to that compassion in prayer and worship, but also through manifesting that compassion in the world through our own compassion.

Summary and Looking Forward

Summary

The primary goal of this project is to develop an understanding of compassion within the Orthodox Christian tradition as a fundamental disposition and virtue in human life generally and in Orthodox Christian life in particular. As a reminder, the sense of compassion that I am developing is not simply restricted to Orthodox Christians. Rather, we are looking at the capacity for compassion that belongs to us by nature—a natural compassion—and is brought to a fullness and perfection in Orthodox spiritual life in our striving to become like Christ or living icons of Christ.

In this chapter, we have seen that terms such as "compassion," "sympathy," "mercy," "pity," and "empathy" have a variety of meanings in contemporary English. There are similar terms in Hebrew and Greek as well. But if we want to develop an understanding of compassion, it is important to sort out relations

---

[128]Cf. Philem 1.7, "because the *splanchna* of the saints." The KJV and Douay-Rheims Bible use "bowels." The NKJV and NASB use "heart." See also Philem 1.20 and 1 Jn 3.17.

[129]Cf. NASB, American Standard Version, and the English Revised Version. However, none of these bibles or any other English or American translations that I can find translate *splanchna eleous* in reference to God with "heart of compassion."

between compassion and other things such as sympathy, pity, or mercy. I have tried to do this in a general way so far, which provides the basis for the analysis of compassion in Chapter 5. I also spent some time developing the understanding of our *splanchna* (viscera) and the *kardia* (heart) as the locus of compassion and the range of passions that counter it. I noted that in the Orthodox tradition, the heart is the holistic center—physical, mental, and spiritual—of our existence. As a reminder, I have discussed compassion in this chapter as an emotional affective state that involves affectivity, understanding, and intentions, whether or not it occurs with any frequency or regularity. In Chapter 5, I will develop the sense of compassion as a stable disposition and a virtue, and I will distinguish it from compassion as a simple emotion that lacks any clear understanding or intentionality. I will now briefly discuss some key indicators from this chapter that will provide the basis for the analysis of compassion in Chapters 5 and 6.

Looking Forward

1) Compassion involves not just some awareness of suffering or distress, but it also provides an impetus to action to assist and be with people. Like the Greek *sympatheia* in the strong sense, compassion involves a suffering or bearing with others. Indeed, God's compassion manifests itself as a solidarity with us and all of creation that does not forsake us. This indicator will be developed in Chapter 5 when I discuss the structure of compassion as a disposition.[130]

2) Compassion involves not only action but also intentions and some understanding of people. We are moved by compassion primarily or even exclusively for the sake of others and not ourselves. I briefly touched on this matter in discussing the difference between pity and compassion. This is important for developing a sense of compassion as a virtue, since our intentions are crucial to determining whether or not we are living and acting virtuously. Our discussion so far provides an indicator for developing, in Chapter 5, the sorts of intentions that can belong to compassion both as a virtue beautiful in itself or for various prizes, and thereby distinguish compassion from pity and other self-aggrandizing passions and dispositions.[131]

3) In sharp contrast to pity, compassion fundamentally rejects denigration, stigmatization, and the social marginalization and oppression that follow from them. This means that compassion, like pity, involves ways of perceiving and

---

[130]See above, p. 39. See Chapter 5, pp. 194, 202, 231.
[131]See above, p. 55. See Chapter 5, pp. 217–27.

understanding others. I will take up this matter in Chapter 5 to discuss the way in which compassion does not involve an "examination" or judgment of others but is a holistic affirmation of the humanity and uniqueness of each person. This indicator will also be central in Chapter 6 to show how compassion is connected with justice.[132]

4) Another key indicator is that both compassion and pity involve dealing with human vulnerability: both the vulnerability of those who suffer and, most especially, our own vulnerability. Compassion involves coming to terms with our own vulnerability in a way that pity does not: in compassion we accept our vulnerability; in pity we often deny it or turn away from it. We often consider vulnerability in relation to particular situations or conditions such as vulnerability to poverty, assault, or abandonment. But is there a more fundamental vulnerability that belongs to us simply as created, finite beings that provides a basis for a universal compassion that is directed to all people (and indeed all creation), independently of whether someone is actually suffering or in some particular distress? We will discuss this point in detail in Chapter 5 in the section that discusses coming to terms with vulnerability.[133]

5) Compassion and mercy are not the same thing. Merciful actions can arise from pity and compassion. Moreover, people can act compassionately on behalf of others for the sake of obtaining justice for people and not simply being merciful. This indicator will be central in Chapter 6 in discussing the relation between compassion and justice.[134]

6) Compassion is not simply a free-floating emotion but is central to our life of repentance. As we saw, compassion (along with a number of other affective dimensions of our lives) is located in the viscera and, especially in the Orthodox Christian tradition, in the heart as the holistic center of our personhood. The heart unites the physical, mental, and spiritual dimensions of ourselves. It is also a battleground between good and evil. I have touched upon the ways in which various toxic passions and attitudes undermine compassion but also the ways in which compassion can prevent these passions and heal us from them. Compassion, then, would play a vital role in repentance—the forward-looking project in which, with the grace of the Holy Spirit, we strive to become living icons of Christ. This indicator will also show up in various places in Chapters 3 and 4.

---

[132]See above, pp. 57–61. See Chapter 5, pp. 197–98. See Chapter 6, pp. 241–43.
[133]See above, pp. 61–62. See Chapter 5, pp. 205–210.
[134]See above, pp. 64–65, 66. See Chapter 6, pp. 243–44, 247–55.

It will also be developed in various ways throughout Chapter 5, particularly in the discussion of how compassion is perfected through obtaining the state of dispassion.[135]

7) Compassion and tears: St Isaac the Syrian describes a person with a merciful heart as one who "sheds tears" at the sight of suffering. Of course, grief, sorrow, and tears can often accompany compassion in response to suffering. But what is the connection between compassion and tears? Must compassion always involve tears? Can compassion be limited to tears? The brief mention of a connection between compassion and tears in this chapter provides an indicator to be developed in the discussion of this topic in Chapter 5.[136]

[135]See above, pp. 72–73. See Chapter 5, pp. 181–85.
[136]See above, p. 68. See Chapter 5, pp. 194–97.

CHAPTER 3

Compassion in the Divine Liturgy and in Holy Scripture

In the previous chapter, I tried to provide a sketch of a conceptual map for understanding compassion, mercy, sympathy, and so forth. Providing these sorts of maps is important since, whether we like it or not, our personal and collective experience and understanding of reality is shaped by our concepts and ideas.[1] Compassion itself, however, is not a concept. It is something real, the experience and manifestation of which are vital for our lives. In the Orthodox tradition, the experience and manifestation of compassion are framed in a theological setting that involves intellectual inquiry and also, and most importantly, experiential awareness. This experiential theological setting is grounded in what God and Christ reveal to us and that we accept on faith, the teachings and Holy Tradition of the Orthodox Church, our worship, our prayer life and experience, the witness of people who manifest compassion, and so forth.

As I mentioned earlier, if developing a compassionate disposition and virtue is integral to attaining to a likeness to Christ and, thus, to God, we need to begin with some understanding of what divine compassion involves. Rather than begin with some theoretical explanation of this compassion, as Orthodox Christians we should begin with our experience of God's—the Trinity's—and Christ's compassion. Each of us has—one may hope—his own personal experience of this compassion. But there are two principal "places" where the Church offers us an experience of divine compassion that we share. First, we have the personal and communal lived experience of this compassion in the divine services and sacraments of the Church, and especially in the Divine Liturgy. Second, we have a shared, revealed source for our indirect experience of divine compassion in human history in the Old and New Testaments.

---

[1] Of course, our experiences can lead us to change and revise our concepts and the words we use to express them.

In order to show the profound and vital role of compassion in the Orthodox Christian tradition, I want to start in the first section of the chapter with the experience and manifestation of compassion in the Divine Liturgy, since that Liturgy grounds Orthodox Christian worship and experience.

> The Holy Eucharist is called the "sacrament of sacraments" in the Orthodox tradition. It is also called the "sacrament of the Church." The Eucharist is the center of the Church's life. Everything in the Church leads to the Eucharist, and all things flow from it. It is the completion of all of the Church's sacraments—the source and the goal of all of the Church's doctrines and institutions.[2]

The principal manifestation of the compassion of the Trinity in the Divine Liturgy takes place in the consecration and distribution of the gifts of bread and wine as the Body and Blood of our Lord, Jesus Christ. But in that Liturgy, we are also called to manifest compassion in our own lives: what is often called the "liturgy after the Liturgy."

Orthodox Christianity does not arise spontaneously, as it were. It develops as the New Covenant that emerges from the Old Covenant of the Jewish faith. As we will see, the Anaphora (Eucharistic) Prayer of the Liturgy of St Basil makes special mention of how God's compassion is manifest throughout the Old Testament and continues in the New Testament. Moreover, one of the central terms to express God's compassion in the Liturgy, *oiktirmos*, traces back to the Septuagint's use of that term to translate the Hebrew term *racham* ("compassion" in the Old Testament). Hence, in the second section of the chapter, I will turn to the manifestation of God's compassion in the Old Testament. I will pay special attention to God's theophany to Moses on Mount Sinai[3] in which God reveals himself as compassionate (*rachuwm, oiktirmōn*), and merciful (*channon, eleēmōn*) and shows that compassion and mercy fundamentally belong to his name—that is, himself. I will also briefly discuss God's injunctions in the Old Testament that we are to show compassion to one another.

God's compassion for the Israelites as a people is extended to all people in the promise of the Suffering Servant, whom Christians identify as the promised Messiah, Christ.[4] The compassion manifest in Christ's Incarnation—the eternal Son of God who becomes human as the fully divine and fully human Jesus

---

[2]Thomas Hopko, *The Orthodox Faith* (Crestwood, NY: St Vladimir's Seminary Press, 2016), 2:38.
[3]Ex 33–34.
[4]Is 49.8–12.

Christ—continues and develops the compassion (*racham*) that God shows to the Israelites. Hence, in the third section, I will consider the reality of compassion in the New Testament: Christ's compassion towards us and our responsibility to manifest that compassion in our own lives.

While we can read, discuss, and meditate on the Bible "on its own," the Church incorporates many biblical texts in the services of the Church such as gospel and epistle readings, prokeimenon verses, and psalms. In our services, these biblical texts "come alive," as it were, to guide us, enrich our worship, and to provide a scriptural anchor for these services. Hence, the fourth section of this chapter will continue the discussion of compassion in the New Testament with a discussion of the gospel lessons that precede the start of Great Lent in the Orthodox Christian tradition.

I will conclude this section with a brief discussion of the role of repentance and compassion in Great Lent. Great Lent is a time to focus our life on repentance (*metanoia*) in response to what Christ endures for us in his life that leads to his suffering and death on the cross, and what is accomplished through that death at Pascha, the feast of the Resurrection of the Lord. Repentance is not simply a backwards-looking matter of acknowledging wrong-doing and seeking forgiveness. It is fundamentally an ongoing, forward-looking project of a change of heart or mind in which, with God's grace, we try to refashion our lives in conformity with Christ. Repentance is fundamentally a process of forgiveness and healing that is crucial to our own cooperation with deification—becoming a living icon of Christ in this life and in the next. I hope to show that the gospel lessons in the *Triodion* (the service book for Great Lent) for the Sundays that precede the start of Great Lent provide a rich source for illuminating how the cultivation of a compassionate disposition is vital for the project of repentance: reshaping our lives to become living icons of Christ, which is the fundamental vocation we have as human beings.

In the final section of the chapter, Summary and Looking Forward, I will provide a brief review of this chapter and point out of several indicators about compassion in this chapter that will be developed in Chapters 5 and 6.

Compassion in the Divine Liturgy

'It is time for the Lord to act (*poiēsai*).'

This verse from Psalm 118.126 comes at the very beginning of the Divine Liturgy.[5] The deacon says this to the priest just before the opening invocation of the Liturgy: "Blessed is the Kingdom of the Father and of the Son and of the Holy Spirit." What sort of action do we believe God will accomplish in the Liturgy? We find an indication in the Prayer of the First Antiphon that comes at the end of the Great Litany:

> *Priest:* O Lord our God, whose dominion is incomparable and glory incomprehensible, whose mercy (*eleos*) is immeasurable and love for mankind (*philanthrōpia*) ineffable: O Master, look upon us and upon this holy house in your loving kindness (*eusplanchnian*, or compassion) and grant (*poiēson*, or impart) to us and to those who pray with us your abundant mercy (*ta eleē*) and compassion (*tous oiktirmous*).[6]

This prayer is very often said silently or in a low voice by the priest. "Impart" (or similar words such as "grant" or "bestow") translates *poiēson*. Like *poiēsai* from Psalm 118.26, it is a form of the verb *poieō*, which has the basic sense of acting, making, or producing something. However, "impart your abundant mercy and compassion" does not quite catch a nuance of the Greek. The terms *ta eleē* and *tous oiktirmous* are plural in number. Although such terms are often translated as singular terms in English—"mercy" and "compassion"—the prayer literally requests

[5]*Service Books,* 26. Some OCA editions of the Divine Liturgy use "It is time to begin the service of the Lord" (*Divine Liturgy, Chrysostom,* 25). For discussions of this phrase, see Matthew Steenberg, "The Church" in *The Cambridge Companion to Orthodox Christian Theology,* ed. Mary B. Cunningham and Elizabeth Theokritoff (Cambridge: Cambridge University Press, 2008), 121 and 133; Elizabeth Theokritoff, "From Sacramental Life to Sacramental Living: Heeding the Message of the Environmental Crisis," *Greek Orthodox Theological Review* 44.1–4 (1999): 513; Lawrence Farley, "It Is Time for the Lord to Act: The Significance of Assembling," Orthodox Church in America, <https://oca.org/reflections/fr.-lawrence-farley/it-is-time-for-the-lord-to-act-the-significance-of-assembling>, April 20, 2020.

[6]The Orthodox Greek Orthodox Archdiocese of America, *The Divine Liturgy of St John Chrysostom,* <https://www.goarch.org/-/the-divine-liturgy-of-saint-john-chrysostom>, April 20, 2020, mod. The translation of *eusplanchnia* as "loving kindness" is used by the Greek Orthodox Church although the term *eusplanchnia* is variously rendered by "tender compassion." Cf. St Nicholas Russian Orthodox Church, "Divine Liturgy of St John Chrysostom English, with parts in Slavonic (in Russian letters)," <https://www.orthodox.net/services/sluzebnic-chrysostom-es.pdf>, April 20, 2020. One version of the Divine Liturgy used by The Orthodox Church in America has: "Look down on us . . . with pity" (*Service Books,* 33). This prayer is read during the divine liturgies of St John Chrysostom and St Basil the Great. As a brief note, it is not clear whether "tender compassion" adds anything to the translation of *eusplanchnia* simply as "compassion."

God to bring forth or impart his "mercies" and "compassions." In fact, these plural English words are often used throughout the Divine Liturgy as translations of these Greek terms.

Compassion is often taken to be an "emotion" or "feeling" that moves someone to act on behalf of another. But surely, we are not asking that God simply bring forth or manifest various "feelings" that he might have. We are not asking God simply to "show sympathy" to us or "feel sorry" for us. Rather, the plural terms clearly refer to merciful actions and compassionate actions on behalf of those at the Liturgy. This Prayer of the First Antiphon that concludes the Great Litany asks God "in" or "because of" (*kata*)[7] his "tender compassion" (*eusplanchnia*) to bring forth or show among those present at the Liturgy his merciful actions (*ta eleē*) and his compassionate actions (*tous oiktirmous*), which are expressions of his divine energies of mercy and compassion. For what sort of divine compassionate actions do we hope in the Divine Liturgy?

Once again, we find an answer to our question in the Prayer of the Proskomedia:

> O Lord God Almighty, who alone are holy, who accept a sacrifice of praise from those that call upon you with their whole heart. Accept also the prayer of us sinners, and bear it to your holy altar, enabling us to offer unto you gifts and spiritual sacrifices for our sins and for the errors of the people. Make us worthy to find grace in your sight that our sacrifice may be acceptable unto you, and that the good Spirit of your grace may rest upon us, and upon these Gifts set forth, and upon all your people.
>
> *Exclamation:* Through the compassions (*oiktirmōn*, compassionate actions) of your Only-Begotten Son, with whom you are blessed, together with your most holy and good and life-creating Spirit, now and ever, and unto the ages of ages. Amen.[8]

The priestly exclamations to prayers during the Liturgy serve to conclude both the public petitions and the priestly prayers that constitute a particular litany. As

---

[7] "In" (*kata*) can also mean "according to" in the sense that we ask God to act a) "by means of" or "because of" his tender compassion and b) "in conformity with" his tender compassion. References to compassion, mercy, or *philanthrōpia* in Orthodox services always, so far as I can tell, involve thanking God, Christ, the Theotokos, or the saints for some action on our behalf or they involve petitioning them to act on our behalf. The reader can see this exemplified in the collection of hymns in Chapter 4.

[8] Or, Prayer of the Litany of Supplication. This prayer follows the Great Entrance during the Divine Liturgy of St John Chrysostom and is read by the priest (*Service Books*, 61).

with the priest's prayer at the end of the Great Litany, this Prayer of the Proskomedia is often said in a low voice or "silently." Among the actions in this prayer the priest bids the Trinity to take, the principal one is "that the good Spirit of your grace may rest upon us, upon the gifts set forth, and upon all of your people." The priest asks God to do this "through the compassions [compassionate actions]" of the Trinity. "Through" translates *dia* and has the causal sense of "by means of." This petition refers to the Epiclesis, the conclusion of the Anaphora Prayer, when the priest prays to the Father to send his Holy Spirit to change the gifts of bread and wine into the Body and Blood of the Lord.[9] This is clearly the primary divine action that expresses the entire purpose of the Liturgy: Christ's sharing of himself with the faithful in the eucharistic meal. Here are the consecratory words said by the priest at the Epiclesis in the Divine Liturgy of St John Chrysostom:

> *Priest:* Send down your Holy Spirit upon us and upon these Gifts set forth. (*Then, blessing the Lamb with the sign of the cross*): And make (*poiēson*) this Bread the precious Body of your Christ . . . (*And blessing the chalice with the sign of the cross*): And that which is in this Cup the precious Blood of your Christ . . . (*And the priest, blessing both the Holy Things says*): Changing them by your Holy Spirit (*to which the deacon responds*: Amen! Amen! Amen!).[10]

The Liturgy began with the declaration: "It is time for the Lord to act (*poiēsai*)." The compassionate and merciful actions that we asked God to impart or bring forth (*poiēsai*) at the end of the Great Litany are in fact fulfilled when the Holy Spirit makes or changes (*poiēson*) the bread and wine to be the Body and Blood of the Lord.[11] In the Liturgy of St Basil, the Holy Spirit is invoked to "bless, hallow, and show (*anadeixai*)" the bread and wine (the "antitypes") to be the Body and Blood of the Lord. "Showing" does not merely mean to make something appear but to bring forth, manifest, and to proclaim that, in being blessed and hallowed, the bread and wine are the Body and Blood of the Lord.[12]

As we saw in the Prayer of the Proskomedia, the actions of the clergy and a fortiori of the faithful are efficacious precisely because of God's compassion, which enables them to perform the Liturgy. Indeed, the very action of offering

[9]Liturgy of St John Chrysostom.

[10]*Service Books*, 70–71 mod. Words in italic are rubrics that indicate the actions the priest or others perform.

[11]The Epiclesis culminates the entire action that God takes throughout the Anaphora Prayer. It is not a kind of single moment detached from the consecratory prayers that precede it.

[12]Robert Taft, SJ, "Ecumenical Scholarship and the Catholic-Orthodox Epiclesis Dispute: Donohu Lecture 1996," *Ostkirchliche Studien* 45 (1996): 6–7.

the Liturgy is not accomplished simply by the clergy or the people but by Christ himself as the one High Priest of the Church. Christ is "the one who offers and the one who is offered."[13] The Liturgy of St Basil illustrates this in the prayer that precedes the consecratory words of the Epiclesis.

> Therefore, Most holy Master, we also your sinful and unworthy servants, whom you have permitted to serve at Your holy altar, not because of our own righteousness (for we have done nothing good on earth), but because of your mercy (*eleē*, merciful actions) and compassion (*oiktirmous*, compassionate actions), which you have richly poured out on us . . .[14]

The entire Liturgy—as a divine mystery (*mystērion*) or sacrament—is an expression of the compassionate actions of God—the Trinity—and Christ since the service itself, as the mystery of the eucharistic Gifts, takes place in the time (*kairos*) in which heaven meets earth. "The liturgy is served on earth, and this means in the time and space of 'this world.' But if it is served on earth, it is accomplished in heaven, in the new time of the new creation, in the time of the Holy Spirit."[15] The declaration that opens the Liturgy—"It is time for the Lord to act"—does not primarily indicate an ordinary time, e.g., 9:30 a.m. (EST), but rather the fullness of time, an eschatological time in which Christ makes himself present to us in his eucharistic Gifts and lifts us, as it were, out of ordinary clock time "into" a sacred time that joins heaven and earth. Or, put another way: the action of the Lord, the Trinity, in the Liturgy sanctifies the ordinary time of human life that is drawn into the fellowship (*koinōnia*) of the divine life "from which" Christ is present to us in the Liturgy itself and especially in the eucharistic Gifts. None of the actions of the clergy or the faithful, as important as they are—for there is no liturgical service apart the community that celebrates the Liturgy—can draw us into the sacred time in which the divine eucharistic mysteries are made present and accessible to us. It is only God's action that accomplishes this.

God's compassionate actions in the Divine Liturgy—celebrated by a particular Orthodox Christian community at a particular service—do not constitute an "isolated" event but rather a manifestation of God's compassion expressed throughout human history. The beautiful Anaphora Prayer to the Father in the Divine Liturgy of St Basil frames the Liturgy in the context of salvation history.

---

[13] *Service Books*, 57, 127 mod. from "the Offerer and the Offered." Prayer of the *Cherubic Hymn* said silently by the priest before the Great Entrance in both divine liturgies of St John Chrysostom and St Basil the Great.

[14] *Service Books*, 145 mod. and my italics.

[15] Alexander Schmemann, *The Eucharist* (Crestwood, NY: St Vladimir's Seminary Press, 1987), 218.

St Basil begins the prayer by remembering our creation and subsequent fall. But he then notes:

> For you did not turn yourself away forever from your creature, whom you made, O Good One, nor did you forget the works of your hands. Through the tender compassion of your mercy (*splanchna eleous*), you visited him in various ways. [16]

St Basil quotes Luke 1.78 where Zachariah prophesies the coming of Christ who "gives knowledge of salvation to his people by the forgiveness of their sins through the *splanchna eleous* of our God through which the Dayspring from on High shall visit us." The various ways in which God visited people before Christ[17] culminate when "the fullness of time had come, you [the Father] spoke to us through your Son himself."[18] St Basil's prayer then recites the key events of Christ's visitation to humans: the Incarnation "so that he might liken us to the image of his glory,"[19] and the key events of his earthy life, especially his cross, death, and Resurrection. Although Christ departs from his earthly life at the Ascension, gifts from his visitation remain: "he has left behind for us these things [bread and wine] of his saving passion, which we have set forth according to his command."[20] At each celebration of St Basil's Divine Liturgy, the compassion through which the Father has visited us in various ways throughout human history is connected with the Divine Liturgy in the blessing, hallowing, and showing of the bread and wine to be the Body and Blood of Christ.

As I noted earlier, *splanchna eleous* refers to a visceral mercy or compassion related to the verb *splanchnizomai*—a movement as to the viscera in which one is moved by compassion. This verb is used in the Synoptic Gospels uniquely of Christ and some characters in his parables.[21] Two examples of the use of this term are important for understanding the compassionate actions that we pray God to impart or show forth in the Divine Liturgy.[22]

---

[16] *Service Books*, 141.

[17] That is, through the prophets, the Law, angels as guardians, and saints.

[18] *Service Books*, 141

[19] *Ibid.*, 141.

[20] *Ibid.*, 142.

[21] See below, pp. 103–105 for further discussion.

[22] For a more complete discussion of the eucharistic interpretation of these events and their connection with the divine compassion and love of the Trinity as expressed in Orthodox Christian Icons of the Trinity, often referred to as *The Hospitality of Abraham*, see John D. Jones, "The Church as Neighbor," 17–21. Cf. Paul Meyendorff, "The Sacrament of Hospitality: A Liturgical Understanding of Hospitality and Communion," *St Vladimir's Theological Quarterly* 62.1 (2018): 131–144.

The feeding of the Four Thousand. In the accounts of this event in Matthew 15.32–39 and Mark 8.1–9, Christ is moved by compassion towards the people who have come to hear him, and he is not willing to let them depart without feeding them.[23] Thus, Christ multiplies the gifts of seven loaves and fish, the only food the disciples have at hand, so that the disciples can feed the people. This event has a double meaning (a) as a corporate compassionate action of Jesus and the disciples whereby people who are physically hungry are fed and (b) as an anticipation or prefiguration of the Eucharist. As Christ, moved by compassion, physically fed the four thousand, so Christ, who is the Bread of Life, feeds the faithful at the Divine Liturgy with the spiritual gifts of his own Body and Blood.

The parable of the good Samaritan. In this well-known parable, the good Samaritan, in contrast to the priest and Levite, is the one who, moved by compassion, tends to the wounded man by the side of the road. Although the parable is given in response to the question of the young man who wants to know "who is my neighbor," Jesus provides the parable to show the young man what it is to be a neighbor. To be a neighbor in the true sense is to be one who is moved by a compassionate disposition to draw near, to visit, and offer assistance and mercy as kindness to anyone who is afflicted or vulnerable.

As I mentioned in Chapter 1, there is a patristic tradition that interprets the parable of the good Samaritan as about Christ himself.[24] Orthodox icons for this parable represent the good Samaritan as Christ. Origen identifies Christ, the good Samaritan, as our neighbor.[25] St Clement of Alexandria answers the young man's question "Who is my neighbor" by answering:

> The Savior himself ... who has had mercy on us ... who cuts out the passions thoroughly by the root ... brought the oil which flows from the compassion (*splanchna*) of the Father, and bestowed it copiously. He it is that produced the ligatures of health and of salvation that cannot be undone—Love, Faith, Hope.[26]

Blessed Theophylact beautifully develops this same idea: "Our Lord and God ... journeyed to us.... He did not just catch a glimpse of us as He happened

[23]Mt 15.32 and Mk 8.2–3.

[24]See above, p. 21 n. 6.

[25]Origen, quoted in *Origen: Homilies on Luke, Fragments on Luke, The Fathers of the Church: A New Translation*, trans. Joseph T. Lienhard (Washington: Catholic University of America Press, 1996), 94.

[26]Clement of Alexandria, *Who Is the Rich Man That Shall Be Saved?* [*Liber quis dives salvetur*] 29, trans. William Wilson (ANF 2: 599; PG 2:633D–635A). Some editions have "compassions of the Spirit" for "compassions of the Father."

to pass by. He actually came to us and lived together with us and spoke to us. Therefore, He at once bound up our wounds."[27] The compassionate actions and works of mercy, which we pray that the Father, Son, and Holy Spirit will bring forth in the Liturgy, are themselves the expression of the compassion that Christ exercises as the good Samaritan. His compassion is expressed in his neighborliness to us in having taken on our own nature in order to live among us; to bear our sins, burdens, and afflictions; and to remain with us and not forsake us. This neighborliness continues right up to the service of a Divine Liturgy when Christ, who is the one who is offered and the one who offers, invisibly visits us again in his true and precious Body and Blood in the consecrated eucharistic Gifts. These gifts, although eaten by the faithful, are never consumed or destroyed, but they sanctify those who have partaken of them.[28] The neighborliness and hospitality that Christ's compassion expresses is a central indicator for the analysis of a compassionate disposition in Chapter 5.[29]

The Trinity imparts its compassionate actions to us during the Liturgy. But what about our response to these actions: our "liturgy after the Liturgy." I will discuss this later at the end of this chapter and again in Chapters 5 and 6. But texts by St John Chrysostom and Metropolitan Anastasios Yannoulatos give profound expression to the scope of what a compassionate liturgy after the Liturgy should involve. The first classic text of Chrysostom shows the deeply liturgical character of Christian compassion both in action and in how we see and understand others. We are not just to give to those who suffer and are afflicted. We are to see and understand them as persons to be honored and we are to resist and oppose those who would denigrate or insult them.

> Would you see his altar also?... This altar is composed of the very members of Christ, and the body of the Lord becomes an altar. This altar is more venerable even than the one which we now use. For it is ... but a stone by nature; but

---

[27] Blessed Theophylact, *The Explanation by Blessed Theophylact of the Holy Gospel According to Luke* [*Ennaratio in Evangelium Lucae*], trans. Christopher Stade (House Springs, MO.: Chrysostom Press, 2004), 119 (PG 123:849A–B, drawn from his commentary on Luke 10.29–37).

[28] Just before placing a portion of the consecrated Lamb in the chalice, the priest raises the Lamb aloft saying "The Holy Things are for the holy." While dividing the Lamb into four parts: one each for the chalice and for clergy taking Communion at the altar, and two for the faithful, he says: "Divided and distributed is the Lamb of God: who is divided, yet not disunited; who is ever eaten, yet never consumed; but sanctifying those who partake thereof" (*Divine Liturgy, Chrysostom*, 76). "Never consumed" means "never destroyed."

[29] See Chapter 5, pp. 192–93. For an excellent discussion about and collection of texts regarding hospitality in the early Church, please see Amy Oden, *And You Welcomed Me: A Sourcebook on Hospitality in Early Christianity* (Nashville, TN: Abingdon Press, 2001).

becomes holy because it receives Christ's Body: but that altar is holy because it is itself Christ's Body ... [which] you may see lying everywhere, in the alleys and in the market places, and you may sacrifice upon it anytime. ... When then you see a poor believer, believe that you are beholding an altar. When you see this one as a beggar, do not only refrain from insulting him, but actually give him honor, and if you witness someone else insulting him, stop him; prevent it.[30]

This liturgy after the Liturgy does not extend only to those who are poor or to those people who are poor and Christians, as Chrysostom's text might suggest. For Archbishop Anastasios, it extends to all people to alleviate personal suffering and social-structural issues of injustice. Noting that because we are not to "escape from life" with the Liturgy but go forward into the world to transform it according to Christ, we are to commit ourselves to "continuous liberation from the powers of the evil that are working inside us" and to orient ourselves to "efforts aimed at liberating human persons from all demonic structures of injustice, exploitation, agony, loneliness, and at creating real communion of persons in love."[31]

God's compassionate visitation with us and creation itself is fulfilled in the Incarnation in which the Son of God takes on human nature and becomes human: the Son of God as Christ, who assumes a personal face in human form. However, this divine compassionate engagement with humans continues God's manifestation of his compassion to the Israelites as found in the Old Testament. Having reflected on our lived experience of divine compassion in the Divine Liturgy, let us turn to our shared indirect experience of divine compassion in the Old Testament.

[30]John Chrysostom, *Homilies on Second Corinthians* 20 (NPNF[1] 12:374; PG 61:539–40). For a discussion of the poor as "altar," see Susan Holman, *The Hungry Are Dying* (Oxford: Oxford University Press, 2003), 60–63.

[31]Archbishop Anastasios (Yannoulatos) of Albania, cited in Ion Bria, "The Liturgy after the Liturgy," *International Review of Missions* 67 (Jan. 1978): 86, 87.

Compassion in the Old Testament

"The Lord, the Lord, God, compassionate, merciful, long suffering and full of mercy."[32]

"Forsake us not who put our hope in you."[33]

The first Old Testament reference to God's compassion (*racham, oiktirmos*)[34] occurs before and during God's theophany to Moses on Mount Sinai.[35] Moses had come down from Mount Sinai with the first tablets of the Law only to find that the Israelites had forsaken God in order to worship a golden calf.[36] God had warned Moses that he would discover this when he descended the mountain and that, since the Israelites had forsaken God for an idol, God threatened to consume or destroy them.[37] Moses successfully implores God to relent from this threat.[38] Indeed, rather than consuming them, God subsequently commands Moses to tell the Israelites to continue their journey to the land he promised them. Yet God only indicates that he will send his angel with them.[39] God declines to go with the Israelites himself because, if he does, he will destroy or consume them.[40]

While God has withdrawn from his initial anger, which threatened to destroy the Israelites, the question of what judgment might befall the Israelites is still undetermined by God. The crucial issue is whether God will forgive the Israelites—that is, whether they can be reconciled to God after the idolatry of the Golden Calf so that God himself and not just an angel, who in this case would be a surrogate, will continue to go with them.

> Unforgiven Israel's fate is revealed in 33.1–5, wherein they will still be granted Canaan, but their idolatry has destroyed the basis for their relationship with God. Consequently, he will no longer remain in their midst (33.3). Worse than destruction, worse than purging by death, and worse than a plague, Israel's judgment for their idolatry is their existence without God, "a punishment

---

[32] Ex 34.6 (NASB translation of the MT).
[33] From the Prayer of the Second Antiphon and Prayer before the Ambo. *Service Books*, 36, 96 (*Liturgy of St John Chrysostom*) and 106, 170 (*Liturgy of St Basil*).
[34] Ex 33.19.
[35] Ex 34.4–6.
[36] Ex 32.15–20.
[37] Ex 32.7–10.
[38] Ex 32.11–14.
[39] Ex 32.34; 33.2.
[40] Ex 33.3.

... that negates every announcement, every expectation, every instruction" so far in Exodus.[41]

An indication of God's withdrawal of his presence occurs when Moses removes the Tabernacle of Testimony a substantial distance from the camp.[42] God continues to be present to Moses by talking to him "face to face as someone might speak to his friend"[43] so that Moses continues to find favor in God's sight. Moses, however, wants confirmation from God that both he and the Israelites have found favor with God such that God himself will go with Moses and the Israelites and lead them. Initially God pledges to send his presence and give rest to Moses as an individual: "I myself will go before you, and give you rest."[44] Moses, however, wants God to accompany the Israelites as a community or nation and to make them distinctive: "Unless you yourself should go with us, do not lead me from here."[45] Moses then presses God to send his presence both for him and his people, which God promises to do.[46]

In response to God's pledge, Moses makes the bold, yet humbly-phrased, request to see God's glory. Some commentators take Moses to be requesting a personal mystical experience since he has found favor in God's sight.[47] Yet Moses' constant intervention with God on behalf of the Israelites and his own steadfast commitment to them show that he is acting on their behalf in a compassionate manner.[48] For example, when God indicated that he would destroy the Israelites

---

[41] Aaron Sherwood, *The Word of God Has Not Failed: Paul's Use of the Old Testament in Romans* (Bellingham, WA: Lexington Press, 2015), Kindle Edition, location 1822. For my reading of Exodus 33–34, I have relied on Sherwood, Kindle Edition, locations 1796–1903, and John Piper, "Prolegomena to Understanding Romans 9:14–15: An Interpretation of Exodus 33.1," *The Journal of the Evangelical Theological Society* 22.3 (September 1979): 203–8.

[42] Ex 33.7.

[43] Ex 33.11.

[44] Ex 33.14. "You" in this verse is singular.

[45] Ex 33.15.

[46] Ex 33.16–17.

[47] Cf. Gregory of Nyssa, *The Life of Moses* 219–225, trans. Abraham Malherbe and Everett Ferguson (New York: Paulist Press, 1978), 110–112. St Gregory interprets this entire section in terms of a "mystical experience" and makes no mention of God's revelation of himself as compassionate and merciful. For some contemporary commentators who see Moses' request as a blessing for himself, see Ellicott's *Commentary for English Readers* and *The Pulpit Commentary* for Ex. 33.18. Both commentaries can be found at BibleHub, <https://biblehub.com/commentaries/exodus/33-18.htm>, April 20, 2020.

[48] Cf. Rabbi David Rosen, "Moses in the Jewish Tradition," in *Moses in Three Monotheistic Faiths* (Jerusalem: PASSIA Publication, 2003), 5, <https://www.rabbidavidrosen.net/wp-content/uploads/2016/02/Moses-in-the-Jewish-Tradition.pdf, 2>, April 20, 2020. Gregory of Nyssa, *Life of Moses* (PG 44:324C) makes reference to Moses' compassion (*sympatheia*).

and make of Moses a new people, Moses sticks by the Israelites and reminds God of the promise he made to Abraham, Isaac, and Israel (Jacob).

Moses does not want a new people to be based on him. He wants God to remain with the Israelites and not abandon them by destroying them or sending them on their journey without him. His request to see God's glory, then, is not simply for his own enlightenment. Rather, he desires to secure assurance about God's promise to go with the Israelites and his people given that God had earlier threatened to destroy them because "they are a stiff-necked people."[49] He desires, in other words, "to look into the depths of God's goodness for the assurance he needed to believe such an amazing concession."[50]

God indicates that he will appear to Moses to let his glory[51] pass by Moses while calling on his own name: the name of the Lord. God indicates to Moses that "I will be merciful (*chanan, eleēsō,*) to those to whom I show mercy (*chanan, eleō*) and I will show compassion (*racham, oiktirēsō*) to those to whom I will show compassion (*racham, oiktirō*)."[52] The text certainly shows God's sovereignty: his compassionate and merciful actions are entirely a matter of his discretion and cannot be compelled.[53] Hence, that declaration alone does not guarantee that God will be merciful and compassionate to the Israelites given their idolatry or whether he will destroy them. Israel sits on a "knife edge."[54] In addition, it is especially important to note that God's declaration to Moses follows a formula known as *idem per idem*. In particular, Exodus 33.19 in the Hebrew has the same sort of construction as Exodus 3.14. In that text, God responds "I will be who I will be"[55] to Moses' request to know his name in case the Israelites want to know who has sent Moses to them. The *idem per idem* formula in both Exodus 3.14 and 33.19 refers to what God expresses about himself—being, compassion, and mercy—as (belonging to) the name or the reality of God.[56] Even though the linguistic connection between

---

[49]Ex 33.3, 5.

[50]Piper, "Prolegomena to Understanding Romans 9:14–15," 208, n. 12.

[51]Ex 33.19, 22. The MT has goodness (v. 19) and glory (v. 22).

[52]Ex 33.19.

[53]"So then, it is not of him who wills, nor of him who runs, but of God who shows mercy" (Rom 9.16). This is St Paul's observation on the meaning of Ex 33.19, which he quotes in Rom 9.15.

[54]Sherwood, *The Word of God Has Not Failed*, Kindle Edition, location 1867–77.

[55]The translation of Exodus 3.14 in the Septuagint misses this nuance with its well-known translation: "I am who am" (*ego eimi ho ōn*).

[56]Temper Longman III and David Garland, eds., *The Expositors Bible Commentary* (Grand Rapids, MI: Zondervan, 2009), 371. Cf. Sherwood, *The Word of God Has Not Failed*, Kindle Edition, location 1862–68, where he notes that the formula also indicates that actions expressed by this formula are done at the discretion of the one who acts.

Exodus 3.14 and 33.19 is lost in the Septuagint, nevertheless, Church Fathers such as St Gregory of Nyssa identify compassion and mercy among the names of God that signify his divine energies—that is, God himself in relation to creation.[57]

The explicit link between the compassion and mercy of God with his name takes place in the theophany described in Exodus 34.5–27. There God appears to Moses and calls on his name:

> And the Lord passed by before his face, and proclaimed, "The Lord, [The Lord], God,[58] compassionate (*rachuwm, oiktirmōn*), and merciful (*channon, eleēmōn*), long-suffering, and very merciful, and true, and keeping righteousness[59] and mercy for thousands, taking away iniquity, and unrighteousness, and sins; and he will not clear the guilty; bringing the iniquity of the fathers upon the children, and to the children's children, to the third and fourth generation."[60]

In response, Moses bows down and tells the Lord:

> If now I have found grace before you, O Lord, I pray, let my Lord go with us, for the people are stiff-necked, and you shall take away our sins and our iniquities, and we shall be yours.[61]

God's theophanic revelation to Moses is significant because he gives first place, as it were, to his compassion and mercy in contrast to an earlier revelation to Moses in which divine anger and justice took first place.[62] In the Jewish tradition, Exodus 34.6–7 reveals the Thirteen Attributes of God's Mercy, which play

---

[57] St Gregory of Nyssa, *Contra Eunomium* 2.1.151–152 (NPNF[2] 5:265; PG 45:534A–B). See Chapter 5, p. 206 for the text.

[58] The Septuagint, in one version at least, has *Kyrios, ho Theos* ("The Lord God"). The MT, however, duplicates "Lord" to have "the Lord, the Lord, God." However, the Greek text for the Polyglot translation and for the CCAT translation both have "The Lord, the Lord, God" (*kyrios, kyrios ho theos*). Eusebius (in the *Eclogae Phopheticae*, 1.12 43) cites this version of Exodus 34.6 as does Cyril of Jerusalem, who uses the repetition of Lord to signify that Exodus 34.6 discloses both the Father and the Son as God. The duplication is also important since it is used in the Jewish tradition in counting the thirteen attributes of God's mercy. For Eusebius see T. Gaisford, *Eusebii Caesariensis Eclogae Propheticae* (Oxford: Typographeo Academico, 1842), reprinted in PG 22:1021–1262; for Cyril of Jerusalem, see *Catechetical Lectures* 10.8 (NPNF[2] 7:59; PG 33:672).

[59] The phrase keeping *dikaiosynē* (justice or righteousness) is not found in the Hebrew. Note that *dikaiosynē* can be translated both as "justice" and as "righteousness."

[60] Ex 34.6–7.

[61] Ex 34.9. Given that God has already affirmed that Moses has found favor in his sight, the conditional "if" can also be understood as "since" ("Notes on Ex 34.9," *Ellicott's Commentary for English Readers*, <https://biblehub.com/commentaries/ellicott/exodus/34.htm>, April 20, 2020.)

[62] See Ex 20.5 in particular.

a very important role in Jewish services and prayer.[63] The thirteen attributes are counted and named in various ways. The first five are: "The Lord!," "The Lord!," "God," "Compassionate," and "Gracious (or Merciful)." However, the thirteenth, "who cleanses," is obtained by reversing the textual sense of "he will not clear the guilty" to mean "he will pardon or he will cleanse."[64]

But these "attributes" of mercy and compassion seem to be offset by what appears to be a form of intergenerational punishment in which God visits the sins of the fathers on the children up to the third or fourth generation.[65] Such punishment seems to amount to a kind of unjust retribution whereby God will punish children for sins committed by their parents and not by the children themselves, sins for which they bear no personal guilt. This is referred to as the "sour grapes theology" later in the Old Testament: "Parents eat sour grapes and their sons' teeth are blunted."[66] The prophets Jeremiah and Ezekiel both declared that God rejects this position.

> And the word of the Lord came to me, saying, son of man, what do you mean by this parable among the children of Israel, saying, the fathers have eaten sour [or, unripe] grapes, and the children's teeth have been set on edge? This parable shall no more be spoken in Israel.[67]

In other words, children will be punished only for sins they commit including those that are imitations of the sins of the parents. Exodus 34.7 has been taken in this sense by both Jewish and Christian theologians.[68] Even apart from the

---

[63]In revealing his Attributes of Mercy, God renews the covenant between himself and the Israelites that was shattered with their worship of the Golden Calf. The Thirteen Attributes also are a prayer given to the Jewish people to recite in asking for forgiveness in a number of services throughout the year. See Ezra Bick, *In His Mercy: Understanding the Thirteen Midot* (Jerusalem: Koren Publishers, 2011) and Kindle Edition, location 79. See also Yonatan Grossman, "The Thirteen Attributes of Mercy," <https://www.etzion.org.il/en/thirteen-attributes-mercy>, April 20, 2020).

[64]Ronald Eisenberg, "Thirteen Attributes of Mercy" in *Jewish Traditions: JPS Guide* (Philadelphia: Jewish Publication Society, 2004), 180–2, also at <https://www.myjewishlearning.com/article/the-13-attributes-of-mercy/>, April 20, 2020. Cf. Dovie Schochet, "What Are the 13 Attributes of Mercy?: Understanding the *Yud Gimel Midot Harachamim*," <https://www.chabad.org/parshah/article_cdo/aid/3609722/jewish/What-Are-the-13-Attributes-of-Mercy.htm>, April 20, 2020.

[65]". . . bringing the iniquity of the fathers upon the children, and to the children's children, to the third and fourth generation." Ex 34.7.

[66]Ezek 18.2.

[67]Ezek 18.1–3. See, Jer 38.29–30. "In those days they shall certainly not say, the fathers ate a sour [unripe] grape, and the children's teeth are set on edge. But every one shall die for his own sin: and the teeth of him that eats the sour grape shall be set on edge" (Jer 31.29–30, MT).

[68]Cf. Cyril of Alexandria, *Commentary on Amos* [*In Amos prophetam*], in *Commentary on The Twelve Prophets*, trans. Robert Hill (Washington: The Catholic University of America Press, 2008), 2:16–17 (PG 71:421–22);

"sour grapes" interpretation of Exodus 34.7, the important point is that in his theophany to Moses, God reveals that the scope of his compassion and mercy outstrip his anger and willingness to punish. In contrast to visiting the sins of the fathers on the sons up to the third or fourth generation, he keeps mercy for "thousands"—that is, indefinitely or, in parallel with Deuteronomy 7.9, "a thousand generations." Indeed, Rashi glosses "thousands" as "two thousand generations" and notes that the attribute of God's "goodness exceeds the attribute of retribution by a ratio of one to five hundred"[69] and that his retribution extends "only to those who hate me."[70]

This interpretation neatly corresponds with several Old Testament texts in which God's compassion is said to endure forever: "Will a woman forget her child so as not to have compassion (*racham, eleēsai*) on the offspring of her womb? But if a woman should forget these, I will not forget you."[71] God's theophany, then, is meant to assure Moses that he will be with the Israelites as his chosen people given the close connection between his compassion and mercy and his very name.

Why is the assurance of God's compassion and mercy so important not just for Moses as an individual but for the Israelites as a people? As we saw, in Exodus 33.19, God leaves Moses in a state of tension, since his mercy and compassion are not "automatic" and cannot be compelled. There are, after all, more than a few flashes of divine anger and wrath in the Old Testament.[72] This wrath often takes the form of a threat to forsake the Israelites. Indeed, at times God actually abandons them but always *after* the Israelites have previously forsaken God—that is, after they have ignored his commandments and turned to idolatry instead of worshiping God.[73] We see a dramatic instance of this when God foretells the Israelites' unfaithfulness and threatens a wrath-filled response to it. Speaking to Moses just before his death,

John Chrysostom, *Homilies on John* 56 (NPNF[1] 14:198–99; PG 59:306); Bobrinskoy, *Compassion*, 78–9; Rabbi M. Shamah, "Parashat Yitro Part IV: Visiting Iniquity of Fathers upon Sons," *Sephardic Institute* (March 2011): 5; Rabbi Zev Farber, "Punishing Children for the Sins of their Parents," *The Torah.com: A Historical and Contextual Approach*, <http://thetorah.com/punishing-children-for-the-sins-of-their-parents/>, April 20, 2020.

[69] Avroham Yoseif Rosenberg, ed., *The Complete Jewish Bible with Rashi Commentary*, <http://www. chabad.org/library/bible_cdo/aid/9895#showrashi=true>, April 20, 2020.

[70] Cf. Ex 20.5.

[71] Is 49.15; cf. Ps 24(25).6–7, Is 54.10, and Lam 3.22.

[72] See, e.g., Ex 22.24, 32.10; Num 11.33; Deut 28.28; Josh 23.16, Judg 2.1, 3.8; Pss 20.9–10, 105.40–41; Is 66.15; Lam 2.1–4; and Ezek 43.8 regarding the anger of the Lord and its destructive consequences for the Israelites or for those who turn against the Lord.

[73] See e.g., 2 Kg 17.18–20 and 2 Chr 36.14–21.

The Lord said to Moses, "Behold, you shall sleep with your fathers, and this people will arise and go a whoring after the strange gods of the land into which they are entering: and they will forsake me, and break my covenant, which I made with them. And I will be very angry with them in that day, and I will leave them and turn my face away from them, and they shall be devoured; and many evils and afflictions shall come upon them."[74]

In several texts, one sees a connection between this sort of wrath and a lack of compassion. Indeed, the lack or absence of compassion by God or humans is linked with an unbridled anger and savagery that leads to the destruction of others.[75] On the other hand, there are numerous times when God pledges not to forsake or abandon the Israelites. In many of these texts there is no explicit relationship between the pledge not to forsake the Israelites and God's compassion.[76] But there are a several passages in the Old Testament where God's promise not to forsake or turn away from the Israelites is linked specifically with his compassion.[77] These texts are important both because they testify to the enduring character of God's compassion and the scope of God's compassion as shown by the compassionate actions for all people that God will work through his suffering servant.[78] These texts are also important because they indicate something fundamental about the nature of compassion in general. Namely, God's compassion is expressed as a commitment to or solidarity with his people. God will not forsake them even though their actions do not merit this compassion and mercy, although there is a final judgment against those who forsake or hate God.[79]

The great public, penitential prayer of the Levites in Nehemiah 9.6–31 invokes a continuous remembrance of God's compassionate promise not to forsake the Israelites despite their constant infidelity to God. The affirmations of God's ongoing compassion and solidarity with the Israelites punctuate the recitation of the history of God's blessing to the Israelites and their rebellion against and forsaking

---

[74]Deut 31.16–17. For other texts see 2 Kg 22.17, Jer 12.7, Lam 5.20, and Ezek 9.9.

[75]These texts draw on the root ḥ-w-s [Strong 2347: chûwç] that is variously translated as "compassion" or "pity" in English translations of the MT but most often in the Septuagint by "to spare" (phaedomai): see Deut 7.16; 1 Sam 24.10; Is 13.18; Jer 13.14; Ezek 5.11, 7.9; and 16.5.

[76]Cf. Deut 31.6, 1 Kg 6.13, Ezra 9.9, Ps 9.10, and Is 41.17.

[77]Deut 4.31, 2 Kg 13.23, 2 Chr 30.9, and Is 54.7–10.

[78]See below, p. 97 for a discussion of this text. For Christians, the text about the suffering servant is interpreted to mean that the radical claim of God's compassion not to forsake human beings is fulfilled in the Incarnation, life, death, and Resurrection of Christ.

[79]We will discuss this aspect of compassion in relation to human compassion when I take up the question of whether there are limits to compassion; see Chapter 6, pp. 247–55.

of him. His compassion for the Israelites always trumps his anger towards them just as God revealed to Moses in Exodus 34.6–7. The text is rather lengthy. It is not read in any Orthodox Christian worship services. There are few patristic references to this text. Yet, the profound and pervasive acknowledgement of and thanks for God's compassion towards us that is found in Orthodox Christian liturgies and other services[80] finds a beautiful anticipation in this penitential prayer.

> You are the only true Lord. You made the heaven ... the earth, and all things that are in it, the seas, and all things in them. ... You are the Lord God. You chose Abram and brought him out of the land of the Chaldeans and gave him the name of Abraham. You found his heart faithful before you, and you made a covenant with him to give to him and to his seed the land of the Canaanites ... and you have confirmed your words, for you are righteous. You saw the affliction of our fathers in Egypt, and you heard their cry at the Red Sea ... and they passed through the midst of the sea on dry land. You cast those that were about to pursue them into the depths ... You guided them by day by a pillar of cloud, and by night by a pillar of fire, to enlighten for them the way wherein they should walk. Also, you came down upon Mount Sinai ... and gave them right judgments, and laws of truth, ordinances, and good commandments. ... But they and our fathers behaved proudly, and hardened their neck, and did not heed your commandments. They refused to listen ... and they appointed a leader to return to their slavery in Egypt (vv. 6–17).
>
> But you, O God, are merciful and compassionate (*oiktirmōn, rachuwm*), long-suffering, and abundant in mercy, and you did not forsake them. (v. 17)
>
> And still further they even made a molten calf for themselves, and said, these are the gods that brought us up out of Egypt. They wrought great provocations. (v. 18)
>
> Yet you in your great compassions (*oitirmois, racham*, or "compassionate actions") did not forsake them in the wilderness. You did not turn away from

[80]From the First Kneeling Prayer for the Vespers of Pentecost: "Do you yourself, O Greatly-merciful One, who love mankind, hear us in that day when we call upon you, and especially on this day of Pentecost. ... Hearken now unto us. ... Accept us who fall down before you and cry, We have sinned. ... You are our God. But as our days have been spent in vanity, we have been stripped of your help, we have been deprived of every defense. But having boldness on account of your compassions (*oiktirmois*), we cry out: Remember not the sins and ignorance of our youth ... And when our strength fails, forsake us not. ... Measure our transgressions according to your compassions (*oiktirmois*), setting the abyss of your compassion (*tēn abysson tōn oiktirmōn sou*) against the multitude of our iniquities. ... Visit us in your goodness; deliver us from the power of the devil" (*The Great Book of Needs*, 2:342 mod.).

them the pillar of the cloud by day to guide them in the way, nor the pillar of fire by night to enlighten for them the way wherein they should walk. And you gave your good Spirit to instruct them, and you did not withhold your manna from their mouth, and you gave them water in their thirst. You sustained them forty years in the wilderness.... You did not allow anything to fail them.... Moreover, you gave them kingdoms, and divided nations to them.... And they took lofty cities, and inherited houses full of all good things.... (vv. 19–25)

So, they ate, and were filled, and grew fat, and rioted in your great goodness. But they turned, and revolted from you, and cast your Law behind their backs; and they slew your prophets.... Then you gave them into the hand of those that afflicted them ... and they cried to you in the time of their affliction.... (vv. 25–27)

And you heard them from your heaven, and in your great compassions (*oiktirmois, racham*) gave them deliverers, and saved them from the hand of those that afflicted them. (v. 27)

But when they rested, they committed evil again before you ... so you left them in the hands of their enemies and they ruled over them.... (v. 28)

And you heard them from heaven and delivered them in your great compassions (*oiktirmois, racham*). (v. 28)

And you testified against them to bring them back to your Law. They did not listen to you but sinned against your commandments and your judgments.... Yet you bore with them many years. You testified to them through your Spirit by the hand of your prophets: but they did not heed them. So, you gave them into the hand of the nations of the land. (vv. 29–30)

But in your many compassions (*oikrirmois, racham*), you did not appoint them to destruction and you did not forsake them. For, you are strong, and merciful, and compassionate (*oiktirmōn, rachuwm*) (v. 31).

God's compassion, however, is much more than a "negative" pledge not to forsake the Israelites. It also shows the positive action that one would expect from compassion: action to forgive the Israelites—or at least the faithful remnant among them—and to reconcile them to God according to his covenant with them and in light of his compassion (*racham*).[81]

[81]Deut 30.3; Is 14.1; Jer 12.15, 30.18, 42.12; and Zech 1.16. Cf. Bobrinskoy, *Compassion*, 55.

In the Old Testament, explicit references to God's compassion are most often focused on the Israelites as a people. His compassion for them is linked to his covenant with them as his chosen people, his ongoing commitment to forgive their sins even though they forsake him, as well as to restore them fully to the land promised to them. God's compassion and mercy for mankind in general is implicitly extended to non-Israelites through the many injunctions that God gives to the Israelites to care for strangers, the poor, and others.[82] The texts in which God is said to hear the cry of the poor (the *anawim*),[83] to free the prisoners, give sight to the blind, to uphold widows and orphans, indicate that God is aware of human suffering and affliction and acts to relieve it for people generally and not just the Israelites.[84] But the main explicit focus of God's compassion *(racham)* is upon a people—the Israelites—and not just to individuals. In this sense, it seems to me at least, that there is no mention of God's compassion for the Egyptians, Assyrians, and the many smaller tribes that populated the earth.

Nevertheless, in the prophecies of Isaiah, we find that God's compassion is extended to all nations and people through the suffering servant, which Christian faith identifies as Jesus Christ. This servant is the one who is called "to raise up the tribes of Jacob, and to restore the preserved of Israel." He is "a light to the Gentiles," who will be "God's salvation to the end of the earth."[85]

> Thus says the Lord, "In an acceptable time have I heard you. . . . I have formed you and given you as a covenant to the nations to establish the earth and to inherit the desert heritages: saying to those that are in bonds, 'Go forth'; and to those that are in darkness 'Show yourselves.' They shall be fed in all the ways. . . . But he that has compassion [*racham, eleos*] on them shall comfort them, and by fountains of waters he shall lead them. . . . Rejoice, you heavens and let the earth be glad. Let the mountains break forth with joy because the Lord has had compassion [*racham, eleos*] on his people and has comforted the lowly ones of his people."[86]

---

[82]Cf. Ex 22.20; Lev 19.33–34, 23.22; Deut 10.19; Ps 146.9; and Jer 7.6.

[83]The Hebrew *anawim* carries the meanings of those who are poor in an economic or social sense and those who submit themselves to God in a spirit of humility. God's compassion to the *anawim* is to those who are poor in the first sense and not just in the latter. Cf. Jones, *Poverty and the Human Condition*, 24–28.

[84]Cf. Howard Culbertson, "Poverty: Bible Verses on Caring for the Poor," Southern Nazarene University, <https://home.snu.edu/~hculbert/poor.htm>, April 20, 2020 for an extensive compilation of Old and New Testament passages relating to God's concern for those who are afflicted and distressed, especially those who are poor. There is, so far as I know, no corresponding compilation in print.

[85]Is 49.6.

[86]Is 49.8–13.

If explicit texts about God's compassion abound in the Old Testament, there are very few texts that mention compassion (*racham*) shown by men or women or how such compassion models or is supposed to model, if you will, God's compassion. In the previous chapter, I mentioned God's exhortation and command to the Israelites to be compassionate, merciful, and just.[87] But we find examples of compassion shown by men and women in Psalm 102.13, which is the regular first antiphon in the Divine Liturgy (in the Slav tradition). God's compassion is likened to the compassion fathers, or parents, show for their children: "As a father shows compassion (*racham, oiktirei*) for his children so God shows compassion (*racham, oiktirēsen*) for those that fear him." God wonders whether mothers can forget their children and the compassion they show them.[88]

There are, however, two notable examples in the Old Testament, where compassion (*racham*) is exhibited by individuals. When he sees his brother Benjamin for the first time in many years after his brothers sold him into slavery, Joseph's "bowels (*racham, ta entera* in LXX)[89] yearned for his brother." Along with compassion, *racham* has the second sense of womb, or in this case, bowels or viscera. Joseph, that is, was moved by compassion at the sight of his brother.[90] He utterly forgives the brothers who sold him into slavery, reconciles himself to them, and provides them with food and other resources to return home and care for Jacob. In the *Testaments of the Twelve Patriarchs*,[91] Simeon takes special note of Joseph's compassion: "But Joseph was a good man and he had the Spirit of God in him, being compassionate (*eusplanchnos*) and merciful (*eleēmōn*), he did not bear malice against me; but he even loved me, as his other brothers."[92] Zebulun cites Joseph's compassion towards his brothers and exhorts his children to show compassion and not malice towards others.[93]

In 1 Kings [3 Kings LXX] 3.16–28, Solomon threatens to use a sword to cut a small baby in two to determine the child's true, biological mother. While the woman who pretended to be the mother tells Solomon to kill the baby so that

[87] See Chapter 1, p. 22 for the text from Zech 7.9–10.

[88] Is 49.15

[89] Gen 43.30.

[90] The Orthodox Jewish Bible has "And Yosef made haste, for his compassion was stirred upon ... his brother," <https://www.bibliatodo.com/en/the-bible/orthodox-jewish-bible/genesis-43>, April 20, 2020.

[91] *The Testaments of the Twelve Patriarchs* is an apocryphal work of Jewish and Christian origins purportedly providing the deathbed testaments of the sons of Jacob. Jacob's youngest son, Joseph, was betrayed by his brothers and sold into slavery in Egypt. I will make extensive use of some of this material, especially the *Testament of Zebulun*, in Chapter 5, pp. 185–87, 191–97. See Chapter 5, pp. 175–76 for more information about the *Testaments*.

[92] *Testament of Simeon* 4.4 (*Testaments* 115; Greek 19–20).

[93] *Testament of Zebulun* 8.4 (*Testaments* 268; Greek 126).

neither woman can have it, the birth mother tells Solomon: " 'I pray you, my lord,' for her bowels yearned over her son, 'give her the child, and do not at all slay it.' "[94] This is a fairly common translation of the text. However, the Hebrew for "her bowels yearned" is the same as the description of Joseph's response to seeing Benjamin. The Hebrew plays on the double meaning of *racham* as compassion and as womb or bowels. So, we find translations such as "she was stirred with compassion for her son,"[95] "compassion for her son burned within her,"[96] and "her compassion was kindled towards her son."[97]

Although compassion need not be accompanied with the sort of intense, gut-wrenching, distress that Joseph and the mother experience, both texts express the visceral, affective source of compassion that animates a person. The two texts seem to provide some correspondence with the distinctive term that is applied to Jesus in the Synoptic Gospels: moved by compassion (*splanchnizomai*), since this Greek verb plays on the double meaning of *splanchna*: viscera or heart, in the New Testament, and compassion.

Compassion in the New Testament

There are a several references to compassion throughout the Epistles that echo Old Testament themes and vocabulary. St Paul describes God as the Father of compassion (*patēr tōn oiktirmōn*).[98] Compassion is also one of the virtues we are to adopt ("clothe ourselves in") that are already present in Christ. They are integral to how we are to live in light of our Baptism:

> If then you were raised with Christ ... set your mind on things above, not on things on the earth. For you died, and your life is hidden with Christ in God (vv. 1–3) ... since you have put off the old man with his deeds, and have put on the new man who is renewed in knowledge according to the image of him who created him (vv. 9–10). ... Therefore, as the elect of God, holy and beloved, put on the bowels of compassion (*splanchna oitkitrmou* or "tender compassion" [NASB]), kindness, humility, meekness, longsuffering; bearing with one another, and forgiving one another. If anyone has a complaint

---

[94] 1 Kg 3.26. The Septuagint has *mētra* (womb) for *racham*.
[95] New American Bible Revised Edition.
[96] New Revised Standard Version.
[97] 1599 Geneva Bible.
[98] 2 Cor 1.3; cf. Rom 12.1 and Phil 2.1, which link compassion (*oiktirmos*) with God.

against another; even as Christ forgave you, so you also must do. But above all of them put on love (*agapē*), which is the bond of perfection (vv. 12–14).[99]

The characteristics or virtues that Paul exhorts us to adopt echo the "compassion formula" by which God reveals his name to Moses in Exodus 34.6–7. Our salvation comes by putting on Christ.[100] Salvation is a restoration to fullness of life and, hence, the restoration of the fullness of relationships between ourselves and God, one another, and creation itself. In putting on Christ, the image of God, in which we are created, is restored so that we are "set on" the path to attaining the likeness to God (what Orthodox Christians call deification). In Colossians 3, St Paul tells us that to put on Christ is to embrace and manifest the very characteristics of God that he identifies as belonging to his name and his glory. That is, we are to acquire "the bowels of compassion and the tenderness of the Father."[101]

For Orthodox Christian faith, this is what it means to become a living icon of Christ. When God created human beings, he said "let us create man according to our image (*kat' eikona*) and according to our likeness (*kath' omoiōsin*)."[102] In the passage from St Paul above, he indicates that those who have put on Christ are "renewed in knowledge according to the image (*kat' eikona*) of him who created"[103] them. In both texts, *eikona* (*eikōn*) is normally translated as "image." But that is the same Greek word by which we refer to the icons that we paint. In contrast to those icons, human beings are living icons (*eikones*) of Christ (the Word)[104] who created all things. Our task is to become like Christ, which as St John of Damascus indicates, means acquiring the virtues, which include being compassionate, merciful, and so forth. We produce painted icons of Christ, whom we worship, and icons of the Theotokos and the saints because we venerate the Theotokos and the saints—those living icons of Christ—who shine forth in their likeness to Christ as our "God-bearing (*theophoroi*) fathers and mothers."[105]

---

[99]Col 3.1–14. For exhortations with similar language, cf. Eph 4.32, Phil 2.1–2, and 1 Pet 3.8. The NKJV has "tender mercies" for *splanchna oiktirmou*. See Chapter 2, pp. 68–70 for a discussion of this phrase. On the connection between putting on Christ and acquiring virtues, see Nonna Verna Harrison, *God's Many Splendored Image: Theological Anthropology for Christian Formation* (Grand Rapids, MI: Baker Academic Publishing, 2010), 68–69.

[100]Rom 13.14 and Gal 3.27.

[101]Bobrinskoy, *Compassion*, 87.

[102]Gen 1.26.

[103]Col 3.10.

[104]Jn 1.3.

[105]For example, the seventh Sunday after Pascha commemorates our Holy and God-bearing Fathers of the First Ecumenical Council of Nicaea.

We find a similar theme in the Jewish tradition that builds on the idea of "calling by [or, on] the name of the Lord." Here is an illustration of this theme in the *Sifre* to Deuteronomy, *Piska* 49. Citing Deuteronomy 11.22, "To walk in all his ways" and Joel 2.32, "It shall come to pass, that whosoever shall call by the name of the Lord shall be delivered," the author poses the question: "How is it possible for man to be called by the name of the Lord?" Drawing on Exodus 34.6, the author identifies being compassionate and merciful as belonging to the ways of the Lord. So, the author answers his question in this way: "Rather, as God is called 'compassionate,' so should you be compassionate, as the Holy One, blessed be he, is called 'merciful,' so too should you be merciful." By calling by the name of the Lord in this way—that is, by being compassionate and merciful as God is compassionate and merciful—we will be delivered (Joel 3.5) and God will prepare us for this glory (Is 43.7).[106]

This text compares very nicely with the text from Colossians that I cited above as well as Jesus' command "Be merciful (*oiktirmones* or compassionate) just as your Father also is merciful (*oiktirmōn* or compassionate)"[107] In putting on Christ (St Paul) and "being called by the name of the Lord" (*Piska* 49), we are to "put on" divine compassion and mercy for ourselves and face the world by being compassionate and merciful to others. Our human compassion and mercy are to reflect God's—Christ's—compassion and mercy and, for the immediate purposes of this book, they are to be understood in light of this divine compassion and mercy.

Christian faith takes the Incarnation of the Son of God as Jesus Christ to be the fulfillment of God's promise in the Old Testament to redeem and save all people because of his compassion (*racham*) and mercy (*chanan*). One might expect that the New Testament would emphasize the Incarnation as the principal expression of God's compassion. John 3.16 expresses that promise in the well-known verse, "God so loved the world that he sent his only begotten son into the world." This verse emphasizes God's *agapē* for us and the world itself as the basis for the Incarnation. As Fr Bobrinskoy writes:

> Divine love—true love—is by nature a sacrificial oblation. . . . Such trinitarian love also creates free beings, called to divine love . . . This is his divine kenosis—prior to the advent of sin—his overabundance of love. . . . Kenotic

---

[106] *Sifre: A Tannaitic Commentary on the Book of Deuteronomy*, trans. Reuven Hammer (New Haven: Yale University Press, 1986), 105–6. I modified the translation slightly as it used "merciful" for *racham* and "gracious" for *chanan*. I used "compassion" and "merciful" respectively to be consistent in how I translate these terms. "Called by" also has the sense of "called on."

[107] Lk 6.36.

sacrifice springs from divine roots. Suffering appears later, when this divine love is questioned, ridiculed, rejected.[108]

In the hymns of the Church, as I mentioned earlier, the language of compassion, mercy, and *philanthrōpia* are used to express the divine impetus for the Incarnation far more often than love (*agapē*). The use of the former terms in the hymns of the Church does not reflect a diminishment of the primacy of divine love but perhaps reflects what St Gregory the Theologian observes: "*Philanthrōpia*, compassion, and mercy are vital parts of God's *agapē*."[109]

The Incarnation of Christ refers not just to the moment at which the Son of God assumed flesh at the conception of Jesus (celebrated on the Feast of the Annunciation of Mary). Taken soteriologically or with reference to our salvation, the Incarnation refers to the entire "event" by which human beings are sanctified and all of creation is redeemed. As the priest prays during the Anaphora Prayer in the Liturgy of St John Chrysostom, it refers to, "all those things which have come to pass for us: the cross, the tomb, the resurrection on the third day, the ascension into heaven, the sitting at the right hand, and the second and glorious coming."[110]

There are no references to the Incarnation in the New Testament that explicitly use the language of compassion (*oiktirmos, sympatheia,* or *eusplanchnia*). There are, however, two texts that are worth noting. The first is contained in the prophecy of Zachariah at the birth of John the Baptist. He proclaims that John will be the Prophet of the Most High, who will give people the knowledge of salvation "by the forgiveness/remission of sins through the tender mercy (*splanchna eleous*) of our God with which the Dayspring from on high shall visit us."[111] Titus 3.4 refers to the Incarnation as expressive of the kindness and *philanthrōpia* of God our Savior. This is the first occurrence of *philanthrōpia* (love of man or mankind) in Scripture to describe the "robust" compassion, mercy, and love of God.

The text from Colossians 3 that I cited earlier links key virtues that we are to develop with the same characteristics we find in God and Christ. However, the language used in the Synoptic Gospels to refer to Christ's compassion is singular and distinct both in relation to the Old Testament and to the Epistles. In these

---

[108]Bobrinskoy, *Compassion*, 56–7. See Chapter 5, pp. 206–209 for the discussion of the Incarnation and God's mercy and compassion as embedded in the very project of creation and not just as a response to human sinfulness.

[109]*Oration* 14.5 (FOC 107.42; PG 35.864B).

[110]*Service Books*, 68. The same text with a slight variation in wording occurs during the Divine Liturgy of St Basil (144). Cf. Bobrinskoy, *Compassion*, 59.

[111]Lk 1.78.

Gospels, the term that describes Christ's compassion and which Christ uses to describe the compassion of significant characters in some of his parables is the verb *splanchnizomai*. This verb is not found in the New Testament Epistles. So far as the *splanchna* are identified as the seat or source of compassion, the term has the sense of "being moved by compassion." The term does not appear in this sense in the Septuagint, but we find a variant at Proverbs 17.5 in an addition to the Hebrew text as we have it today: "He that laughs at the poor provokes him that made him; and he that rejoices at the destruction of another shall not be held guiltless: but he that is moved by compassion (*episplanchnizomenos*) shall find mercy (*eleēthēsetai*)."[112] On the other hand, the term is not used in classical Greek literature or philosophy although it is used in the *Testaments of the Twelve Patriarchs*, which seems to be the first text in which *splanchnizomai* is used in the sense of "being moved by compassion." Nevertheless, although the Synoptic Gospels clearly parallel the *Testaments of the Twelve Patriarchs* in using *splanchnizomai*,[113] I will defer looking at the *Testaments of the Twelve Patriarchs* until Chapter 5, for it has one of the most extensive discussions on compassion in the genre of Later Jewish Hellenic and Greek patristic literature and it will provide a very important basis for understanding the nature of compassion as a disposition.

The term *splanchnizomai* is used in all of the Synoptic Gospels. Mark, Matthew, and Luke all use the term in reference to particular healing miracles of Christ: raising the son of the Widow of Nain back to life,[114] the healing of a leper,[115] and the healing of two blind men.[116] Mark records that the father of a son possessed by a demon appeals to Jesus to heal his son "But if you can do anything, have compassion on us and help us."[117] Both Mark 8.2 and Matthew 15.32 take note of the fact that for the feeding of the four thousand, Jesus was moved by compassion for the crowds that had heard him teach but had nothing to eat. For the feeding of the five thousand, Matthew notes that Jesus was moved by compassion and healed the sick.[118] In Mark's version of the same event, Jesus is moved by compassion "because they were as sheep not having a shepherd: and he began to

---

[112]Prov 17.5 LXX. The last clause ("but he that. . . .") is not found in the MT or in any English translations based on the MT.

[113]*Testaments* (English) 254–55.

[114]Lk 7.13.

[115]Mk 1.41. Accounts of the healing of the leper appear in Mathew 8.1–4 and Luke 5.12–16, although no reference is made to Jesus being moved by compassion.

[116]Mt 20.34.

[117]Mk 19.22.

[118]Mt 14.14.

teach them many things."[119] Jesus was moved by compassion for the same reason when he encountered a multitude.[120] His response was the first commissioning of the disciples.[121] In Jesus' parables, the father of the prodigal son is moved by compassion to welcome him home.[122] The good Samaritan is moved by compassion to attend to the man beaten and left by the road.[123] The king, in the parable of the unmerciful servant, is moved by compassion when one of his servants begs for more time to repay what is, in essence, an unpayable debt.[124]

I provided some discussion of the nature of Christ's compassion in my earlier discussion of the feeding of the four thousand and in the parable of the good Samaritan.[125] I will provide some further discussion in the next section of this chapter. In general, we can note that in each of the instances where specific reference is made to Jesus' being moved by compassion or in which he describes characters in his parables as being moved by compassion, compassion moves him to immediate action on behalf of someone regardless of whether he takes the initiative (such as when he raises the deceased son of the Widow of Nain) or in response to requests from those in distress (as in the healing of the two blind men). We observe the same immediate response in the three parables in which someone is moved by compassion: the good Samaritan's response of assistance for the man robbed, beaten, and left by the road; the father for the prodigal son on his return; and the king for the servant who begs mercy from him.

In each of these instances, neither Jesus nor the characters in his parables seem concerned about determining whether the people that are assisted are somehow responsible for their distress. Neither Jesus nor the writers of the Gospels give any indication that he is concerned with examining whether people merit his assistance. This lack of "examination" contrasts rather starkly with Aristotle's description of when *eleos* (pity or compassion) is justified "by the sight of some evil, destructive or painful, which befalls one who does not deserve it."[126] Moreover, while *eleos* for Aristotle is properly directed to someone who is one's equal in some social or filial sense and does not seem to extend to the equality we all have as human beings by nature, Jesus' compassion as exemplified in the parable of the

[119]Mk 6.34.
[120]Mt 9.36.
[121]Mt 10.1–8.
[122]Lk 15.20.
[123]Lk 10.33.
[124]Mt 18.27.
[125]See above, pp. 85–86.
[126]Aristotle, *Rhetoric* 2.8.

good Samaritan is, "without borders." It expresses his profound sense of neighbor-liness to all people, which is precisely the point Jesus makes to the young man who challenges Jesus to answer the question "Who is my neighbor"?[127] Put another way: Christ's compassion without boundaries reflects the equality of honor we share with him in light of our common humanity, which in his Incarnation, he shares with us. I will draw on this feature of Jesus' compassion in Chapter 5 in developing the structure of a compassionate disposition as assisting people "without judgment."

Given that references to Christ's being moved by compassion are relatively few in number in the Gospels, it might seem that these references simply take note of a particular emotion that arises from time to time in Jesus. Neverthe-less, we must remember that the Incarnation and Christ's entire earthly ministry reflect Christ's compassion as the incarnate Son of God, which is (as I mentioned earlier) the reason that the Orthodox Christian tradition identifies Christ as the good Samaritan.[128] Being moved by compassion is not an occasional emotion for Christ but a fundamental disposition, if you will, by which he came into and lived in our world.[129]

Compassion in the Gospel Readings on the Sundays before Great Lent

To close the discussion of compassion in the New Testament, I want to return, as it were, to revisit the theme of compassion in Orthodox Christian liturgical experience. I want to link several gospel texts in the liturgical cycle—namely, the preparation for Great Lent—to highlight the role compassion should play in our lives. Reflecting on the Gospels in this way will integrate our experience of com-passion in the Divine Liturgy and the manifestation of compassion in the New Testament.

During the four weeks prior to the start of Great Lent, there are fixed gospel lessons and other service material designed as preparations for the journey through Great Lent to Pascha and beyond to Pentecost and the Feast of All Saints.[130] They

---

[127]John D. Jones, "Opening the Doors of Compassion: Cultivating a Merciful Heart," *In Communion* (Spring, 2012): 7, <https://incommunion.org/2012/09/13/opening-the-doors-of-compassion-cultivating-a-merciful-heart-by-fr-john-d-jones/>, April 20, 2020.

[128]See above, pp. 85–86.

[129]The hymns of the Church that commemorate Christ's compassion make this abundantly clear. See Chapter 4, hymns H-1 to H-54.

[130]Briefly: the point of repentance is to work with the grace of the Holy Spirit, which was bestowed on the Church at the Feast of Pentecost, in order to grow in likeness to Christ—that is, become living icons of Christ. The Feast of All Saints is the Sunday after Pentecost, on which we commemorate the men and women

are the first Sundays in the service book of the Triodion: a) The Sunday of the Publican and the Pharisee,[131] b) The Sunday of the Prodigal Son,[132] c) The Sunday of the Last Judgment,[133] d) and The Sunday of Forgiveness[134] and the Expulsion of Adam and Eve from Paradise. In the Slavic lectionary, the first Sunday before the start of the Triodion is called Zacchaeus Sunday, named for the gospel story of the encounter between Jesus and Zacchaeus.[135]

The four pre-Lenten Sundays and the Sunday of Zacchaeus provide a valuable perspective on the centrality of relationships in our lives and how the repair of broken relationships is a major concern for the life of repentance. These Sundays of preparation also implicitly point to a central role for compassion in the life of repentance. Hence, these gospel lessons, which are read within the Divine Liturgy, provide significant guides for our liturgy after the Liturgy as we face the world.

The Sunday of Zacchaeus

The Sunday of Zacchaeus focuses on the encounter between Jesus and a chief publican or tax collector named Zacchaeus, who is very rich.[136] Publicans were generally despised in the Roman Empire including Judea and other areas around Jerusalem. Collecting taxes in Israel for the occupying forces of the Roman Empire, these publicans were often viewed as traitors by the Jewish people. The Roman system allowed publicans great freedom to overcharge people when collecting taxes, and to engage in a wide range of fraudulent and exploitive practices.[137] In the gospel account, Zacchaeus desires to see Jesus while Jesus is traveling through Jericho. Given his height and the large crowd, Zacchaeus climbs a tree in order to see Jesus. It is not clear from the gospel account what explicitly motivates Zacchaeus to see Jesus or even whether he planned to actually meet him face to face. Whatever plans Zacchaeus might have had, Jesus takes the initiative to establish a relationship him. He calls Zacchaeus down from the tree and invites himself to stay and dine at Zacchaeus' house. While the crowd

---

who through their own lives and the work of the Holy Spirit are recognized by the Church as our God-bearing (*theophoroi*) fathers and mothers, as well as the Theotokos who is the God-bearer in the flesh.

[131]Lk 18.9–14.

[132]Lk 15.11–32.

[133]Mt 25.31–46.

[134]Mt 6.14–21.

[135]Lk 19.1–10.

[136]Lk 19.1–10.

[137]For a general account of publicans in Jesus' time, see Alan D. Campbell, "The Monetary System, Taxation, and Publicans in the Time of Christ," *The Accounting Historians Journal* 13.2 (Fall 1986): 131–35.

grumbles and is indignant because Jesus is associating with a sinner, whom they found despicable, Jesus effectively extends an offer of hospitality and friendship to Zacchaeus.[138]

Zacchaeus is filled with joy because Jesus will be a guest at his house. Moreover, he also makes a spontaneous expression of repentance, which is not merely a mental gesture of contrition but a positive set of actions designed both to redress the unjust ways in which he has treated people and to distribute money to those who are poor.[139] In response to Zacchaeus' repentance, Jesus comments that "today salvation has come to this house."[140] In the most fundamental sense, this means that Jesus has come to Zacchaeus' house. However, salvation is the process of our restoration to the fullness of life. Thus, Zacchaeus' commitment to a newfound relationship with Jesus is the beginning of the process of his own salvation. As part of his project of repentance, if he wants to become like Jesus, Zacchaeus must act to restore broken relationships and refashion his relationships with people by treating them decently and justly.

Zacchaeus cannot accomplish his own salvation. That requires divine action and grace. But he does have to accept and contribute to it through the way he lives. The efficacy of the saving restoration that Jesus offers to him depends on whether Zacchaeus follows through with his response to that offer for the rest of his life. Given the ways in which his relationship to others has been defined by greed, what is at stake for him is not merely embarking on performing a set of good works. He has to reframe how he currently views other people, from regarding them in a purely instrumental manner to be exploited for his own personal gain, to viewing them as his neighbors. More specifically, Zacchaeus has to learn how to be a neighbor to others as Jesus has been a neighbor to him. Jesus' encounter with Zacchaeus is a vignette of the parable of the good Samaritan: Jesus does not simply ignore him or reject him as the crowd does. Rather, he draws near to Zacchaeus to offer salvation to one who was lost.[141] If Zacchaeus is to follow Christ and be healed, he has to adopt the sort of "befriending"

---

[138]Lk 19.8. Jesus is not at all averse to taking the initiative in connecting with people who are socially marginalized or socially despised, ostracized, ritually impure, and so forth; see Mt 8.1–11, Lk 13.10–17, and Jn 5.2–9, 4.1–26. In all of these cases, Jesus' openness to people cuts through the denigrating stereotypes or invidious distinctions by which they are viewed by others.

[139]Lk 19.8. Compare Zacchaeus' actions with John the Baptist's admonitions to people about what they needed to do to "bring forth works worthy of repentance" (Lk 3.8). Nearly all of these actions concern how people are to share with each other as well as eliminate the exploitation of others (Lk 3.11–14).

[140]Lk 19.9.

[141]Lk 19.10.

hospitality and openness towards others—the compassion towards others—that Jesus has shown towards him.

The Sunday of the Publican and the Pharisee

In the parable of the publican and the Pharisee,[142] Zacchaeus effectively reappears in the person of the publican. Jesus tells this parable to "some who trusted in themselves that they were just and despised others."[143] The parable focuses on how one might seek to justify oneself before God. Justification here has a sense of presenting oneself in a certain way that entitles one to be treated in certain ways. The publican is so profoundly contrite that he makes no effort to claim that any characteristic traits he has or actions he performs justify any claim against God. All he can do is ask for a divine mercy that overlooks all of the ways he has sinned.[144] The Pharisee, on the other hand, seeks to justify himself before God through the ways he has kept the Law: "I fast twice a week; I give tithes of all that I possess."[145] But the Pharisee prefaces his own attempt at justification at the expense of the publican and others by negatively contrasting himself to them. "God, I thank you that I am not like other men—extortionists, unjust, adulterers, or even as this tax collector."[146] He seeks to puff himself up before God by despising the publican and others.

The Greek term for despising others, *exoutheneō*, occurs in several New Testament texts where it shows the kind of denigrating action that can arise from this attitude.[147] In Romans 14.3, Paul makes a point of saying that those who eat certain foods should not despise or judge those that do not eat them. Later in the same chapter, he chastises those who judge or despise their brother.[148] St Paul also writes in 1 Corinthians 1.28 that God chooses those who are despised to "bring to nought" or deprive the "things that are" of their force, influence, and power.

In Mark, Jesus comments that he must suffer many things and be despised.[149] Luke 23.11 gives one example when Herod and his soldiers treated Jesus with contempt and mocked him by putting a robe on him. Pilate's soldiers treated him with

[142] Lk 18.9–14.

[143] Lk 18.9. This verse, which introduces the parable, is not included in the Orthodox Christian lectionary when the parable is read during the Liturgy.

[144] Lk 18.13.

[145] Lk 18.12.

[146] Lk 18.11.

[147] The term is also translated as "to show contempt," "to ridicule," or "to set at nought."

[148] Rom 14.10.

[149] Mk 9.12.

similar contempt, although the word *exoutheneō* is not used, when they scourged him, mocked him, and placed the crown of thorns on his head.[150] Crucifixion throughout the ancient world was a brutal form of agonizing physical punishment designed to publicly humiliate and degrade those who were crucified.[151]

No one, including the Pharisee, can justify himself before God in terms of personal accomplishments alone. Despising others in the bargain only further undermines the Pharisee's attempt to justify himself before God. The interior attitude of despising people, which is expressed by the Pharisee, is precisely the sort of attitude that can lead to mistreating people or rejecting them, personally and socially. Human beings, both individually and collectively, devise all kinds of strategies in order to justify certain social, political, economic, or other privileges for themselves, appealing to certain kinds of characteristics they posses and, simultaneously, by denigrating or despising others who ostensibly lack these characteristics.

One need consider only the many inappropriate and unjustified ways in which groups or individuals can use race, gender, ethnic identity, intelligence, religious affiliation, or any range of characteristics, to justify certain privileges or benefits for themselves and also to justify denying or excluding those benefits to others because of their purported inferiority. The characteristics by which people are despised can be "reified" or objectified in such a way that people are "defined" by those characteristics as defectively human. The reader can recall Lt Hofmiller's rejection of the possibility that a crippled person like Edith could ever love someone.[152] In this case, then, despising people provides the basis for stigmatizing them. Of course, privileged groups and individuals can easily use the basis of privilege to support justification before the divine or to show how they are blessed by God precisely because of the privileged positions they claim to have.[153]

The sort of disdain for others that the Pharisee displays for various groups precludes him from developing any sense of real fellowship (*koinōnia*) or community with them and ultimately with God: you cannot really love God if you despise and

---

[150]Mt 27.26–31, Mk 15.15–20, and Jn 19.1–3.

[151]See the masterful study by Martin Hengel, *Crucifixion in the Ancient World and the Folly of the Message of the Cross* (Philadelphia: Fortress Press, 1977).

[152]Zweig, 313–14.

[153]The struggle with and condemnation of phyletism within the Orthodox Church comes to mind, especially when ethnic identity is wedded to church identity in an exclusionary way. Phyletism was condemned at the Council of Constantinople in 1872 and defined as "racial discrimination, ethnic feuds, hatreds and dissensions within the Church of Christ." Ecumenical Patriarch Bartholomew, *Speaking the Truth in Love* (New York: Fordham University Press, 2010), 359. See *ho horos tēs topikēs Synodou tou 1872*, <http://www.oodegr.com/oode/biblia/ethniki/A4.htm>, April 20, 2020 for the Greek text of the definition.

denigrate your neighbor.[154] One final comment: not despising people does not mean that we should not point out moral failure or weakness. Jesus certainly was not shy about pointing out the ways in which people mistreated others or failed to follow God's commands.[155] It is one thing to be morally and spiritually frank with people. It is quite another to despise people in the sense of rejecting the basic worth or value that they have as human beings. Blessed Theophylact makes this point in his commentary on Jesus' encounter with Zacchaeus: while publicans and especially chief publicans were an "abomination" because they lived off the "tears of the poor," Jesus did not despise Zacchaeus.[156] That is, Jesus refused to let Zacchaeus be defined by his activities as a publican or "boxed into" his identity as a publican.

The Sunday of the Prodigal Son

If the parable of the publican and the Pharisee presents a kind of snapshot of two people with two quite different stances towards God, themselves, and others, the parable of the prodigal son[157] develops contrasting ways of relating to God by comparing the journey of a young son, who rejects his father and then returns to him, with the older brother who remains home. In this familiar story, there is a father who is very wealthy and has two sons. The younger son decides to leave home and insists on taking his inheritance before his father dies. Having insulted his father, he severs his relationship with his father, brother, and everyone else on the estate by wandering off to a foreign land where he spends all of his money on prodigal or wasteful living.[158] A famine arises and, since he is without resources and there is no one willing to help him,[159] he ends up slopping pigs in order to stay alive. He ends up with nothing to eat but the pigs' food because evidently even the owner of the pigs will not give him any food. He comes to his senses and

---

[154] 1 Jn 4.20.

[155] Jesus does this in a general way in the Sermon on the Mount (Mt 5.21–48); cf. Mt 9.4–5, 23.2–4, and Mk 3.4, 7.6–9, and 11.15–17.

[156] Theophylact, *Gospel according to St Luke*, 246 (PG 123:1020, drawn from commentary on Luke 19.35–43). There are, to be sure, stronger and weaker senses of despising. Weaker senses might include disliking someone very much or a strong disapproval of someone. But stronger senses include treating or viewing people as "nought" or "nothing" in ways that can run from exceptional contempt to outright stigmatization.

[157] Lk 15.11–32.

[158] Lk 15.13. For an excellent discussion of the centrality of relationships and reconciliation in the parable, see Ted Bobosch, "The Prodigal Son and Brother," Fr Ted's Blog: Meditations of An Orthodox Priest. Entry posted February 24, 2008, <https://frted.wordpress.com/2008/02/24/the-prodigal-son-brother/>, accessed April 20, 2020.

[159] Lk 15.16. Note that the text says that no one would give him anything. It does not say that no one had anything to give to him.

remembers life on his father's estate and the way in which his father generously provided for everyone.[160] He decides to return to his father, admit his wrongdoing, beg forgiveness, and plead to be accepted as one of the servants and no longer as a son.

Before he gets home, the father sees him at a distance, is moved by compassion, and runs out to greet him.[161] He welcomes him and restores him to his status as his son. He throws a grand party for the return of his son. But the older brother is upset and complains to his father about the unfair way the father is treating him. The older brother points out that while he remained home and has been completely faithful and obedient to the father, the father had never thrown a party for him.[162] The father tries to reach out to the older brother in order to reconcile him with his brother but the parable ends without providing the older son's response.

The parable portrays the younger brother as self-indulgent and wasting his inheritance in profligate living. Moreover, the people with whom he associates in spending his inheritance also seem to be self-indulgent. No one, at least, seems to be possessed of a spirit of generosity towards him since the parable notes when a famine struck, despite his extreme hunger, "no one gave him anything."[163] The young man finds himself utterly isolated and abandoned in what amounts to a kind of hell.

It is tempting to think of hell as an extremely crowded place where people are tormented, tortured, and punished by demons. Certainly, one finds this portrait in Western literature and paintings as well as in various apocryphal accounts about the next life in the early Church. This portrait is also found in the Byzantine icon of the Last Judgment.[164] But another conception of hell is that of complete isolation in which one is cut off from any active engagement with God or with others. Or, perhaps more precisely, hell is being profoundly aware of the presence of God's love and the painful recognition that, having willfully rejected that love

---

[160]Lk 15.17.

[161]Lk 15.20.

[162]Lk 15.29.

[163]Lk 15.16.

[164]Dante's *Inferno* and the depictions of hell by Hieronymus Bosch come to mind for Western Christian depictions. For the early patristic tradition, see A. M. R. James, trans., "The Apocalypse of Peter [*Apocalypsis Petri*]," The Akhim Fragment, sections 21–34, in *The Apocryphal New Testament* (Oxford: Clarendon Press, 1924), <http://www.earlychristianwritings.com/text/apocalypsepeter-mrjames.html>, April 20, 2020. See also Boris K. Knorre, *Icon of the Last Judgment: A Detailed Analysis* (Clinton, MA: Museum of Russian Icons, 2013), 11–17, <http://www.museumofrussianicons.org/wp-content/uploads/2016/09/KnorreLastJudgment-Final.pdf>, April 20, 2020.

during one's life, one is cut off—one has cut oneself off—from participating in it.
St Isaac of Nineveh writes:

> Those who are scourged in Hell are tormented with the scourgings of love.
> Scourgings for love's sake, namely of those who perceive that they have sinned
> against love, are more hard and bitter than tortures through fear. The suffer-
> ing which takes hold of the heart through the sinning against love is more
> acute than any other torture. . . . Love works with its force in a double way. It
> tortures those who have sinned, as happens also in the world between friends.
> And it gives delight to those who have kept its decrees. Thus it is also in hell.
> I say that the hard tortures are grief for love.[165]

Hell is being cut off from community and fellowship with other people, with
all the bodiless powers (the angels), with all living things, and with God. The
pigsty in which the young man finds himself is akin to the state of the rich man
in the parable of the rich man and Lazarus:[166] Having utterly neglected Lazarus
during his life, the rich man finds himself after his death in a state where he lacks
the resources to relieve the pain caused by his thirst. No one else in his condition is evidently able or willing to help him, and while he can communicate with
Abraham to beg for mercy,[167] Abraham can only talk to him but is prevented
from helping him.[168]

It is important to note that even in hell, the rich man is stuck in his egoistic
attitude towards Lazarus. He cannot manage to apologize to Lazarus or to ask for
his forgiveness for having neglected him. He is only interested in Lazarus as a kind
of use-object to bring him some water[169] or to be sent to scare his brothers, who
are still alive, into not neglecting those who are in need.[170] It is not clear that he is
concerned that his brothers' care for the poor for their sake but simply that they
give to the poor so they can avoid his situation. Having lived by a kind of narcis-
sistic egoism, the rich man dies cemented as it were into that same egoism.

---

[165]Isaac of Nineveh [Isaac the Syrian], *Mystic Treatises* 27 (136); cf. *Ascetical Homilies*, 141, where the tor-
tures of hell (Gehenna) are described as "bitter regret." Cf. Thomas Hopko, *The Orthodox Faith*, 4:180 and
Georges Florovsky, *Byzantine Fathers*, trans. Raymond Miller (Vaduz, Liechtenstein: Büchervertriebsanstalt,
1987), 238.

[166]Lk 16.19–31.

[167]Lk 16.24.

[168]Lk 16.26.

[169]Lk 16.24.

[170]Lk 16.27–28.

It is worth noting, by way of some contrast, that Evagrius of Pontus believed the rich man showed "pity" (likely, *eleos*) to his brothers. Moreover, Evagrius writes: "Pity (*to eleein*, or to show mercy) is the most beautiful germ of virtue." Evagrius makes this claim because the germs or seeds (*spermata*) of virtue are never completely eliminated from us even after death since those seeds belong to us by nature as God created us.[171] If we grant that the rich man is really concerned for his brothers and not himself, we might regard has action as a moment of compassion and not pity as I am using those terms. But given his attitude to Lazarus as a use-object, it is still not clear he is really interested in his brothers' showing any genuine compassion to those who are poor.

As a slight digression: Evagrius is among those who subscribe to what is called universal resurrection, restoration, or salvation (*apokatastasis*)[172] in which, in light of God's mercy and compassion, all things are ultimately restored and brought to the fullness of life. If so, then even though the rich man is in hell, there might still be some hope for him and the possibility of some repentance. While *apokatastasis* is an extremely attractive view of and hope for God's mercy and compassion for all people, it is generally discredited in the Orthodox Christian tradition—at least as something that in this life we can know that God will do. After all, in response to the rich man's requests that Lazarus be sent to provide him with water, Abraham declares that "between us and you there is a great gulf fixed, so that those who want to pass from here to you cannot, nor can those from there pass to us."[173]

In any event, in contrast to the rich man, the prodigal son gets a second chance in this life in "coming to his senses."[174] Since he has not yet perished, he has a chance to repent or to undergo a radical change of heart and mind. In the parable, the beginning of his repentance consists in acknowledging the ways in which he has sinned against his father, in order to seek forgiveness. But before he arrives home and has a chance to apologize, his father, moved by compassion, forgives the son and restores him to his former place in his house.[175] As with Jesus' interaction

---

[171]See Evagrius Ponticus, *Kephalaia Gnostica: A New Translation of the Unreformed Text from the Syriac* 1.40, trans. Ilaria L. E. Ramelli (Atlanta: Society of Biblical Literature Press, 2015), 36, 43–44. *Eleos* might be the most beautiful gem of virtue but "pity" in the English translation likely is not.

[172]Ibid., lxxxi–lxxxvi.

[173]Lk 16.26. For a general discussion of this theme in the Orthodox Christian tradition, see Kimberly Patton, "Can Evil Be Redeemed? Unorthodox Tensions in Eastern Orthodox Theology," in *Deliver us From Evil*, ed. M. David Eckel and Bradely Herling (London: Continuum International Publishing Group, 2008), 186–206. See Chapter 5, pp. 219–20 for Chrysostom's description of hell and his likely rejection of *apokatastasis*.

[174]Lk 15.17.

[175]Lk 15.20–22.

with Zacchaeus, the father's compassion for his son is expressed as a gesture of hospitality. Open-ended hospitality towards others in fact is a fundamental mark of compassion as we will see in Chapter 5.[176]

Many of the hymns for the Sunday of the Prodigal Son focus almost exclusively on exhorting us to identify with the prodigal son so that our journey through Great Lent will be like the returning prodigal son, begging forgiveness from the Father's compassion so that we not be rejected or sent back to the pigsty. "With the words of the Prodigal I cry aloud: I have sinned, O Father; like him, receive me now in your embrace and reject me not."[177]

In the parable, however, the young son is welcomed home. We could take the young man's return home as an example of the fullness of salvation—our entry into eternal life. Yet we can also understand it as a spiritual rebirth akin to Baptism. In Baptism we are not simply saved in some final sense but we are graced with the Holy Spirit to begin the process of our salvation. The crucial question then is: How ought the young son view and treat others after his welcome home party has ended? What does his repentance as a change of mind and heart involve? In particular, how will he repair all of the relationships that he severed when he left home and how will he forge new relationships with others?

His older brother is certainly not an ideal role model. The older brother complains about what he believes is the unfair way in which his father is treating him in throwing a party for the younger brother. He justifies himself to his father by pointing out how his actions contrast with those of "this son of yours,"[178] whom he does not seem to want to recognize as his brother. He essentially rebukes his father by claiming that he has been treated unjustly.

Having been left to manage the work of father's estate without the help of the younger brother, the older brother is probably justified in his anger towards the younger brother. But the complaint of the older brother amounts to an envy-motivated "whine" that the father is not treating him fairly. It is really no skin off his nose that the father is throwing a lavish feast for the son. The father has not deprived the older brother of anything. He has not prevented the older son from doing anything he wants or enjoying anything to which he is entitled. The father is acting out of a spirit of generosity that seems to characterize his dealings with his children and his servants. The older brother, whatever his other virtues might

---

[176]See Chapter 5, pp. 192–93. See Chapter 4, pp. 139–40 where I will also provide a brief discussion about hospitality.

[177]Sunday of the Prodigal Son, Matins, Ode 3, Troparion (*LT* 116).

[178]Lk 15.30.

be, wants justice in a narrow sense—a kind of quid pro quo. He seems to lack any sense of compassion or willingness to forgive his younger brother or to reconcile himself with him.

St Ephrem the Syrian alludes to the lack of compassion shown by the older brother in his rebuke of a monk who evidently despised another monk. Stressing Paul's exhortation that no matter what we do or how pious we are, if we do not have love, we are nothing,[179] as well as the injunction from 1 Thessalonians 5.15,[180] he then adds this comment:

> For the Lord of glory did not reject the prodigal son, but came toward him, as having been raised from the dead, and put the best garment on him . . . rejoicing at finding his lost son. He attended to his other distressed son, imploring him: "Son, you are always with me and everything I have is yours . . ." Compassionate actions [*oiktirmonai*] must take the lead with the brotherhood. And you, brother [the monk whom Ephrem is addressing], do not despise [others] but imitate the son who repents and returns.[181]

Both of the sons need to move towards repentance. The younger son has started on that journey on his way home, but the parable does not provide the details about how he concretely works out that repentance in terms of repairing broken relationships and building new relationships. So too for the older brother. Both of the brothers need an attitude adjustment, if you will, a change of mind and heart (repentance in the literal sense) towards living for others as does the father.[182] The next two Sundays before Lent—the Sunday of the Last Judgment and the Sunday of Forgiveness—provide crucial guidelines and divine commands for how the two sons and the rest of us ought to live in light of the compassion shown by the father in the parable. The parable of the unmerciful servant provides a key link between the parable of the prodigal son and the Sunday of the Last Judgment and the Sunday of Forgiveness.

---

[179] 1 Cor 13.2.

[180] "See that no one renders evil for evil to anyone, but always pursue what is good both for yourselves and for all."

[181] Ephrem Syrus, *Sermones paraenetici ad monachos Aegypti* 26 (K. G. Phrantzolas, Ὁσίου Ἐφραίμ τοῦ Σύρου ἔργα, vol. 3 [Thessaloniki: To Perivoli tis Panagias, 1990], specific text retrieved from <http://stephanus.tlg.uci.edu/Iris/Cite?4138:036:104178>, April 20, 2020.

[182] It is possible that the older brother is ordinarily as generous and compassionate to others as is the father. His father's treatment of his brother may simply have "pushed a button." The parable leaves this undetermined.

The Sunday of the Last Judgment

The parable of the unmerciful servant[183] compares the Kingdom of God to a gift economy. The servant who receives compassion and mercy from the king is expected to share that compassion and mercy with others if he wants to remain in the kingdom. The gift economy of the Kingdom of God is grounded existentially and ontologically in our relationship with God since we are created in the image of God with the task of attaining to the likeness of God in becoming a living icon of Christ. That is, if we understand ourselves as living icons of Christ, then we seek through our own compassion to become bearers of Christ's compassion, forgiveness, and mercy in the world.

But while the parable of the unmerciful servant is focused on showing compassion and mercy in forgiving others, it also can be extended to our use of the material and other gifts that we receive from God. This is what is presented in the gospel for the Sunday of the Last Judgment.[184] That parable is preceded by other parables that address how we manage the gifts and resources that God gives us. The parable of the Last Judgment extends the boundaries of sharing our resources to those who are "least"—typically those who have little social status or power and who are often neglected within a society.

St Gregory the Theologian eloquently expresses the divine expectation that we use our resources and gifts to show kindness and compassion precisely because of our fundamental reality as images—icons—of Christ, that is, in Gregory's language, "a son of God and fellow heir with Christ" (cf. Rom 8.17):

> Recognize the source of your existence, of your breath of life, your understanding, your knowledge[185] of God (itself the greatest of all gifts) . . . recognize that you have become a son of God, fellow heir with Christ, if I may be so bold, even a very god. Where did you obtain all these things? . . . Who, without listing them individually, endowed you with all the things that lift humans above the rest of creation? Is it not he who now in return and exchange for everything asks that you show *philanthrōpia* [kindness or humanity] to your fellow man? Can we then not be ashamed if we, after all we have received from him and hope yet to receive, will not grant him even this one thing, *philanthrōpia* [kindness or humanity]?[186]

---

[183]Mt 18.21–35.

[184]Mt 25.31–46.

[185]Knowledge here is not simply cognitive understanding but the lived, personal knowledge of someone based upon experience and a relationship with that person.

[186]Gregory the Theologian, *Oration* 14.23 (FOC 107.56; PG 35:888).

… which our human nature, learning piety and kindness (*philanthrōpia*) from our equality in weakness (*asthenia*), has given to compassion (*to sympathes*) the force of law.[187]

The criteria for judgment and condemnation in the parable of the Last Judgment, then, do not simply concern whether or not we perform "alms" or works of mercy understood simply as external actions.[188] They concern whether or not in our own repentance we embrace and reflect the compassion of the father of the prodigal son towards others, the non-judgmental hospitality Christ showed to Zacchaeus, and of course the compassion Christ shows to us in his Incarnation.

The Sunday of Forgiveness

The gospel text for the Sunday of Forgiveness includes: "For if you forgive men their trespasses, your heavenly Father will also forgive you. But if you do not forgive men their trespasses, neither will your Father forgive your trespasses."[189] It duplicates the lesson of the parable of the unmerciful servant although it focuses on compassionate actions that aim at reconciliation and rebuilding a broken relationship through forgiveness rather than relieving someone of a debt that cannot possibly be repaid. How we view people is crucial for this kind of forgiveness. The affective hardness that underlies the Pharisee's attitude of despising the publican, the crowd's rejection of Zacchaeus as a "sinner," and the older brother's evident disowning of his younger brother, preclude any genuine sense of reconciliation or community with the people they despise. There may be legitimate reasons for anger towards others or for setting limits as we restore relations with others. But that is different from the kind of hardened attitude that simply writes people off or views them as incapable of change since one views them as "defined" by various negative characteristics.

Finally, as Fr Bobrinskoy warns, there can be an egoism that creeps into forgiveness that must be avoided: "I discover that when I forgive, I view myself to be at the center of things: it is I who forgive, for it is me who has been wounded.

---

[187]Gregory the Theologian, *Oration* 14.15 (FOC 107.49–50; PG 35:876). Cf. Bobrinskoy, *Compassion*, 86: "the human being is, by nature, by virtue of vocation, a 'being of communion,' a sharing being and—when faced with what the world has become and what the human being has undergone [suffering]—a being of compassion."

[188]Georges Florovsky, "The Meaning of the Great Fast," in *LT*, 19–20.

[189]Mt 6.14–15.

When I forgive, it is always the me that is praised."[190] Forgiveness that stresses this sort of egoism amounts to a forgiveness borne of pity and not compassion.

The Beginning of Great Lent

Great Lent begins on the Monday following the Sunday of Forgiveness. Fasting and other ascetic practices of disciplining our passions are crucial for Orthodox spiritual life during Great Lent. But they are not solely inwardly directed. St Peter of Damaskos writes that like wealthy individuals who renounce their possessions for whoever wants them and make themselves servants to others, "He who fasts likewise does so for love's sake, so that others may eat what he would otherwise have eaten."[191]

To be sure, the extended fasts during Great Lent as well as before the Feast of the Nativity are a time for turning inward through self-discipline and repentance to soften our heart, opening it for the sanctifying work of the Holy Spirit. Always completely dependent upon the grace of the Spirit, we seek to work with him to refashion our own lives, centering them entirely on the love of Christ—and, thus, the Trinity.[192] But we do not and cannot refashion our own lives in relation to God apart from our relationships with other people. On the very first Monday of Great Lent, we are enjoined by Isaiah (1.16–17): "Cease to do evil; learn to do good; seek justice, correct oppression; defend the fatherless, plead for the widow." This injunction and warning is repeated in Isaiah 58.6–7, which is read on the Wednesday of the sixth week of Great Lent: "Is not this the fast that I choose: to loose the bonds of wickedness . . . to let the oppressed go free, to share bread with the hungry, and bring the homeless poor into your house."[193]

These injunctions are emphasized in Orthodox liturgical texts:

> While fasting with the body, brethren, let us also fast in spirit. Let us loose
> every bond of iniquity. Let us undo the knots of every contract made by vio-
> lence. Let us tear up all unjust agreements. Let us give bread to the hungry

---

[190]Bobrinskoy, *Compassion*, 80. See, 73–81 for his extended meditation on forgiveness.

[191]St Peter of Damaskos, *Twenty-Four Discourses* 15 (*Philokalia* 3: 253–54; Greek 3:147).

[192]As we remind ourselves throughout the Divine Liturgy and many other worship services when we commemorate the Theotokos and the saints in various litanies: "Let us commend ourselves and each other and all our life to Christ our God" (e.g., Great Litany, *Service Books*, 33).

[193]It might seem that I have shifted the tenor of our relationship to our neighbor from compassion and mercy to justice. But, as we will see in the next chapter, some hymns commemorate the compassion of the saints for doing exactly what is commanded as a matter of seeking justice in the readings from Isaiah. See Chapter 4, Hymns H-63, H-65, and H-70, pp. 163, 164, 165.

and welcome to our house the poor who have no roof to cover them, that we may receive great mercy from Christ our God.[194]

The compassionate actions of the father towards his prodigal son and Jesus' compassion and hospitality towards Zacchaeus are linchpins of the gospel lessons for the pre-Lenten Sundays. Zacchaeus' spontaneous act of restitution and generosity as well as the humble repentance of the publican and the prodigal son are key human responses to God's compassion towards us. But Zacchaeus' actions cannot be a one-time gesture. The publican cannot remain standing in the portico simply begging God's mercy. Rather while begging for God's mercy, he has to go back to his own life and change how he has lived. So too for the prodigal son since, as I pointed out earlier, we need not assume that his life comes to an earthly end after he gets home. By way of contrast, without a fundamental change in how they "see" and "understand" people, the hardened attitudes of the crowd towards Zacchaeus, the Pharisee towards the publican, the older son towards his brother, and the evident indifference of the goats towards those in need,[195] may allow at most for a kind of self-aggrandizing pity towards others. As with Lt Hofmiller's pity towards Edith in Zweig's *Beware of Pity*, whatever assistance these people might provide to others is countered by the despising attitudes they have towards them.

Great Lent, then, is a time in which we respond with humility and gratitude towards the compassion God shows to us and also aim to express that compassion in our dealings with others. As we will see, cultivating a robust sense of compassion towards others is itself integrally connected with the various interior ascetic activities of Lent, since their purpose is to lead us to a condition of dispassion—a way of life in which we reject all of the self-serving passions that block our relationship with Christ and the Trinity, with one another, and with the world around us.[196] Cultivating a robust sense of compassion towards others is also integrally connected with our response to the Divine Liturgy and the eucharistic Gifts of the Body and Blood of Christ.

As the Divine Liturgy expresses the inherent compassionate neighborliness of the Trinity towards us, our gratitude for the eucharistic Gifts must be fundamentally reflected in our own liturgy after the Liturgy. In the living out of this Liturgy

---

[194]First Week of Lent, Wednesday, Vespers, Sticheron at *Lord, I Call* (*LT* 235). Repeated in Chapter 4 as hymn H-87.

[195]Mt 25.41–44.

[196]See Chapter 5, pp. 203–205.

we try, with God's grace and support, to be true neighbors to other people—all
people—enacting our compassionate imitation, as best we can, of the compassion
bestowed on us by the Trinity and Christ. With this in mind, we will examine
in the next chapter the liturgical hymns that commemorate the compassion of
Christ, the Theotokos, and other saints, as well as those hymns that exhort us to
be compassionate.

Summary and Looking Forward

Summary

We are created in the image and likeness of God and, as St John of Damascus
notes, compassion is a fundamental virtue to be acquired in attaining a likeness
to Christ. If this is so, we need to begin with an understanding of God's—the
Trinity's—and Christ's compassion for its own sake, of course, but also for identifying the paradigmatic source for the capacity for compassion that belongs to us
by nature as human beings and that is brought to a fullness in Orthodox Christian life. I hope that I have accomplished that in this chapter beginning with the
manifestation of God's compassion in the Divine Liturgy, which is central to
Orthodox Christian life and theology. I then moved to consider God's compassion in the Old Testament and how that prefigures Christ's compassion in the
New Testament. I also briefly explored the fundamental role of compassion in
our life-long project of repentance, with a reflection on the gospel readings for
the Sundays preceding the start of Lent. I will now briefly discuss some key indicators from this chapter that will provide the basis for the analysis of compassion
in Chapters 5 and 6.

Looking Forward

1) The Divine Liturgy is the central sacrament or mystery of the Church in which
divine compassion is manifested principally in the consecration of the gifts of
bread and wine as the Body and Blood of Christ and in their reception by the
faithful for healing, forgiveness, and our ongoing life of repentance. This indicator will provide the context for the analysis of compassion at the very beginning
of Chapter 5.[197]

---

[197] See above, pp. 80–87. See Chapter 5, pp. 179–81.

2) The compassion exercised in the Divine Liturgy continues the compassionate healing ministry of Christ as expressed in the parable of the good Samaritan. Christ is, for Orthodox Christians, the paradigmatic good Samaritan. In his compassion, he shows what it is to be a neighbor. We have a second key indicator: Neighborliness—drawing near to others to be with them—is a fundamental feature of compassion. We will find references to neighborliness and compassion throughout Chapters 5 and 6.[198]

3) The concept of the "liturgy after the Liturgy" expresses how our actions in the world after the Liturgy should reflect the compassion and love we have received through the Liturgy and the eucharistic Gifts. This characterization of our life in the world reflects one principal way in which compassion in Orthodox Christian life builds on and develops the natural compassion that we have by nature; namely, living compassionately is an integral part of becoming a living icon of Christ. This indicator will receive explicit mention towards the end of Chapter 5 and the Epilogue.[199]

4) The account of the feeding of the 4,000 has a double meaning as an action of feeding people who are physically hungry and as prefiguring the feeding of the faithful in the Liturgy with the eucharistic Gifts. I noted that in feeding the four thousand, Christ and his disciples exercise compassion in a collective manner. This raises the question of how and in what sense compassion can be expressed collectively by people; that is, the sense in which we, in an organized manner, show compassion. I will explore this matter in Chapter 6.[200]

5) I noted that the ascetic activities of Great Lent are important for the development of compassion since these activities are designed to lead us to a state of dispassion. I will develop this theme in Chapter 5.[201]

6) In his theophany to Moses on Mount Sinai (Exodus 34.4–6), God reveals that compassion, mercy, long suffering, and so forth belong to his very name—that is, his reality or, in the Orthodox Christian tradition, his energies. This compassion continues to be shown to the Israelites even when they abandon him as the long text from Nehemiah 9.6–31 made clear. The compassion that God shows to the Israelites is extended to all people through the promise of the suffering servant, whom Christians identify as Christ. Divine compassion expresses itself as a steadfast solidarity or fellowship and community with all people. I will develop

---

[198]See above, pp. 85–86. See Chapter 5, pp. 192–93, 203, 232. See Chapter 6, p. 243.
[199]See above, pp. 86–87. See Chapter 5, p. 232. See Epilogue, p. 259.
[200]See above, p. 85. See Chapter 6, pp. 243–47.
[201]See above, pp. 118–9. See Chapter 5, pp. 203–205.

this aspect of human compassion in Chapter 5 in the analysis of compassion as a disposition.[202]

7) The text from Colossians 3.1–14 that exhorts us to "put on Christ" with compassion, mercy, and love, provides a basic scriptural justification for viewing compassion as a virtue. Moreover, as I pointed out, the characteristics we are to acquire in putting on Christ echo the "compassion formula" by which God characterizes himself as compassionate, merciful, and so forth. I will discuss the sense in which compassion is a virtue in the third section of Chapter 5.[203]

8) I noted Fr Bobrinskoy's observation that the divine love and kenotic sacrifice of the Son of God are present at the very creation of the world and not simply in response to sin. This raises the question of whether God's compassion is exclusively a response to the consequences of human sin or more fundamentally something present at the very creation of the world. I will explore this idea in Chapter 5 when I take up the theme of coming to terms with vulnerability. This will provide a basis for arguing for a universal compassion that accepts the vulnerability of all created things as created and responds to it.[204]

9) In the reflection on the gospel lessons for the Sundays prior to the start of Great Lent, there was an ongoing contrast between compassion and the visceral denigration, despising, and stigmatization of people. The latter were reflected in the behaviors and attitudes of the crowd towards Zacchaeus, the Pharisee in the parable of the publican and the Pharisee, and the older brother in the parable of the prodigal son. Three indicators for further analysis can be drawn from this reflection.

One key indicator was that these people illustrated that despising people in the strong sense of denigration and stigmatization is not simply an action. More fundamentally, it involves ways of understanding people that rejects the fullness of their humanity and dignity. This indicator will provide a key for the discussion in Chapter 5 about the nature of a compassionate disposition as a disposition "without judgment."[205]

A second indicator is that denigration and stigmatization undermine and can destroy neighborliness and community between those who stigmatize and those who are stigmatized. On the other hand, Christ approaches Zacchaeus with a welcoming, non-judgmental hospitality. Christ does this throughout his earthly

---

[202]See above, pp. 91, 95–96, 97. See Chapter 5, pp. 193–94, 201–202.
[203]See above, pp. 99–100. See Chapter 5, pp. 211–33.
[204]See above, pp. 101–102. See Chapter 5, pp. 209–210.
[205]See above, pp. 117, 119. See Chapter 5, pp. 197–200.

ministry. The father in the parable of the prodigal son responds to the younger son in the same way in being moved by compassion. This indicator will also be developed in Chapter 5 in examining the contrast between compassion as non-judgmental affirmation of others and the array of toxic passions that accuse people in advance of being inferior and even sub-human in a way that supports harming and exploiting people or, at best, exhibiting a form of condescending pity towards them.[206]

For a third indicator, I pointed out that the task for Zacchaeus, the publican, and the prodigal son was to move forward from the mercy or forgiveness they initially receive and rework or refashion their own lives to reflect the compassion and mercy that has been extended to them. That reworking is fundamental to the forward-looking process of repentance that is pervasive throughout Great Lent. As the reader will see, developing this theme will reverberate throughout much of Chapter 5 and the Epilogue.[207]

10) I briefly noted a similarity between Old Testament commands to treat people justly and the veneration of some saints who are regarded as compassionate for treating people in the same way. This indicator raises the question about the relation between compassion and justice that I will discuss in chapter 6.[208]

11) I noted that Jesus and the characters in his parables who are moved by compassion to assist others do so without any indication of making judgements as to peoples' worthiness for compassion, and without reservation. This is a very important indicator for developing the structure of a compassionate disposition as "without judgment."[209]

---

[206]See above, pp. 106–110, 119. See Chapter 5, pp. 183–85, 197–200.
[207]See above, p. 118. See Chapter 5, pp. 225–27. See Epilogue, p. 258.
[208]See above, pp. 79, 118–20. See Chapter 6, pp. 235–46.
[209]See above, p. 104. See Chapter 5, pp. 197–99.

CHAPTER 4

The Celebration of Compassion in the Hymns of the Church

There is not a single liturgical service in the Orthodox Church which does not use chanting and singing extensively. Why is this so? . . . The Orthodox Liturgy begins with the exclamation: "Blessed is the Kingdom of the Father, and the Son, and the Holy Spirit. . . ." The Kingdom of God, experienced in the Liturgy, is an expression of divine beauty: singing, hymnography, iconography, ritual, solemnity are all part of what is experienced by the faithful as the epiphany or manifestation of "heaven on earth."[1]

The experience of "heaven on earth" in the Divine Liturgy flows into all of the services of the Church. The hymns of the Church play a substantive role in this experience. Hence, to fill out the experiential dimension of the theological framework for understanding and responding to compassion, I will devote this chapter to presenting a very small set of selected hymns that focus on the celebration of the compassion of Christ, the Theotokos, and various saints. The organization of the chapter is straightforward.

In the first section, I will briefly lay out the order of Orthodox Christian worship services that are part of the daily cycle of worship, along with the Divine Liturgy.[2] I will also note the various texts that are used for the hymns and other variable texts for these services. In the second section, I will discuss the nature and role of chanting or singing in these worship services. Along with prayer, chanting and singing sacred music, in its own way, can help center us in the heart and open us to a holistic experience of compassion.

---

[1]David Drillock, "Liturgical Song in the Worship of the Church," *St Vladimir's Theological Quarterly* 41.2–3 (1997): 183.

[2]There are a number of other worship services in the Orthodox Christian Church: sacramental services such as Baptism and Marriage, as well as occasional services such as the funeral service, akathists, and molebens. *The Great Book of Needs*, 4 vols (South Canaan, PA: St Tikhon's Seminary Press, 1999–2002) contains the texts for a number of these services. For this project, I am focusing primarily on hymns contained in services of the daily cycle and the Divine Liturgy.

In the third section, I will focus first on a selection of hymns that celebrate Christ's compassion in the principal feasts of the Lord and also in his healing ministry on earth. I will then turn to the celebration of the compassion of the Theotokos and of several selected saints who are venerated for their compassion. Finally, I will present some of the hymns that remind us of our responsibility to care for others.

In the fourth section of the chapter, Summary and Looking Forward, I will provide a brief review of this chapter and point out several indicators about compassion in this chapter that will be developed in Chapters 5 and 6.

Orthodox Worship Services

Centered on the Pascha of our Lord and Savior Jesus Christ, the Orthodox Church is essentially eucharistic in nature. Pascha is at the heart of all of the divine services of the Church: "This is the chosen and holy day, first of Sabbaths, king and lord of days, the feast of feasts, holy day of holy days. On this day we bless Christ forevermore."[3] At the heart of that Paschal Liturgy, as with every Liturgy, is God's divine compassionate action in which the Holy Spirit changes the gifts of bread and wine to be the precious Body and Blood of our Lord. All of the other worship services and sacraments (mysteries) of the Church throughout the year, whether eucharistic or not, radiate out from and point back to the Paschal Liturgy.

Since the references to God's compassion, mercy, and *philanthrōpia* pervade Orthodox worship services, let me provide a very brief outline of these services. Vespers marks the end and beginning of each liturgical day. For example, the change of the liturgical day from Thursday to Friday takes place at the Vespers served on Thursday evening. Vespers is followed by Compline, a service that generally precedes the time before retiring for the night. In the middle of the night, there is a set of midnight prayers. Very early in the morning—around daybreak—the service of Orthros or Matins is celebrated. This service is followed by the Hours, which are services of psalms and prayers.[4] There are four Hours: First,

---

[3] Pascha, Matins, Paschal Canon, Ode 8, Irmos. *The Paschal Service* (Syosset, NY: Orthodox Church in America, Department of Religious Education, 2000), 36. [This publication and others by the Department of Religious Education of the Orthodox Church in America are now published through St Vladimir's Seminary Press.—*Ed.*]

[4] In the Russian tradition, a vigil is often served (every Saturday evening and on the eve of all vigil-rank services) that combines Vespers, Matins, and the First Hour. The full cycle of these services each day is often celebrated in monasteries, which is one of the great gifts of the monastic life to the Church.

Third, Sixth, and Ninth.[5] Outside Lent, the Divine Liturgy can be celebrated daily; but it is not part of the daily cycle.[6] It takes place in the Kairos in which the Lord acts in the mystical, mysterious joining together of heaven and earth "outside" time. The time for the Divine Liturgy is not strictly linked to a particular clock time as part of the daily cycle.

Each of these services contains fixed and variable texts. The fixed texts are built into the templates for given services: e.g., the Great Litany for Vespers, Matins, and the Divine Liturgy; the Prayer of the Hours for the Hours; Psalm 103 and *Gladsome Light* for Vespers. In addition, each service contains variable texts drawn from various "cycles." The *Menaion* contains the variable texts for each day of the month. For each day, one finds a particular set of hymns for the saint or saints commemorated on that day, as well as for the major and minor feasts of the Lord and of the Theotokos that are assigned to a fixed date on the calendar: e.g., the Nativity of Christ (Dec. 25), the Birth of the Theotokos (Sept. 8), the Transfiguration of Christ (Aug. 6), and the Dormition of the Theotokos (Aug. 15).[7] The *Octoechos* contains the variable texts for each day of the week according to the tone for the week. There are eight tones or modes—melodic sequences—in the Orthodox Christian Church. The first tone begins with the first week of Pascha. The tones rotate in order throughout the year.

There is also the long period of movable feasts determined each year by the date of Pascha. All Orthodox Christians follow the determination of Pascha according to the traditional Julian calendar. The texts for the period prior to Pascha are drawn from the *Triodion*. They include the four Sundays prior to the

---

[5] The First Hour is served in the morning around 6–9 a.m. It commemorates Christ's being brought before Pilate. The Third Hour is served around 9 a.m. to noon. It commemorates Pilate's judgment that Christ be crucified and his mocking and scourging as well as the descent of the Holy Spirit on the Apostles at Pentecost. The Sixth Hour is served around 12–3 p.m. It commemorates Christ's journey to Golgotha and the Crucifixion. The Ninth Hour is served around 3–6 p.m. It commemorates Christ's Passion and Death. *A Manual of the Orthodox Church's Services,* trans. Dimitrii Sokolov (New York: Wynkoop Hallenbeck Crawford, Co., 1899), 36, 39.

[6] During Great Lent, the daily Divine Liturgy, which is essentially resurrectional in nature, is replaced by the Pre-Sanctified Liturgy, which is penitential in focus. In the Pre-Sanctified Liturgy, which does not contain the consecratory Anaphora Prayer, the eucharistic Gifts are served from Gifts sanctified at an earlier Divine Liturgy (on a Saturday or Sunday, when Liturgy can be served in Great Lent).

[7] I will provide dates for fixed feasts as celebrated by Orthodox Christians who use the Gregorian or Revised Julian calendar. Many Orthodox Christians use the traditional Julian calendar. There is currently a thirteen-day discrepancy between them: e.g., the Feast of the Nativity is celebrated on Dec. 25 on the Gregorian Calendar and Jan. 7 on the Julian calendar (or, rather, both celebrate the feast on Dec. 25, but Dec. 25 on the Julian calendar falls on Jan. 7 on the Gregorian calendar). All Orthodox Christians use the dates from the Julian calendar for the movable feasts that are centered on the Feast of Pascha. For further information on this matter see: *FM* 563–4 and Alkiviadis Calivas, *Essays in Theology and Liturgy* (Brookline, MA: Holy Cross Orthodox Press, 2001) 2:125–42.

start of Great Lent—the Sundays of the Publican and the Pharisee, the Prodigal Son, the Last Judgment, and the Sunday of Forgiveness and the Expulsion of Adam and Eve from Paradise; the six weeks of Great Lent that conclude with the Divine Liturgy on Palm Sunday; and Great and Holy Week that begins with the Bridegroom Matins (often served on the evening of Palm Sunday), which is the first service for Great and Holy Monday, and ends with the Vesperal Liturgy of Great and Holy Saturday. The variable texts for the services for Pascha through the Sunday of All Saints, which follows Pentecost, are taken from the *Pentecostarion* or *Flowery Triodion*. On any given day, then, and depending upon the feast for the day, the variable texts for a given service will be taken from one or more of these volumes.

Although the services from the daily cycle may be served by a priest alone, the Divine Liturgy always requires two people: the priest and at least one other person. All of the services are part of the public worship of the Church—the mystical Body of Christ—a fulfillment of the compassionate action resulting from the Incarnation of the Son of God. There is a profound sense in which human salvation or deification is corporate—the communion of saints—and never merely personal. Hence, while there are many hymns in the Church that appeal to God's compassion to save the individual, God's, Christ's, compassion is expressed in a prior sense towards the Church as the people of God.

The plan of the divine services reflects St Paul's injunction to "pray without ceasing"[8] as an activity of the Church in public through corporate prayer and not only in personal prayer. Moreover, Fr Georges Florovsky emphasizes that while private prayer allows one to enter into an "intimate and direct conversation with the Living God and acquire the Holy Spirit,"

> "Private devotions" are inevitably but a preparation for, and a sequel to, "corporate worship." They always are pointing beyond themselves. *Prayer is intrinsically subordinate to sacraments.* . . . Accordingly, the ultimate "encounter" is realized also in a *sacramental* way, in the mystery of the Holy Eucharist.[9]

Fr Florovsky's observation has a direct bearing on our experience of God's compassion and mercy in the Liturgy and in our public worship services. At the core of personal prayer is the very "simple" yet profound Jesus Prayer: "Lord Jesus Christ, Son of God, have mercy on me the sinner." The divine services of the

---

[8]1 Thess 5.17.
[9]Georges Florovsky, "Orthodox Services and their Structure" (*FM* 38).

Church provide a corporate or communal[10] expression of this prayer: "Lord Jesus Christ, Son of God, have mercy on us sinners," which is reflected in the myriad occasions when the response to various litanies is "Lord, have mercy," which is likely the most frequently uttered response in Orthodox services.

Indeed, even the prayers of the services of the hours, which do not contain litanies and are often said in private prayer, take us beyond a merely personal experience of and prayer for God's mercy: Consider this section of the Trisagion Prayers: "Holy God, Holy Mighty, Holy immortal, have mercy on *us*... Most holy Trinity, have mercy on *us*. Lord, cleanse *us* from our sins. Master, pardon *our* iniquities. Holy God, visit and heal *us* for your Name's sake" (my emphasis). To repeat, the divine mercy and compassion that we receive and for which we give thanks as individuals is embedded in the mercy and compassion extended by God to the Church, as the people of God, and the whole of creation.

Chanting, Singing, and Worship as Celebration

Orthodox services are sung or chanted, especially the Divine Liturgy.[11] Indeed, liturgical chant, as Anatoly Grindenko says, "is an image, or icon, of the singing of the angels. . . . [T]he aim of liturgical chant, which is an icon living only in time, is to go through physical sound into the invisible world."[12] The ancient prayer for chanters well exemplifies the sort of disposition that should undergird chanting: "Help us to cleanse ourselves, in body and soul, in clear thoughts and calm spirit, and that through singing that we dress ourselves in light of love and life, in communion with you and all the saints."[13] We are also enjoined to avoid vanity and making judgments about ourselves (and presumably other people).

The services of the Church are a primary setting in which we offer praise to God. In chanting or singing the services, including the hymns, theology comes alive, since the "vantage point is no longer outside the event to which it refers,

---

[10]"Corporate" here means people united together in a community and not merely a collection of individuals arranged like a pile of marbles in a heap.

[11]St Ignatius evidently regarded this chanting as an antiphonal response between the clergy and the people—not just, as is often the case, a choir or chanter that often assume the responsibility for all of the sung responses while the congregation remains silent and hopefully in prayer. See Dimitri Conomos, "Orthodox Byzantine Music," entry posted November 15, 2012, <http://www.asbm.goarch.org/articles/orthodox-byzantine-music/>, April 20, 2020 and Everett Ferguson, "Congregational Singing in the Early Church," *Acta Patristica et Byzantina* 15.1 (2004): 144–59.

[12]Anatoly Grindenko (Founder and Director), "Liner Notes," *Meditation: Chants for Great Lent* with the Moscow Russian Patriarchate Choir, recorded 1999 on Opus 111, compact disc.

[13]National Forum of Greek Orthodox Church Musicians, "Prayers for Church Musicians," <http://churchmusic.goarch.org/events/churchmusicsunday/prayers/>, April 20, 2020.

but rather the event itself, made present liturgically and encompassing worshippers past, present and future."[14] The chanting and singing of and listening to the hymns, as well as the entire service, serve to center us in our heart in order to experience and participate in the saving acts of God's compassion of which the mysteries—that is, the sacraments—are vital.[15]

The chanted character of the services and, thus, of the hymns embedded in them, serves to orient us away from our heads to our hearts, in which, through the grace of the Holy Spirit, we can experience ourselves and one another in community (*koinōnia*) in an integrated and holistic manner—body, mind or intellect (*nous*), and spirit—in the presence of God.[16] In this way, they lead us to the deep affective, visceral, and spiritual or heart-centered source of compassion.[17]

The Incarnation is itself the mystery that undergirds, if you will, all of the mysteries of the Church and of the services of the daily and weekly cycles. It is, then, not surprising that hymns that celebrate the Incarnation as an expression of God's compassion, *sympatheia*, mercy, and *philanthrōpia* are pervasive throughout the services of the Church. The compassionate saving event of the Incarnation extends from the conception in the flesh of the Son of God at the Annunciation of the Theotokos; through his crucifixion, Resurrection, and Ascension; to Pentecost; and finally to his second and glorious coming—the general resurrection and the restoration of creation and of the righteous or the just to the everlasting fullness of life in communion with the Trinity.

Hymns Celebrating and Invoking Compassion

I do not plan to offer a comprehensive survey of all the references to Christ's compassion in the hymns of the Church.[18] I want to focus on those hymns that

[14]Bogdan G. Bucur, "'The Feet that Eve Heard in Paradise and Was Afraid': Observations on the Christology of Byzantine Hymns," *Philosophy and Theology* 18.1 (2006): 18.

[15]Cf. Constantine Carnavos, "Knowing God through Icons and Hymnody," *Greek Orthodox Theological Review* 23.3–4 (1978): 282–98 and Dimitri Conomos, "Early Christian and Byzantine Music: History and Performance," Archdiocesan School of Byzantine Music, Greek Orthodox Archdiocese of America, Nov. 11, 2012, <http://www.asbm.goarch.org/articles/early-christian-and-byzantine-music-history-and-performance/>, April 20, 2020.

[16]At the very beginning of the Anaphora Prayer, the priest blesses the people: "The grace of our Lord Jesus Christ, and the love of God the Father, and the communion (*koinōnia*) of the Holy Spirit be with you all" (2 Cor 13:13). Of course, as the heart is the "battle ground of good and evil," we may also be aware of all of the passions and attitudes that divide and separate us from one another that require forgiveness and for which we petition God in the Prayer before Communion.

[17]The heart-centered source of compassion can all too often be disrupted by toxic passions and thoughts that can open us to repentance or, alas, drive us away from our worship.

[18]I do, however, want to provide a somewhat robust selection. I think it is important to document and collect at least a brief selection of these hymns. Read together, they provide a powerful theological—that is,

express his compassion in the great feasts of the Lord, Holy Week, and Pascha. I have made a particular attempt to include some hymns that link the mystery or paradoxical, wondrous nature of the Incarnation of the Son of God with his compassion.[19] Here are some extracts from these hymns:

H-11. He who dwells in the light that no man can approach and who upholds all things, in his ineffable compassion (*eusplanchnian*) is born of a Virgin.[20]

H-32. He who made the lakes and springs and seas, wishing to teach us the surpassing value of humility, girded himself with a towel and washed the feet of the disciples, humbling himself in the abundance of his great compassion (*hyperbolē eusplanchnias*).[21]

H-37. Today the Master of the creation and the Lord of Glory is nailed to the cross and his side is pierced.... He who wraps the heaven in clouds is smitten upon his back ... that in his compassion (*eusplanchnos*) he may save the world from error. [22]

H-39. Today he who is in essence unapproachable, becomes approachable for me, and suffers his passion, thus setting me free from passions.... I venerate your compassion (*eusplanchnia*): glory to you, O longsuffering Lord.[23]

It is extremely important to keep in mind the paradoxical, wondrous character of the compassion of Christ's Incarnation that is so beautifully and eloquently expressed in these and many other hymns.[24] They open us to a mystery that is beyond the rational intellect: we cannot wrap our heads around it through any kind of conceptual thinking or rational analysis. Rather, with mind in the heart, these hymns call to us remember and celebrate the way in which his Incarnation bridged the gap between the uncreated and created and established a solidarity with all mankind—especially those who are the least and the most despised among us—and creation itself. Christ's compassion for us, whose divine nature is

experiential—encounter with divine and human compassion in our worship services and our response to it. I have numbered the hymns for ease of reference.

[19] See Bogdan Bucur, "The Feet that Eve Heard in Paradise and Was Afraid," 8–9 for a discussion of this distinctive feature of Orthodox Christian Hymns. A number of hymns with this feature are also given in his article (5–9).

[20] Forefeast of the Nativity (Dec. 24), Matins, Exapostilarion (*FM* 216).

[21] Great and Holy Thursday, Matins, First Sessional Hymn after Ode 3 (*LT* 549–50).

[22] Third Sunday of Lent (Sunday of the Cross), Matins, Procession of Cross from altar to analogion, Sticheron (*LT 349*).

[23] Great and Holy Friday, Royal Hours, Third Hour, Sticheron (*LT* 604).

[24] See hymns H-5, H-9, H-13, H-15, H-37, and H-39 for other examples.

utterly different from ours, is a profound lesson for those who despise and reject
their fellow man, with whom they share the same common human nature and
equality of honor, or who simply provide assistance to others out of a condescending pity that accepts and does not challenge the degraded status imputed to them.
Compassion for all persons who share our common nature, I would add, ought
not be something paradoxical or wondrous for us.

For our own human response to Christ's compassion, I will then turn to the
hymns that venerate the Theotokos and selected saints for their compassion.
Finally, although relatively few in number within Orthodox services, I want to
acknowledge those hymns that exhort us to be compassionate, merciful, and
"philanthropic" in imitation of Christ and also admonish us for our lack of
compassion.[25]

The Great Feasts of Christ, Pascha, and Holy Week[26]

H-1. No hymn can recount the multitude of your many mercies [*oiktirmōn*,
or compassionate actions]. For though we offer unto you, O holy King, songs
numberless as the sand upon the seashore, yet we do nothing worthy of the
blessings you have given us, who cry unto you: Alleluia![27]

I will order the feasts according to the events of Christ's life and not according
to their sequence in the church year, which begins on September 1. For example,
I will begin with the Feast of the Annunciation, when the Son of God is incarnate in the womb of the Virgin even though the feast day for the Annunciation
is on March 25. Although I have interspersed my brief observations about each
feast prior to presenting the hymns for the feast, these hymns collectively have a
remarkable integrity and beauty. The reader might find it worthwhile at some
point simply to read through these hymns in an uninterrupted sequence; this
will amplify the pervasiveness of our commemoration of Christ's compassion,

---

[25]Throughout these hymns, you will often find the expression "in his compassion." The Greek word, *kata*,
translated as "in," has the stronger, causal sense of "according to" or "because of."

[26]For discussions of the meaning of the feasts of the Lord, see *FM* 46–66; A Monk of the Eastern Church
(Lev Gillet), *The Year of the Grace of the Lord: A Scriptural and Liturgical Commentary on the Calendar of the
Orthodox Church*, trans. Deborah Cowan (Crestwood, NY: St Vladimir's Seminary Press, 1980); Hierotheos
of Nafpaktos, *Feasts of the Lord: An Introduction to the Twelve Feasts and Orthodox Christology*, trans. Esther
Williams (Levadia, Greece: Birth of the Theotokos Monastery, 2003); and Paul Evdokimov, *The Art of the Icon:
A Theology of Beauty*, trans. Steven Bigham (Redondo Beach, CA: Oakwood Publications, 1990), 269–344.

[27]Lenten Akathist to the Theotokos, Kontakion 11 (*LT* 435).

which is manifest throughout his entire earthly ministry and, in fact, from all eternity.[28]

FEAST OF THE ANNUNCIATION OF THE THEOTOKOS (MARCH 25)

H-2. Today is the beginning of our salvation, the revelation of the eternal mystery! The Son of God becomes the Son of the Virgin, as Gabriel announces the coming of Grace. Together with him let us cry to the Theotokos: Rejoice, O Full of Grace! The Lord is with you![29]

In the Old Testament, God's compassion for the Israelites amounts to a pledge to restore them to the Promised Land. As we saw in the previous chapter, however, that compassion was to be extended to all people through the Suffering Servant. God's promise of sending the Suffering Servant, the Messiah, is fulfilled in the Incarnation of Christ, which is commemorated in the Feast of the Annunciation. The compassion God exhibits towards Israel now takes on a profoundly personal or hypostatic character: Born of the Virgin, the Son of God puts on the form and nature of a creature, which, as created, is profoundly different from his own divine nature and, as fallen, has been corrupted and estranged from God through sin.[30] His compassion and love for us—and indeed the whole of creation—is expressed in his kenosis, his "emptying" of himself to take the form of a servant.[31]

By compassionately taking on human nature at the very beginning of human life in which we are all profoundly vulnerable and dependent on others, Christ invites his Mother to cultivate the deep sense of *racham*—compassion as the womb-like love a mother has for a child and God has for his creation.[32] There is one stunning text from Clement of Alexandria in which he expresses the womb-like love and compassion that God as Mother has for us:

[Behold] the mysteries of love. And then you shall look into the bosom of the Father, whom God the only-begotten Son alone has declared. And God

---

[28]But one must always remember that these hymns are embedded in various worship services, which are their proper home.

[29]Troparion of the Annunciation, Tone 4 (*Service Books*, 284).

[30]"Thus, man fell into slavery when he was estranged from his proper place. The place of the heart is virtue and knowledge from which man was estranged when he fell into evil and ignorance and came to be a slave. For the one who sins is a slave of sin." Evagrius, *Expositio in Proverbia Salomonis*, in C. Tischendorf, ed., *Notitia editionis codicis bibliorum Sinaitici* (Leipzig, 1860), 116.

[31]Phil 2.7.

[32]See Chapter 5, p. 209 for further discussion of this key indicator for coming to terms with our vulnerability in compassion.

himself is love (*agapē*); and out of love to us became feminine (*ethērathē*). In his ineffable essence he is Father; in his compassion (*sympathēs*) for us he became Mother. The Father by loving became feminine: and the great proof of this is he whom he begot of himself; and the fruit brought forth by love is love. For this also he came down. For this he clothed himself with man. For this he voluntarily subjected himself to the experiences of men, that by bringing himself to the measure of our weakness whom he loved, he might correspondingly bring us to the measure of his own strength.[33]

Selected Hymns for the Feast of the Annunciation

H-3. Showing compassion [*katoikteirēsas*] upon that which he has made and bending down in his tender mercy [*splanchnois tois oikeiois*], the Maker hastens to dwell in the womb of a Maiden, the Child of God. To her the great Archangel came, saying to her: "Hail, O thou who art full of divine grace, our God is now with thee. Be not afraid of me, the chief commander of the armies of the King. For thou hast found the grace that thy mother Eve once lost: and thou shalt conceive and bring forth him who is one in essence with the Father."[34]

H-4. Having reached the city of Nazareth, Gabriel now salutes thee, the living City of Christ the King, and he cries aloud to thee: "Hail, thou who art blessed and full of divine grace. Thou shalt hold in thy womb God made flesh, and through thee in his compassion [*eusplanchnia*], He shall call back mankind to its ancient state. Blessed is the divine and immortal fruit of thy womb, who through thee grants the world great mercy."[35]

H-5. Let the heavens be glad and the earth rejoice: for the Son, who is coeternal with the Father, sharing his throne and like him without beginning, in his compassion [*oikton*] and merciful love for mankind [*philanthrōpon eleon*]

---

[33] Clement of Alexandria, *Who is the Rich Man that Shall Be Saved?* 37 (ANF 2: 601; PG 9:641). See also Kathleen E. McVey, "Ephrem the Syrian's Use of Female Metaphors to Describe the Deity," *Zeitschrift für Antikes Christentum /Journal of Ancient Christianity* 5.2 (2006): 261–88. For a very interesting study of the presence of feminine language about God in the patristic and broader Christian tradition, see Mimi Haddad, "Evidence for and Significance of Feminine God-Language from the Church Fathers to the Modern Era," *Priscilla Papers* 18.3 (2004): 3–11. The Septuagint, alas, misses the connection in the Hebrew between *racham* (compassion) and *rechem* (womb) since *mētron* (womb) bears no etymological connection to *oiktirmos* and *eleos*, the Greek terms often used to translate *racham* (compassion).

[34] Annunciation of the Theotokos, Small Vespers, Sticheron at *Lord, I call* (*FM* 437 mod.).

[35] Annunciation of the Theotokos, Small Vespers, Sticheron at *Lord, I call* (*FM* 438).

has submitted himself to emptying, according to the good pleasure and the counsel of the Father; and he has gone to dwell in a virgin's womb that was sanctified beforehand by the Spirit. O marvel![36] God is come among men; he who cannot be contained is contained in a womb; the Timeless [One] enters time; and, strange wonder! His conception is without seed, his emptying is past telling: so great is this mystery.[37]

H-6. The coeternal Word of the Father without beginning, not being parted from the things on high, has now descended here below, in his infinite compassion [*eusplanchnia*] taking pity [*oiktos*][38] upon fallen men; and assuming the poverty of Adam, he has put on a form that is alien to him.[39]

H-7. Making known the mystery that had been hid of old, O Maiden, Gabriel once cried out to you: Rejoice, O palace of God, wherein having dwelled He shall deify all mortals, since He is compassionate [*eusplanchnos*].[40]

FEAST OF THE NATIVITY OF CHRIST: CHRISTMAS (DECEMBER 25)[41]

At his Nativity, the incarnate Son of God was made visible to the world in the flesh. Although the Incarnation itself took place at the Annunciation of the Theotokos, the manifestation of Christ's Incarnation to the world takes place at his Nativity when he is "born in the flesh." Many of the hymns for this feast express the wondrous—or more aptly, paradoxical—nature of the Incarnation and Nativity: "Today the Virgin gives birth to the Transcendent One (*ho hyperousios*—the one beyond being and essence), and the earth offers a cave to the Unapproachable One (*ho aprositos*)!"[42] In his Incarnation and Nativity, the Son of God, who

---

[36] The Greek here literally means *paradox*, as I discussed in the previous section.

[37] Annunciation of the Theotokos, Vigil, Litya, *Glory* Sticheron when the feast falls on Saturday or Sunday (*FM* 443).

[38] Christ's kenosis is not a condescending pity in which someone remains aloof from those who are assisted. This is a pity framed by compassion in which someone willingly enters into the lives of others to bear with them in their struggles and, in the case of Christ, to suffer with them and for them. Here is one example of a traditional meaning of "pity" that overlaps the meaning of "compassion" as I have tried to develop it. But see H-8 below where *oiktos* is translated as compassion.

[39] Annunciation of the Theotokos, Matins, Praises, Sticheron (*FM* 459 mod.).

[40] Synaxis of Archangel Gabriel (Mar. 26), Matins, Canon, Ode 3, Theotokion (*Menaion*, March, 115). Repeated same service July 13. *Menaion* here and throughout refers to Holy Transfiguration Monastery, *The Menaion*, 12 vols. (Boston: Holy Transfiguration Monastery, 2005).

[41] The Feast of the Nativity was not celebrated as such in the early Church until about the fourth century. The emphasis in the early Church was on the Feast of the Theophany with which the Feast of the Nativity is closely linked theologically and liturgically. See A Monk (Gillet), *Year of Grace*, 66, 96–97, n. 1.

[42] Kontakion of the Nativity (*Service Books*, 277).

fashions the entire cosmos, humbles himself to take on human flesh and to experience and live in the human condition. In becoming one with us, he becomes a brother to us.

The revelation of God's compassion towards Moses on Mount Sinai confirmed to Moses that God himself, and not merely an angel, would accompany the Israelites, and that he would not forsake them. This confirmation, this promise, is realized for the whole of humanity and creation in the Incarnation and Nativity of Christ that manifests Christ as Emmanuel—"God with us."[43] This is a fundamental meaning of compassion towards others: that in being moved by compassion towards others we are with them, suffering with them (that is, at least undergoing their struggles with them), in a solidarity or fellowship (*koinōnia*) with them. The following hymns for the Incarnation reveal this fundamental aspect of compassion that I will develop in Chapter 5: compassion as a fundamental disposition and orientation towards people for establishing fellowship, community, or solidarity with them. Compassion undergirds neighborliness towards all people, as the parable of the good Samaritan makes abundantly clear.

Selected Hymns for the Feast of the Nativity of Christ

H-8. Ye mountains and ye hills, ye plains and valleys, ye peoples, tribes, and nations, and all things that have breath, shout with jubilation, be filled with divine gladness; for the Redemption of all is come, the timeless Word of God made subject to time because of His compassion [*oiktos*].[44]

H-9. With uprightness of mind let us lift up our voice in song, celebrating the Forefeast of Christ's Nativity. For He who is equal in honor with the Father and the Spirit, has from compassion [*splanchna*] clothed Himself with our nature, and makes ready to be born in the city of Bethlehem. The shepherds with the angels sing the praises of His ineffable Nativity.[45]

H-10. Thou bearest, O my Son, the likeness of the Father. How then is it that Thou, becoming poor, hast assumed the likeness of a servant? How shall I lay Thee in a manger of beasts, Who beyond reason deliverest all men from unreason? I hymn Thy compassion (*to eusplanchnon*).[46]

[43]Mt 1.22–23 drawing on Is 7.14.
[44]The Sunday before the Nativity of Christ (Dec. 18–24), Matins, Canon of the Forefeast, Ode 6, Troparion (*Menaion*, December, 130).
[45]Forefeast of the Nativity (Dec. 24) Vespers, Sticheron at *Lord, I call* (*FM* 199).
[46]Forefeast of the Nativity (Dec. 24), Matins, Second Canon of the Forefeast, Ode 8, Troparion (Menaion,

H-11. He who dwells in the light that no man can approach and who upholds all things, in his ineffable compassion [*eusplanchnia*] is born of a Virgin. He is wrapped in swaddling clothes as a babe and laid in a cave in a manger of dumb beasts. Let us hasten to Bethlehem to worship him with the Magi, bringing as our gifts the fruits of our virtuous deeds.[47]

H-12. What mysteries beyond mind and speech! God in his compassion [*eusplanchnia*] is born on earth, putting on the form of a servant that he may snatch from servitude to the enemy those who with fervent love cry out: Blessed art Thou, O Savior who lovest mankind.[48]

H-13. Before your birth, O Lord, the angelic hosts looked with trembling on this mystery and were struck with wonder: for you who have adorned the vault of heaven with stars have been well pleased to be born as a babe; and you who hold all the ends of the earth in the hollow of your hand are laid in a manger of dumb beasts. For by such a dispensation has your compassion [*eusplanchnia*] been made known, O Christ, and your great mercy (*eleos*): glory to you.[49]

H-14. He who rules the heights of heaven, in his compassion (*eusplanchnia*) has become such as we are, born of a Maiden who has not known man. The Word who before was wholly outside matter, in these last times has assumed the material substance of the flesh so that he might draw unto himself fallen Adam, the first-formed man.[50]

THE PRESENTATION OF CHRIST IN THE TEMPLE (FEBRUARY 2)

Forty days after she gave birth, Mary, Joseph, and Jesus traveled from Bethlehem to Jerusalem in accordance with Mosaic Law, which required that Mary present herself for purification and present Jesus as her first-born male child.[51] Jesus expresses his humility in submitting to the Mosaic Law that he himself had given. The hymns below well express this presentation as an example of Christ's humility of his Incarnation. This feast also commemorates the encounter with Jesus

December, 196). Hopefully, today we would recast references to "(dumb) beasts" simply as "animals" or "animals without reason."

[47]Forefeast of the Nativity (Dec. 24), Matins, Exapostilarion (*FM* 216).

[48]Forefeast of the Nativity (Dec. 24), Matins, Praises, Sticheron (*FM* 217).

[49]Eve of the Nativity (Dec. 24), Royal Hours, Third Hour, Sticheron before the Prokeimenon (*FM* 231).

[50]Nativity of Christ, Matins, Second Canon, Ode 3, Troparion (*FM* 272.)

[51]Lev 12.2–8 regarding Mary, and Ex 13.12 and Num 18.15 regarding Jesus.

of St Simeon and Anna the Prophetess, both of whom recognized Jesus as the promised Messiah.

Selected Hymns for the Feast of the Presentation of Christ in the Temple

H-15. Today he who once gave the Law to Moses on Sinai submits himself to the ordinances of the Law, in his compassion [*eusplanchnos*] becoming for our sakes as we are. Now the God of purity as a holy child has opened a pure womb, and as God he is brought as an offering to himself, setting us free from the curse of the Law and granting light to our souls.[52]

H-16. O Treas'ry of the ages, Who art the Life of all things, Who didst once engrave on the tablets the Law upon Mount Sinai, for my sake didst Thou become a babe and madest Thyself subject to the Law, so that Thou mightest deliver and free all men from bondage unto the old Law. Glory be to Thy compassion [*euplsanchnia*], O Saviour. Glory be unto Thy Kingdom. Glory be to Thy dispensation, O only Friend of man.[53]

FEAST OF THE THEOPHANY, THE BAPTISM OF THE LORD (JANUARY 6)

Christmas often seems like a "self-contained" event. In our culture, the "holiday" is celebrated as a time for gift giving and for giving a nod at least to the value of "peace and good will for all people." But often the day after Christmas, life for many people returns back to "normal" with Christmas a mere memory. Traditional Orthodox icons of the Nativity, however, always represent the Nativity of the Lord as pointing beyond itself. If one looks closely at many icons of the Nativity, the swaddling clothes and manger in which the baby Jesus is laid in fact resemble the winding sheets of the deceased when they are laid in a tomb. This is not done for macabre effect or because of an obsession with death but because Christ's Incarnation for our sake takes place for our salvation. That salvation is accomplished over the course of Christ's life on earth culminating in his death on the cross and his Resurrection at Pascha.[54] Accordingly, Orthodox Christian icons of the Nativity reveal the

---

[52]Presentation of Christ, Vespers, Litya, Sticheron (*FM* 412).

[53]Forefeast of the Meeting in the Temple (Feb 1), Matins, Canon of the Martyr, Ode 3, *Glory . . . now and ever* Sessional Hymn (*Menaion,* February, 8). See also, Synaxis of Symeon and Anna (Feb. 3), Matins, Sessional Hymn after First Reading from the Psalter (*Menaion*, February, 23) and Holy Great Martyr Theodore the Commander (Feb. 8), Matins, Sessional Hymn after First Reading from the Psalter (*Menaion*, February, 52).

[54]Cf. Paul Evdokimov, *The Art of the Icon: A Theology of Beauty,* 278–79.

trajectory of Christ's compassion—his suffering with and for us—that "drives" the Incarnation from its inception. The Baptism of the Lord is a central event in that trajectory.

The Baptism of the Lord is the first major event in Christ's adult life that is recorded in the Gospels. It expresses the paradox of his humility in accepting to be baptized by John.

> **H-17.** Being of one throne with the Father and the Spirit, I have as Mine escort the armies of the Angels; yet I in My compassion [*eusplanchnia*] did accept hospitality [*exenisthēn*] in a little cave when I was born in Bethlehem; so then, lend thy right hand to Me that I may now in Myself wash clean away the trespasses of the world.[55]

In his humanity, Christ embraces human neediness and vulnerability so that we can offer hospitality and compassion to him. But the hospitality that we can offer him—directly by his contemporaries or indirectly by us through service to others—reflects the hospitality that the Trinity and Christ offer to us.

This feast is also one of the principal trinitarian theophanies mentioned in the gospel. Christ's Baptism is the first of two recorded instances where the Father and the Holy Spirit are present with the Son.[56] His transfiguration is the second event.[57] Rublev's famous icon of the Trinity is known as *The Hospitality of Abraham* since it is based on the event in Genesis where Abraham offers hospitality to the three strangers who visit him near the oak at Mamre.[58] The eucharistic chalice on the table where the three "angels" are sitting implicitly expresses the realization that the divine compassion for us and the world that leads to the Incarnation is also fundamentally an act of divine hospitality.

The Greek word for hospitality, *philoxenia*, literally means a love of strangers. Showing hospitality to strangers—which included those who were vulnerable and in need—was a common expectation throughout much of the ancient world. A chief mark of hospitality in the ancient world was that hosts invited strangers into their dwellings to provide for them and also, if only briefly, offered fellowship

---

[55]Forefeast of the Theophany (Jan. 4), Matins, Praises, Sticheron (*Menaion,* January, 48). Regarding *exenisthēn*: the verb *xenizō* means to welcome or receive someone as a guest (Strong's G3579). Its immediate connection with hospitality (*philoxenia*) is made in Hebrews 13.2 "Do not neglect to show hospitality (*philoxenia*) to strangers, for by this some have entertained (*xenisantes*) angels without knowing it" (NASB). See also hymn H-63.

[56]Mt 3.16–17, Mk 1.10–11 and 3.22.

[57]Mt 17.5, Mk 9.7, and Lk 9.24–35.

[58]Gen 18.1–13.

and a sense of community (*koinōnia*) with them.[59] The compassionate hospitality that Christ offers in the Incarnation is also patterned on the compassionate hospitality of the father of the parable of the prodigal son who, seeing his wayward son at a distance, rushes out to greet the son and welcome him home.

The Baptism of Christ prefigures our own Baptism through the Holy Spirit. Our Baptism is the mystery, or sacrament, of the Church in which we are welcomed home to begin our own journey into the Kingdom of Heaven. During the service for Baptism, we pray for the "grace of redemption, the blessing of Jordan" to sanctify the baptismal water through the indwelling or "descent of the Holy Spirit."[60] At the Great Blessing of the Waters, which takes place on the Feast of the Theophany, the Priest prays in a similar manner:

> For you, O Master, for the sake of your compassion [*eusplanchnia*, or tender-hearted mercy] could not endure to behold the race of man tormented by the devil; but you came and saved us.... You sanctified the streams of the Jordan, sending down from heaven your Holy Spirit, crushing the heads of the dragons that lurked therein.... Do you yourself, O King, the Lover of Mankind, come now through the descent of your Holy Spirit, and sanctify this water.[61]

Selected Hymns for the Feast of the Theophany (Baptism) of Christ

H-18. Ye angelic hosts, go ye on the way before us; make your way from Bethlehem to the River Jordan; and come forth, O thou Baptist John, abandon the wilderness. Make ready, O river, and rejoice, and let all the earth be filled with gladness, for Christ cometh now and purgeth Adam's sin away, since He is compassionate [*eusplanchnos*].[62]

H-19. When mankind had departed far from God, the Word of God took pity [*katoiktirō*, or showed compassion] and appeared as a man; and through

---

[59]See Kevin D. O'Gorman, "Dimensions of Hospitality: Exploring Ancient and Classical Origins," in *Hospitality: A Social Lens*, ed. Conrad Lashley, Paul Lynch, and Allison Morrison (Oxford: Elsevier, 2007), 17–32.

[60]"The Office of Holy Baptism" (*The Great Book of Needs*, 1:34)

[61]The Great Sanctification of Waters of Holy Theophany (*The Great Book of Needs*, 1:313–14). The timing for this service varies depending on the day of the week the feast falls (303). [By tradition, when both the eve and the feast fall on consecutive weekdays, the Great Sanctification takes place on both the eve and the feast itself.—Ed.]

[62]Forefeast of Theophany (Jan. 2), Matins, Praises, Sticheron (*Menaion*, January, 26).

deifying Baptism, He maketh mankind His own in a manner befitting God, and leadeth it back up to the dignity of the archetype.[63]

H-20. Thou, the Child of the Father Who is without beginning from before eternity, comest unto the child of Zacharias asking for Baptism, O Compassionate One [*eusplanchnos*], that Thou mightest make us sons of God by grace.[64]

H-21. Word of God, Thy poverty passeth thought and measure! For I know that Thou, in behalf of me, the fallen, because of Thy compassion [*oiktos*] hast with Adam thus clothed Thyself, making new again all sprung from Adam; and I, obeying Thy commandment, with faith cry to Thee: Blessed art Thou Who hast appeared, our God, glory be to Thee.[65]

H-22. When he saw you, O Master, draw near to him, John the Forerunner was amazed, and as a faithful servant he cried out in fear: "What is this humility, O Savior? What is this poverty that you have put on? In the wealth of your goodness and compassion [*eusplanchnia*], you have raised up man from his humiliation, by clothing yourself in him!"[66]

THE TRANSFIGURATION OF CHRIST (AUGUST 6)

H-23. On the mountain you were transfigured, O Christ God. And your disciples beheld your glory as far as they could see it; so that when they would behold you crucified, they would understand that your suffering was voluntary, and would proclaim to the world that you are truly the Radiance of the Father![67]

Celebrated on August 6, the Transfiguration[68] takes place just prior to Christ's final entrance into Jerusalem to undergo his passion and death on the cross. This is a major feast in the Orthodox Church since it is a principal trinitarian theophany. But it is also the event in which Christ was transfigured to manifest the uncreated

---

[63]Forefeast of Theophany (Jan. 3), Matins, Ode 5, Troparion (*Menaion*, January, 33).

[64]Forefeast of Theophany (Jan. 4), Matins, Canon of the Forefeast, Ode 1, Troparion (*Menaion*, January, 41).

[65]Forefeast of Theophany (Jan. 5), Matins, Praises, Sticheron (*Menaion*, January, 60).

[66]Synaxis of John the Baptist (Jan. 7), Great Vespers, Aposticha, Sticheron (*FM* 39). The Greek text literally reads "since you were compassionate."

[67]Kontakion for the Transfiguration, Tone 7 (*Service Books,* 287).

[68]Mt 17.1–8, Mk 9.2–9, and Lk 9.28–36.

light and glory of his divinity. The feast played a central role in the hesychast con-
troversies in the time of St Gregory Palamas, since it provided a basic justification
for the hesychastic conviction that in this life we are able to see the uncreated
glory of God.[69] The transfiguration has always been a festival of the uncreated
light in the Orthodox tradition. But the Transfiguration is also fundamentally
linked to the cross and the Resurrection. As Chrysostom notes, Christ reveals his
divine glory to his disciples,

> [t]o show the glory of the cross, and to console Peter and the others in their
> dread of the passion, and to raise up their minds. Since having come, they
> [Moses and Elias] by no means held their peace, but" spoke," it is said, of the
> "glory which he was to accomplish at Jerusalem" (Lk 9.31); that is, of the pas-
> sion, and the cross; for so they call it always.[70]

The Transfiguration provides consolation to his disciples in the face of Christ's
passion because it points beyond the cross to the "splendor of the resurrection"[71]
and the "beauty of the divine kingdom."[72] The transfiguration of Christ's humanity on Mount Tabor shows "the exchange mortal men will make with your glory
at your second and fearful coming."[73]

Compared with feasts such as the Nativity of the Lord or the Theophany,
there are very few references to Christ's compassion in the hymns for the Transfiguration. My own research shows there is little emphasis on the theme of Christ's
compassion either in commentaries on the event of the Transfiguration or on the
icons of the Transfiguration. Indeed, the uncreated glory revealed at the Transfiguration seems to be linked with God's power and majesty. One author notes
the opposition between Christ's glory that the disciples witnessed on Mount
Tabor with Christ's extreme humility on the cross by contrasting the description
of Christ on Mount Tabor—"the Lord's face was altered, shining like the sun,
and . . . his clothes became brilliant white"—with the humiliation and torture
Christ experienced at his crucifixion.[74]

---

[69]See Gregory Palamas, "Sermon on the Transfiguration 1," *Saint Gregory Palamas: The Homilies*, ed. and
trans. Christopher Veniamin (South Canaan, PA: Mt. Tabor Publishing, 2009), 272. For a detailed discussion
on the uncreated light, see St Gregory Palamas, *Triads* 3.1.9.9–36 in *Gregory Palamas, The Triads [Pro hesychas-
tis]*, trans. John Meyendorff and Nicholas Gendle, (Mahwah, NJ: The Paulist Press, 1982), 69–92.

[70]John Chrysostom, *Homilies on Matthew* 56 (NPNF¹ 10:346; PG 58:551).

[71]Transfiguration of Christ, Great Vespers, Sticheron at *Lord, I call* (*FM* 470).

[72]Transfiguration of Christ, Matins, Second Canon, Ode 7, Troparion (*FM* 490).

[73]Transfiguration of Christ, Matins, First Sessional Hymn (*FM* 478). Cf. Introduction (*LT* 63).

[74]Steven C. Salaris, "Preaching Christ Crucified at the Feast of the Transfiguration," <http://ww1.antio-
chian.org/node/21286>, May 27, 2022.

Drawing on Moses' presence with Christ at the Transfiguration, the Church, however, provides a crucial link between the glory of God revealed at the Transfiguration and the glory of God revealed on the cross. Exodus 33 and 34, which describes God's self-manifestation of his glory to Moses on Mount Sinai, is read for both feasts. This hymn from the Matins for the Transfiguration implicitly mentions the event: "The Glory that once overshadowed the tabernacle[75] and spoke with your servant Moses, Master, was a figure of your Transfiguration that ineffably shone forth as lightning upon Tabor."[76] The glory of the Lord overshadows the tabernacle both before[77] and after Moses sees the glory of God on the Mount Sinai.[78]

Even though God had assured Moses that he would send his presence with Moses and the Israelites, Moses asks to see God's glory to understand his willingness to remain with a stiff-necked people—Moses' own words—whom God is otherwise prepared to destroy.[79] The selection of the text at Good Friday ends at the point where God has declared that he "will be compassionate to whom he will be compassionate"[80] and, that while Moses cannot see his face and live, God will nevertheless pass by him to reveal his glory.[81] The text read during Great Vespers at the Transfiguration continues with God's actual manifestation of himself to Moses in which he calls on his own name: "The Lord, the Lord, God, compassionate, merciful . . ."[82]

The following hymn implicitly indicates that the glory of the Lord that was revealed to Moses on Mount Sinai is the same glory revealed to Moses on Mount Tabor in the person of Christ himself.

H-24. Christ now cometh forth to reveal Himself evidently to Moses, and to show him His ineffable glory by speaking directly with him face to face on Mount Tabor. Let us keep the forefeast with jubilation.[83]

---

[75]This seems to refer to the portable tent that Moses moved about. It should be distinguished from the tabernacle described in Exodus 26.1.

[76]Transfiguration of Christ, Matins, Canon 2, Ode 3, Troparion (*FM* 484).

[77]Ex 33.8–11.

[78]Ex 34.9.

[79]See Chapter 3, pp. 89–90.

[80]Ex 33.19.

[81]Ex 33.19.

[82]Ex 34.6.

[83]Forefeast of the Transfiguration (Aug. 5), Matins, Canon of the Forefeast, Ode 1, Troparion (*Menaion, August*, 32).

In Exodus 33.13, Moses asks God, "reveal yourself to me that I may clearly behold you." God's revelation of himself on Mount Sinai as "The Lord, the Lord, God, compassionate . . ." is now clearly revealed to Moses on Mount Tabor in the person of Christ, the incarnate Son of God. Indeed, Eusebius interprets the manifestation of God to Moses on Mount Sinai as the Lord (the Son of God) passing by Moses and calling upon his Lord, the Father: "The Lord that descended in the cloud, and stood by Moses in the name of the Lord, called Another beside himself, who is twice called Lord. . . . [I]t is not Moses, as might be supposed, but the Lord himself who calls another Lord his Father."[84]

It is precisely the very same glory of the compassionate and merciful God that is revealed to the disciples on Mount Tabor. The placement of the text from Exodus 33–34 for the Great Vespers for the Feast of the Transfiguration thus indicates that the manifestation of God's glory, compassion, and mercy to Moses on Mount Sinai is an anticipation of the Transfiguration and also that the Transfiguration manifests that same divine compassionate glory in and through the person of Christ. The theophany of the Transfiguration thus manifests the compassion that underlies and drives, as I have indicated, the entire "event" of Christ's Incarnation from his conception at the Annunciation to his "second and glorious coming." However, the divine glory and compassion of Christ manifest at his transfiguration is the same divine glory and compassion manifest at his crucifixion. The hymns for Great and Holy Friday will make this very clear. As Fr Florovsky notes: "The Transfiguration is par excellence the feast of Christ's divine glory."[85]

Selected Hymns for the Feast of the Transfiguration of Christ

> **H-25.** Ye whose minds are set on Heaven, come and let us be changed today with a change unto better things; and, being conformed to Christ in all godly rev'rence, we shall all rejoice, being led up from the earth below unto the virtues sublime and lofty height. For Christ, the Saviour of our souls, hath now transfigured disfigured man for His tender compassion's [*oiktos*] sake, and on Tabor hath made him shine.[86]

> **H-26.** O Thou Who hast sanctified the whole world with Thy light, Thou wast transfigured upon a high mountain, O Good One, showing Thy disciples Thy

---

[84]Eusebius, *Demonstration of the Gospels* [*Demonstratio evangelica*] 2.5.17. Eusebius: *The Proof of the Gospel*, ed. and trans. W. J. Ferrar (Eugene, OR: Wipf and Stock Publishers, 2001), 260 (PG 22:396).

[85]Georges Florovsky, "Orthodox Services and their Structure," *FM* 61.

[86]Transfiguration of the Lord, Small Vespers, Sticheron at *Lord, I call* (*Menaion*, August, 39); and Martyr and Archdeacon Laurence (Aug. 10), Vespers, Sticheron at *Lord, I call* (*Menaion*, August, 6).

sovereignty, that Thou dost redeem the world from transgression. Where-fore we cry unto Thee: O Compassionate Lord [*eusplanchne kyrie*], save our souls.[87]

PALM SUNDAY

Following on the heels of the raising of Lazarus from the dead, Jesus enters Jerusa-lem for the last time. The entry is victorious: children throw down their garments before him and wave palm branches. He receives the praise: "Hosanna! Blessed is he who comes in the name of the Lord."[88] But the pomp and majesty that nor-mally accompanies a royal entry is replaced with humility and meekness. "O you who ride on the cherubim and are praised by the seraphim, you have sat, O gra-cious Lord, like David on a foal, and the children honored you with praise fitting for God."[89] The humility and meekness that mark Christ's entry into Jerusalem thus continue the paradoxical and wondrous expression of the compassion that informs his Incarnation as the suffering servant, the one willing to suffer with and for us (*com-passio*): "Surely he has borne our griefs and carried our sorrows; yet we esteemed him stricken, smitten by God, and afflicted."[90]

Selected Hymns for the Feast of Palm Sunday

There are three hymns celebrating Christ's compassion on Palm Sunday. The first two bracket the feast, being read at Great Vespers for Palm Sunday and also at the Vespers for Palm Sunday evening. The third, also read at the Vespers for Palm Sunday evening, announces the beginning of Holy Week and the extension of Christ's compassion through Palm Sunday to the Crucifixion.

H-27. Rejoice and be glad, O city of Zion; exult and be exceeding joyful, O Church of God. For behold, your King has come in righteousness, seated on a foal, and the children sing his praises: Hosanna in the highest! Blessed are you who show great compassion [*oiktirmōn*]: have mercy upon us.[91]

[87]Transfiguration of the Lord, Vespers, Entreaty (Litya), Sticheron (*Menaion*, August, 41); and Matins, Sticheron after Ps 50(51) (*Menaion*, August, 43). See also, Holy Apostle Matthias (Aug. 9), Vespers, *Glory . . . now and ever* Sticheron at *Lord, I call* (Menaion, August, 61).

[88]Mk 11.9 and Jn 12.13; cf. Mt 21.9 and Lk 19.38.

[89]Palm Sunday, Great Vespers, Aposticha, Sticheron (*LT* 492); Palm Sunday Evening, Great Vespers, Aposticha, Sticheron (*LT* 505).

[90]Is 55.4. Read twice on Great and Holy Friday, at both Sixth Hour and Vespers.

[91]Palm Sunday, Great Vespers, Aposticha, Sticheron (*LT* 491 mod.); and Palm Sunday Evening, Vespers, Sticheron at *Lord, I call* (*LT* 505).

H-28. The Savior has come today to the city of Jerusalem, to fulfil the Scriptures; and all have taken palms into their hands and spread their garments before him, knowing that he is our God, to whom the cherubim sing without ceasing: Hosanna in the highest! Blessed are you who show great compassion [*oiktirmōn*]: have mercy upon us.[92]

H-29. Passing from one divine feast to another, from palms and branches let us now make haste, you faithful, to the solemn and saving celebration of Christ's passion. Let us behold him undergo voluntary suffering for our sake, and let us sing to him with thankfulness a fitting hymn: Fountain of tender mercy [*pēgē tēs eusplanchnias*, or compassion] and haven of salvation, O Lord, glory to you![93]

PASSION WEEK (EXTREME HUMILITY)

Christ Jesus, who, being in the form of God, did not regard equality with God a thing to be grasped but emptied himself, taking the form of a bond-servant, and being made in the likeness of men. Being found in appearance as a man, he humbled himself by becoming obedient to the point of death, even death on a cross.[94]

Humility is fundamental to the Incarnation of the Son of God. In the hymns and other Orthodox Christian writings, his emptying of himself (*kenōsis*) is referred to as his condescension. But we must keep in mind that "condescend and condescension always mean our Lord's overlooking of the infinite distance between Him and us in His infinite love and humility, without any of the connotation of patronizing arrogance usually implied in modern usage."[95] That is, although Christ assumes the weakness of human nature in his Incarnation, the humility of his condescension is not a matter of "weakness" but of the strength and courage that belongs to true humility.[96]

---

[92]Palm Sunday, Great Vespers, Aposticha, Sticheron (*LT* 492 mod.); and Palm Sunday Evening, Vespers, Sticheron at *Lord, I call* (*LT* 505).

[93]Palm Sunday Evening, Vespers, Aposticha, Sticheron (*LT* 505–6). *Pēgē* also has the sense of being a source of something.

[94]Phil 2.5–8 (NASB).

[95]"Introduction" (*Menaion*, September, 14).

[96]Humility is a key indicator for the subsequent analysis of compassion. See Chapter 5, pp. 200–202 for its role in the perfecting of a compassionate disposition.

Selected Hymns for Passion Week (Extreme Humility)

H-30. Moved by your tender mercy [*eusplanchnia*, or compassion], O Christ our Benefactor, you of your own will go forth to meet your passion, wishing to deliver us from the passions and from condemnation in hell. Therefore we all sing the praises of your holy sufferings and we glorify your deep self-abasement.[97]

H-31. Humbling yourself because of your compassion, O Master, you have spoken with kindness to your fallen sons. For in your love for mankind you go out to meet the sinful, and embracing them you grant them salvation. And if any man reproaches you for this, in your tender love you are not angry with him, for you alone are measureless in mercy.[98]

H-32. He who made the lakes and springs and seas, wishing to teach us the surpassing value of humility, girded himself with a towel and washed the feet of the disciples, humbling himself in the abundance of his great compassion [*hyperbolē eusplanchnias*] and raising us from the depths of wickedness, for he alone loves mankind.[99]

H-33. Humbling yourself in your compassion [*eusplanchnia*], you washed the feet of your disciples, teaching them to take the path which as God you followed. And Peter, who at first refused to be washed, yielded then to the divine command, and earnestly entreated you that we may be granted your great mercy.[100]

H-34. In your compassion [*eusplanchnia*], you humbled yourself and were lifted on the cross, raising up with yourself him who had fallen of old through eating from the tree. Therefore, you are glorified, O Lord alone supreme in love, and we sing your praises forever.[101]

GREAT AND HOLY FRIDAY

Christ's crucifixion is remembered throughout the Church year and, indeed, every day during the Sixth and Ninth hours. The primary remembrance takes

---

[97]Great and Holy Monday, Compline, Sessional Hymn (*LT* 520 –21).

[98]Second Week of Great Lent, Sunday, Matins, Canon Ode 8, Troparion (*LT* 326). Greek text not found.

[99]Great and Holy Thursday, Matins, First Sessional Hymn after Ode 3, Troparion (*LT* 549–50).

[100]Great and Holy Thursday, Matins, Second Sessional Hymn after Ode 3 (*LT* 550).

[101]First Week of Great Lent, Friday, Matins, Canon, Ode 8, Irmos (*LT* 269).

place on Great and Holy Friday. But the cross itself is the special object of veneration on two other major feasts: The Great Feast of the Elevation of the Cross (Sept. 14) and the Veneration of the Cross on the third Sunday of Great Lent, as well as on the Feast of the Procession of the Cross (Aug. 1). Naturally, we venerate the cross because of Christ who suffered and died upon it. But we venerate the cross for the way in which Christ transforms it from an instrument of death and degradation to an instrument and symbol of self-sacrificial love that is at the heart of our salvation and deification.

For the Orthodox Christian tradition, Christ's crucifixion is not reducible to a penal or forensic atonement in which, since none of us individually or collectively can satisfy God's demand for retribution because of our sins, God's only Son becomes incarnate to serve as the victim who can suffer punishment and "right the scales of justice" between God and humans. In the following hymns the reader will see that Christ's compassionate suffering on the cross is oriented towards healing those who are wounded by sin to bring them into the fullness of life. Moreover, the wondrous, paradoxical reality of the Incarnation once again resonates through these hymns.

Selected Hymns for Great and Holy Friday

H-35. With the psalmist, O Master, we now behold the footstool on which your undefiled feet rested, your precious cross, exalted this day with love. And with devotion lifting it on high, we beseech you crying: O, you who sanctified all people by your divine cross, let us share in your ineffable compassion [*eusplanchnia*] and your grace.[102]

H-36. The cross is raised on high, and urges all the creation to sing the praises of the undefiled passion of him who was lifted high upon it. For there it was that he killed our slayer, and brought the dead to life again: and in his exceeding goodness and compassion [*eusplanchnos*], he made us beautiful and counted us worthy to be citizens of heaven. Therefore, with rejoicing, let us exalt his name and magnify his surpassing condescension.[103]

H-37. Today the Master of the creation and the Lord of Glory is nailed to the cross and his side is pierced; and he who is the sweetness of the Church tastes gall and vinegar. A crown of thorns is put upon him who covers the

---

[102]Elevation of the Cross (Sept. 14), Small Vespers, Sticheron at *Lord, I call* (*FM* 131)
[103]Elevation of the Cross (Sept. 14), Great Vespers, Sticheron at *Lord, I call* (*FM* 133.)

heaven with clouds. He is clothed in a cloak of mockery, and he who formed man with his hands is struck by a hand of clay. He who wraps the heaven in clouds is smitten upon his back. He accepts spitting and scourging, reproach and buffeting; and all these things my Deliverer and God endures for me that am condemned, that in his compassion [*eusplanchnos*], he may save the world from error.[104]

H-38. When the soldiers mocked you, O Lord, before your death upon the precious cross, the heavenly hosts were struck with wonder. For you, who have adorned the earth with flowers, were arrayed in a crown of shame; and you, who wrapped the firmament in clouds, were clothed in a robe of mockery. Thus in your providence, O Christ, you have made known your compassion (*eusplanchnia*) and great mercy: glory to you.[105]

H-39. Today he who is in essence unapproachable, becomes approachable for me, and suffers his passion, thus setting me free from passions. He who grants light unto the blind is spit upon by the mouths of the transgressors, and he gives his back to scourging for the sake of those that are captives. When the pure Virgin his Mother saw him upon the cross, she cried out in pain: "Woe is me, my Child: what is this that you have done?"... I sing the praises of your passion, I venerate your compassion (*eusplanchnia*): O longsuffering Lord, glory to you.[106]

H-40. Joseph with Nicodemus took you down from the tree, O you who clothe yourself with light as with a garment; and looking upon you dead, stripped, and without burial... he lamented, saying... "How shall I bury you, my God? How shall I wrap you in a winding sheet? How shall I touch your most pure body with my hands? What song at your departure shall I sing to you, O Compassionate [*oiktirmon*] Savior?"[107]

BETWEEN THE CRUCIFIXION AND PASCHA

The two events of the crucifixion and Resurrection are inextricably linked: Christ endures the cross for the sake of Pascha. There would be no Pascha—the trampling

---

[104]Third Sunday of Lent (Sunday of the Cross), Matins, Procession of Cross from altar to analogion, Sticheron (*LT* 349). The Greek word for error (*planē*) has the sense of "going astray." Falling into sin is an "error" not just in the cognitive sense of a mistake but in the lived sense of wandering astray from God.

[105]Great and Holy Friday, Royal Hours, Third Hour, Sticheron (*LT* 604).

[106]Third Sunday of Lent (Sunday of the Cross), Matins, Theotokion after Praises (*LT* 349).

[107]Great and Holy Friday, Vespers, Aposticha, *Glory... now and ever* Sticheron (*FM* 615–6).

down of death by death—apart from the cross. The first hymn for this section provides Christ's striking response to his mother's profound grief and sorrow over his death.[108] It is also, as it were, his own response to his agonizing cry on the cross: "My God, my God, why have you forsaken me."[109] The second, *Having Beheld the Resurrection of Christ*, is the beautiful hymn celebrating Christ's compassion and love for us as the link between the cross and the Resurrection. It is recited at every Divine Liturgy by the priest after the distribution of Communion, it is sung at Matins for Sunday, during the Canon for Pascha just prior to the Divine Liturgy of Pascha, and in the Paschal Hours.

H-41. Do not lament for Me, O My holy Mother, seeing Me, thy Son and God, suspended on the Tree, Who once suspended, upon the floods, earth unsupported and Who have formed all creation with My hand. For I shall arise again and shall be glorified and I shall crush Hades' sovereignty by My great power; yea, Hades' might I shall utterly destroy and all held captive by its wickedness I shall ransom for I am compassionate [*eusplanchnos*], and shall free them all, granting the eternal Kingdom unto them.[110]

H-42. Having beheld the resurrection of Christ, let us worship the holy Lord Jesus, the only Sinless One! We venerate your cross, O Christ, and your holy resurrection we praise and glorify; for you are our God, and we know no other than you; we call on your name. Come, all you faithful, let us venerate Christ's holy resurrection! For, behold, through the cross joy has come into all the world. Let us ever bless the Lord, praising his resurrection. By enduring the cross for us, he has destroyed death by death![111]

---

[108]While this exact hymn is not found during Holy Week, a close variant is: "Weep not for Me, O Mother, beholding in the sepulcher the Son whom you conceived without seed in your womb. For I shall rise and shall be glorified, and as God I shall exalt in everlasting glory those who magnify you with faith and love" (Great and Holy Saturday, Matins, Canon, Ode 9, Irmos (*LT* 651).

[109]Ps 21(22).1.

[110]Martyr Paramon and 370 Martyrs in Bithynia (Nov. 29), Vespers, Theotokion of the Cross at *Lord, I call* (*Menaion*, November, 216). See also, Wonderworkers and Unmercenaries Cyrus and John (Jan. 31), Matins, Praises, Theotokion of the Cross (*Menaion*, January, 277);* Finding of the Sacred Relics of the Holy Martyrs in the Quarter of Eugenius (Feb. 22), Vespers, Theotokion of the Cross at *Lord, I call* (*Menaion*, February, 125);* The Holy Forty-Two Martyrs of Amorion (Mar. 6), Matins, Aposticha, Theotokion of the Cross (*Menaion*, March, 24);* Hieromartyr Basil of Ancyra (Mar. 22), Vespers, Theotokion of the Cross at *Lord, I call* (*Menaion*, March, 92); and Octoechos Tone 4 Friday, Vespers, Theotokion at *Lord, I call* (*Great Octoechos* 3: 280).* (* = "and unto My own Father I shall lead them, as the Friend of man [*philanthrōpos*]" replaces "and shall free them all, granting the eternal Kingdom unto them.")

[111]Divine liturgies of St John Chrysostom and St Basil after the distribution of Communion (*Service Books*, 85 and 166).

THE FEAST OF THE PASCHA OF OUR LORD

The icon for Pascha is the harrowing of hades[112] which shows Christ "doing the work" of the resurrection: "trampling down death by death and upon those in the tombs bestowing life."[113] Through his death on the cross, Pascha represents Christ's compassionate pursuit of human beings into the depths of hell in order to find them and restore them to life. "You descended to earth to find Adam, but you did not find him on earth, O Master, and you went to search for him in hades."[114] There is one reference to Christ's compassion at his Resurrection in the services for Pascha (Nocturns). But the theme radiates throughout the year in the Sunday Resurrection Kontakion, Tone 3, and the Resurrection Troparion, Tone 8.

Selected Hymns for the Feast of the Pascha of our Lord

H-43. On this day you rose from the dead, O Compassionate One [*oiktirmon*], leading us from the gates of death. On this day, Adam exults as Eve rejoices; with the prophets and patriarchs they unceasingly praise the divine majesty of your power.[115]

H-44. You descended from on high, O Compassionate One [*eusplanchnos*]! You accepted the three-day burial to free us from our passions! O Lord, our Life and Resurrection, glory to you![116]

H-45. Isaiah, as he watched by night, beheld the light that knows no evening, the light of your Theophany, O Christ, that came to pass from tender love [*sympathēs*, or compassion] for us; and he cried aloud: "The dead shall arise and those that dwell in the tomb shall be raised up, and all those born on the earth shall rejoice exceedingly."[117]

---

[112] An image of this icon can be found at <https://oca.org/fs/icons-of-great-holy-pascha>, April 20, 2020.

[113] Paschal Troparion: "Christ is risen from the dead, trampling down death by death and upon those in the tombs bestowing life."

[114] Great and Holy Saturday, Matins, Lamentations, First Stasis, verse 25, cited in Bobrinskoy, *Compassion*, 54–55 when he quotes this hymn to show the profound depth of solidarity with humankind that animated the compassion of the Incarnation.

[115] Octoechos Tone 3, Resurrection Kontakion (*Divine Liturgy, Chrysostom*, 151 mod.).

[116] Octoechos Tone 8, Resurrection Troparion (*Divine Liturgy, Chrysostom*, 156 mod).

[117] Great and Holy Saturday, Matins, Canon, Ode 5, Irmos (*LT* 648) See also, Nocturns of Pascha, Ode 5, Irmos (*The Paschal Service*, 12–3); Sunday Before the Nativity of Christ (December 18–24), Compline, Ode 5, Irmos (*Menaion*, December, 129); Forefeast of the Nativity (Dec. 24), Compline, Ode 5, Irmos (*FM* 206); Forefeast of Theophany (Jan. 5), Compline, Ode 5, Irmos (*FM* 298–99); and Octoechos, Tone 6, Sunday, Matins, Ode 6 Canon of the Theotokos, Irmos (*Great Octoechos* 3:190).

H-46. O Master of all, incomprehensible Maker of heaven and earth, by Thy Passion upon the Cross Thou hast become a well-spring of dispassion for me; and by accepting burial and arising in glory, Thou didst raise up Adam also with Thine almighty hand. Glory to Thine arising on the third day, whereby Thou hast granted unto us life everlasting and forgiveness of sins, since Thou alone art compassionate [*eusplanchnos*].[118]

H-47. Rising from the grave as from sleep, O Compassionate One [*oiktir-mon*], Thou hast rescued all from corruption; and creation is confirmed in the Faith by the Apostles who preached Thine Arising. O God of our Fathers, blessed art Thou.[119]

THE FEAST OF THE ASCENSION OF CHRIST

Nevertheless, I tell you the truth. It is expedient for you that I go away; for if I do not go away, the Comforter will not come to you; but if I depart, I will send him to you.[120]

By his own design, Christ's Pascha points beyond itself to his Ascension, and thence, to Pentecost. The Feast of the Ascension of Christ is celebrated forty days after Pascha. The compassion that "drives" the Incarnation is oriented to sending and restoring the gift of the Holy Spirit that was diminished and lost through sin. The theology of the Ascension is so well-laid out in the following two hymns, not much more must be added by way of introduction except to emphasize that it is the same earthly body—which Christ assumed in order to live, suffer, and die—that is glorified, raised from the dead, and taken into heaven at the Ascension. These hymns express Christ's compassion for us with the Greek term *sympatheia*. They have been translated with "compassion," which English translations of Orthodox Christian hymns often use for *sympatheia*. Both hymns well illustrate how the Greek word *sympatheia* can signify a person's engagement in the life of another in order to suffer with and for the other.

---

[118]Sunday of All Saints, Great Vespers, Aposticha, Sticheron (*Pentecostarion*, 267). See also Octoechos, Tone 8, Sunday, Great Vespers, Aposticha, Sticheron (*Great Octoechos* 4:164). *Pentecostarion* here and throughout refers to Holy Transfiguration Monastery, *The Pentecostarion* (Boston: Holy Transfiguration Monastery, 2014).

[119]Sunday of All Saints, Matins, Canon of the Cross and the Resurrection, Ode 7, Troparion (*Pentecostarion*, 277). See also Octoechos, Tone 8, Sunday, Matins, Ode 7, Canon 2, Troparion (*Great Octoechos* 4:186).

[120]Jn 16.7, from Christ's farewell discourse to his disciples prior to his crucifixion.

Selected Hymns for the Feast of the Ascension of our Lord

H-48. Without being separated from the bosom of the Father, O most sweet Jesus, after living as a man with those upon the earth, Thou wast taken up in glory today from the Mount of Olives. And raising up our fallen nature by Thy compassion [*sympathēs*], Thou didst seat it together with the Father. Wherefore, the heavenly orders of the Bodiless were ... seized with trembling, and they magnified Thy love for mankind [*philanthrōpia*]. With them, we on earth also glorify Thy condescension toward us, and Thine Ascension from us.[121]

H-49. Adam's nature, which had gone down into the lower parts of the earth, Thou hast renewed in Thyself, O God, and Thou hast led it up above every principality and power today. For since Thou didst love it, Thou didst seat it together with Thyself; since Thou hadst compassion [*sympathēsas*] on it, Thou didst unite it to Thyself; since Thou hadst united it to Thyself, Thou didst suffer with it; and enduring the Passion, though Thou art impassible, Thou didst glorify it. [122]

THE FEAST OF PENTECOST

At the Feast of the Theophany, Christ's Baptism, the Holy Spirit in the form of a dove lighted on Christ to confirm that he is the Messiah, the one sent by God. On the day of Pentecost, Christ sent the Holy Spirit upon the apostles and disciples and those with them in the upper room, including the Theotokos and the women who were with Jesus during his life.[123] Hardly incidental to the compassionate impetus of Christ's Incarnation, Pentecost is integral to that compassion. It validates the promise Christ made to the disciples not to forsake them and to be with them always,[124] which, as we have seen earlier, is exactly the promise that

[121]Ascension of the Lord, Vespers, *Glory . . . now and ever* Sticheron at *Lord, I Call* (*Pentecostarion*, 190). See also, Seventh Week after Pascha (Week of the Fathers), Wednesday, Matins, Aposticha of the Praises, *Glory . . . now and ever* Sticheron (*Pentecostarion*, 223); and Seventh Week after Pascha (Week of the Fathers), Friday Vespers, *Glory . . . now and ever* Sticheron at *Lord, I Call* (*Pentecostarion*, 225).

[122]Ascension of the Lord, Litya (Entreaty), Sticheron (*Pentecostarion*, 191). See also Seventh Week after Pascha, Monday, Vespers, Aposticha, Sticheron after *Glory . . . now and ever* (*Pentecostarion*, 221).

[123]The icons for Pentecost show the apostles receiving the tongues of fire as do the hymns for the feast, although the Theotokos appears in some icons in the center seat in the middle of the icon. Acts 1.15, however, describes the hundred and twenty individuals in the upper room. They included the women, the Theotokos, and Jesus' brother (Acts 1.14). St John Chrysostom explicitly indicates that all of them received the Holy Spirit in the form of a tongue of fire. John Chrysostom, *Homilies on the Acts of the Apostles* 4 (NPNF[1] 11:25; PG 60:43).

[124]Mt 28.20.

God gives to the Israelites in the Old Testament as the expression of his compassion and mercy for them. Indeed, as Fr Bobrinskoy observes, the sign of God the Father's compassionate forgiveness of human sinfulness is the gift of the Holy Spirit.[125]

> H-50. O Lord, as the Apostles saw Thee being lifted up in the clouds, O life-giving Christ, they were filled with sorrow and wept with lamentation, saying with grief: O Master, leave not as orphans us Thy servants whom Thou hast loved in Thy mercy [oiktos], since Thou art compassionate [eusplanchnos]. But as Thou didst promise, send us Thine All-holy Spirit, to illumine our souls.[126]

Moreover, Pentecost is a feast of rebirth and renewal in the pouring out of the Holy Spirit upon human beings to restore them to the possibility of the fullness of life. Pentecost is the birth of the Church with its sacraments or mysteries.[127] Baptism is also a feast of rebirth and renewal in the gift of the Holy Spirit that renews the person who is baptized "after the image of him who created him/her; that being buried, after the pattern of [Christ's] death, in Baptism, he/she, in like manner, may be a partaker of [Christ's] resurrection."[128]

Selected Hymns for the Feast of Pentecost

> H-51. Grant speedy and lasting consolation unto Thy servants, O Jesus, when our spirits are despondent. Be Thou not parted from our souls in affliction; be Thou not far from our minds in adversities, but do Thou ever anticipate our needs. Draw nigh unto us, draw nigh, O Thou Who art everywhere present, and even as Thou art ever with Thine Apostles, so do Thou also unite to Thyself us who long for Thee, O Compassionate One [oiktirmon], that, being united with Thee, we may praise and glorify Thine All-holy Spirit.[129]

> H-52. After Thy rising, O Christ, from nether Hades, and after Thy divine Ascension to the height of Heaven, Thou didst send down Thy glory unto

---

[125] Bobrinskoy, *Compassion*, 76.

[126] Ascension of the Lord, Small Vespers/Great Vespers, Sticheron at *Lord, I call* (*Pentecostarion*, 189–90). See also Leavetaking of the Ascension (Friday of the Seventh Week of Pentecost), Vespers, Sticheron at *Lord, I call* (*Pentecostarion*, 225).

[127] All of the sacraments and "all the benedictions and intercessions are irruptions of the divine power of healing, of forgiveness, and of consolation" (Bobrinskoy, *Compassion*, 63).

[128] *The Great Book of Needs*, 1:35.

[129] Pentecost, Matins, Canon, Ode 6, Ikos (*Pentecostarion*, 243); and also for the Monday and Saturday after Pentecost (*Pentecostarion* 258 and 263).

the disciples, renewing an upright Spirit in those God-seers, O Merciful [*oiktirmon* or compassionate] Saviour; and like a tuneful harp, they proclaimed clearly unto all, as with a plectrum divine, Thy melodies with mystic strains, and Thy holy economy.[130]

H-53. The Spirit, the All-holy Lord, do Thou renew in us, O God, Whom in old time Thou, Most Merciful [*oiktirmon*, or compassionate], didst send to strengthen Thy disciples, so that they might accomplish Thy saving will throughout the world, O Lord.[131]

Christ, the Compassionate Healer of Human Illness

In Chapter 3, I briefly discussed the gospel texts in which Christ's healing of people from various physical and mental infirmities is motivated by his compassion.[132] I mentioned that while only a few gospel accounts explicitly indicate that he was moved by compassion, compassion was not simply a "feeling" that occasionally arose in Christ. As we have seen in the previous hymns, Christ's compassion for us pervades and guides the entire event of the Incarnation, of which his earthly ministry and healing miracles are a vital component. Not surprisingly, this aspect of Christ's compassion is noted throughout the service of Holy Oil or Unction, the sacrament of healing in the Orthodox Christian Church (in Greek tradition served on Great and Holy Wednesday).[133]

There are references to compassion in a number of hymns and prayers in the service. One hymn notably makes reference to the oil of compassion: "O Master who ever comfort the souls and abodes of man with the oil of compassion [*elaiō tēs eusplanchnias*] and who preserve the faithful with oil: Do you yourself now show compassion [*oiktirēson*] through the oil to them that draw near unto you."[134] During this service, those who are in need of healing—physical, mental, or spiritual—are anointed with oil that has been blessed during the service. In addition to hymns and prayers, there are scriptural references to compassion in the parable of the good Samaritan, which is one of the readings for the service, as well James 5.10–16 (also one of the readings), which notes that the Lord is

---

[130]Pentecost, Matins, Kathisma after the Polyeleos (*Pentecostarion*, 241); and also for Friday after Pentecost, Matins, Sessional Hymn after First Reading of the Psalter (*Pentecostarion*, 262).

[131]Wednesday after Pentecost, Matins, Praises, Sticheron (*Pentecostarion*, 260).

[132]See Chapter 3, pp. 103–105.

[133]For the text of the service see St Tikhon's Seminary Press, "The Office of Holy Oil (Anointing)," in *The Great Book of Needs*, 1:189–236.

[134]The Office of Holy Oil, Canon, Ode 1, Troparion (*Great Book of Needs* 1.193 mod.).

compassionate and merciful, thus repeating the beginning of the "compassion formula" from Exodus 34.6.[135]

The most significant feasts of Christ's healing compassion occur on three Sundays during the period from Pascha to Ascension: the Sunday of the Paralytic, the Sunday of the Samaritan Woman, and the Sunday of the Man Born Blind.[136] In each of these events, Christ takes the initiative to approach someone and offer healing both physical and spiritual even though they are at the margins of society: the paralytic who lies by the pool of Bethesda for thirty-eight years ignored by those around him; the Samaritan woman, for whom Jews had great animosity and who comes to the well to draw water at the heat of day rather than with the other women in the morning; and the man born blind who has been reduced to living as a beggar.

Each service features a hymn that acknowledges Christ's compassion.[137] These three events manifest Christ's compassion and neighborliness. The healing of the paralytic in particular provides a striking resemblance to the parable of the good Samaritan. The paralytic had been lying by the Pool in Bethesda for thirty-eight years trying to get into the waters when the angel descends on it so that he could be healed. He is unable to move himself to the pool and he tells Jesus that no one has bothered to help him. Just like the man beaten by the side of the road, who is ignored by everyone except the good Samaritan, the paralytic is ignored by everyone but Jesus. The following hymn from the Sunday of the Paralytic expresses the neighborliness and hospitality that underlie Christ's compassion throughout his earthly healing ministry and, as I will argue in Chapter 5, they constitute the core of compassion.

> H-54 With your pure hand, you created man; you came to heal the sick, O compassionate [*eusplanchnos*] Christ. By your word you raised the paralytic at the Sheep's Pool, you cured the pain of the woman with the issue of blood. You had mercy on the Canaanite woman's daughter. You did not reject the request of the centurion. Therefore, we cry to you: "Glory to you, O Almighty Lord!"[138]

[135]For the meaning and purpose of this service, see Thomas Hopko, *The Orthodox Faith*, 2:43–45.

[136]The events are respectively recorded in Scripture: Jn 5.1–15, Jn 4.5–42, and Jn 9.1–38.

[137]Third Sunday after Pentecost (Sunday of the Paralytic), Matins, Canon of the Paralytic, Ode 4, Troparion (*Pentecostarion*, 99) and Matins, Exaposteilarion (*Pentecostarion*, 103); Fourth Sunday after Pentecost (Sunday of the Samaritan Woman), Great Vespers, *Glory* Sticheron at *Lord, I call* (*Pentecostarion*, 128) and Matins, Canon of the Samaritan Woman, Ode 8, Troparion (*Pentecostarion*,139); Fifth Sunday of Pentecost (Sunday of the Blind Man), Great Vespers, Sticheron at *Lord I Call* (*Pentecostarion*, 156) and Matins, Canon of the Blind Man, Ode 3, Troparion (*Pentecostarion*, 162).

[138]Fourth Sunday after Pascha (Sunday of the Paralytic), Vespers, Sticheron at *Lord, I call* taken from OCA

The Compassion of the Theotokos

H-55. It is truly meet to bless you, O Theotokos, ever blessed, most pure, and Mother of our God. More honorable than the Cherubim and more glorious beyond compare than the Seraphim, without corruption you gave birth to God the Word. True Theotokos we magnify you.[139]

Orthodox Christians venerate the Theotokos as first among the saints. She is venerated as the one who preeminently fulfills the human vocation: realizing through the grace of God what it means to be made in the image and according to the likeness of God. In the Orthodox Christian understanding, she is the first one who received the fulness of the gift of deification or theosis. While venerated as the Mother of God (Theotokos, properly "God-bearer"), she is also a human woman, not a goddess. We venerate her Annunciation since it is through her acceptance of bearing the incarnate Son of God that our salvation is wrought. She is, however, subject to the same liability to death and corruption that is the consequence of ancestral sin. Even granting the traditional belief that she is without personal sin, she cannot "save herself"—that is, bring herself into the everlasting fullness of life with the Trinity, which is the fruit of the resurrection.

The Orthodox Feast of the Dormition (August 15) commemorates the falling asleep in the Lord, i.e., the death, of the Mother of God. She lies in the grave for three days. Yet, the profound importance of the feast is that through the grace of Christ, she is raised from the dead and translated into everlasting life even before the general resurrection. That is, she is brought into the fullness of attaining to the likeness of the incarnate Christ.[140] Moreover, as we will see, in being brought into the fullness of life, she continues to face us and our world and bestow her compassion on us.

She has the same calling as every other human: "to love the Lord your God with all your heart and mind and to love your neighbor as yourself" (or to love others as Christ has loved us). Her life is dedicated to God in a unique manner: she

service texts for this Sunday, <http://oca.org/liturgics/service-texts, 2019–0519-texts-yy.docx>, May 5, 2019. [Note: The service texts on the OCA website combine all cycles applicable to a given year and date; they are usually available for several weeks before and after a specific day's service.—*Ed.*]

[139] Hymn to the Theotokos at the conclusion of the Anaphora Prayer (Divine Liturgy of St John Chrysostom, *Service Books*, 71). It is replaced by special hymns to the Theotokos on special feasts. Also see Office of Holy Oil, Canon, Ode 9, Theotokion (*Great Book of Needs* 1:200). An abbreviated version of the hymn beginning at *More honorable than the Cherubim* is part of the conclusion of many services, including Vespers, Matins, and the Hours.

[140] See *FM* 63–64; Thomas Hopko, "The Feast of the Dormition," *Orthodox Faith* 2:136–38; and A Monk (Gillet), *Year of Grace*, 242–44.

is the one who bears the Son of God in the flesh. She is the God-bearer (*Theotokos*, "the woman who gave birth to God). However, what she is graced to accomplish in a unique way belongs to all of us created in the image and according to the likeness of God: to become God-bearers (*theophoroi*) in our witness to our life in Christ and the Trinity.

I have found very few texts or hymns that refer to the compassion the Theotokos showed for others while she was alive. A letter attributed to St Ignatius of Antioch (but regarded as written by an anonymous author), remarks that "she sympathizes (*condolet*) with the wretched and the afflicted as sharing in their afflictions, and is not slow to come to their assistance."[141]

In her deification, the Theotokos preeminently attains to the likeness of God that perfects the image of God, of Christ, in which she, along with every other human, is created. In her deified state, then, she is most completely a living icon of Christ who reflects Christ's love and compassion back to the world. In her deified state, then, she faces the world and does not forsake it:

> **H-56.** In giving birth you preserved your virginity. In falling asleep you did not forsake[142] the world, O Theotokos. You were translated to life, O Mother of Life, and by your prayers, you deliver our souls from death.[143]

The recognition of and appeal to the compassion she shows is found most typically in hymns about her and in many accounts of her miraculous interventions in human affairs. For example, in Sophronius' *Life of Saint Mary of Egypt*, Mary refers to the encouragement she received from the compassion (*eusplanchnia*) of the Theotokos, which allowed her to enter into a church after her way had been blocked by an invisible force.[144] In the Lenten Akathist to the Theotokos, she is hailed as "earth yielding a rich harvest of compassion" (*sympatheia*).[145] We call upon her to always be near us as merciful and compassionate (*sympathēs*).[146]

---

[141]St Ignatius of Antioch, *Epistle of Ignatius to St John the Apostle* (spurious letter; ANF 1:124; PG 5:941).

[142]It is perhaps worth noting that the Greek word is related to the more intensive term *enkataleipō* (forsake or abandon) that is used in the Old Testament, where God's compassion for the Israelites is linked to his promise not to forsake them (cf. Lev 26.43 and Deut 4.31). The latter word is also the same word used in the Divine Liturgy in the priest's Prayer of the Second Antiphon and the final Prayer before the Ambo: "Forsake [*enkatalipēs*] us not who put our hope in you" (*Divine Liturgy, Chrysostom*, 33, 85.)

[143]Feast of the Dormition of the Theotokos, Troparion (*Divine Liturgy, Chrysostom*, 241).

[144]St Sophronius, *Life of Mary of Egypt* (*Vita sanctae Mariae Aegytiae*) 24 (PG 87:3713).

[145]Lenten Akathist to the Theotokos, Ikos 3 (*LT* 424).

[146]Akathist Hymn to Theotokos and Small Compline, Prayer to the All Holy Theotokos. See Holy Trinity Monastery, *The Unabbreviated Horologion*, 2nd ed. (Jordanville, NY: Printshop of St Job of Pochaev, 1997), 247.

It is not surprising that we find a number of hymns that venerate the compassion of the Theotokos. The earliest hymn to the Theotokos, dating from about AD 250, cites her compassion for us.

H-57. Beneath your compassion [*eusplanchnia*] we take refuge, O Theotokos: despise not our petitions in distress: but deliver us from peril, for you alone are pure and alone blessed.[147]

Not only do we venerate her compassion, but we constantly call on her to act towards us based on that compassion, *sympatheia*, and mercy. As with the hymns that celebrate the compassion, *sympatheia*, *philanthrōpia*, and mercy of the Lord, we chant these hymns in part to invoke or take note of actions done on our behalf because of her compassion. But in celebrating her compassion towards us, we are also called to show that compassion to others. We honor her not just through hymns but by actually showing compassion and mercy to others:

... after all, she is truly, after God, the holiest of all beings, for like always delights in like! Let us do her homage by our mercy [*eleos*] and our compassion [*sympatheia*] for the poor. For if God is honored by nothing so much as by mercy (*eleos*), who can deny that his mother is glorified, too, by the same thing? She has opened up to us the unspeakable depth of God's love for us![148]

This text of St John of Damascus provides a perspective for understanding two principal prayers to the Theotokos, which are said by all clergy in the Entrance Prayers before the Divine Liturgy, as well as the faithful in other services.

H-58 O Blessed Theotokos: open the doors of compassion [*eusplanchnia*] to us whose hope is in you, that we may not perish but be delivered from adversity through you, for you are the salvation of the Christian people.[149]

---

[147]Theotokion for final prayers in daily vespers during Lent (*LT* 90 mod.); and Octoechos Tone 5, Saturday, Matins, Praises, *Glory . . . now and ever* Sticheron (*Great Octoechos* 3:192). For information about this hymn see Henri de Villiers, "The Sub Tuum Praesidium," New Liturgical Movement, Thursday, February 3, 2011, ‹http://www.newliturgicalmovement.org/2011/02/sub-tuum-praesidium.html#.XI8ctihKhjE›, April 20, 2020.

[148]John of Damascus, *On the Holy and Glorious Dormition and Transformation of our Lady Mary, Mother of God and Ever-Virgin* 16 (*On the Dormition of Mary: Early Patristic Homilies*, tr. Brian Daly, PPS 18 (Crestwood, NY: St Vladimir's Seminary Press, 1998), 220; PG 96:744.

[149]Divine Liturgy, Priest's Entrance Prayers (*Service Books*, 7 mod.); Octoechos, Tone 6, Thursday, Matins, *Glory . . . now and ever* Troparion after First Sessional Hymn (*Great Octoechos* 3:269); Great Compline, Theotokion after Prayer of Manasses (*Horologion*, 226); Midnight Prayers Weekdays and Saturdays, Second Theotokion after Psalm 133 (*Horologion*, 18 and 37); Service of Holy Oil (Unction), Theotokion before Psalm 5 (*The Great Book of Needs*, 1:192).

H-59. Make us worthy of your compassion [*eusplanchnia*], O Theotokos, Fountain of Loving Kindness [*sympatheia*]. Look on us sinful people and reveal your power as always, for we have put our hope in you. "Rejoice!" we cry to you, as once did Gabriel, the leader of the bodiless hosts.[150]

The first and most common way to understand these prayers is that we are asking the Theotokos to open the gates of her compassion for us or to make us worthy of her compassion. But there is another sense: We ask her to open the gates of our compassion to others; and we pray that she might make us worthy of showing compassion to others.

H-60 O Theotokos, abundantly grant me great strength to look each day with a cheerful purpose and kindly disposition upon the poor, strangers, or the many who are in need. Enable me to bear voluntary poverty to draw near to God.[151]

If this second reading seems forced, remember Christ's illustration in the parable of the unmerciful servant of the gift economy that is the Kingdom of God. The servant would have remained in the kingdom, through his own compassion, if he had passed on the gift of compassion he received from the king; namely, if he had showed compassion to his fellow servant as the king had shown compassion to him.[152] He refused to do that and, as Blessed Theophylact observed, excluded himself from the kingdom.[153] So too, as I noted earlier, a basic realization of the Jesus Prayer is that one does not keep praying for Christ's mercy and simply bask in the mercy that is received. Rather, recognizing the great compassion and mercy that Christ bestows on us, we should bear witness to that compassion and mercy through bestowing our own mercy and compassion upon others.

Here follow two of the hymns to the Theotokos that invoke or honor her compassion, sympathy, and mercy.

---

[150]Divine Liturgy, Clergy Entrance Prayers, Veneration of the Icon of the Theotokos (*Service Books*, 7 mod.); Octoechos, Tone 2, Monday, Matins, First Kathisma, Theotokion (*Octoechos* 1:97); First Week of Great Lent (Sunday of Orthodoxy), Monday, Matins, Second Kathisma, Theotokion (*LT* 189); First Week of Great Lent, Monday, Matins, Theotokion after the Second Reading from the Psalter (*LT* 189).

[151]Octoechos, Tone 1, Friday, Vespers, Sticheron at *Lord, I call*; cf. *Great Octoechos*, 1:129.

[152]Mt 18.21–35.

[153]Theophylact, *The Explanation by Blessed Theophylact of the Holy Gospel According to Matthew* [*Ennaratio in Evangelium Matthaei*], trans. Christopher Stade (House Springs, MO: Chrysostom Press, 2006), 160 (PG 193:348A, on Matthew 18.28–30).

H-61. I have recourse to your holy protection, O spotless Virgin Mother, as to a harbor of salvation, and I entreat you be moved with compassion [*splanchnistheti*] for me. Do not reject your servant, but save me in my present affliction, for you are compassionate [*sympathes*, or sympathetic] by nature. O Mother of the Most High God, intercede continually and save your faithful servants from all adversity.[154]

H-62. O blessed Theotokos, you see those on earth, and feel and suffer with us [*sympatheia*] in our lowliness. Be moved by compassion [*splanchnizo*] for your people in distress. Pray for us constantly, lest we perish in our sins. O Virgin undefiled and all-holy, intercede for the salvation of our souls before the God who is always ready to forgive.[155]

The hymns to the Theotokos invoke her compassion most frequently for the forgiveness of our sins. Yet one need only consider the many icons of the Theotokos that honor the various ways in which she befriends us—both individually and collectively. Discussion of those icons is beyond the scope of this project. But the Orthodox Church in America website has an extensive collection of the Icons of the Theotokos and the events they commemorate. The interested reader is encouraged to browse this collection.[156]

The Compassion of the Saints

Typically more than one saint is venerated on each day of the year—our "venerable and God-bearing fathers and mothers." More than a few are venerated for their compassion. Those venerated for their compassion in the hymns—and there are many whom we recognize for their compassion who are not explicitly mentioned in this way[157]—bear or manifest God's compassion to the world through

[154]Octoechos, Tone 2, Wednesday, Vespers, Sticheron at *Lord, I call* (*Great Octoechos* 1:251 mod.); and Paul the Confessor (November 3), Vespers, Aposticha, Theotokion (*Menaion*, Nov., 38).

[155]Cheese Fare Week, Friday, Matins, Kathisma Theotokion after Second set of Psalms (*LT Supp.* 43 mod.); Octoechos, Tone 7, Tuesday, Matins, Kathisma Theotokion after Third Reading from the Psalter (*Great Octoechos* 3:63).

[156]Orthodox Church in America (OCA), "Icons of the Theotokos." <https://oca.org/saints/icons-mother-of-god>, April 20, 2020. So far as I know, there is no comparable print publication of this material. For information about the collections for the icons used on the website, see "Icons of the Mother of God," <https://www.oca.org/fs/attributions>, April 20, 2020.

[157]Two notable examples are St Basil the Great and St John Chrysostom. The Orthodox Christian tradition also has a long tradition of "unmercenary saints": those who provided medical treatment of various kinds to people without any monetary compensation. For very good sources of information for these saints, see Georgia Hronas, ed. and trans., *The Holy Unmercenary Doctors: The Saints Anargyroi Physicians and Healers of the*

their own compassion. In this brief section, I will draw attention to some of them. I have arranged this material according to order of the church year, which begins in September. Before providing the hymns, I want to make three observations about them and the saints they celebrate.

First, the saints in these hymns are not commemorated for particular compassionate or merciful actions. They are commemorated primarily for a profound depth and constancy of mercy, compassion, and sympathy that radiates from within them.[158] Thus one hymn, H-63, describes St John the Merciful as "the imitator of Christ and well-spring of mercy [*pēgē eleous*], [who] floods the needy with great compassions of his tender loving-kindness [*eusympathētatos oiktirmos*]."[159] In these saints, we venerate compassion and mercy perfected as a fundamental disposition that holistically orients them to care for others. I will refer to this trait of the saints when I discuss the sense in which compassion is a virtue.[160]

Second, in two of the hymns below, H-74 and H-75, a saint commended for compassion is likened to an angel on earth. I cannot find any direct references in the service texts to angels as compassionate or merciful, but there are two relevant references in patristic texts. St Nilus of Sinai distinguishes between those angels that are "kind, philanthropic, compassionate, and sympathetic" with those merciless angels who punish sinners.[161] Dionysius the Areopagite refers to "philanthropic angels, who take compassion on nations and invoke what is good on their behalf."[162] The awareness of the compassion of angels in the hymns is expressed obliquely through those saints who live like angels on earth. These hymns imply that while living like the angels may involve renouncing the world in becoming dispassionate, it does not mean forsaking the world and our neighbors.

Third, in several of the hymns below, you will also note the scope of the compassion of some saints through caring for diverse groups, e.g., "succor of those in distress, feeder of the hungry, help of the oppressed; protector of widows and

---

Orthodox Church, Translated from the Greek Great Synaxaristes of the Orthodox Church (Minneapolis: Light and Life Publishing Company, 1999) as well as Agioi Anargyroi, "Synaxis of the Unmercenary Saints" <http://full-of-grace-and-truth.blogspot.com/2008/10/synaxis-of-holy-unmercenaries.html>, April 20, 2020.

[158] See hymns H-64, H-65, H-68, H-70, H-71, H-73, H-74, and H-75 for this and similar expressions. See H-61 for the reference to the Theotokos as compassionate by nature. See H-69 for the same reference to Righteous Father George, Metropolitan of Mytilene.

[159] See H-29 where Christ is referred to as the "fountain of compassion" (*pēgē tēs eusplanchnias*).

[160] See Chapter 5, 226–27; 231–33.

[161] Saint Nilus of Sinai, *Epistle* 164 (*Epistola 164, Vorioni Ecdico*) (PG 79:280).

[162] Dionysius the Areopagite *Epistle* 8.1; Dionysius the Areopagite, *The Works of Dionysius the Areopagite*, trans. John Parker (London and Oxford: James Parker and Co., 1897), 151; online at: <https://www.ccel.org/ccel/d/dionysius/works/cache/works.pdf>, April 20, 2020 (PG 3:1085C).

visitation of all the sick, unfailing covering of the naked and miserable."[163] This text resonates with a similar text in Psalm 145.7–9, which is the second antiphon for the Sunday Liturgy in the Slav tradition.

> The Lord executes justice for the oppressed; He gives food to the hungry. The Lord sets the prisoners free ... The Lord raises up those who are bowed down ... The Lord protects the strangers; He supports the fatherless and the widow.[164]

God's expectation that we do these same things is also contained in two powerful texts from Isaiah that we hear during Great Lent.[165] We often think of justice and compassion as at least in strong tension, if not actually opposed to each other, especially if we limit compassion to being merciful to people—that is, helping them in ways to which they have no rightful claim or simply being kind to them. Is that the case with the compassion of these saints? Or can it be a manifestation of executing justice? I will discuss the relation between compassion and justice in Chapter 6.

ST JOHN THE MERCIFUL/ALMSGIVER (NOVEMBER 12)[166]

H-63. John, the great shepherd and luminary of the Alexandrians, the imitator of Christ and well-spring of mercy [*pēgē eleous*], floodeth the needy with the great compassions of his tender loving-kindness [*eusympathētatous oiktirmous,* or abundant sympathy of his compassions]. Come, ye poor in spirit, let us fill ourselves by imitating his cheerfulness. For like Abraham of old, through his brotherly affection and love of compassion [*phileusplanchnōs*], he gave hospitality [*xenia*] to Christ in the person of the poor, and hence was counted worthy of the beatitude;[167] and with boldness he intercedeth that our souls find mercy.[168]

---

[163]Cf. H-64 for John the Merciful and also H-65 and H-70.

[164]Ps 145.7–9. The phrase "executes justice for the oppressed" is also translated as "executes judgment for the oppressed"—that is, a judgment on behalf of the oppressed; namely, to secure justice for them.

[165]See Chapter 3, p. 118 for these texts.

[166]For an account of his life, see <https://oca.org/saints/lives/2018/11/12/103286-st-john-the-merciful-patriarch-of-alexandria>, April 20, 2020. For information about the printed sources for this and the other lives of the saints on the Orthodox Church in America's website provided below, see "The Lives of the Saints." <https://www.oca.org/fs/attributions>, April 20, 2020; see also *Three Byzantine Saints: Contemporary Biographies of St Daniel the Stylite, St Theodore of Sykeon and St John the Almsgiver,* trans. Elizabeth Dawes and Norman H. Baynes (Crestwood, NY: St Vladimir's Seminary Press, 1996), 199–262.

[167]Mt 5.7. "Blessed are the merciful, for they shall obtain mercy."

[168]St John the Merciful (Nov. 12), Vespers, *Glory* Sticheron at *Lord, I call* (*Menaion*, November, 85).

H-64. Rejoice, giver most rich to the poor, well-spring of mercy [*pēgē eleous*], overflowing of sympathy [*brysis tēs sympatheias*]; swift uprighting of the fallen, succour of those in distress, feeder of the hungry, help of the oppressed; protector of widows and visitation of all the sick, unfailing cov'ring of the naked and mis'rable: righteous Father John, who dost stand in the Heavens' heights, look with thy gaze of mercy and attend to us from on high, and importune Christ the Saviour that He might send down upon our souls His rich and great mercy and a share in His divine and eternal love for man.[169]

ST PHILARET THE MERCIFUL (DECEMBER 1)[170]

H-65. Rejoice, giver most rich to the poor, wellspring of mercy [likely, *pēgē eleous*], overflowing of sympathy [likely, *brysis tēs sympatheias*]; swift uprighting of the fallen, succour of those in distress, feeder of the hungry, help of the oppressed; protector of widows and visitation of all the sick, unfailing cov'ring of the naked and mis'rable: law of diligence, and abyss of beneficence; matchlessly cheerful giver who dispensest abundantly that which is needful and fitting to all that faithfully run to thee. O thrice-blessed Father, intercede with Christ to grant His great mercy to our souls.[171]

H-66. From the wealth of your faith in God, You distributed your riches to the poor, O Philaret. Your life was adorned with compassion [*eusplanchnia*]. And you glorified the Giver of mercy. Implore him to have compassion [*oiktirmōn*] and mercy on those who praise you![172]

ST NICHOLAS OF MYRA (DECEMBER 6)[173]

H-67. The fruit of thy manly exploits, O righteous Father, hath cheered the hearts of the faithful; for what man would not marvel, upon hearing of thine immeasurable humility, thy patience, thy cheerful kindness towards the poor,

---

[169]St John the Merciful (November 12), Vespers, Aposticha, Sticheron (*Menaion*, November, 86).

[170]For an account of his life see, ‹https://oca.org/saints/lives/2019/12/01/103453-righteous-philaret-the-merciful-of-amnia-in-asia-minor›, April 20, 2020.

[171]St Philaret the Merciful (December 1), Vespers, Aposticha, Stichcron (*Menaion*, December, 271). Given as supplemental service in the volume. I could not find the Greek text.

[172]Troparion for St Philaret the Merciful (OCA translation, ‹https://oca.org/saints/troparia/2019/12/01/103453-righteous-philaret-the-merciful-of-amnia-in-asia-minor›, April 20, 2020).

[173]For an account of his life see, ‹https://oca.org/saints/lives/2019/12/06/103484-st-nicholas-the-wonderworker-and-archbishop-of-myra-in-lycia›, April 20, 2020.

thy compassion [*sympathēs*] for the afflicted? Thou taughtest all men in a fashion befitting godliness, O Hierarch Nicholas; and now, as thou hast put on the unfading crown, intercede in behalf of our souls.[174]

ST PHILOTHEI (FEBRUARY 19)[175]

H-68. O Philothei, thou, like Tabitha in Joppa, wast a faithful handmaid and disciple of thy Christ, for thy whole life, thou wast seen to be adorned with good works; thou, like a spring, didst pour forth about thyself streams of thy rich mercy [likely, *eleos*] and abundant sympathy [likely, *sympatheia*]; thou didst disperse all thy wealth abroad and didst distribute it in the hands of the poor, O righteous one, who, having striven, wast received by Christ, unto Whom thou didst lend all thou didst disperse. Do thou therefore entreat Him to enlighten and to save our souls.[176]

RIGHTEOUS FATHER GEORGE, METROPOLITAN OF MYTILENE (APRIL 7)[177]

H-69. Having the compassion of mercy [*oiktos tou eleous*] ever dwelling with thee by nature [*emphyton*, or inborn], thou becamest a workshop of abundant sustenance to the poor.[178]

ST MACARIUS OF CORINTH (APRIL 17)[179]

H-70. We know thee to be a mercy-spring [likely, *pēgē eleous*], a most compassionate [likely, *sympathestatos*] soul, consolation of sufferers, feeder of the fatherless, widows' helper and champion, the strength and solace of them that fall in sin, the refuge healing deniers of Christ's Name, and a most excellent

---

[174]*St Nicholas of Myra (December 6)*, Entreaty (Litya), *Glory* Sticheron (*Menaion*, December, 36). "Manly" also has the sense of "noble."

[175]For an account of her life see, <http://pemptousia.com/2011/11/st-philothei-angelou-venizelou-athens-1522–1589-printed-pemptousia/>, April 20, 2020.

[176]St Philothei (Feb. 19), Matins, Praises, Sticheron (*Menaion*, February, 183). Given as supplemental service in volume. I could not find the Greek text.

[177]For an account of his life see, <https://oca.org/saints/lives/2019/04/07/101023-st-george-the-confessor-the-bishop-of-mytilene>, April 20, 2020.

[178]Righteous Father George, Metropolitan of Mytilene (Apr. 7) Matins, Ode 5, Troparion (*Menaion*, April, 36).

[179]For an account of his life see, <https://oca.org/saints/lives/2018/04/17/101134-venerable-makarius-of-corinth>, April 20, 2020.

trainer unto contest with wise words and deeds for the holy Martyrs, O divine
Macarius.[180]

ST SAMPSON THE HOSPITABLE OF CONSTANTINOPLE (JUNE 27)[181]

H-71. Let us extol sacred Sampson; for imitating the compassion [*eusplanch-nia*] of God, he was filled with sympathy [*sympatheia*, or compassion] for the
ailing and became raiment for all the naked.[182]

H-72. In thy great sympathy [*sympatheia*], thou becamest the enrichment of
the poor and a physician of the sick, raising up for their sakes an illustrious
hospital to purge their maladies.[183]

ST ELIZABETH THE NEW MARTYR (JULY 5)[184]

H-73. Emulating the Lord's self-abasement on the earth, thou didst forsake
royal mansions to serve the poor and disdained, overflowing with compassion
for the suffering. And taking up a martyr's cross, thou in meekness didst perfect the Saviour's image within thee. Wherefore, with Barbara, entreat Him
to save us all, O wise Elizabeth.[185]

ST MACRINA, SISTER OF ST BASIL THE GREAT (JULY 19)[186]

H-74. Even at thy death, thy holy face shone brightly with splendid light, O
Macrina most laudable; for Christ made thee glorious as His comely virgin,
as completely Godlike, as full of mercy, radiant, divinely eloquent, great in

---

[180]St Macarius of Corinth (Apr. 17), Vespers, Sticheron at *Lord, I call* (*Menaion*, April, 142). Given as part
of supplemental service in the volume. I could not find the Greek text.

[181]For an account of his life see, <https://oca.org/saints/lives/2019/06/27/101828-st-sampson-the-hospi-
table-of-constantinople>, April 20, 2020.

[182]St Sampson the Hospitable of Constantinople (June 27), Matins, Canon, Ode 3, Troparion (*Menaion*,
June, 133).

[183]St Sampson the Hospitable of Constantinople (June 27), Matins, Canon, Ode 5, Troparion (*Menaion*,
June, 135).

[184]For an account of her life see, <https://oca.org/saints/lives/2019/07/18/101915-grand-duchess-eliza-
beth>, April 20, 2020. For some details the Mary and Martha Convent/Hospital she founded as well as the
"Rule of St Elizabeth the New Martyr," see her work, Elizabeth Feodorovna (St Elizabeth the New Martyr),
The Martha-Mary Convent: and Rule of St Elizabeth the New Martyr, trans. St Elizabeth Convent (Jordanville,
NY: The Printshop of St Job of Pochaev, 2005).

[185]St Elizabeth the New Martyr (July 5), Troparion (*Menaion*, July, 199). Given as supplemental service
in the volume.

[186]For an account of her life see, <https://oca.org/saints/lives/2019/07/19/102055-venerable-macrina-the-
sister-of-st-basil-the-great>, April 20, 2020.

sympathy [*sympathēs*, or compassionate]. For thou hadst lived upon the earth the selfsame life which the Angels lead and wast well-pleasing unto God in the brilliancy of thy life.[187]

ST SYMEON OF EMESA, THE FOOL FOR CHRIST'S SAKE (JULY 21)[188]

H-75. Lowly in thy thinking, filled with love for God, great in sympathy [*sympathēs*, or compassion], brimming over with charity [*agapē*, or love] wast thou, O blest Symeon, meek and very humble, living all thy days like an angel walking on the earth, having a life that was truly heavenly. Hence, Father, Son, and Holy Spirit came and took up Their rest in thee, since, O Father inspired of God, thou wast pure and beyond reproach.[189]

THE GREAT MARTYR AND HEALER ST PANTELEIMON (JULY 27)[190]

H-76. All who love Martyrs must honour with praise the memory of godly Panteleimon, mercy's image and namesake; striving by compassion [*sympatheia*] to imitate Him Who alone is incomp'rable in His compassions [*oiktirmos*] and mercies [*eleos*], he hath received much divine grace from Him as the prize.[191]

Our Response to Christ's Compassion

Besides commemorating and venerating Christ's compassion for us, there are many hymns throughout the Church year and in all of the major service books in which we invoke Christ's compassion to forgive our sins, to save us, and to respond favorably to our compunction and repentance. But our relationship to Christ in repentance is integrally connected with our relationship to our neighbor and to the world around us. Once again, we cannot really say that we love God, whom we cannot see, if we cannot love our neighbor whom we do see.[192]

---

[187] St Macrina, Sister of St Basil the Great (July 19), Vespers, Sticheron at *Lord, I call* (*Menaion*, July, 110).

[188] For an account of his life see, <https://oca.org/saints/lives/2018/07/21/102065-venerable-simeon-of-emessa-the-fool-for-christ>, April 20, 2020.

[189] St Symeon of Emesa, the Fool for Christ's Sake (July 21), Vespers, Sticheron at *Lord, I call* (*Menaion*, July, 127).

[190] For an account of his life see, <https://oca.org/saints/lives/2019/07/27/102099-greatmartyr-and-healer-panteleimon>, April 20, 2020.

[191] The Great Martyr and Healer St Panteleimon (July 27), Vespers, Aposticha, Sticheron (*Menaion*, July, 161).

[192] 1 Jn 4.20.

Our response to God's compassion for us involves not just giving thanks for that compassion but radiating that compassion, through our compassion, in the world around us. There are some, but relatively few hymns, that remind and exhort us about this. Many but not all of these hymns are found in the *Triodion*. In a number of these selections, there is reference to the importance of *eleēmosynē* in our lives. This term is often translated simply as "alms" or "alms-giving," which often has the narrow sense of giving money or sharing our wealth with others. But *eleēmosynē* cannot be restricted in this way. God performs *eleēmosynas*[193] and this refers in a broad sense to "works of mercy" or "acts of compassion."[194] Yet it makes a great deal of difference, indeed all the difference, whether these actions merely express a self-serving pity that keeps others "at bay" or whether they express a compassionate concern for others that bears with them in community (*koinōnia*). Fr Florovsky's observation about the "deep meaning" of *eleēmosynē* is most apt:

> The second-century Shepherd of Hermas insists that the money saved through fasting is to be given to the widow, the orphan, and the poor. (*Similitudes* 5.3.7) But almsgiving means more than this. It is to give not only our money but our time, not only what we have but what we are; it is to give a part of ourselves.... For the mere giving of money can often be a substitute and an evasion, a way of protecting ourselves from closer personal involvement with those in distress. On the other hand, to do nothing more than offer reassuring words of advice to someone crushed by urgent material anxieties is equally an evasion of our responsibilities.[195]

In some of the hymns, the "motive" for personal acts of compassion often seems to be personal salvation: "Be compassionate so that you will be saved."[196] If we frame the purpose of such actions to be solely our own personal salvation, then a subtle egoism creeps into such actions, since compassion in any genuine sense is an orientation towards others for their sake. It is not clear that we are really performing acts of compassion any more than we are following Christ's commandment to love others as he loved us if we love others only because it

---

[193] Ps 102.6. This is the first antiphon of the Divine Liturgy on Sunday in the Slav tradition.

[194] The translation of "acts of compassion" is used in the English editions of the *Philokalia* and the *Lenten Triodion*. See, e.g., *LT* 312, 685 and *Philokalia* 1:39, 40; 2:339, 353; 3:158.

[195] Georges Florovsky, "The Meaning of the Great Fast" (*LT* 19–20). Fr Florovsky's observation provides a very important indicator about what a compassionate disposition involves and what runs counter to it.

[196] See hymns H-77, H-81, H-83, H-84, and H-85.

will lead to our salvation. I will explore this issue in the next chapter since these exhortations need not have this egoistic sense.[197]

Selected Hymns for our Response to Christ's Compassion

H-77. Knowing the commandments of the Lord, let this be our way of life: let us feed the hungry, let us give the thirsty drink, let us clothe the naked, let us welcome strangers, let us visit those in prison and the sick. Then the Judge of all the earth will say even to us: "Come, you blessed of my Father, inherit the kingdom prepared for you."[198]

H-78. Let us now set out with joy upon the second week of the Fast; and like Elijah the Tishbite let us fashion for ourselves from day to day, O brethren, a fiery chariot from the four great virtues; let us exalt our minds through freedom from the passions; let us arm our flesh with purity and our hands with acts of compassion [*eleēmosynē*]; let us make our feet beautiful with the preaching of the Gospel; and let us put the enemy to flight and gain the victory.[199]

H-79. With their tongues, the dogs licked the sores of Lazarus the beggar, showing towards him in a greater compassion [*sympathesteros*] to the poor man than the rich man did.[200]

H-80. Rich and lacking compassion [*asplanchnos*], my mind has despised and cast out faith in your commandments before the gates, O Lover of mankind. But as sympathetic [*sympathēs*] and a lover of compassion [*philoiktirmōn*] raise it up as once in compassion [*sympathēs*] as you raised up your friend Lazarus, who was four days dead.[201]

H-81. We have all learned the meaning of this parable of the Lord. Let all of us, then, hate the rich man's lack of compassion [*asplanchnos*], that we may escape punishment and rejoice forever with Abraham.[202]

---

[197]See Chapter 5, p. 226.

[198]Sunday of the Last Judgement, Litya, *Glory* Sticheron (*LT* 151).

[199]First Week of Great Lent, Sunday (Sunday of Orthodoxy), Vespers, Sticheron at *Lord, I call* (*LT* 312). The phrase "and our hands. . . . of the Gospel" is not in all Greek editions but needs to be supplied, otherwise four virtues are not listed (*LT* 312, n. 22).

[200]Fifth Week of Great Lent, Sunday (St Mary of Egypt), Matins, Ode 4, Troparion (*LT* 453 mod.)

[201]Fifth Week of Great Lent, Sunday (St Mary of Egypt), Matins, Ode 9, Troparion (cf. *LT* 459).

[202]Fifth Week of Great Lent, Sunday (St Mary of Egypt), Matins, Ode 9, Troparion (*LT* 459).

H-82. As brethren in Christ, let us acquire brotherly love, and let us not be lacking in compassion (*asympathēs*) for our neighbor, lest for money's sake we be condemned like the unmerciful [*aneleēmōn*] servant, and like Judas express remorse to no purpose.[203]

H-83. Raised on high through acts of compassion [*eleēmosynē*], as though upon the Mount of Olives, let us make ready for the invisible coming of Christ to us, as we praise, bless and exalt him above all forever.[204]

H-84. Let us make haste to wash away through fasting the filth of our transgressions and through acts of mercy [*eleos*] and love of humanity [*philanthrōpia*] for those in need, that we may enter into the bridal chamber of the Bridegroom Christ, who grants us great mercy.[205]

H-85. Yoking love with compassion [*sympatheia*], O ye faithful, let us make haste to offer up our prayer to Christ, that he may raise us from the grave of our secret passions.[206]

H-86. Have mercy on me, O God, have mercy on me! Why do you wrong the poor man? Why do you withhold the worker's pay? Why do you not love your brother? Why do you pursue lust and pride? Therefore, abandon all these things my soul, and repent for the sake of the kingdom of God.[207]

H-87. While fasting with the body, brethren, let us also fast in spirit. Let us loose every bond of iniquity. Let us undo the knots of every contract made by violence. Let us tear up all unjust agreements. Let us give bread to the hungry and welcome to our house the poor who have no roof to cover them, that we may receive great mercy from Christ our God.[208]

---

[203] Great and Holy Friday Matins, Troparion after the Second Gospel reading (*LT* 575–6.). The reference to Judas is to Mt 27.3. The Greek word, translated here as "remorse," *metamelomai*, also can mean "repent" and is translated that way in the *LT*. But in this passage, Judas expresses remorse or repentance to the chief priests for having betrayed Jesus. That was to no purpose since the chief priests simply disregarded him (Mt 27.4). Judas, however, did not express remorse or repentance to God and ask for forgiveness.

[204] Sixth Week of Great Lent, Wednesday, Matins, Second Canon, Ode 8, Troparion (*LT Supp.* 286).

[205] Cheese Fare Week, Tuesday, Vespers, Aposticha, Sticheron (*LT Supp.* 14 mod).

[206] Sixth Week of Great Lent, Thursday, Matins, First Canon, Ode 5, Troparion (*LT Supp.* 293).

[207] Canon of Repentance, Ode 4, Troparion (*Horologion*, 341).

[208] First Week of Lent, Wednesday, Vespers, Sticheron at *Lord, I Call* (*LT* 235).

Summary and Looking Forward

Summary

This chapter has presented a selection of the many Orthodox Christian hymns that commemorate and celebrate the compassion of Christ, the Theotokos, and many saints. There are also hymns that exhort us to be compassionate to others and to shun a lack of compassion. Hymns, of course, are written for worship and thanksgiving and not for conceptual, philosophical, or theological analysis. But the hymns I have presented radiate a vibrant understanding of compassion and provide several indicators or clues about compassion that I will develop in a more formal manner in Chapters 5 and 6.

Looking Forward

1) Chanting, if done musically and prayerfully, is a centering experience in which we get the mind or intellect out of our head and into our heart. Chanting and prayer can open us to the holistic "place" in our lives, our heart, in which we experience compassion and love and, thus, can experience ourselves and others in communion or fellowship (*koinōnia*). Of course, since the heart is the battleground of good and evil, our chanting, worship, and prayer can be disrupted by an array of toxic passions that separate and divide us from others. We saw examples of this battle in the hymns at the end of Chapter 4 that exhorted us to be compassionate and merciful to people and to avoid a lack of compassion. I will discuss the issue of centering ourselves in our heart as a basis for opening ourselves to compassion in Chapter 5.[209]

2) The paradox of the Incarnation and compassion: Christ's Incarnation bridges the gulf between heaven and earth in which the eternal Son of God, while remaining eternal, becomes incarnate as Jesus Christ fully identifying himself with all of humanity, especially with those who are the least and most despised among us. The One beyond being, the Transcendent One, draws near and becomes our neighbor to live with us and heal us. This same paradoxical aspect of these hymns is repeated in many of the hymns commemorating his voluntary suffering and death on the cross. He offers redemption, salvation, and deification to all. The compassion that animates Christ is fundamentally non-judgmental and free of any stigmatization. It provides a key indicator for the structure of our compassion as a disposition and virtue.[210]

[209]See above, pp. 129–30. See Chapter 5, pp. 169–70.
[210]See above, pp. 136–7, 148–49. See Chapter 5, pp. 183, 197–200.

3) Christ's Incarnation is a kenosis that is grounded in humility. From the moment of his Incarnation in Mary's womb, the Son of God in his compassion takes on and accepts the weakness of human nature. This is reflected, for example, in the hymns for the Annunciation and the Nativity, and it receives a pointed emphasis in the hymns for the Extreme Humility of Christ. In Chapter 5, I will develop the role of humility in perfecting a compassionate disposition through dispassion and coming to terms with our vulnerability.[211]

4) Moreover, the humility of Christ's kenosis is expressed in his fundamental solidarity with us and our willingness to serve others for their sake, e.g., **H-15** and **H-29**. In Chapter 5 I will develop how humility, as an elimination of pride and arrogance, contributes to compassion.[212]

5) At his Incarnation in the womb of the Theotokos, Christ invites his mother to embrace the womb-like love connected with the Hebrew understanding of *racham*. Her compassionate care for her child embraces the profound vulnerability and utter dependence of any child in the womb. This indicator will be developed in Chapter 5 when we discuss how compassion entails coming to terms with our vulnerability as created beings.[213]

6) By embracing human vulnerability and interdependence in the Incarnation, Christ allows us to offer compassion and hospitality for him. His Incarnation is itself an expression of the divine hospitality that is reflected in the icon *The Hospitality of Abraham*. This indicator provides a key for discussing the nature of a compassionate disposition as a fundamental openness and hospitality towards others. This will be developed in Chapter 5 in discussing the structure of a compassionate disposition.[214]

7) One key indicator in Chapter 3 was that compassion is a steadfast and constant orientation towards others. We see this manifest once again in the commemoration of Christ's compassion present throughout the entire event of his Incarnation. Moreover, along with Christ, several saints and the Theotokos are venerated as fountains or wellsprings (*pēgē*) of compassion. This will provide support for the analysis of compassion as a stable disposition or virtue that we are to acquire.[215]

---

[211] See above, pp. 134–35, 136–7. See Chapter 5, pp. 200–210.
[212] See above, p. 147. See Chapter 5, pp. 201–202.
[213] See above, pp. 133–34. See Chapter 5, p. 209.
[214] See above, pp. 139–40. See Chapter 5, pp. 192–93.
[215] See above, pp. 146, 160, 163–64. See Chapter 5, pp. 187, 214–16.

8) In her *theosis*, the Theotokos continues to face our world, interceding for us and also rendering assistance through her compassion. The same is true of many saints that we venerate. This fact emphasizes the importance of our facing the world in this life and manifesting compassion in our "liturgy after the Liturgy." I will discuss this towards the end of Chapter 5 and in the Epilogue after Chapter 6.[216]

9) Compassion and justice: Some of the saints are commemorated for their compassion and mercy in feeding the hungry, helping the oppressed, and so forth (cf. **H-64**, **H-65**, and **H-70**). These actions parallel God's commands in the Old Testament to seek justice for people. Does compassion involve only mercy in these actions? Does compassion replace doing justice? Can compassion for people assist them by seeking justice for them? This issue will be discussed in Chapter 6.[217]

10) Fr Florovsky observed that the "deep meaning" of *eleēmosynē* is not simply giving money at a distance but giving part of ourselves with an openness to a personal relationship with those we assist. This provides a key indicator for the structure of a compassionate disposition as an openness to others that bears with them and does not flee from them. It is for this reason that *eleēmosynē* is probably better rendered as "works or mercy" or "works of compassion" than simply "almsgiving."[218]

* * *

In Chapter 2, I provided a conceptual sketch of the "lay of the land" for exploring compassion in relation to sympathy, mercy, and pity. We also briefly discussed how the heart is the holistic center of our existence. In this chapter and Chapter 3, I discussed various references to the manifestation of divine and human compassion in Scripture and Orthodox Christian worship services. Throughout these chapters, we have found a number of clues or indicators in the Orthodox Christian tradition about the nature and role of divine and human compassion. It is time to move on and fill out the details of the "lay of the land" and tackle the questions: What is it to be moved by compassion? What is the role of compassion in human life—in general, as a natural compassion—and in Orthodox Christian spiritual life in particular? It is to be hoped that our responses to these questions

---

[216]See above, pp. 158–60, 164–65. See Chapter 5, pp. 232–33. See Epilogue, pp. 258–59.
[217]See above, pp. 164, 165–66. See Chapter 6, pp. 241–47.
[218]See above, p. 168. See Chapter 5, pp. 193–94.

will also provide an answer to the very "practical" question that animates this project: "Why should we care about being compassionate as human beings and also as Orthodox Christians?"

CHAPTER 5

Moved by Compassion

I n this chapter, I will set forth the basic structure of compassion as a disposition and virtue that is of central importance for our lives. I will now begin to pull together the many indicators about the nature of compassion I have previously highlighted in the Summary and Looking Forward sections of Chapters 2–4, and discuss them more fully and systematically.

Before I provide a brief outline of the chapter, let me provide some background on a principal, although likely less well known, work that I will employ in this chapter, especially in the section dealing with the structure of compassion as a disposition: the *Testaments of the Twelve Patriarchs*. This work is an early pseudo-epigraphical text that purports to be a set of death-bed testaments by the twelve sons of Jacob.[1] Various versions of the text were composed from the early centuries before to early centuries after Christ. It reveals both Jewish and Christian sources.[2] Versions of the *Testaments* exist in Hebrew and Greek.[3] It appears to have had an influence on the New Testament and the early Church.[4]

The Testament of Zebulun contains perhaps the most sustained description of compassion in ancient Jewish (Hebrew and Greek) and early Christian literature. Moreover, along with the Synoptic Gospels, the *Testaments*—especially the *Testament of Zebulun*—are the first texts to make any significant use of *eusplanchnia* (compassion) and *splanchnizomai* (being moved by compassion) in discussing and describing compassion.[5] Most patristic sources and the Synoptic Gospels mention compassion or discuss it in short texts. As the reader will see, however, the *Testament of Zebulun* is a rich source for an extended description of what

[1] In the biblical account, Jacob's youngest son Joseph was his favorite son although the target of a good deal of envy and hatred by his older brothers. Eventually, they plotted to kill him but ended up selling him into slavery in Egypt (Gen 37.1–36).

[2] For issues about dating the manuscript see, Elias Bickerman, "The Date of the *Testaments of the Twelve Patriarchs*," *Journal of Biblical Literature* 69.3 (Sept. 1950): 245–60; *Testaments* (English) 82–83.

[3] See *Testaments* (Greek) ix–liii, for a discussion of the various manuscripts.

[4] See *Testaments* (English) 67–82 and A. W. Argyle, "The Influence of the *Testaments of the Twelve Patriarchs* upon the New Testament," *Expository Times* 63.8 (May 1952): 256–58.

[5] *Testaments* (English) 254–55.

compassion involves. So too are some of the other Testaments that provide excellent descriptions of toxic passions that undermine compassion. As a final note, although clearly theocentric in its orientation, Zebulun's description of compassion can be described as what might be regarded as a "natural compassion."[6] The Testament of Zebulun is, in my own estimation, clearly consistent with the understanding of compassion in the Greek patristic and Byzantine tradition.

There are three major sections to this chapter: Preliminary Considerations, Compassion as a Disposition, and Compassion as a Virtue.

The first section takes up three preliminary considerations that will set the stage for the remainder of the chapter.

- First, in order to provide a framework for this chapter, I will begin by briefly discussing the Orthodox Christian understanding of the wages of sin as corruption and death, and how the compassion of the Incarnation and our own developed compassion in a lifelong process of repentance address the reality of sinfulness.[7]

- Second, as the heart is the holistic center of our lives, which plays the central role in repentance, I will develop the notion of the heart that was presented in Chapter 2; and drawing on the Testaments of the Twelve Patriarchs, I will proceed to a brief discussion of the contrast between compassion and the passions that arise out of and produce a sclerotic heart and viscera.

- Third, I will provide a brief analysis of compassion as a simple, raw emotion that, as we will see, is fundamentally different from compassion as a disposition.

The second section of the chapter, Compassion as a Disposition, contains the core of my analysis of the nature of compassion. It is divided into three parts: 1) the nature of a disposition, 2) the structure of a compassionate disposition, and 3) perfecting a compassionate disposition.

- The nature of a disposition. I will briefly develop what a disposition involves and contrast that to what the lack or absence of a disposition can involve.

---

[6]For some references to the idea of a natural compassion in patristic authors see: Athanasius, *Arian History* 62 (NPNF[2] 4:293; PG 25:768); John Chrysostom, *Homilies on Philippians* 4 (NPNF[1] 13:201; PG 62:210); *Homilies on 2 Corinthians* 10 (NPNF[1] 12:30; PG 61:472); Cyril of Alexandria, *Commentary on the Gospel of Luke*, Homily 58, trans. R. Payne Smith from Syrian text (Oxford: Oxford University Press, 1859), 265; Eusebius Pamphilius, *Church History* 10.8 (NPNF[2] 1:385; PG 20:897) and *The Life of Constantine* 1.54 (NPNF[2] 1:497; PG 20:968–69); and Maximus the Confessor, *Four Hundred Texts on Love* 2.32 (*Philokalia* 2:51; Greek 2:19).

[7]Of course, the effects of sin are decisively healed only through the Resurrection of Christ.

- The structure of a compassionate disposition: First, as we have seen repeatedly, compassion is a way of orienting ourselves to others—a fundamental openness to others—in which we are willing to bear with them and act for their sakes and affirm them in the fullness of their humanity and in their uniqueness as persons. As a disposition, it is a steadfast tendency to think, act, and live in a certain way. Drawing on a key text from the *Testament of Zebulon*, in the first part of this section, I will show that the structure of the disposition of compassion has three central aspects:

    (a) it is a dispositional openness, hospitality, and receptiveness towards others;[8]

    (b) it is constituted by an alert sensitivity to suffering that leads one to bear with and suffer with others;[9] and

    (c) it is manifest without any examination or judgment about others.[10]

This last feature of compassion is crucial in distinguishing compassion from pity. Also, in discussing compassion as an alert sensitivity to suffering, I will offer a brief excursus on the relation between compassion and tears since tears and sorrow often accompany a compassionate response to suffering.

- Perfecting a compassionate disposition: It is one thing to have a disposition, it is another to try to perfect it. I will begin this part with a brief discussion on the role of humility in perfecting the disposition of compassion. After that, I will discuss two chief traits for perfecting compassion that are found in the Orthodox Christian tradition: dispassion and coming to terms with human vulnerability.

    First, compassion in any full sense requires attaining a state of dispassion. Acquiring dispassion is vital in centering ourselves on God and on turning us away from the toxic passions that lead us to be indifferent to others or simply manipulate them for our own purposes.

    Second, I will develop a fundamental dimension of vulnerability that belongs to us simply as created beings independently of whether we had ever sinned. I will do this by exploring a position in the Orthodox Christian tradition that takes the Incarnation—and thus God's compassion and mercy— to be embedded in the very creation of things rather than just as

[8]See pp. 192–93 below.
[9]See pp. 193–97 below.
[10]See pp. 197–200 below.

a response to sin. This discussion will in fact broaden the framework I will sketch in the first section of this chapter that understands the Incarnation and compassion as a response to sin.[11]

The third and final section of the chapter, Compassion as a Virtue, develops the sense in which a compassionate disposition is a virtue—a steadfast character trait that is integral to our natural well-being as well as our salvation and deification. There are five parts to this section.

- First, as I pointed out earlier, virtue involves the intentions or reasons for action. Virtue is not simply a matter of a certain kind of action. Pity and compassion, as we have seen, differ in their intentions but not necessarily in particular actions. But are acting for the sake of others and for our own sake intrinsically opposed? Some think they are. Hence, I will sketch two diametrically opposing views—psychological egoism and pure altruism[12]—that deny we can simultaneously act for our own interests and the interests of others. Neither of those views, however, fits with the idea of compassion as a virtue: We are to extend compassion for the sake of others without any hope of reward, yet in doing so we promote our own human flourishing and efforts to attain to a likeness to Christ.

- In the second part of this section,[13] I will lay out the notion of virtue as a stable character trait that conforms to our nature and is vital for our own holistic flourishing or well-being and deification. I will draw on a key text of St John Chrysostom, who distinguishes between virtue as intrinsically good independent of "rewards" (virtue as beautiful in itself) and virtue as an instrumental good employed only to obtain certain "prizes."

- In the third part of this section, I will discuss two "prizes" within the patristic tradition for compassionate assistance to others that are basically self-interested and amount to pity. One presumed prize arises from fear of punishment; namely, failure to be compassionate will merit some extrinsic punishment by God while being compassionate will merit the prize of avoiding such punishment. Another presumed prize is redemptive

---

[11]This, however, is the dominant view one finds in much Orthodox Christian theology, liturgical texts, and hymns.

[12]Pure altruism is the view that in acting for the interests of others, one has utterly no regard for one's own interests.

[13]See pp. 213–7 below.

almsgiving;[14] namely, being compassionate somehow provides "merits" for the forgiveness of past sins. I will discuss how pursuing only these prizes, or prizes like them, in assisting others can amount to pity, as I am using the term, and not compassion.

- The fourth part of the section will examine what it means to pursue a compassionate virtue simply for the sake of itself or as beautiful for itself. This analysis will also resolve the question as to whether we can be compassionate for the sake of others while simultaneously and consciously contributing to our own well-being and salvation.[15]

- The fifth part of this section will develop a specifically Orthodox Christian understanding of the virtue of compassion. The discussion of compassion to this point can apply with some modifications to a strictly natural compassion—the capacity for compassion that we have by nature—as well as a Christian expression of compassion. In the latter case, compassion explicitly or consciously arises out of and is oriented towards a love for God and Christ and our desire to imitate that love in acting for the sake of others. Hence, I will explore the specifically Orthodox Christian sense of the virtue of compassion: being moved by compassion for the sake of Christ and our fellow humans that is integral to attaining to a likeness to God: becoming a living icon of Christ.[16]

Preliminary Considerations

The Wages of Sin, Repentance, and Compassion

After he finished creating the cosmos, God declared it to be good.[17] The initial goodness of creation meant that humans and the cosmos were placed on a path for bringing them into the fullness of life as the fullness of an ever-living communion

---

[14]See pp. 221–25 below.

[15]See pp. 225–27 below.

[16]See pp. 227–33. The merciful heart for St Isaac the Syrian extends compassion and mercy to all of creation or at least all living things and not only our fellow human beings. Zebulun provides an echo of this view, as we will see. Nevertheless, for this project, I am focusing on compassion specifically directed to all human beings. Surely, we can, and hopefully do and should, show compassion to beings that are not human. But that means we must view them as valuable in and of themselves and not merely as things to serve human interests. Exploring that view in the Orthodox Christian tradition is simply beyond the scope of the present work. If the reader is interested in my own view on this matter, please see my article: "Humans and Animals: Compassion and Dominion," *Anglican Theological Review* 63 (1981): 259–72.

[17]Gen 1.31.

with God and one another. Created in the image and according to the likeness of God and placed in the Garden of Eden, the first humans were good but not fully perfected. They were like children according to some Church Fathers.[18] Created with free will, their own free acceptance of their dependence on God as well as their faith and trust in him was crucial to their own development.[19] When he gave Adam the command that allowed him and anyone else to eat of any tree in the garden except the tree of the knowledge of good and evil, God gave them the option to remain faithful to him or to go their own way—that is, to die.[20] In choosing to sin, Adam and Eve essentially chose to pursue their life independently of God. That is, they attempted to become gods or god-like on their own.[21] The disastrous effect of that choice, as God warned, was death: a spiritual death or voluntary separation from God[22] and the unleashing of a Pandora's Box of self-aggrandizing passions that drove them away from God. They sealed their fate, as St Symeon the New Theologian points out, by doubling down on their initial transgression and refusing to repent and seek forgiveness when God offered them the chance to do so.[23]

Their sin broke up a life-giving relation between them and God, and it simultaneously poisoned their own relation to one another. Rather than personally accepting responsibility for their choice, they played the "blame game" when God offered them the opportunity to repent. Adam blamed Eve and implicitly blamed God for creating Eve. Eve blamed the serpent.[24] Their relation with the world around them was also disrupted. They were banished from paradise[25] because they both, however unwittingly, rejected living there. Their initial spiritual death was subsequently followed by a physical death in which the body and soul were separated when the body perished. The wages, or consequences, of this sin was

---

[18]Irenaeus, *Against Heresies* 4.38.1 (ANF 1, 521; *Sources chrétiennnes* 100:952–56). Text is cited in M. C. Steenberg, "Children in Paradise: Adam and Eve as 'Infants' in Irenaeus of Lyons," *Journal of Early Christian Studies* 12.1 (2004): 1–35, which provides a detailed discussion of this topic. See also, Theophilus, "Theophilus to Autolycus" 2.25 (ANF 2:104; PG 6:1092).

[19]The Greek word for sin, *hamartia,* basically means to miss the mark or to wander off target. In its deepest reality, sinfulness amounts to idolatry: choosing something or someone other than God as the ultimate center of one's life.

[20]Gen 2.17.

[21]Gen 3.1–6.

[22]Gen 2.17. See, Maximus the Confessor, *Four Hundred Texts on Love,* 2.93 (*Philokalia* 2:65; Greek 2:27).

[23]Symeon the New Theologian, *Homily* 66 (*The Banishment and Repentance of Adam and Every Christian*), in *The First Created Man,* trans. Seraphim Rose (Platina, CA: St Herman of Alaska Brotherhood, 2001), 107–11.

[24]Gen 3.11–13.

[25]Gen 3.22–23.

actual corruption and death for themselves and for all humanity; this is called Ancestral Sin in the Orthodox Christian tradition.[26] The tragedy and horror of this sin—the radical destruction of communion (*koinōnia*) between people and God and among people—is seen almost immediately in fratricide: Cain's jealous murder of his brother Abel.[27]

In the Orthodox Christian faith, God's response to this tragedy through the Incarnation is fundamentally therapeutic and rehabilitative (restorative) in nature. Our response to the gift of the Incarnation is fundamentally a matter of repentance (*metanoia*)—the willingness to undergo the lifelong process of a holistic transformation of our lives that aims, with God's grace, to rebuild and renew the relationships between ourselves and God—the Trinity—and Christ, ourselves and our fellow humans, ourselves and the created world, and our own relation to our own self.[28]

The Heart-Centered Struggle between Good and Evil

The Orthodox Christian faith stresses the centrality of the heart in our lives, especially in the activity of repentance. It is not simply the seat of emotions but the holistic center of our existence: "the meeting place between the Divine and the human, between the spiritual and the physical, between God's grace and our freedom ... the place of Divine Indwelling."[29] It was created to be a wellspring of life. Corrupted by sin, however, it is a toxic source of passions that destroy us. The heart (*kardia*) is where we must center ourselves in our engagement with God and

---

[26]Cf. Rom 5.12. This understanding of sin stands in marked contrast to the notion of Original Sin, a guilt that we all inherit from Adam and Eve. See Michael Prokurat, et al., *Historical Dictionary of the Orthodox Church,* 29. For a very extensive analysis of these two models and the differences between them, see the three-part article: David Weaver, "From Paul to Augustine: Romans 5.12 in Early Christian Exegesis," *St Vladimir's Theological Quarterly* 27.3 (1983): 187–206; "The Exegesis of Romans 5.12 among the Greek Fathers and Its Implication for the Doctrine of Original Sin: The 5th–12th Centuries, Pt 2," *St Vladimir's Theological Quarterly* 29.2 (1985): 133–59; and "The Exegesis of Romans 5.12 among the Greek Fathers and Its Implication for the Doctrine of Original Sin: The 5th–12th Centuries, Pt 3," *St Vladimir's Theological Quarterly* 29.3 (1985): 231–57.

[27]Gen 4.8.

[28]Cf. Bobrinskoy, *Compassion,* 126–7.

[29]Bishop Kallistos (Ware), "Enter the Heart," 8. Please see the earlier discussion in Chapter 2, pp. 68–73, about the *splanchna* (viscera) and *kardia* (heart). As a reminder: while *splanchna* and *kardia* are not identical, the *splanchna* include the heart, and modern translations of the New Testament at times render *splanchna* as "heart" rather than "bowels." However, the understanding of the heart (*kardia*) in the Orthodox Christian tradition is more holistic—uniting body, soul, and spirit—than *splanchna*. In going through the chapter, the reader should bear in mind the difference yet overlap between *splanchna* and *kardia*. Also, while "bowels" is used in the translation of *splanchna* is some quotations, the reader should bear in mind that "bowels" in this context has the sense of viscera, as I discussed in Chapter 2, and not simply the intestinal tract.

with one another—the merciful, compassionate heart that St Isaac of Nineveh describes.[30] As we will see, this is particularly important since compassion fundamentally counters those visceral stances by which we despise, denigrate, or stigmatize other people.

Let me turn, then, to a brief discussion of compassion and the toxic passions that "dwell" in the viscera or "bowels," and heart: e.g., the sclerotic viscera of the envious person, the voracious viscera and heart of the predatory person, the "bowels" of mercy—the visceral mercy—of the compassionate person; that is, heart-motivated compassion. Of course, in the physiological sense, sclerosis or hardening can affect all of the organs in the viscera including the heart. In the transferred sense, visceral sclerosis[31] refers to an affective and cognitive hardening by which we recoil from others and block developing any sense of community or fellowship (*koinōnia*) with them through stances such as:

- indifference towards people (e.g., the rich man's attitude towards Lazarus);

- objectification of people as mere use objects (e.g., Zacchaeus' greed before his encounter with Christ);

- striking back aggressively to harm people (e.g., think of how people strike back at others whom they hate);

- delegitimating and/or marginalizing people (e.g., through stigmatization and denigration towards others that can result in social isolation and persecution of them when, as marginalized, they live at the fringes of society or are placed in ghettos, as was the case of the Jews in Nazi Germany);

- Condescending pity that denigrates those who are the objects of pity (e.g., Lt Hofmiller's reduction of Edith to "the crippled girl" who, like all disabled people, he believed was incapable of showing genuine love).

Affective and cognitive sclerosis of the viscera and the heart is diametrically opposed to the neighborliness towards others that the good Samaritan shows to the stranger who was beaten. That is, compassion arises out of a visceral and

[30]Isaac of Nineveh, *Mystic Treaties* 74 (*Mystic Treatises*, 341). See Chapter 2, p. 68 for the text.

[31]In Scripture and in the patristic tradition, the Greek phrase for a hardened heart (*sklērokardia*) normally seems to refer to obstinacy with respect to God. The English term "hardhearted," however, can refer to those who lack any sense of sympathy or compassion for others. The English term takes on a meaning that the Greek above does not seem to have. See below, p. 184, for the use of a hard heart in this sense in the *Testaments of the Twelve Patriarchs*.

heartfelt, better motivated, openness to others that acts for the sake of others. It lies at the basis of neighborliness towards people. We often think of compassion as an emotion. Today, we might locate the source of emotions in the brain and suspect that locating or referring emotions to our viscera or the heart is an outdated view of human emotions and affectivity. But regardless of the neurological source of our emotions, there is a good experiential reason to keep our discussion of compassion and its contrast to other affective states linked to a traditional focus on the viscera (*splanchna*) or the heart (*kardia*).

When I studied classical piano many years ago, my teacher would often try to pry me loose from overly technical but rather lifeless performances by telling me to play more musically. In part, she was telling me to play with more feeling. But more fundamentally, she was telling me to get out of my head and center myself mid-body because the energy for a musical performance is visceral and affective in nature and not just head-oriented. This does not mean that musical performance is located in irrational emotions, for there is a musical intelligence that goes with musical playing but it is not the intelligence of ordinary discursive or analytical reasoning.[32]

More to the point: to play musically requires that one be centered, as it were, mid-body so that the musical energy has a holistic character to it. Like musical energy, the energy of compassion—rooted in the presence of the Holy Spirit in the heart—is also centered "mid-body": the Greek verb "moved by compassion" (*splanchnizomai*) refers to an affective movement of the viscera (*splanchna*). Developing a compassionate disposition requires becoming centered in the heart, as the Orthodox Christian tradition understands it, so that body, mind, and spirit are united in a holistic dispositional orientation towards others for their sake. In developing this sort of disposition, one must strive for dispassion in order to counter and overcome all kinds of self-aggrandizing and "other-negating" visceral passions that wreak havoc upon us and those around us as well as separate us from God.

Why should we care about this? Surely, the claims of justice for equality, fairness, and impartiality can be met by simply rationally affirming that the equality of all human beings is rooted in a common human nature. That would be sufficient if history were not littered with any number of people and groups who rationally or dogmatically proclaim the equality of all people while accepting all

---

[32]You can conceptually analyze a musical score from now until the end of time and never be able to make the simplest decision about phrasing. That comes only by playing and listening to the music, whether mentally or in actual performance.

kinds of denigrating and invidious distinctions about various groups of people
that undermine or even deny them the dignity and equality of honor (*homotimos*) or "primary equality of rights" (*protē isonomia*)[33] that are the foundation
of treating people justly. The source of these invidious distinctions and stigmas
is not solely rational or located in the "head"; it is profoundly visceral and affective. One need simply listen to the toxic, visceral language that has pervaded and
corrupted social and political discourse in the United States in recent years to
verify this assertion. Compassion for others, I will suggest, provides a powerful
lived, visceral, or affective and embodied antidote to the profoundly toxic, negative, destructive and visceral energy of denigration that reason and concepts by
themselves do not provide.

We get a very good illustration of how these toxic passions produce sclerotic
hearts and viscera by initially looking at several toxic visceral responses described
in the *Testaments of the Twelve Patriarchs* by some of Zebulun's brothers. They
give an apt illustration of what the lack of compassion involves. Zebulun's brother
Simeon, for example, confesses to murderous envy towards his brother Joseph:

> My heart (*kardia*) was hard (*sklēra*); my liver was immovable (*akinēta*); and
> my bowels (*splanchna*) were without sympathy (*asympathēs*, or compassion-
> less) because valor (*andreia*, or courage)[34] also has been given from the Most
> High to men, in their souls and in their bodies. And at that time I was jealous
> of Joseph, because our father loved him; and I set my liver against him to kill
> him because the prince of deceit sent the spirit of jealousy and blinded my
> mind so that I did not regard him as a brother and did not spare Jacob my
> father.[35]

Unable to experience any *sympatheia* for Joseph, Simeon has no compassion
for him. His visceral envy precludes his ability to behold Joseph as his brother.[36]
This affective visceral hardness drives the animosity towards Joseph by some of
the other brothers. Filled with hatred and anger towards Joseph, Gad confesses
the constant desire to murder Joseph because he believes that Joseph is favored by
his father and because of Joseph's dreams:

[33]See Chapter 2, p. 57 n. 81.

[34]One might wonder whether this sort of "courage" in battle leads to a vindictiveness and vengeance that
violates any respect for the people one fights in battle.

[35]*Testament of Simeon* 2.2–7 (Testaments 111; Greek 16).

[36]Later in his Testament, Simeon regrets this action, cautions his children against envy, and praises Joseph
for being a good and compassionate person (*Testament of Simeon* 4.4 [*Testaments* 115; Greek 19–20]).

And the spirit of hatred was in me; and I did not want to see Joseph, neither with the eyes nor with the ears.... Now I confess my sin, children, that very often I wanted to kill him, because I hated him in my soul, and there was in me altogether no mercy (*eleos*) towards him.[37]

Driven by covetousness, Gad and Dan are more than willing to sell Joseph into slavery and keep an inordinate share of the proceeds.[38] The sclerotic affective hardness in these individuals displays an array of what we might call aggressive and hostile self-aggrandizing and other-rejecting passions. Simeon's lack of sympathy is more fundamental than a failure of "fellow-feeling." It marks a substantive rejection and disaffiliation of Joseph as a brother. The disaffiliating "energy" of Simeon's envy, which dehumanizes Joseph in Simeon's eyes—he is no longer a "brother"—"clears the way" for unjust aggressive actions towards Joseph and Jacob.

While "brother" in these texts is used in the ordinary familial sense, it is clear that when such passions are directed to other people who are unrelated, they effectively prevent interaction with them as fellow humans—as our brothers and sisters. Lack of sympathy or compassion (*asympatheia*), then, precludes any sense of communion or fellowship (*koinōnia*) with others. The visceral hardness that underlies this *asympatheia* amounts to an affective and cognitive delegitimizing of people that can express itself in cold, calculated actions or spontaneous actions to destroy, consume, and exploit others. It can also render people utterly indifferent to others who suffer or are in distress. We will see the stark contrast between these toxic passions and Zebulun's compassion when I discuss compassion as a disposition.

Compassion as a Simple Emotional Response to Another's Suffering

What about compassion? On the one hand, compassion or pity can be viewed as a simple but passionate, gut-wrenching feeling of distress at another person's affliction.[39] Whatever assistance is offered is largely automatic or instinctual. Help might be offered but without any clear intention to help. Or, compassion might be a strong emotional state that wells up at times within us that moves us,

---

[37] *Testament of Gad* 1.9–2.2 (*Testaments* 321; Greek 160).

[38] *Testament of Gad* 2.1 (*Testaments* 321; Greek 160) and *Testament of Dan* 1.4–5 (*Testaments* 277; Greek 131).

[39] For a literary portrayal of this sort of pity that is very close to Zebulun's description below, see Elizbeth Von Arnim, *The Princess Priscilla's Fortnight* (New York: Charles Scribner's Sons, 1914), 255.

with some degree of understanding and intentionality, to assist others.[40] More fundamentally, compassion might be a stable and persistent dispositional stance towards others. The *Testament of Zebulun* presents descriptions of the first and the last views.

The first description of compassion as a simple, raw emotion seems to describe Zebulun's initial reaction of extreme agitation in response his brothers' attempt to kill Joseph. In response to Joseph's requests to his brothers to show him mercy and compassion for his father's feelings, Zebulun indicates that he was moved to *oiktos* and that he began to weep (or, *oiktos* overcame my heart).[41] He then continued: "My liver was poured out within me in and the whole substance of my feelings (*splanchna* or, viscera) was weakened up to my soul."[42] He then notes that he wept along with Joseph and that "my heart throbbed and the joints of my body were shaken and I was not able to stand."[43]

It is not completely clear whether Zebulun is describing what we might call a powerful, largely involuntarily, gut-wrenching, reaction of grief and pain that overwhelmed him or what might be described as compassion or pity. The key to understanding this reaction depends on the meaning of *oiktos*. The term can mean either lamentation and weeping, or pity, or compassion.[44]

The variant reading—*oiktos* overcame my heart—seems to fit with Zebulun's own description of his liver pouring out of him. Since the liver was the organ for fighting, Zebulun indicates that the fight, quite literally, went out of him. Being utterly overwhelmed by his emotions, he was simply rendered immobile and was unable even to get up. His weeping with Joseph would seem to be an almost uncontrollable sobbing at the same time that Joseph is sobbing. Zebulun does not describe himself as having sympathy with Joseph in the sense that his sobbing is the kind of intentional suffering with or bearing another's suffering that goes along with compassion.

On one reading of the text, Zebulun's response lacks the kind of intentionality that we normally think belongs to compassion: compassion moves one to deliberately render assistance to someone for that person's sake. Zebulun's reaction, however, seems to preclude any such assistance, since he is largely paralyzed, as it were, because of his reaction, more precisely his body's reaction, to this event.

[40] I focused on this sense of compassion in Chapter 2.
[41] Variant reading: *Testaments* (Greek) 118, n. 22.
[42] *Testament of Zebulun* 2.4 (*Testaments* 258 mod.; Greek 118).
[43] *Testament of Zebulun* 2.5 (*Testaments* 258; Greek 118).
[44] *Testaments* (English) 259, n. 2,4.

Zebulun indicates that he wept with Joseph. When Joseph sees that Zebulun is weeping with him, Joseph runs and hides behind Zebulun for protection. And indeed when Ruben sees them both weeping together, he indicates that they should not kill Joseph but throw him in a dry well until they decide what to do with them.[45] But Zebulun does not describe this "weeping with" Joseph as a result of or for the sake of some kind of *sympatheia* or suffering with and on behalf of Joseph, although it might be.[46] If *oiktos* in this text means compassion or pity, it seems to be "little more than instinctive distress caused by, rather than at, the suffering of others."[47]

On the other hand, prior to describing this scene, Zebulun indicates that through many tears he warned his brothers against harming Joseph.[48] This seems to suggest a minimal intentionality to his extreme grief and weeping. If so, his compassionate reaction of grief—even though it immobilized him—is in effect an inchoate protest against the injustice of his brothers' plan to murder Joseph. In either event, Zebulun seems to be describing compassion or pity (*oiktos*) as an almost involuntary, spontaneous reaction of pain and grief to someone's affliction.[49] Hence, when taken as a simple, non-cognitive emotion, compassion is neither the affective state that we described in Chapter 2, and certainly not something that would qualify as a disposition.

Compassion as a Disposition

The Nature of a Disposition

In Chapter 1, I indicated that a disposition was a settled state or condition of a person. Before proceeding to the analysis of compassion as a disposition, let me expand upon what a disposition is. Dispositions typically refer to attitudes, mental states, or any of the ways in which we typically and consistently orient ourselves to the world, to ourselves, or to God. Dispositions might be "inherent" in a person. Someone might have always had a cheery disposition, or be simply a mean-tempered person. I will not get bogged down in a nature/nurture argument

---

[45] *Testament of Zebulun* 2.5–7 (*Testaments* 258; Greek 118–19).

[46] For a somewhat similar analysis of this section of Zebulun's account, see Françoise Mirguet, *An Early History of Compassion*, 51–52.

[47] Roger Crisp, "Compassion and Beyond," *Ethical Theory and Moral Practice* 11 (2008): 240. Crisp thinks this describes the "compassion" that babies can show in response to the crying of other babies.

[48] *Testament of Zebulun* 1.7 (*Testaments* 256; Greek 117).

[49] *Oiktos* need not be limited to this minimalist conception of compassion. Cf. the use of this term in hymns H-5, H-6, H-7, H-21, and H-26 where it refers to Christ's compassion.

about the sources of dispositions. I am merely noting that some people have dispositions that have a lifelong and an evidently unlearned character about them. Some dispositions, on the other hand, are learned. To become adept at being a philosopher, I had to train myself to develop critical and analytical attitudes that consistently approached problems and arguments employing certain methods, attitudes, and so forth. We can get a more developed idea of the nature of a disposition by contrasting a disposition with some examples of what would not count as a disposition. I will use a compassionate disposition as an example.

First, suppose someone who is not compassionate—that is, not a compassionate person—performs compassionate actions. To begin: What do we mean when we call someone a compassionate person in the sense that they have a compassionate disposition? We regard others as compassionate persons because that is a settled way in which they orient themselves to others. So too, we regard others as truthful persons because their settled, predominant tendency or attitude is to tell the truth to people. People's dispositions are, if you will, the "default" ways—the predominant ways—in which they orient themselves to the world around them or to God.

People who are not compassionate might be simply indifferent to compassion because they are indifferent to suffering, or they might be hostile to compassion because they believe it is a weakness or mistake to treat people compassionately.[50] We do not observe them frequently manifesting compassion to people nor would they acknowledge that they do so.

It is entirely possible, of course, that such people may on occasion act compassionately. Their compassion might be a simple raw emotion of the type Zebulun experienced when Joseph was threatened. Of course, compassion in any robust sense is not just about an action but about the intentions that direct the action. So this occasional compassionate action might be the sort of affective response to someone we discussed in Chapter 2. The people we are describing might be so affected by a particular occasion of distress, that their awareness of that distress leads them to deliberately care for someone else for that person's sake. There is no reason why people who are not compassionate, as I have characterized, might for some reason and in some situations manifest compassion. But if such people manifest compassion only sporadically or occasionally, it seems clear that they

---

[50]Of course, if people are not compassionate persons, in the sense that they never do anything compassionate or never have any compassionate feelings or affective states, then by definition, they could never act compassionately.

do not have a compassionate disposition and are not compassionate people. Of course, if these compassionate actions become more settled and consciously supported by the affective and cognitive states that belong to compassion, then the person may be on the way to developing a compassionate disposition or becoming a compassionate person.

Second, suppose someone is a compassionate person but at times does not treat people compassionately. In one case, there are times when, despite my compassion for other peoples' distress, I am precluded from showing compassion to them. I might have a legal obligation to punish someone. Even though I am moved by compassion for that person's situation and extenuating circumstances, my legal obligations may preclude me from treating him or her in a way that I believe would manifest compassion. I will discuss some other examples like this in Chapter 6 on the relation between compassion and justice. In a second case, I may not manifest compassion to someone because I think such compassion would be a mistake. For example, if what I would regard as a compassionate response to someone would only enable that person to perpetuate self-destructive behavior, I might not treat him or her in what I would regard as a compassionate manner. That raises the complex issue as to whether there are limits to compassion. I will also discuss this issue in Chapter 6.

To sum up this example: if there are limits or constraints on manifesting compassion, then persons who are otherwise compassionate by disposition may determine that it is not good for them to act on their compassion, or they may accept that they are precluded by other responsibilities from manifesting a compassionate response.[51] But these sorts of situations clearly do not mean that such persons cease to have a compassionate disposition as the predominant way in which they orient themselves to other people.

Third, people who are devoted to caring for people in a compassionate manner may suffer from compassion fatigue: the physical and mental exhaustion and even the inability to continue caring for people that results from extended experience of and care for people suffering from traumas, disasters, prolonged ill health, or other emergencies. This sort of fatigue, sadly, affects first responders, e.g., in dealing with the prolonged covid pandemic. Whether this sort of fatigue permanently undermines a compassionate disposition depends on a number of

---

[51]This does not mean that anyone is ever justified in not holistically affirming others in their humanity and in their uniqueness as persons.

factors both personal and institutional—namely, whether assistance and support is provided to first responders to care for themselves.[52]

Fourth and finally: the more likely reason that some people who are compassionate might treat some other people without compassion is that having a compassionate disposition does not mean that they have a perfect compassionate disposition. Our sinfulness can easily get in the way of our attempt to manifest compassion. We may at times fail to treat people compassionately even though we normally would. For example, our anger at them gets in the way of our compassion for them; they might do something that "pushes a button" that leads us to push them away, and so forth. Actions like this do not preclude people from having a compassionate disposition: a settled and default orientation to others. It does mean that they have to work to perfect that disposition, so they are not tripped up by events or feelings or thoughts that lead them away from being compassionate. For Orthodox Christians, this work would be part of the process of repentance. Of course, if their desire to be compassionate is constantly tripped up by events, feelings, or thoughts, we might say they have a desire to be compassionate that has not yet developed into a compassionate disposition.

Dispositions and virtues are not unconditional—that is, it is not the case that you either have them perfectly or you do not have them at all. All of us can have stronger or weaker dispositions and virtues. But at the very least, for example, if we look at a range of possible responses to suffering such as pity, compassion, indifference, and hostility, one would expect people with a compassionate disposition to respond to suffering in a compassionate manner[53]—both in actions and in their attitudes and intentions—consistently and reliably. Their response to suffering by default would be a compassionate response. We can likely give clear examples of people who have compassionate dispositions and of people who do not have such dispositions. But determining borderline cases—the point at which a compassionate disposition "fizzles out" or has not yet been reached—is likely a grey area.

As we proceed, please remember that I am developing the structure of a compassionate disposition in terms of what I believe is fundamental and essential to such a disposition and is manifest in a robust and steadfast manner, as we saw in

---

[52]For an excellent discussion of this issue, see Fiona Cocker and Nerida Joss, "Compassion Fatigue among Healthcare, Emergency and Community Service Workers: A Systematic Review," *International Journal of Environmental Research and Public Health* 13.6, 618, <https://doi.org/10.3390/ijerph13060618>, July 20, 2021. See Chapter 6, pp. 246–47.

[53]What that involves is the topic of the next part of this section.

Chapter 4 with Christ, the Theotokos, and various saints. Still, I am certainly not trying to portray a compassionate disposition in an absolute sense; namely, people either have that disposition perfectly or they do not have it at all.

The Structure of a Compassionate Disposition

Let me now turn to the analysis of the structure of compassion as a disposition. A key text from the *Testament of Zebulun* will anchor my discussion in this section. In contrast to Zebulun's initial description of his compassion, his subsequent exhortation to his sons to treat all people with compassion (*eusplanchnia*) displays a considerably more sophisticated description of compassion that is far more akin to the ways in which the Synoptic Gospels describe Christ, and in which Christ himself portrays certain characters in parables, as moved by compassion: for example, the parable of the good Samaritan and the parable of the prodigal son. The passage is rather long, but Zebulun's discussion is perhaps one of the most extended descriptions of compassion from this period and well beyond. Also, he presents those to whom he manifests compassion simply as people in need. He does not undertake the sort of ghoulish, tragic presentation of poor and other people one finds later in the fourth century. He does not dramatically portray the distress of the people he feeds in order to move his sons or anyone else to a sense of compassion.

Please note that I am leaving the Greek terms below marked with an asterisk (*) untranslated for the moment. I will unpack their meaning in the discussion following this text. From the *Testament of Zebulun* concerning mercy and compassion:

> 5.1 And now, my children, I bid you to keep the commands of the Lord, and to show mercy (*poiein eleos*) upon your neighbor, and to have compassion (*echein eusplanchnian*) towards all, not towards humans only, but also towards animals without reason....[54]

> 6.1–5. I was the first who made a boat to sail upon the sea, for the Lord gave me understanding and wisdom therein. I let down a rudder behind it, and I

[54]Zebulun's reference to animals and perhaps the rest of creation echo themes found in other Jewish texts. For example, Philo the Jew describes Moses as legislating or commanding humanity or kindness (*philanthrōpia*) not only to humans but to animals, and even to plants. Philo of Alexandria, *On Virtues* [*De virtutibus*], *Humanity* [*Philanthrōpia*] 15, 16, 18–20. Philo of Alexandria, *On Virtues, Introduction, Translation, and Commentary*, Walter Wilson, trans. (Leiden: Brill, 2011), 66–73. See *Testaments* (English), 264, n. 5 ,1 for a discussion of this issue.

stretched a sail on an upright mast in the midst. Sailing in it along the shores, I caught fish for my father's house until we went into Egypt; and being moved by compassion (*splanchnizomenos*), I gave of my fish to every person who was a stranger. And if someone was a stranger, or sick, or aged, I boiled the fish and dressed them well, and offered them to all people as every person had need, (*synagōn**) and (*sympaschōn**). . . .

7.2 Do you therefore, my children, from what God gives to you, be moved with compassion to show mercy (*splanchnizomenoi eleate*) *adiakritōs** to all people. Give to every person with a good heart. And if for a time you do nothing to give the person who is in need, *sympaschete** [with him] with bowels of mercy (*splanchnois eleous* or a visceral mercy). [55]

DISPOSITIONAL HOSPITALITY

Three core characteristics and features of compassion are suggested by the meaning of the terms *synagōn*, *sympaschōn* (and the related term *sympatheia*), and *adiakritōs*. The Greek word *synagōn* usually has the sense of bringing people together. A synagogue, for example, is a place where people come together for worship. One might think that Zebulun is bringing people together to organize a meal program for the purpose of feeding them. But in this particular text, *synagōn* appears to be connected with the distinctive use of the term in Matthew 25, the parable of the last judgment. To the "sheep" (those who are righteous or just) Christ says that when he was a stranger (*xenos*), they took him in or welcomed him (*synēgagete*).[56] But to the "goats," he says they did not welcome him and take him in.[57] They made no effort to be a neighbor (*plēsion*) to Christ. The sheep, on the other hand, came towards him (*ēlthen pros*) as a neighbor (*plēsion*);[58] the goats did not. *Synagōn* in this sense is an openness to others in which one comes towards them, or welcomes them,[59] in a gesture of support. *Synagōn* here is hospitality (*philo-xenia*) in the literal sense: love of the stranger. For Zebulun this *synagōn*

---

[55] *Testament of Zebulun 5.1, 6.1–5, and 7.2 (Testaments 263, 265 mod.; Greek 123, 124–25).*

[56] Mt 15.35.

[57] Mt 25.43.

[58] So too, when the good Samaritan is moved by compassion on seeing the man beaten by the side of the road, he comes towards (*proselthōn*) him (Lk 10.34) as a neighbor (*plēsion*). Remember, the point of this parable is to show the young man what is involved in being a neighbor: not just one who is nearby others but one who comes towards others.

[59] This is how *synagōn* is translated in *Testaments* (English) 265.

extends to everyone. The closest word we might find in Greek is *phil-anthrōpia* in the sense of a dispositional kindness or humanity towards others.

Being moved by compassion is fundamentally a dispositional movement towards others in a gesture of friendship and hospitality. Notice that Zebulun gives fish to everyone he encounters that has need of food while he is sailing along the shores. He indicates a persistent attentiveness to people who might need fish. That persistent attentiveness is the sign of an underlying dispositional orientation to others. It emerges from the viscera and a heart that, even if grieving over the suffering of others, are open to and receptive of others. After all, *splanch-nizomai* has the transferred or metaphorical sense of an affective movement of the viscera in which we go out to others in order to assist them. If this seems a bit fanciful, then simply contrast the affective openness and receptiveness you might feel towards a good friend or someone you seek to comfort with the constricted visceral recoiling against or aggressiveness towards those whom you fear, despise, or who threaten to harm you.[60] The Dalai Lama, it is worth noting, observes that his compassion towards all people always involves greeting every person as if they were old friends.[61]

AN ALERT SENSITIVITY TO SUFFERING THAT
MOVES ONE TO SUFFER OR BEAR WITH OTHERS

The dispositional openness to others in compassion is grounded in a sympathy (*sympatheia*) for others that is an alert sensitivity to the suffering of others, but that is not threatened by that suffering. Zebulun, like the good Samaritan, is aware of his surroundings and alert to people who are suffering or in distress. This sensitivity to suffering moves him towards others to assist them. Zebulun offered fish to "all people as every person had need . . . *sympaschōn* . . ." In using this word, Zebulun indicates that he is literally "suffering with those" (*sym-paschō*) to whom he not only gives fish but he also prepares the fish he gives.[62] This term is related to *sym-patheia* but it has the explicit sense of opening oneself to the suffering of

---

[60]There is, of course, a kind of visceral openness of the predator or manipulator. That openness, however, is a voracious, dissembling openness that wants to consume, exploit, or subjugate others. Being moved by this sort of voraciousness, this person's hands might be open to the other but merely as a kind of bait to draw the other person close enough so that the open hand can be closed in order to aggressively snatch them.

[61]Tezin Gyatso, "Compassion and the Individual," <http://www.dalailama.com/messages/compassion>, April 20, 2020

[62]The term can also have the sense of "having compassion" on people or "having sympathy" with them. See ANF 8:24 and *Testaments* 265 respectively.

others in the sense of bearing with them while assisting them. It also means that Zebulun does not flee or retreat from others.[63]

Clearly Zebulun is not undertaking the suffering of others by making himself hungry and depriving himself of food. Rather, he bears with them in the sense that he turns away from what he has been doing (catching fish) to attend to them. He does not just give people raw fish; he cleans, prepares, and serves the fish when needed. Moreover, he is open and responsive to the suffering and distress others experience. In this suffering or bearing with them, he creates, if only for a brief moment, some sense of community or fellowship (*koinōnia*) or, to use a modern term, a sense of solidarity with them.[64]

So far, we have two basic features of being moved by compassion: compassion is (a) a dispositional openness or hospitality to others in which one comes towards people; and (b) a sensitivity to suffering that prompts a willingness to bear or suffer with people in their suffering while not retreating or fleeing from them by rejecting them or simply passing them by. Compassion, then, refers to affective and embodied dispositions or orientations that move individuals out beyond themselves towards others in a welcoming, open-handed gesture of hospitality and service.

Excursus on Compassion and Tears

Although Zebulun portrays his compassion for people as a movement towards others that acts on their behalf, there are times when he has nothing to give them and is unable to assist them. So, he writes:

> If for a time you do not have anything to give the person who is in need, suffer with him in bowels of mercy [*sympaschete autō en splanchnois eleous*]. I know that (once) my hand did not find anything for the present to give to him who was in need, and for seven stadia I walked with him and wept and my bowels were moved towards him in sympathy [*sympatheia,* or compassion].[65]

---

[63] *Testaments* 265 translate *sympaschōn* as "having sympathy."

[64] See Françoise Mirguet, *An Early History of Compassion,* 53, who makes a similar point in reference to Zebulun's description of how he comports himself towards others when he has nothing to give them. I discuss this section of the *Testament* below, pp. 194–97. Recall Fr Florovsky's observation about the deep meaning of *eleēmosynē,* Chapter 3, p. 168.

[65] *Testament of Zebulun* 7.3–4 (Testaments 265; Greek 126).

Shedding tears for others or grieving for others[66] especially when there is no other way to assist them is a theme that runs throughout the patristic and Orthodox Christian tradition. Blessed Theophylact writes: "Not only with money does one show mercy [*eleein*] but also with words. And should you have nothing at all to give, show mercy with tears."[67] In a contemporary vein, Fr Thomas Hopko also writes: "Spiritual acts of mercy are a necessity for everyone. . . . Not all can work and assist. But all can pray, all can weep, and all can express co-suffering love with mercy for all, without discrimination or condition."[68]

These tears in response to the suffering of others are not a kind of weepy sentimentality for others or a condescending pity. After all, while weeping, Zebulun walked seven stadia with the person he could not assist. The weeping certainly expresses some sort of grief and fellow-feeling or sympathy with the poor person. However, Zebulun's weeping also is obviously connected with his taking time from what he was doing to be present for a while (seven stadia is roughly one mile in our measure) in a supportive manner. What is really crucial to Zebulun's action is that his weeping expresses an intentional compassionate co-presence with someone.[69]

This willingness to be compassionately present to someone if only to console them or bear with them is a basic feature of a robust expression of compassion. It is fundamentally connected and in line with Zebulun's earlier description of providing fish for people by welcoming them and suffering with them. This compassionate co-presence is a way to establish, if only for a time, a *koinōnia* (fellowship) with a person who is in need or otherwise suffering. We see the same sort of compassionate action when someone simply comforts another person or is silently present to and with another person who is undergoing some sort of distress when there is nothing to say and nothing to do but weep with and for the person. This weeping is done not merely in the sense of weeping alongside another person— recall Lt Hofmiller's relation to Edith—but weeping and mourning with and for them in a neighborly manner.

---

[66] These sorts of tears, of course, are different from the spiritual tears by which we grieve before God over our own weakness and imperfection.

[67] Theophylact, *The Gospel According to Matthew*, 45 (PG 123:188D, commentary on Mt 5.7). Theophylact's observation about showing mercy obviously extends to manifesting compassion.

[68] Thomas Hopko, "On Stewardship and Philanthropy: Forty Sentences" in *Good and Faithful Servant: Stewardship in the Orthodox Church*, ed. Anthony Scott (Crestwood, NY: St Vladimir's Seminary Press, 2003), 143.

[69] Cf. Mirguet, *An Early History of Compassion*, 53.

This sort of mourning, grief, or weeping can assume a global character. The paradigmatic expression of this is the agony for the world that Christ experiences in his prayer in the Garden of Gethsemane.[70] It is captured in St Isaac the Syrian's famous description of a merciful heart: "a heart on fire for the whole of creation. . . . By the strong and vehement mercy that grips such a person's heart, and by such great compassion, the heart is humbled and one cannot bear to hear or to see any injury or slight sorrow in any in creation."[71]

While expressed through tears and grief, compassion cannot remain caught up in them when action on behalf of others is possible. In his preface to his *Commentary on Ezekiel*, St Jerome notes how the work on the commentary was delayed because of the inundation of refugees from the sack of Rome. The following text shows how his response and that of his brothers to the suffering that they witnessed was initially confined to tears and grief but was supplemented with action on behalf of the refugees. The change in response was driven by their decision to set aside their own all-consuming work of writing a commentary on Ezekiel, which initially prevented them from helping the refugees:

> We cannot relieve these sufferers: all we can do is to sympathise with them, and unite our tears with theirs. The burden of this holy work was as much as we could carry; the sight of the wanderers, coming in crowds, caused us deep pain; and we therefore abandoned the exposition of Ezekiel, and almost all study, and were filled with a longing to turn the words of Scripture into action, and not to say holy things but to do them.[72]

A remarkable section from a letter attributed to Sulpitius (Suplicius) Severus to his sister comments on how the injunction to "weep with them that weep"[73] cannot limit compassion for others simply to weeping or grieving for them. This text is eminently worth quoting and, indeed, does not require any commentary.

> The precept which has been given us is "to weep with them that weep". . . .
> [But] to weep with one that weeps, and at the same time to refuse to help him that weeps when you can, is a proof of mockery, and not of piety. In short,

---

[70]See Archbishop Lazar Puhalo, "The Moral Grief and Co-Suffering of Love of Christ in Gethsemane," <http://www.clarion-journal.com/clarion_journal_of_spirit/2016/06/the-moral-grief-and-co-suffering-love-of-christ-in-gethsemane-lazar-puhalo.html>, April 20, 2020.

[71]Isaac the Syrian, *Homily 71* (*Ascetical Homilies*, 344–45). This is the translation from the Greek text of the Homily.

[72]Jerome, *Commentary on Ezekiel*, Preface to Book 3 (NPNF[2] 6:500; PL 25:75–6).

[73]Rom 12.15.

our Savior wept with Mary and Martha, the sisters of Lazarus, and proved the infinite compassion (*misericordiam*) within him by the witness of his tears. But works, as the proofs of true affection soon followed, when Lazarus, for whose sake the tears were shed, was raised up and restored to his sisters. This was sincerely to weep with those who wept, when the occasion of the weeping was removed.[74]

AN OPENNESS TO ALL PEOPLE WITHOUT EXAMINATION

So far, we have seen that compassion is a dispositional openness to others that is alert to suffering. But what is the scope of this openness; to whom is it directed? Once again, we get an excellent indication from Zebulun. While he talks about specific groups such as strangers, those who are sick, or those who are aged, in fact, he directs this openness towards everyone, not just people but even animals. Indeed, as we have seen, he tells his children to "be moved by compassion to show mercy *adiakritōs** to all people." The sense of the Greek term in this context is without making an examination or without making distinctions: impartiality. It can also mean "without hesitation."[75] Compassion, I would argue, involves being open to others without going through an initial mental account of whether they are somehow at fault or whether they are good or bad—that is, one extends compassion without hesitation and without reserve. This basic appeal to an openness to all people without discrimination [*adiaphorōs*] is echoed by St John Chrysostom when he admonished elites who refused to provide any assistance to poor people unless they somehow "passed muster" of their examination as to whether were worthy of assistance.[76] The poor seemed to always fail this examination much to St John's exasperation. St Theodoros the Great Ascetic links this attitude of welcoming others without examination with the hospitality of Abraham in the Old Testament:

> Accepting the task of hospitality, the patriarch used to sit at the entrance to his tent (cf. Gen 18.1), inviting all who passed by, and his table was laden for all comers including the impious and foreigners, without discrimination (*mē diakrinomenos*)."[77]

[74]Sulpitius Severus, *Epistle 2 to Claudia on Virginity* 6 (NPNF[2] 11:60; PL 20:231).

[75]*Testaments* (English) 265 (for this use in the translation of the passage) and 267 n. 7.2 for a discussion of the merits of this translation. Although the Greek term is not used in the references to Christ or characters in his parables being moved by compassion, those texts certainly show that their compassion was given without hesitation (see Chapter 3, pp. 103–104).

[76]John Chrysostom, *Commentary on Hebrews* 1.1 (NPNF[1] 14:422; PG 63:95–96).

[77]Theodoros the Great Ascetic, *A Century of Spiritual Texts* 85 (*Philokalia* 2:32; Greek 1:320).

In one sense, of course, there are very often practical limitations to the assistance we can give to others. Demands placed on us may exceed the resources we have. We may have to determine and even triage levels and types of distress in order to assist some people instead of or before others. We may have responsibilities to some people that put limitations on what we can offer to others. We may, as do many people in helping professions, suffer compassion fatigue. We may also have to protect ourselves and others from those who would harm us. In these and many other cases, compassionate actions may have to be practically circumscribed by an examination or assessment of what we can do.

Often we cannot actually and effectively assist people unless we know something about them and their circumstances. It would make little sense to provide food to others without making some effort to determine something about their health condition, allergies, and even religious beliefs or other matters that might place limits on the foods they can eat. Approaching others without discrimination (*adiaphorōs*) cannot possibly mean approaching others as bare instantiations of a human form devoid of any particular characteristics.

I suggest that this appeal to an openness to others "without examination" means that we do not make some prior examination or accusation about the worthiness of people for assistance. If so, Zebulun's admonition contrasts sharply with Aristotle's description of *eleos* (translated variously as "pity" or "compassion"), which should only be experienced towards those whose misfortune is not their own fault. Moreover, I suggest that this approach to others without examination is best set against the background of the many "passions and thoughts" by which we sort people out both socially and individually according to various prejudiced distinctions or according to the range of self-aggrandizing passions that we experience such as hatred, envy, greed, fear, and so forth.

In particular, for my immediate purposes: the many affective-cognitive states by which people are stigmatized and denigrated contain what might be called social and psychological *a priori* accusations. Stigmatization and denigration fundamentally *a priori* (that is, prior to encountering them) "accuse" people at the core of their being as being defective in their humanity. That is, they provide the cognitive and affective "viewpoint" within which, regardless of physical proximity, we flee—mentally, affectively, and spiritually—from people (or better, have already fled from them before we even encounter them) because we view or interpret them as defective and unworthy of inclusion in any truly human relationships. They are viewed as at best "children" and at worst fundamental threats to ourselves, to others, and to the community.[78]

Simeon's sclerotic viscera (*sklērosplanchnon*)[79] and immovable liver lead him to lay his hand on Joseph, to set upon him, in order to destroy him. He is like those "who harden the viscera (or heart) of hospitality" [*ta tēs philoxenias splanchna sklērounontes*].[80] He does this because in his envy and lack of sympathy or compassion for Joseph, he has already accused Joseph of unworthiness as a brother. In several texts, Chrysostom links the lack of sympathy (*asympatheia*) and the lack of compassion (*asplanchnia*) with inhumanity or lack of humanity (*apanthrōpia*).[81]

On the other hand, one of the basic terms to describe compassion in the New Testament, in early literature like *The Testaments of the Twelve Patriarchs*, and throughout the Greek patristic and Byzantine tradition is *eusplanchnia*. It is often translated simply as "compassion" but also as "tender compassion," "tender mercy," and so forth. *Eusplanchnia* and *eusplanchnos* have literal meanings of "good and healthy (*eu*) viscera (*splanchnos*)."[82] Compassion as *eusplanchnia*, then, has the sense of healthy or well-ordered viscera that are open to others, willing to bear with them, and are not threatened by them. These viscera, and by extension, the heart, are well-ordered when the self-aggrandizing passions that disrupt and destroy our relationships with others are controlled and even eliminated. Compassion in this sense is open to others *adiakritōs* (without examination or accusation).

To sum up: I have drawn on Zebulun's description of compassion to develop a sense of compassion as a disposition that involves a welcoming, hospitable, non-accusatory openness to others, arising from an alert sensitivity to their suffering, that bears with them in suffering, vulnerability, and distress, and in which one acts for their sake. At its core, compassionate acceptance of other persons without

---

[78]See Chapter 2, pp. 57–61 for the earlier discussion on the dynamics of stigmatization.

[79]The term is coined by Michael Choniates, *Oration* 22 (S. P. Lampros, ed., Μιχαὴλ Ακομινάτου τοῦ χωνιάτου τὰ σωζόμενα [Michaēl Akominatou tou choniatou ta sōzomena] [Athens: 1879–1880], 2:367).

[80]Carolus de Smedt, Franciscus van Ortroy, et al., *Analectica Bollandiana* (Brussels: Polleunus et Ceuterick, 1906), 25:225. The phrase is contained in the hagiography of Neophytus Inclusus, a 13th-century Cypriot monk.

[81]John Chrysostom, *Non esse ad gratiam concionandum* (PG 50:656) and *In Eutropium* (PG 53:395) for the former and *De paenitentia* 2 (PG 60:699) for the latter.

[82]Henry Liddell and Robert Scott, *A Greek English Lexicon* "eusplanchnia," <http://www.perseus.tufts.edu/hopper/text?doc=Perseus%3Atext%3A1999.04.0057%3Aentry%3Deu)splagxni%2Fa>, April 20, 2020 and "*eusplanchnos*," <http://www.perseus.tufts.edu/hopper/morph?l=eu%29%2Fsplagxnos&la=greek&can=eu%29%2Fsplagxnoso&prior=eu)splagxni/a#lexicon>, April 20, 2020.

examination and, more fundamentally, without accusation, seeks to establish a communion or community (*koinōnia*) with them that affirms the wholeness of their humanity, their uniqueness as persons, and the equality of honor due to them. "Non-accusatory" means an affirmation (both affective and cognitive or rational) of the fullness of the equality of honor to which all humans are due. "Non accusatory" implicitly challenges and rejects the passions and thoughts that give rise to and support the "accusations of defectiveness" that underly denigration and stigmatization.[83]

Perfecting a Compassionate Disposition

People can have and exercise dispositions in more or less robust and complete ways. My disposition to pray regularly to God can be disrupted or can suffer from periods of neglect. My disposition to treat my colleagues in a professional manner can wax or wane because of stress. My disposition to be compassionate to people can be circumscribed because sometimes I get greedy with people, or there are some individuals or groups that "push a button" or annoy me so that I push them away and at most pity them. But what is involved in perfecting a compassionate disposition?

HUMILITY AND COMPASSION

As a preface to discussing dispassion and dealing with our own vulnerability as central in perfecting a compassionate disposition, let me note the important role that humility plays in developing and perfecting compassion. At its core, humility involves a radical and honest acceptance of ourselves before God and before our fellow humans and creation.[84] We are, first of all, to be humble before God. This involves an honest and ongoing repentance over our sinfulness—and how that has estranged us from God—as well as profound thanks for the blessings that God has given us, especially through Christ's Incarnation, to restore us to the fullness of life. Humility is a fundamental virtue that leads us away from pride and arrogance. Humility, thus, is a "gateway to dispassion"[85] that allows us to stand in

---

[83]Of course, this is precisely the point of the parable of the good Samaritan. Freed from the animus that drives Samaritans and Jews apart, the good Samaritan makes himself unhesitatingly a neighbor of the man (likely an Israelite) beaten and lying by the side of the road.

[84]For an excellent summary of the Orthodox Christian understanding of humility, see Hopko, *Orthodox Faith*, 4:71–73.

[85]Peter of Damascus, *Twenty-Four Discourses* 9 (*Philokalia* 3:237–8; Greek 1:134). He is quoting St John Climacus, *The Ladder of Divine Ascent*, Step 4.

the presence of God and, as we will see below, opens us to the possibility of striving for a perfect love of God, which, through that love and compassion, directs us back to our fellow humans and the whole of creation.

As a "gateway to dispassion," human humility, modeled on God's humility, is a virtue that is integral to developing any full sense of community with God and with each other. As Fr Georges Florovsky observed:

> Despite the obvious difference between God's humility and our humility, the human forms of humility are derived from the very nature of God, just as the commandment to love is rooted in God's love for mankind. God's humility is precisely that, being God, he desires, he wills to be in communion with everything and* everything is inferior to God.[86]

As we have seen, to really be in communion with everyone, we must push back on all of the self-aggrandizing passions and thoughts that harmfully divide and separate us from each other. Acquiring dispassion through humility is, as we will see, central to that endeavor.

In his Incarnation, Christ assumed human existence and in his humility fully accepted and identified with the fragility and vulnerability that marks human existence. But how is humility linked with coming to terms with our vulnerability? The arrogance and pride that separated Adam and Eve from God did not lie initially in the fact that they did not acknowledge their sinfulness. Rather, they refused to accept the reality of their humanity as created beings—their fundamental dependence on God and gratefulness for the love God showed in creating them and the world. Humility allows us to stand in the presence of God not by just admitting our sinfulness before God but also by fully accepting our fundamental reality as created beings: without God, we are simply nothing.

Fr Florovsky notes that all of creation is inferior to God. After all, God is uncreated and the ultimate cause of everything else. But none of our fellow creatures is inferior to us by nature since we all share the same equality of honor. Yet, as St Gregory the Theologian observes, acknowledging this requires that we also accept the "equality of weakness" (*asthenia*)[87] that we have by nature. This weakness marks a fundamental vulnerability that belongs to us simply as created beings. None of us—personally or collectively—has the ability to protect ourselves fully from the array of threats that result in death, suffering, loss, and so

---

[86]Florovsky, *Byzantine Fathers*, 28–29. * = "and" seems to have the sense of "even though."
[87]See below, pp. 209–210.

forth. Surely, the global impact of the covid pandemic has taught us that. We may be able to protect ourselves in a variety of ways through social, political, and economic means, beyond anything that we can provide personally. But that simply emphasizes our profound dependence on other people and our social world that marks our fundamental interdependence as essentially social beings.

Coming to terms through humility with the vulnerability that belongs us by nature does not mean simply resigning ourselves to it. We legitimately strive personally and collectively to create social worlds that support our lives and provide a reasonable guard against threats. But the fear of the vulnerability that marks the human condition and the absurd sense of entitlement that accompanies it, can lead us with pride and arrogance to prop ourselves up, individually and socially, at the expense of others, whom we stigmatize, denigrate, and thereby marginalize, undermining any genuine sense of community and compassion. This is a false pride and arrogance that is actually a form of cowardice. It irrationally fears the human condition and deflects the fear into a rejection and even hatred of other people.[88] The humble and honest acceptance of our vulnerability can both eliminate this fear that poisons human life and reject the resulting evil treatment of people through stigmatization and marginalization and all other unjust means.[89]

> Righteousness casts out hatred, humility destroys hatred. For he who is righteous and humble is ashamed to do what is wrong being reproved not by another but by his own heart, for the Lord knows his soul (*psychē*)*. He does not speak evil of any man.[90]

The personal and collective humble acceptance of our vulnerability is a gateway, as it were, to the full personal and collective acceptance of our fellow humans that belongs to a compassionate disposition. For in our humility, we strive to reflect the humility that Christ manifests in his Incarnation and that leads to his compassionate solidarity with all of humanity and especially with those who are "despised and rejected." It is in this way, then, that humility allows a compassionate disposition to be perfected through coming to terms with our vulnerability.

---

[88]Recall Sartre's description of the Anti-Semite and of all of those who stigmatize others, (p. 62).

[89]The Buddhist monk, Jack Kornfield, gives a beautiful expression to this point within the Buddhist tradition: "Vulnerability and the Tender Heart," <https://jackkornfield.com/vulnerability-and-the-tender-heart/>, April 20, 2020.

[90]*Testament of Gad* 5.3–4 (*Testaments* 328; Greek 164–5). *Testaments* 328 provides "looks upon his (inner) disposition" for "knows his soul."

BEING GROUNDED IN DISPASSION

If compassion is to be perfected as a disposition, then we must be free from all of the self-aggrandizing passions and thoughts that make others simply useful to us or drive them away from us as somehow inferior to us.

In the Orthodox Christian tradition, compassion in the fullest sense requires dispassion (*apatheia*). Dispassion does not mean an apathetic indifference to others because we have shut down all of our desires and emotions. Rather, "Dispassion is a peaceful condition of the soul in which the soul is not easily moved to evil."[91] Pursuing dispassion means ridding ourselves of the self-aggrandizing aspects of our desires. Through dispassion we are rid of the impulsions, desires, thoughts, and images of things that lead us to sin.[92] This sort of dispassion is precisely what is involved in the "death of the self" that, in the Orthodox Christian tradition, does not mean a masochistic belittling of the self. Rather, it involves a discovery of the self through repentance that, through the grace of the Holy Spirit, allows us first of all to strive to attain a perfect love of God and, thus, our neighbor. Citing 1 John 4.20—"He who does not love his brother whom he has seen, cannot love God whom he has not seen"—St Maximus the Confessor writes: "The actualization and proof of perfect love for God is a genuine and willing attitude of goodwill towards one's neighbor."[93]

Dispassion in particular requires the elimination of those passions and fears by which we denigrate and condemn others. St Seraphim of Sarov well illustrates how the tendency to condemn others arises out of our own unwillingness to confront our own failings—which is precisely the starting point for repentance:

> You cannot be too gentle, too kind. Shun even to appear harsh in your treatment of each other. Joy, radiant joy, streams from the face of him who gives and kindles joy in the heart of him who receives. All condemnation is from

[91]Maximus the Confessor, "Four Hundred Texts on Love," 1.36 (*Philokalia* 2:56, Greek 2:6). The collection of writings in the *Philokalia* contains one of the venerable sources of writings about dispassion in Orthodox Christian spiritual life.

[92]Maximus the Confessor, *Various Texts on Theology, the Divine Economy, and Virtue and Vice* [*Capita theologica et oecumenica sive Capita gnostica*] 3.51–52 (*Philokalia* 2:172; Greek 2:136–7).

[93]Maximus the Confessor, *Various Texts* 1.36 (*Philokalia* 2:222; Greek 2:97). See Kallistos Ware, "The Passions: Enemy or Friend?" *In Communion* 17 (Fall 1999) and online October 18, 2004, <https://incommunion.org/2004/10/18/the-passions-enemy-or-friend/>, April 20, 2020 and Bronwen Neil, "'The Blessed Passion of Holy Love': Maximus the Confessor's Spiritual Psychology," *Australian eJournal of Theology* 2 (February 2004): 1–8, <http://aejt.com.au/__data/assets/pdf_file/0005/395672/AEJT_2.8_Neil_Blessed_Passion.pdf>, April 20, 2020.

the devil. Never condemn each other. We condemn others only because we
shun knowing ourselves. When we gaze at our own failings, we see such a
swamp that nothing in another can equal it. That is why we turn away, and
make much of the faults of others. Instead of condemning others, strive to
reach inner peace. Keep silent, refrain from judgement.[94]

Dispassion and the refusal to judge people, which lie at the core of compassion, upends all of the invidious distinctions by which we diminish and marginalize people, as St Macarius reminds us:

Christians . . . ought not to pass judgment of any kind on anyone. . . . But they
should look upon all persons with a single mind and a pure eye,[95] so that it
may be for such a person almost a natural and fixed attitude never to despise
or judge or abhor anyone or to divide people according to categories.[96]

Dispassion involves what Fr Bobrinskoy calls an "oblation of the heart" in
which we share in God's love and compassion. But this means that we must be
open to the suffering of the world: "to confront suffering and evil in all of their
forms" as did Jesus. But this requires an oblation of the heart, which occurs when
"the heart opens itself, when it ceases being hardened, when it fortifies itself with
the spirit of compassion, that it is able to fill itself with the misery of the world."[97]
The word "hardened" translates *blindé*, which has the sense of armored or bul-
letproof. It well describes the state that people with sclerotic viscera and hearts
strive to obtain so they can "protect themselves" and drive away from themselves
others whose vulnerability and suffering threaten them, or when they become
blind and indifferent to their suffering.

St John Chrysostom pinpoints this sort of fear and the havoc it can wreak
on others:

And what is the specious plea of the many [for loving wealth]? I have children,
one says, and I am afraid lest I myself be reduced to the extremity of hunger
and want, lest I should stand in need of others. I am ashamed to beg. . . . [so]

---

[94]St Seraphim of Sarov, quoted in Jim Forest, *Praying with Icons* (Maryknoll, NY: Orbis Books, 2008),
169. Forest does not provide a citation to a text of St Seraphim that contains this quotation. I have not been
able to find one.

[95]Note: the mind and the intellect are in the heart and not divorced from the heart! Judgment here is not
just cognitive but affective as well.

[96]Pseudo-Macarius, *Homily* 15 (*The Fifty Spiritual Homilies*, 111).

[97]Bobrinskoy, *Compassion*, 91. See also the entire section on the oblation of the heart, 90–2.

you cause others to beg? I cannot, you say, endure hunger ... [so] you expose others to hunger? Do you know what a dreadful thing it is to beg, how dreadful to be perishing by hunger? Spare also your brethren! ... [T]o be hungry is neither a disgrace nor a crime.[98]

Eradicating these passions is a matter of watchfulness and spiritual warfare.[99] It is not too surprising that in Orthodox Christian and monastic writings one finds a stress on the spirituality of tears by which we confront and grieve over our own imperfection and struggle towards acquiring dispassion.[100] The fruit of this dispassion for St Maximus the Confessor is perfect love. Drawing on Colossians 3.10–11, where St Paul describes the "new man who is renewed in knowledge according to the image of him who created him, where there is neither Greek nor Jew, circumcised nor uncircumcised, barbarian, Scythian, slave nor free, but Christ is all and in all," [101] St Maximus writes that in reaching the "summit of dispassion [*apatheia*]," those who are "perfect in love"[102] and have reached the "summit of dispassion" eliminate the differences between themselves and others because they have "risen above the tyranny of the passions" and fix their "attention on the single nature of humanity." In this way, they "look on all in the same way ... [showing] the same disposition to all."[103]

COMING TO TERMS WITH VULNERABILITY

Compassion orients us to all people without judgment or prejudicial discrimination. But does compassion direct us to people just when they are undergoing some determinate or particular need, vulnerability, or suffering? Or, is there a more fundamental disposition of compassion that involves an openness towards people, if you will, simply because of their humanity as created persons? Put another way, is compassion something triggered by a particular event of a person in some

---

[98]John Chrysostom, *Homilies on First Thessalonians* 10 (NPNF¹ 13.368; PG 62.458).

[99]This theme runs through the *Philokalia*. Cf. St Hesychios the Priest, for whom in watchfulness, we halt "thoughts at the entrance to the heart. In this way predatory and murderous thoughts are marked down as they approach." *On Watchfulness and Holiness* 6 (*Philokalia* 1.163; Greek 1.142).

[100]John Chryssavgis, "The Spiritual Way," in *Cambridge Companion to Orthodox Christian Theology*, eds. Mary Cunningham and Elizabeth Theokritoff (Cambridge: Cambridge University Press, 2008), 153–55.

[101]Col. 3.11. He also employs Gal. 3.28: "There is neither Jew nor Greek, there is neither slave nor free, there is neither male nor female; for you are all one in Christ Jesus."

[102]St Maximus is speaking of *agapē* (love), but he clearly has in mind *philanthrōpia*, understood as compassion, as the love that we are to show to our fellow humans.

[103]This is not just a conceptual beholding of other people but a lived embodied experience of them. Maximus the Confessor, *Four Hundred Texts on Love* 2.30 (*Philokalia* 2:79; Greek 2:18).

sort of distress or does compassion involve a basic dispositional orientation to people regardless of whether they are in some particular distress?

As we saw in Chapter 4, Orthodox Christian hymns stress God's compassion and mercy as underlying and "motivating" the Incarnation. In these hymns, liturgical texts, and much Orthodox Christian theology, the Incarnation is represented as a response to sin and the fall. If so, then the compassion that drives the Incarnation expresses God's energies as a response to sinfulness. St Gregory of Nyssa seems to capture this idea when he argues that mercy is a divine energy that arises after human sin. While he refers specifically to God's mercy in this text, its extension to God's compassion is clear:

> The Lord is full of "compassion and mercy, long-suffering, and of great goodness" (Ex 34.6). Now what do these words tell us? Do they indicate his energies, or his nature? No one will say that they indicate anything but his energies. At what time, then, after showing compassion and mercy, did God acquire his name from their display? Was it before man's life began? But who was there to be the object of mercy? Was it, then, after sin entered into the world? But sin entered after man. The energy, therefore, of showing mercy, and the name itself, "mercy," came after man.[104]

Yet the idea that the Incarnation is entirely and only a response to sin is balanced in the Orthodox Christian tradition by St Maximus the Confessor and others who argued that the Incarnation was embedded in the very purpose of creation as the "means" by which God chose to bring human beings and creation into the fullness of life. St Nikodimos the Hagiorite, influenced by St Maximus, writes:

> The mystery of the incarnate dispensation of the divine Logos is the beginning of all the ways of the Lord, and that it comes before all creation ... this is the divine purpose that underlines the beginning of existent things, the purpose formed by God before they existed, on account of which all things exist.[105]

[104]Gregory of Nyssa, *Against Eunomius* 2.1.151–152 (NPNF² 5:265 mod.; PG 45:534A–B). See Appendix 2, TDB, for a discussion about interpreting the sense of energy (*energeia*) in this text.

[105]St Nikodimos of the Holy Mountain, "Apology for My Notes on Our Lady Theotokos in the Book of Unseen Warfare," in Panyiotis Nellas, *Deification in Christ: The Nature of the Human Person* (Crestwood, NY: St Vladimir's Seminary Press, 1997), 228, 229. See Bogdan Bucur, "Foreordained from All Eternity: The Mystery of the Incarnation according to Some Early Christian and Byzantine Writers," *Dumbarton Oaks Papers* 62 (2008): 199–216, for a discussion of this text and an excellent historical and systematic discussion of this topic.

On this view, human sinfulness changed the conditions in which the Incarnation took place—as leading to the cross—but not the reality of the Incarnation. Drawing on this tradition, Metropolitan Hierotheos notes that the Incarnation is not a response of "simple compassion" (*eusplanchnia*).[106] The metropolitan does not explain what he means by compassion. He is perhaps thinking of compassion as a response to some form of suffering that arises in our broken world. But if the Incarnation was intended as part of creation regardless of whether humans fell through sin, then perhaps there was an original compassionate or merciful "impetus" for it that would not have been exclusively a response to human suffering that resulted from the fall.

Indeed, in the head-bowing prayer in St John Chrysostom's *Divine Liturgy*, we read: "We give thanks to you, O King invisible, who by your measureless power made all things, and in the greatness of your mercy (*eleos*) brought all things from non-existence into being."[107] Chrysostom expands on this text in his commentary on Philippians[108] and Severianus provides a rather beautiful elaboration of this text in one of his sermons:

> All creation proclaims the mercy and *philanthrōpia* of God as does the governance of creation. For there is nothing among the things that appear which does not proclaim the goodness of God. But indeed, the heaven, the earth, the sea, and all that is visible and invisible came to be, is sustained, and is protected by God's mercy. Therefore, the blessed David suitably proclaims his mercifulness from his *philanthrōpia* when he says: "For our God is merciful and just; our God shows mercy [*racham, eleos*, or compassion]." (Ps 116.5)[109]

Why view creation itself as an act of mercy? All created beings depend utterly and completely on God for their existence. There is a radical contingency to creation: no created being can bring itself into being from nothing and no created being can secure itself from "relapsing" into nothing—utter and complete annihilation. We get a more complete elaboration from St Athanasius on why this is the case:

---

[106]Hierotheos of Nafpaktos, *Feasts of the Lord*, 345.

[107]*Service Books of the Orthodox Church*, 77 mod. This prayer follows the Lord's prayer.

[108]John Chrysostom, *Homilies on Philippians* 4 (NPNF¹ 13: 201, 202; PG 62:212).

[109]Severianus, *Homilia de lotione pedum* in Antoine Wenger, "Une homélie inédite de Sévérien de Gabala sur le lavement des pieds," *Revue des études byzantines* 25 (1967): 225. The last word, *eleei*, in the verse from Psalm 116.5, is often translated as "shows mercy." But since the underlying Hebrew is *racham*, it is plausible, as I will argue below, to translate it as "shows compassion." See the NASB translation of this verse from the MT.

But the reason why the Word, the Word of God, has united himself with created things is truly wonderful, and teaches us that the present order of things
is none otherwise than is fitting. For the nature of created things, inasmuch
as it is brought into being out of nothing, is of a fleeting sort, and weak and
mortal, if composed of itself only. But the God of all is good and exceeding
noble by nature—and therefore is kind (*philanthropōs*). For one that is good
can grudge nothing: for which reason he does not grudge even existence, but
desires all to exist, for the exercise of his loving kindness (*philanthrōpia*).[110]

St Maximus the Confessor teaches that the *logos* (the nature or principle)
of each created being exists from all eternity in the Logos, the Word and Son
of God. The logos of each thing in the Logos, the Son of God,[111] is not yet an
individually existing thing nor can the logos of any created thing bring forth that
thing by itself. It is only through the creative action of the Logos that individual
things come into existence. Moreover, the perfection of things consists in fully
conforming to the logos in terms of which they were created. As Bishop Kallistos
(Ware) remarks, our goal is "to become truly ourselves, to realize the vison that
God has of each one of us from eternity.[112] For humans, this is what we mean by
attaining to the likeness of God in our uniqueness as persons according to which
we were created.

No created beings—not even Adam and Eve prior to the fall—can accomplish
their final end under their own power unless, in and by themselves, they were able
to eliminate or completely protect themselves against the weakness and liability
to mortality and non-existence that belongs to created things as created.[113] On
the view of St Maximus and others who stress that the Incarnation was intended
from eternity as the way in which created things would be brought to their own
perfection—deification for humans and redemption for all created things—then
if things are created out of mercy and *philanthrōpia*—kindness and not just love
of man in a narrow sense—the Incarnation from all eternity expresses that same
mercy and *philanthrōpia*.

"All of creation proclaims the goodness of God" as Severianus wrote. Recall
that when Moses asked God to show him his glory, God promised that he would

---

[110]Athanasius, *Contra Gentes* 3.41 (NPNF[2] 4:26; PG 25:81C).

[111]Cf. Jn 1.1–3.

[112]Ware, "Enter the Heart," 10. He draws on a similar theme in the Jewish tradition.

[113]Maximus has an extended discussion of this idea in *Ambiguum* 7.2. *On the Cosmic Mystery of Jesus Christ: Selected Writings from St Maximus the Confessor*, trans. Paul Blowers and Robert Wilken, PPS 25 (Crestwood, NY: St Vladimir's Seminary Press, 2003), 54–60 (PG 91:1077D–1085A).

manifest himself to Moses so that all of his goodness or glory[114] passed by Moses. And when God's glory passed by Moses and the Lord called on his own name, he revealed himself as compassionate and merciful. In proclaiming God's goodness, all creation then proclaims God's compassion and mercy. It is noteworthy that Severianus cites Psalm 116.5 when he remarks that David proclaims the mercy of God from his *philanthrōpia*: "Therefore, the blessed David suitably proclaims his mercifulness from his *philanthrōpia* when he says: 'For our God is merciful and just; our God shows *eleos* [Greek, "mercy," or *racham*, from Hebrew, "compassion"].'"

In this text, the final word *racham* in the Hebrew is translated in the Greek by a form of the verb *eleeō* in the Septuagint rather than *oikteirō*, which as we have seen is often used to translate *racham*. If we are attentive to the underlying sense of *racham*, God proclaims his mercifulness from his *philanthrōpia* or in this case his *racham* or compassion. *Racham* has the sense of a woman's womb-like love for her child. Isaiah captures the sense of this compassion when God asks: "Can a woman forget her nursing child and have no compassion on the son of her womb? Even these may forget, but I will not forget you."[115] But neither infants in the womb nor nursing children necessarily suffer. They are, however, profoundly vulnerable: unable to sustain themselves in existence and utterly dependent upon others. In this case, we can have compassion (*racham* as *eusplanchnia*) for them as a willingness to bear with and for them, not because they are actually suffering in some way but because, unless God miraculously intervenes, they are vulnerable and without our assistance they cannot survive or flourish.

Created in the image of God, a "trinitarian image," we were created to live in community or communion (*koinōnia*) with one another.[116] The denial of our own vulnerability and interdependence, the pretense to self-sufficiency, is often at the root of a passion-driven egoistic obsession with mammon, wealth, power, prosperity, and so forth. It is not surprising that St Gregory the Theologian chastised those who refused to provide any assistance to lepers precisely because those people relied on human prosperity rather than acknowledging the "weakness" (*asthenia*) and fragility of human nature and all things created—that is, the fact that we are fundamentally vulnerable to all kinds of suffering and death no matter how fortunate or privileged our circumstances.[117] So Gregory writes: "Our

---

[114]"Goodness" is in the MT; "glory" in the LXX.

[115]Is 49.5.

[116]Kallistos Ware, "The Mystery of the Human Person," *Sobornost incorporating Eastern Churches Review*), new series 3.1 (1981): 66.

[117]Gregory of Nazianzus, *Oration* 14.19 (FOC 107:52–3; PG 35:881).

human nature, learning piety and kindness (*philanthrōpos*) from our equality in weakness (*asthenia*), has given compassion (*to sympathēs*) the force of law."[118] Here the fundamental basis for compassion for others in the sense of a *sympatheia* for others—a co-suffering with others—is our own acceptance of the common weakness; that is, vulnerability to suffering and death that we share with others by virtue of being created. That compassion also accepts the fundamental sociality and interdependence that belongs to us by nature as human beings.

Simone Weil eloquently expressed an awareness of this sort of vulnerability that is involved in compassion—not so much the vulnerability of those we assist but coming to terms with our own vulnerability, which means "saying to oneself: 'I may lose at any moment, through the play of circumstances over which I have no control, anything whatsoever that I possess including those things which are so intimately mine that I consider them as being myself.'"[119]

Compassion in this fundamental sense is not simply a response to some particular affliction or even the ways in which some people are vulnerable and powerless in the face of certain threats, for example, small children who live under the threat of violence. Compassion is a dispositional openness towards all human beings in light of the fundamental vulnerability that marks the intersubjectivity, sociality, and interdependence of the human condition regardless of the various ways in which we personally or socially may or may not be subject to some specific forms of suffering.

You might recall Sartre's pointed observation that the real issue for the Anti-Semites was not Jewish people but a "fear of the human condition." As Sartre implied, this fear animates and drives a good deal of denigration and marginalization. If that fear of the human condition undermines and can destroy compassion, then by way of contrast our profound acceptance of what St Gregory the Theologian called our equality in weakness and our refusal to be threatened by it provides the basis for a universal compassion for all humans and, in fact, all created things. This means that if compassion is offered without examination, then compassion is directed even to those who would harm us. Christ does, after all, command us to love our enemies.[120]

[118]Gregory of Nazianzus, *Oration* 14.15 (FOC 107:49–50; PG 35:876).

[119]Simone Weil quoted in Steven Tudor, *Compassion and Remorse: Acknowledging the Suffering Other* (Leuven: Peeters Publishers, 2001), 107. Tudor provides an excellent discussion of this issue, 105–7.

[120]Lk 5.44. See Bobrinskoy, *Compassion*, 67–72. More on this in Chapter 6, pp. 251–55.

Compassion as a Virtue

Compassion, in the Orthodox Christian tradition, should be cultivated as a steadfast disposition or orientation towards others. Since it is a beneficial disposition that imitates divine compassion, it is clearly a candidate to be regarded as a virtue or character trait that contributes to our own perfection and deification. Virtues, as I have mentioned earlier, involve not only actions, but also intentions, or the reasons for the sake of which we do things. So I want to begin this section by discussing various theories of intentions in relation to the possibility of compassionate action.

Theories of Intentions[121] *that Exclude Compassion as a Virtue*

In Chapter 2, I noted that while both pity and compassion involve actions directed to another person, pity and compassion differ in their intentions or goals. One who pities someone may assist that person but does so for his or her own perceived self-interest. Compassion, however, moves us to act on behalf of someone in such a way that we act for the sake of the other person, even if that works against our self-interest in some ways.[122] If we take compassion in the broad sense of a dispositional welcoming of and co-suffering presence with others without examination, we refer to a disposition or virtue that orients us to others for their sake and not just our own self-interest or perhaps without any consideration of our self-interest. If, however, my assistance or actions for another person are done primarily for my sake, then the action is egoistic or selfish in nature. Selfishness in this context does not necessarily mean that I am harming someone else but rather that I do something for another person only and primarily because it promotes my own self-interest. I treat the other person basically as a means to my own self-interest even if I happen to assist him or her: for example, I help someone across the street only because I want applause from the crowd.

---

[121] We often talk about being motivated to be compassionate to others. But motivations are technically different from intentions. I may be motivated by a severe thunderstorm warning to stay in the house and not venture outside. I am staying inside because the warning prompts me to act in this way. But the intention or purpose of staying inside is to remain safe and avoid harm from lightening or torrential rain. Intentions and motivations are both reasons for acting. Motivations "push us," as it were, to act. Still, our intentions are always properly expressed by the goal, purpose, or end that we aim to achieve; namely, the intention of an action is that for the sake of which we do something. But since these terms are often used interchangeably, I will not stress the distinction in this part.

[122] Again, pity and compassion can overlap depending on how we hear and understand these terms, but I am now stressing the division between them.

Some believe that all of our actions are self-regarding. This view is known as psychological egoism: we always or for the most part act to promote what we believe is in our own self-interest.[123] The stronger view that we *always* act to promote our own self-interest makes genuine other-regarding actions impossible. On this view, the psychological egoist would say that no matter how unselfish actions might seem, e.g., soldiers who sacrifice their lives to save their comrades, they are ultimately driven by some self-interested intention, e.g., posthumous fame. The weaker view allows for the possibility of compassionate actions for the sake of others but only provided that we do not in any way act for our own self-interest.

Psychological egoism adopts what we might call an "on-off" light switch approach to human intentions. If I do something for the sake of myself, I cannot do something for the sake of someone else and vice versa. On the other hand, what is called pure altruism, which is a form of compassion, might mean acting for the sake of another person without any regard for one's own interest. On this meaning, altruistic or compassionate actions involve the same "on-off" light switch approach to human motivations and intentions as psychological egoism.

The most straightforward reason for acting compassionately is: I saw someone in distress. I was moved by compassion to help them and I helped them for their sake. Such actions can have a "spontaneous" character to them, e.g., I witness someone who is injured in an accident, and without giving a thought for my own safety, out of compassion I rush immediately to their aid. Or such actions can be carried out over the course of time, e.g., think of people who, moved by compassion, devote their life to serving others in physical and social distress, such as people who out of compassion intentionally devote their lives to victims of socially stigmatized medical conditions. This second example would indicate a compassionate disposition.

In either case, people who perform these actions may not supply any particular self-interested motive in acting, and they may not even see the actions as particularly distinctive about their character as human beings: "I did what anyone else would do." "I did not do anything special."[124] These might be "pure" altruistic actions. Whether there are "pure" altruistic actions, or whether all of our actions

---

[123]Psychological egoism, as a purported factual description of how we act, is quite different from ethical egoism, a moral theory that claims we ought always to act in order to promote only our own actual self-interest. Perceived self-interest is not necessarily the same as actual self-interest. For a good discussion of psychological egoism, see the section devoted to this topic in Andrew Mosley, "Egoism," *Internet Encyclopedia of Philosophy*, <https://www.iep.utm.edu/egoism/>, April 20, 2020.

[124]Kristen Monroe, *The Heart of Altruism*, x–xi, 208–10.

are motivated only by self-interest or shaped only by self-interested intentions, is a highly contestable matter.[125] Compassionate actions, however, need not be so utterly altruistic that persons performing them must be unaware that those actions are their own actions or that they reflect the kind of persons they are or desire to be. This is particularly the case if we think of compassionate actions flowing from a virtue or character trait of compassion. So, let me turn to the discussion of virtue and its relation to human nature.

Virtue and Human Nature

In this part, I will aim to answer these three questions: What is a virtue? What does a virtue have to do with human nature? Why should we care about being virtuous? I will answer these questions in a general way and then apply them to the virtue of compassion.

Consider this quotation from St John Chrysostom:

> For if fear diverts a man from unseemly things, much more should the love of Christ. Difficult is virtue; but let us cast around her form the greatness of the promise of things to come. Indeed those who are virtuous, even apart from these promises, see her beautiful in herself, and on this account go after her, and work because it seems good to God, not for hire; and they think it a great thing to be sober-minded, not in order that they may not be punished, but because God has commanded it. But if anyone is too weak for this, let him think of the prizes.[126]

"Virtue" translates the Greek work *arēte*. In a broader and more basic sense, an *arēte* is a functional excellence: a stable characteristic or trait something requires in order to function well according to its nature or purpose. In classical Greek philosophy (e.g., Plato or Aristotle), one can speak about the *aretai* or functional excellences of a wide variety of natural things (e.g., plants or animals) or human artifacts and tools (e.g., shoes or hammers) in addition to human beings. We can also talk about a wide variety of human endeavors that have their own distinctive excellences: for example, the sorts of characteristics and dispositions required for someone to be a good neurosurgeon, teacher, or mechanic.

[125]See, Richard Kraut, "Altruism," *The Stanford Encyclopedia of Philosophy* (Fall 2020 Edition), Edward N. Zalta, ed., <https://plato.stanford.edu/archives/fall2020/entries/altruism/>, December, 31, 2020.

[126]John Chrysostom, *Homilies on John* 77 (NPNF[1] 14:282–3; PG 59:418).

Yet there are also those stable characteristics and dispositions that are vital to human flourishing or to the realization of our humanity—what we might refer to as moral, intellectual, or spiritual virtues. Vices or evils (*kakia*), on the other hand, are what we might regard as dysfunctional defects. They are characteristics or traits that inhibit or run counter to human flourishing and salvation or deification in light of our common nature. In the patristic literature, covetousness or greed are examples of vices that lead to inhumanity.[127] In the following discussion, the reader might find it helpful to remember that in virtue ethics the inherent goodness of virtue and the inherent evil of vice can be expressed by the adage: "Virtue is its own reward and vice is its own punishment."

Virtue, in a specifically Christian context, is an integral aspect of realizing our own humanity and living according to the likeness of God or becoming a living icon of Christ. Vice or viciousness, on the other hand, manifests sinfulness and fundamentally runs afoul of and expresses a rejection of living according to the likeness of God. At the core of the Christian tradition is the teaching that we are created in the image and according to the likeness of God as expressed preeminently and perfectly in Christ, who is the incarnate Son of God. Rationality and freedom are typically taken to mark the image of God that belongs to our nature, while the perfection of our life according to the likeness of God is found in the virtues.[128] The fruits of the Spirit, for example, are Christian virtues "which literally means those powers and possessions of the mind and the heart which all men should have if they are truly human, fulfilling themselves as created in the image and likeness of God."[129]

God is a Trinity of three persons—Father, Son, and Holy Spirit—whose being is essentially a matter of communion (*koinōnia*).[130] Human beings are not simply individuals but are persons who are fundamentally created to be in relationship with God, with each other, and with the created world. As Bishop Kallistos (Ware) writes:

---

[127]See p. 220 for the quotation from Chrysostom that pointedly describes the character of this inhumanity.

[128]John of Damascus, *On Virtues and Vices* (*Philokalia* 2:341; Greek 2:238).

[129]Thomas Hopko, *The Orthodox Faith*, 4:56. St Maximus the Confessor observes that the virtues of the angels "communicate a goodness" that both imitates God and allows them to "confer blessings on themselves [and] on one another ... thus making them like God." *Four Centuries on Love* 3.33 (*Philokalia* 2:88; Greek 2:32).

[130]John Zizioulas, *Being as Communion: Studies in Personhood and the Church* (Crestwood, NY: St Vladimir's Seminary Press, 2000), 17.

as God is a union of three persons, dwelling in each other through a move-ment of unceasing mutual love, so man becomes fully himself[131]—fully human according to the divine [trinitarian] image—only when living in and for others. We become human by sharing.[132]

In light of the fundamentally social character of human life, it is not surprising to recall the passage from St John of Damascus that I quoted earlier: Human life reflects its likeness to God through the "possession of the principle of virtue and as regards his imitation of God through virtuous and godlike actions.... Such actions consist in being disposed with *philanthrōpia* towards one's fellow humans . . . and in manifesting compassion (*eusplanchnia*) and sympathy (*sympatheia*) to all."[133] Centered on the love of God, human life in any full and complete sense is to be pursued with and for others in a communion or community that respects and affirms the fundamental equality of honor that each person has as an image of God in Christ. The other-regarding virtues of compassion and mercy that St John of Damascus cites are crucial to the realization and fullness of life.

St John Chrysostom notes that virtuous people pursue virtue as "beautiful in herself" independently of any promises or extrinsic rewards. The virtues of compassion or mercy are beautiful in themselves precisely because through them we serve others for their sake and thus both share with them the gifts that God gives us and bear witness to his compassion for us. St John Chrysostom also links being virtuous for its own sake with obeying a command of God. And indeed, God commands us to live in certain ways: "Be merciful [*oiktirmones*, or compas-sionate], as your Father also is merciful [*oiktirmōn*, or compassionate]"[134]; "Deal mercifully and compassionately [*racham, oiktirmōn*] every one with his brother: and oppress not the widow, or the fatherless, or the stranger, or the poor."[135]

God, however, does not give us these commands as kinds of "categorical imperatives" to follow simply for their own sake as duties unconnected with human flourishing and deification. God gives us these commands in order that we might live in the fullest sense of that word both in relation to God and to one another. If we are compassionate and merciful for the sake of God or Christ, then we fundamentally express our love for and gratitude to God and Christ—as

---

[131]Better: human beings become fully themselves.
[132]Kallistos Ware, "Mystery of the Human Person," 66.
[133]John of Damascus, *On the Virtues and Vices* (*Philokalia* 2:341; Greek 2:238).
[134]Lk 6.36.
[135]Zech 7.9–10.

a deeply personal love and not merely as obedience to some impersonal divine command—by caring for others for their sake.

In contrast to those who pursue virtue for its own sake, Chrysostom refers to those who are weak and are motivated by "prizes" that are self-aggrandizing, or who are motivated by fear of punishment. One common feature of urban Christianity in the fourth century is that many Christian bishops such as St John Chrysostom, St Basil of Caesarea, and others made strenuous efforts to persuade wealthy and elite Christians to share their wealth with those who were extremely poor. Even if we allow for some rhetorical exaggeration in the portraits of the wealthy and the poor, it is clear that there were rich urbanites who despised those who were poor, had leprosy, were disabled, were prisoners, or were otherwise socially marginalized.

We find any number of descriptions of these people as exceptionally greedy, envious, and unwilling to share anything with those who were poor.[136] Many of these descriptions of wealthy people follow the brief description that Jesus gives of the rich man in the parable of the rich man and Lazarus.[137] The people that are described in fourth-century homilies are so affectively sclerotic against the poor and other disaffiliated people and so attached to the denigrating language used to describe them, that many of the bishops were trying to persuade those who basically lacked any sense of sympathy (*asympathēs*) or mercy (*aneleēmōn*)[138] to show a bare minimum of pity for people, much less any compassion for them.

Here is part of St Basil the Great's excoriation of grain merchants who exploited parents driven to sell their children into slavery because of a famine. After describing the agonizing "Sophie's choice" of a father who is trapped into letting all of his children die or selling one of them to get money to feed them, Basil writes:

> At length with tears the father goes to sell the dearest loved among his children. But you do not bend before the face of such agony. . . . Hunger drives this suffering man, but you . . . prolong his agony. . . . Tears do not move you

---

[136]For some examples, see John Chrysostom, *Homilies on Hebrews* 11 (NPNF¹ 14:422; PG 62:88); *Homilies on Matthew* 35 (NPNF¹ 11:235–36; PG 57:410); John Chrysostom, *Eight Sermons on the Book of Genesis*, trans. Robert Hill (Boston: Holy Cross, 2004), 92–3 (PG 54:603); and Gregory the Theologian, *Oration* 14.29 (FOC 107.62; PG 25:897).

[137]Lk 16.19–31. Certainly, not all of those who were wealthy behaved in this manner. In fact, there were any number of wealthy men and women who sold everything they had and gave it to the poor.

[138]This is analogous to Simeon's viscera that lacked compassion or sympathy (*sympatheia*) for Joseph. *Testament of Simeon* 2.2–7 (*Testaments* 111; Greek 16).

to pity; nor do his groans of anguish soften your heart. You are immovable and implacable. Money fills your mind.[139]

Since these people had made, or at least tried to make themselves "bullet-proof"[140] against being affected by the suffering of others, they were hardly likely to see compassion for all people as something beautiful in itself. Hence, one finds constant appeals to them to share what they had with people for various prizes or to avoid punishments.[141] In other words, the appeals were designed to awaken them to at least some awareness of the suffering of others that they could address purely or primarily for self-interest, what we today would call pity.

Acting for Self-Interested "Prizes" or Rewards

FEAR OF PUNISHMENT

I suggest that people who are motivated to perform "compassionate" actions for others out of some sort of fear of punishment and for the sake of avoiding punishment are in fact acting out of what I have described a kind of self-regarding pity rather than compassion in any robust sense of that term. We find an example of this latter kind of motivation given by Zebulun. After exhorting his sons to be compassionate to all people and all animals, he adds that because he was compassionate (*eusplanchnia*) to all:

> The Lord blessed me, and when all my brothers were ill, I escaped without illness. For the Lord knows everyone's purpose. Therefore, my children, have mercy in your feelings, because as a man does to his neighbor so will the Lord do to him also. For the sons of my brothers were ill, were (even) dying because of Joseph, because they had not shown mercy in their feelings, but my sons were preserved without illness . . .[142]

---

[139]Basil the Great, *Homily on the Saying of the Gospel according to Luke, 'I will pull down my barns and build bigger ones,' and On Greed* 4; *Sunday Sermons of the Great Fathers*, trans. and ed., M. F. Toal (Chicago: Henry Regnery, 1959), 329 (PG 31:270A–B).

[140]See above, p. 204.

[141]De Vinne, *Advocacy of Empty Bellies*, gives several examples from John Chrysostom and Peter Chrysologus (with the threat of punishment, 110) and Basil the Great and Augustine regarding prizes for almsgiving (97, 98). Cf. Bronwen Neil, "Models of Gift Giving in the Preaching of Leo the Great," *Journal of Early Christian Studies* 18.2 (Summer 2010): 244.

[142]*Testament of Zebulun* 5.2–4 (*Testaments* 263–64; Greek 124). Zebulun oddly seems to draw on a version of the "sour grapes" theology. See Chapter 3, pp. 92–93.

On the face of it, Zebulun seems to introduce a kind of quid pro quo between God and people in terms of showing compassion to others. In addition, he also suggests that God will punish children for the sins, the lack of compassion, of their parents since his brothers' sons remained ill and even were dying *because* their fathers had not shown compassion. His general claim in this text is that we should be "compassionate" to others because if we are not, God will not only punish us with physical illness but he might also punish our children with physical illness or even death.

The punishments to which Zebulun refers are, if you will, "external" in character rather than consequences inherent to the failure of being compassionate. Zebulun's admonition to his children is like telling people not to tell a lie because God might subject them or their children to an acute case of appendicitis. That is much different, for example, from cautioning someone not to lie because they risk developing the character defect of becoming a liar and diminish the realization of their own humanity.

Moreover, "compassion" for others that is motivated by fear of external punishment by God seems to be at best limited or defective. If someone renders assistance to another person strictly because of fear of physical or other punishments by God, then one wonders whether the person is being moved by compassion to assist the other in the spirit of hospitality and willingness to bear or suffer with the other, which Zebulun subsequently indicates shaped his own compassionate response to people. Indeed, towards the end of his *Testament*, Zebulun exhorts his sons to show compassion on everyone because "in the last days God will send his compassion (*to splanchnon*) on the earth and wheresoever he finds bowels of mercy (*splanchna eleous*, a visceral mercy), he dwells in him."[143]

To the extent that fear of punishment predominates in "compassionate" action, the question naturally arises whether people so motivated would be moved by "compassion" if they knew there was no punishment for not being compassionate. Suppose that I am moved by the awareness of another person's distress and I assist that person only so that I avoid being subjected to some physical or other punishment. Is it likely that I would assist the person if I were not afraid of being punished for not assisting him or her? The intention governing the action, then, seems to be a form of self-interested pity rather than compassion since I am acting primarily or even exclusively on what I perceive to be in my self-interest.

---

[143] *Testament of Zebulun* 8.2 (*Testaments* 268; Greek 126).

Chrysostom uses the parable of the rich man and Lazarus to stoke a fear of divine eternal punishment in those who lack any sense of pity or compassion. "Let no one hope for good things if he has not done good things."[144] The fates of the rich man and Lazarus are reversed in the next life. Unwilling to share any of his earthly goods with Lazarus, the rich man finds himself in hades subject to great deprivation where no one is able to help him.[145] The rich man in hell basically wants Abraham to send Lazarus to his brothers to frighten them into giving "alms" to the poor. He shows no interest in Lazarus except as a means to relieve his misery and to frighten his brothers into being charitable in order to save their own skins in the next life. His concern for his brothers is not surprising since, drawing on the parable of the last judgment, Chrysostom writes that in hell there is

> also darkness, and gnashing of teeth, and chains indissoluble, and an undying worm, and fire unquenchable, and affliction, and distress, and tongues scorching like the rich man's; and we wail, and no one hears us; and we groan and gnash our teeth out of anguish, and no one pays attention to us ... all is without pardon ... all that compassion that arises from nature [*ek tēs physeōs sympatheia*] is extinguished.[146]

Those who show no compassion in this life yet have great material benefits will have the tables turned on them. For people without pity (*aneleēmones*), who see no value in assisting others, these portraits of hell might strike fear in them if they believed them.[147] They might assist others, not because they care for them, but simply to avoid gruesome punishments in the next life. At most they would show pity but not compassion in any genuine sense.

These threats of eternal punishment are designed to stoke fear in the hearts of those who would otherwise not assist others in need. They can be contrasted with passages in which the inherent punishment of vices such as greed and extortion

---

[144]John Chrysostom, *Homilies on Second Corinthians* 10 (NPNF[1] 12:330; PG 61:472).

[145]John Chrysostom, *Homilies on Philippians* 2 (NPNF[1] 13:192; PG 62:195).

[146]John Chrysostom, *Homilies on Second Corinthians* 10 (NPNF[1] 12:329–30; PG 61:471–2). Chrysostom seems to depart from Evagrius in this text since he writes that "all that compassion that arises from nature [*ek tēs physeōs sympatheia*] is extinguished," while Evagrius believed that the seeds of virtue were never completely eliminated even in hell: see Chapter 3, p. 113. There is also dispute about whether Chrysostom believed in *apokatastasis* as did Evagrius. For a somewhat positive assessment see, Ilaria Ramelli, *The Christian Defense of Apokatastasis* (Leiden: Brill, 2019), 549–54. For a decidedly negative assessment see James Cook, "'Hear and Shudder!' John Chrysostom's Therapy of the Soul," in *Revisioning John Chrysostom: New Approaches, New Perspectives*, Chris L. de Wet and Wendy Mayer, eds. (Leiden: Brill, 2019), 264–66.

[147]Chrysostom likely thought they did not believe in these punishments since to such people they seem to be "a fable." *Homilies on First Corinthians* 9 (NPNF[1] 12:53; PG 61:81).

are set forth as a loss or diminishment of someone's humanity. This "punishment" contrasts with the inherent "reward" of compassion that is integral to one's full humanity or living according to the likeness of God. In contrast to the humanity of those who are merciful, compassionate, and kind, Chrysostom gives a stark portrayal of how the diminishment of one's humanity—not the image of God but the likeness to God—befalls those who exploit others and refuse to assist them. The text is rather long. But it gives vivid expression to the maxim that virtue is its own reward and vice its own punishment: respectively the realization and enhancement or the diminishment and injury to one's character and humanity.

> [The eyes of the greedy or rapacious person] do not see men as men. . . . He
> does not even lift up his head unto the Lord; but all is money in his account.
> The eyes of human beings are wont to look upon poor persons in affliction,
> and to be softened; but those of the rapacious man, at sight of the poor, glare
> like wild beasts. The eyes of human beings do not behold other people's goods
> as if they were their own, but rather their own [goods] as others; and they
> do not covet the things given to others, but rather exhaust upon others their
> own means: but these [rapacious people] are not content unless they take all
> men's property. . . . How then can [such a person] be human? Do you not see
> we call something humane [*anthrōpinos*] when it is full of mercy [*to eleou
> gemon*] and loving-kindness [*philanthrōpia*]? But when a man does anything
> cruel or savage, inhuman [*apanthrōpos*] is the title we give to such a person. . . .
> [T]he stamp of man as we portray him is his showing mercy. The animals
> without reason are such as they are by nature: but these [greedy and rapacious
> people], endowed by nature with gentleness, forcibly strive against nature to
> train themselves to that which is savage.[148]

This is a long passage to be sure, but extremely important. The inhumanity of those who exploit others solely for personal gain does not lie *simply* in their actions but just as much and perhaps more fundamentally in the ways in which they "see" other human beings. Their inhumanity—or their diminished human-ity—lies in sclerotic hearts and minds that dehumanize others as mere use objects. This applies both to those who refuse to assist others but also, I suggest, to those who merely pity or assist others for personal gain (as Lt Hofmiller acted towards Edith). The harshness of this language looks rather similar to the language of stigmatization since stigmatized people are viewed as defective or sub-human by

---

[148]John Chrysostom, *Homilies on First Corinthians* 9 (NPNF¹ 12:52–53; PG 61:80–81).

those who stigmatize them. Stigmatization, however, locks people in certain roles and reduces them to those roles. Chrysostom is not trying to do that.

> I know that many hate us because of these words; but I feel no hatred towards them; rather I have compassion for [*eleō*, or strive to show mercy to] and lament for those who are so disposed. Even should they choose to strike, I would gladly endure it, if they would but abstain from their savage mind.[149]

Rather, Chrysostom is trying to correct people from what he and the Christian tradition view as self-destructive behaviors, attitudes, and dispositions; namely, vices. He does not at all think that people in this life are locked into those roles or that they are defined by these roles. On the contrary, he is trying to awaken some sense of repentance in them. As I will argue in Chapter 6, this effort to lovingly correct people is a part of the "tough love" that is fully compatible with compassion.[150]

But why be compassionate to others as something inherently good? Because being compassionate is simply part of being a human being made in the image and according to the likeness of God. Think of compassionate people who refrain from taking any great credit for what they do or are indifferent to external rewards because "I did what any normal person would do" or "what else would I do?"[151] People who make these sorts of comments might likely add that it would be inhuman or lacking in humanity not to act in such a way. Cast into a Christian context, they might say: "I'm simply trying to love others as Christ loved me." "I'm simply trying to be the kind of human person that Christ created me to be"—that is, oriented to care for others for their sake.

REDEMPTIVE ALMSGIVING

"Redemptive Almsgiving (works of mercy)" holds out the prize that monetary donations or works of mercy or compassionate actions will somehow "cover over" or wipe clean the past sins one has committed. There are several biblical and patristic texts that seem to affirm that almsgiving covers or removes sins:[152]

---

[149]John Chrysostom, *Homilies on First Corinthians* 9 (NPNF[1] 12:53; PG 61:82).

[150]See Chapter 6, pp. 248–50.

[151]People who offer these sorts of responses, whom Kristen Monroe calls altruists, do not have to embrace any particular religious framework. Indeed, she shows that holding religious beliefs is not a particular predictor of altruists or compassionate people (*The Heart of Altruism*, 121–30).

[152]*Eleēmosynē* is often taken as almsgiving in the narrow sense of distributing money or economic resources to those in need. These texts, however, also apply to *eleēmosynē* in the broader sense of works of mercy or acts of compassion.

- By alms and by faithful dealings sins are purged away.[153]

- Charity (*eleēmosynē,* works of mercy) for your father shall not be forgotten: and instead of sins it shall be added to build you up. In the day of your affliction, it shall be remembered; your sins also shall melt away, as the ice in the fair, warm weather.[154]

- Water will quench a flaming fire; and alms makes an atonement for sins.[155]

- For alms deliver from death, and shall purge away all sin.[156]

- But rather give alms of such things as you have; then indeed all things are clean to you.[157]

- "Nor would the infirmity and weakness of human frailty have any resource, unless the divine mercy, coming once more in aid, should open some way of securing salvation by pointing out works of justice and mercy, so that by almsgiving we may wash away whatever foulness we subsequently contract."[158]

One might understand these texts in terms of a balance sheet approach to salvation. For each person, there is a ledger: one side has room for tabulating the score for sinful actions and the other for tabulating the score for "righteous" actions including "almsgiving." Every time one commits some sin, one receives negative points depending presumably on the particular sin, its seriousness, the intention behind it, and so forth. The same is true for the good things one does, except that for "almsgiving," not only does one get credit for the good actions, one also gets credit, "covers over," or erases corresponding negative scores for bad actions. In fact, if almsgiving or works of mercy cover all sins, then presumably even acts totally unrelated to almsgiving such as murder, rape, or adultery might be "covered over" with the bonus credits from almsgiving. At the last judgment, the ledger "book of deeds" is brought out, the final score weighed, and judgment is rendered.[159] It is not clear why God would impose this sort of bookkeeping

[153]Prov 15.27 (LXX), or 16.6 (MT).

[154]Sir 3.14–15.

[155]Sir 3.30.

[156]Tob 12.9.

[157]Lk 11.41.

[158]Cyprian of Carthage, *On Works and Alms* 1 (ANF 5:476; PL 4:605), discussing the way God allows us to deal with post baptismal sins.

[159]For ancient sources for this idea, see Peter Brown, *The Ransom of the Soul: Afterlife and Wealth in Early*

nightmare on himself or his angels. Rather, as an alternative model, his forgiveness of past sins in response to current almsgiving or works of mercy might simply be a matter of mercy.

In both models, however, the "reward" for works of mercy is "backwards looking." Both models assume some notion of retributive justice relative to our deeds: we ought to be punished according to what we deserve. The accounting model provides an offset for this retribution through some sort of calculation that uses good deeds to "write off" punishment for bad deeds. The compassionate forgiveness of past sins because of good deeds basically offsets the requirements of retributive judgement through mercy. Retribution in and of itself, however, has no interest in whether someone is "rehabilitated" or is willing to undertake a transforming repentance. Having paid one's debt or had it forgiven, one can go one's merry way and sin some more with the idea that future almsgiving will "right the scales." Repentance in this context can simply be a process of confessing to one's misdeeds and then performing some good deed in the future as a way of atoning for or offsetting evil deeds. Good deeds or works of mercy in this sense function simply as a kind of restitution for past misdeeds.[160]

Simply offsetting the demands of retribution to motivate good works or alms misses the fundamental understanding in Orthodox Christianity that salvation—that is, being restored to the fullness of life in relation to God, one another, and the whole of creation—is a matter of healing and transformation, to use a modern term for repentance, through our cooperation with divine grace. Becoming someone who loves God with all one's heart, mind, and soul and who loves one's neighbor as oneself—or, perhaps more radically, loves others as Christ loved us—is a "forward looking" project of character formation and not a matter of maintaining a spiritual spreadsheet of good and bad actions.

Jesus, in Luke 11.41 above, and Cyprian seem to suggest that "giving alms," as a mere action, redeems or cleanses sin. In Luke 11.38, however, a Pharisee criticized Jesus for not ritually washing his hands before a meal. Christ responds that the Pharisees focus on external rituals to the neglect of inner dispositions by allowing themselves to be filled with greed and sin.[161] Jesus' point is that "He who made the outside also made the inside." Cyprian interprets this to mean that unless what is

---

Christianity (Cambridge, MA: Harvard University Press, 2015), 97–98; and Leslie Baynes, *The Heavenly Book Motif in the Judeo-Christian Apocalypses 200 BCE–200 CE* (Leiden: Brill, 2012), 8 and 85–105 for the discussion of the Book of Deeds containing the "heavenly accounting of people's works, good and evil."

[160] This is true only if one focuses on the actions and not the intention.

[161] Lk 11.39.

within (namely, the heart) is cleansed, the actions that one performs will not be cleansed. Conversely, by cleansing the heart, the actions that follow from it will also be cleansed:

> He who shall have cleansed what is within has cleansed also that which is without; and that if the mind is cleansed, a man has begun to be clean also in skin and body. Further, admonishing, and showing whence we may be clean and purged, he added that alms must be produced. He who is compassionate (*misericors*) teaches and warns us that compassion (*misericordia*) must be shown; and because he seeks to save those whom at a great cost he has redeemed, he teaches that those who, after the grace of Baptism, have become foul, may once more be cleansed.[162]

In other words, if we develop a compassionate disposition we must and will show compassion to others—not as an extrinsic addition but as a constitutive part of what a compassionate disposition involves.

Theophylact, moreover, rightly notes that the translation of Luke 11.41 that I used above—"but rather give alms of such things as you have; then indeed all things are clean to you"—is not correct. Jesus, Theophylact says, is quite precise: he says we should give alms of that which is within (*ta enonta*)—namely, the heart—and not just things, material goods, or what we possess (*ta onta*). The proper meaning of Luke 11.40—taking *eleēmosynē* as works of mercy or compassionate actions rather than simply as alms or giving money—is: "Give what is within [the heart] as works of mercy [or, works of compassion] and all things will be clean."[163] In other words, it is not the action alone of assisting someone, whether through money or other means, that constitutes a work of mercy but the intention with which one gives. Purely self-interested giving might express pity for someone but it does not express a work of mercy, which must stem from a compassionate intention (as I have characterized it) and not pity.

To illustrate the importance of intention, St John Chrysostom writes:

> Works of mercy or compassion (*eleēmosynē*) not greed, for that which proceeds from greed endures not, though you give to those who need. For almsgiving is that which is free from all injustice and this makes all things clean.

---

[162]Cyprian of Carthage, *On Works and Alms* 2 (ANF 5:476; PL 4:606).
[163]Theophylact, *The Gospel according to Luke*, 133 (PG 123:869A, commentary on Luke 11.37–41). Contrast the NKJV translation above with the NASB translation of this verse.

This is a thing better even than fasting, or lying on the ground; they may be more painful and laborious, but this more profitable. It enlightens the soul, makes it sleek, beautiful, and vigorous.[164]

Compassion as a Virtue Beautiful in Itself

We can now develop a holistic, therapeutic sense of how works of mercy or compassion can "cleanse sins." Our English word "repentance" translates *metanoia*, which fundamentally means undergoing a change of mind (*nous*) or heart. Repentance is far more than simply "being sorry" for evil things one has done. It involves a process of seeing things in a new way or, equivalently, refashioning the heart, viscera, mind, and intellect (*nous*) from being dominated by self-aggrandizing passions to being redirected to love, compassion, and mercy. Recall my discussion of Zacchaeus in Chapter 3: his sudden repentance in which he restores to others the same or even more than he has taken from them is just the beginning of a true repentance. The principal spiritual and existential challenge that awaits Zacchaeus is whether this initial act of repentance as restitution will lead to a genuine change of heart and mind in which he fundamentally reframes his relationships with God and his fellow humans. Repentance, as Chrysostom pointedly observes, is not primarily "backward looking" but forward looking towards healing and wholeness:

> And repentance involves not doing the same again; for he that again puts his hand to the same, is like the dog that returns to his own vomit ... and like the person in the proverb who cards wool into the fire or draws water into a cask full of holes. It is necessary, therefore, to depart both in action and in thought from what we have dared to do, and having departed, to apply to the wounds the remedies which are the contraries of our sins. For instance: have you been grasping and covetous? Abstain from rapine, and apply works of mercy [*eleēmosynē*] to the wound.... Have you spoken ill of your brother, and injured him? Cease finding fault, and apply kindness.[165]

---

[164]John Chrysostom, *Homilies on John* 82 (NPNF[1] 14:300; PG 59:442). St John is commenting on Luke 11.14. Also see John Chrysostom, *Homilies on Matthew* 19 (NPNF[1] 14:153; PG 57:275); *Homilies on John* 33 (NPNF[1] 14:117; PG 59:192).

[165]John Chrysostom, *Homilies on John* 34 (NPNF[1] 14:121 mod; PG 59:197). See Plato, *Laws* VI, 780c for the reference to the person who cards wool into the fire and Plato, *Gorgias* (493b) and cf. Jeremiah 2.13 for the person who draws water into a cask full of holes (leaky jar) and cf. Jeremiah 2.13 (broken cisterns). Plato uses this image to describe the unrestrained hedonist for whom immediate pleasure is the only good.

Doing works of mercy that flow out of an inner disposition of compassion can "cover past sins" in a healing or therapeutic sense. For example, people who do not exercise or eat properly and suffer the ill effects of such behavior may undergo a process of "repentance," as it were, to refashion how they treat their body. They will undertake a regime of exercise and better eating habits and in the process begin to experience the gradual removal (at least partially) of the effects of the ill health that stemmed from the lack of exercise and good nutrition. To be successful in this new regime, however, they will most likely have to deal with their attitude towards food, what prompts them to eat, what has motivated them to avoid exercise, and so forth. The changed disposition of maintaining exercise and good nutrition does not "cover" the effects of lack of exercise and bad nutrition in some bookkeeping model of point scoring. Rather, the new disposition allows the person to be healed and freed from the attachment to the passions that undermined the good effects of proper exercise and nutrition. Of course, there may be scars or damage from the old bad habits that do not completely disappear.

In the same way, showing compassion and mercy to others can serve to "cover past sins" in the therapeutic sense. In a forward-looking process of repentance or change of mind and heart, one aims at developing, by striving to acquire the Holy Spirit, a compassionate and merciful disposition—a merciful and compassionate heart. This disposition frees one from acting in terms of the self-aggrandizing passions and thoughts that brought about the neglect or mistreatment of people in the first place and separated us from God by not manifesting to others the mercy he shows to us.

Compassion leads us away from ourselves to affirm others and care for their welfare. In a more holistic and Christian sense, by "putting on Christ," being compassionate leads us to understand and experience that our own human flourishing, salvation, and sanctification is interconnected with serving others for their sake. The cultivation of a compassionate disposition allows us, with the grace of God, to seek to love others as Christ loved us, to the extent that through compassion, we become—should consciously aim to become—more fully living icons of Christ who are, as we say of the saints, God-bearing (*theophoroi*) people of God. It is in this way that compassion and the actions that flow from it "cleanse us from our sins." It is in this sense that the compassionate person can value or affirm compassion as beautiful and good in itself.

Our capacity for compassion and mercy is a gift of God that belongs to our very being: the capacity by nature to be compassionate and merciful, which is what the early Christian tradition regards as a natural capacity for sympathy and compassion. The Psalmist writes, "The Lord crowns you with mercy and compassion."[166] Crowns can be bestowed at the beginning or the end of an activity. Crowns symbolizing victory or exceptional performance are awarded at the end of an activity as the symbols or rewards for exceptional performance. Crowns of investiture, which are given when someone undertakes an office, symbolize at least some of the nature or prestige of the office. Monarchial crowns often symbolize the power, majesty, glory, and responsibilities of the office.

In an Orthodox Christian wedding, the sacramental highpoint of the service occurs when the bride and groom are crowned to one another. They receive martyrs' crowns. The basic meaning of "martyr" (Greek *martys*, a "witness," "one who bears testimony") is to faithfully bear witness to something even when that requires self-sacrifice. The bride and groom are crowned to one another in order to indicate they have received God's blessing and strength to manifest through the Holy Spirit the hard work and commitment of self-sacrificial love—Christ's love—that is foundational for the community (*koinōnia*) of a family. In the same way, I think, God crowns us with compassion and mercy to invest us by nature with the capacity to serve one another with virtues that imitate the divine characteristics and energies of mercy and compassion. We are created, after all, "to share" as Metropolitan Kallistos observed. If you do not resonate with the theocentric background for this view, then note that the Dalai Lama makes a similar point: "Ultimately, the reason why love and compassion bring the greatest happiness is simply that our nature cherishes them above all else."[167]

Moved by Compassion for the Sake of Christ and Our Fellow Humans

Compassion, as has been discussed so far, is fundamentally directed towards other people and other living things. But Christian compassion is also expressed for the sake of Christ or out of love for Christ. St Gregory the Theologian concludes a discussion of the spiritual importance of a number of virtues with this:

> Contemplation [*theōria*] is a beautiful thing, as is action [*praxis*]: the one because it rises above this world and advances towards the Holy of Holies and conducts our mind upward to what is akin to it, the other because it welcomes Christ and serves him and confirms the power of love [*philtron*]

[166]Ps 102.8.

[167]Tenzin Gyatso, "Compassion and the Individual," ‹http://www.dalailama.com/messages/compassion›, April 20, 2020.

through good works.... We must regard charity [*agapē*, love] as the first and greatest of the commandments ... its most vital part is love of the poor [*philoptōchia*], compassion [*eusplanchnia*] and sympathy [*sympatheia*] for our fellow humans. Of all things, nothing so serves God as mercy [*eleos*] because no other thing is more proper to God.[168]

Human rationality and freedom are often taken as the defining features of our nature. Rationality can often be limited to our conceptual and cognitive capacities for understanding things. Our increasingly sophisticated understanding of other animals has blurred some of the traditional boundaries between us and them in terms of cognitive abilities. It is, however, the spiritual dimension of our being that is ultimately most distinctive about us. As intrinsically valuable as reason and freedom are for human life, what is really distinctive about us is the gift of being able self-consciously, and thus freely and with understanding, to commend or offer "ourselves, each other and all our life unto Christ our God."[169] As St Gregory pointed out, we do this through *theōria* (the life of prayer and worship) and *praxis* by serving and welcoming Christ through compassion and mercy towards our fellow human beings.

We should note, however, that there are texts where those in need seem to become simply means through which compassionate actions gain some sort of benefit from God. We might give to the poor or assist those in need because we expect that they will pray for us and enhance our status before God. We might assist those in need because they will be porters who will carry our gifts to heaven for spiritual reward. We might give to those in need because at the last judgment they will be called to advocate for or against us.[170] In all of these cases, engaging in compassionate or merciful actions is framed in the context of "economic exchange": those whom one assists cannot repay the assistance in any material or worldly form but they become means by which God can receive our actions and

---

[168]Gregory, *Oration* 14.4–5 (FOC 107.41–2; PG 35:864).

[169]The entire petition reads: "Commemorating our most pure, most holy, most blessed and glorious Lady Theotokos and Ever Virgin Mary with all the saints, let us commend ourselves and each other, and all our life unto Christ our God." In the Divine Liturgy of St John Chrysostom, this is the final petition for the Great Litany, the Little Litanies before the second and third antiphons, and the Litany of Supplication. With some variation in the opening part of the petition, it also is said as the last petition before the Lord's Prayer and the Litany of Thanksgiving at the close of the Divine Liturgy (*Divine Liturgy, Chrysostom*, 31, 32, 34, 59, 72–3, and 84). The same petition occurs throughout the Divine Liturgy of St Basil as well as many other services such as Vespers, Matins, and Compline.

[170]De Vinne, *Advocacy of Empty Bellies*, 98–114, discusses these motivations for "almsgiving" and cites a number of patristic authors, e.g., Augustine, Chrysostom, Gregory of Nyssa, and Clement of Alexandria.

provide benefits (or punishments) far more valuable (or fearsome) than any material or other benefit that could be returned by people in need.

Put another way, these sorts of appeals were ways in which various Church Fathers tried to give some (spiritual) utility and status to individuals and groups who were simply ostracized and denigrated by various elites or simply excluded as members of Roman society. They were ways of rendering visible those who were socially invisible.[171] These appeals, however, can certainly create the impression that we are not really serving or welcoming Christ. Rather, we are simply serving the poor or others in need in order for them to help us gain benefits or avoid divine punishments. These appeals suggest a kind of exchange in which those who are wealthy get a significant return on their investment: the rich give material goods to the poor and the poor aim to provide more valuable spiritual goods in their interventions with Christ. But then the question arises: if people give alms or do works of mercy only for the sake of this sort of return on their investment, would these same people render any assistance apart from that promised return on investment?

Let me be a bit more precise for my purposes. The idea that people can assist others in ways that work to their mutual advantage is ambiguous. I can assist you for your sake because I care for you. We can care for each other to our mutual advantage as well. For, if that care flows out of a virtuous disposition, then even if people gain no other benefit from caring for others, it is to their advantage to do so because of the way in which it expresses their character and humanity. This is so regardless of whether we think of that or even consciously intend to act for that reason.

Egoists, however, who assist others only for self-gain may end up doing what is to their advantage and the advantage of the persons they help. But that is only because their advantage happens to coincide with that of the persons they help and not because they really care about those persons in the sense of acting for those persons' sake. Two ethical egoists can mutually benefit one another even though neither cares about the other for the sake of the other. The problem with the appeals to assist others mentioned above is that if is they are cast entirely in the language of economic exchange, they are perfectly compatible with purely self-interested assistance (pity) rather than compassion.[172]

---

[171] Cf. Holman, "Entitled Poor," 481–82, for the efforts of Christian bishops in the fourth century to create "kinship" ties for those who had no social standing in the Roman Empire.

[172] This is why Chrysostom rejects assistance given to others purely for the sake of vainglory or reputation as counting as a work of compassion or mercy. *Homilies on Matthew* 19 (NPNF[1] 10:131; PG 57:275). Such acts may have the "face" of "mercy" but the intention of cruelty and inhumanity (*apananthrōpia*).

At times, moreover, one finds texts where we are encouraged to give to Christ instead of the poor. Chrysostom, for example, scolds widows who want other people to give alms for them. He comments that they should not disdain to assist the poor themselves because it is really not to the poor that they give but to Christ.[173] Taken at face value, the poor in this case are merely means to give to Christ. One wants to give to Christ but since that cannot be done directly, the poor or other people "in need" serve as proxies for Christ. In this case, Christ seems to appear "behind" the poor. Those in need at best stand as surrogates for Christ, to such an extent that by giving or failing to give to them, one reaps the rewards or punishments that come from showing mercy to Christ himself, or failing to do so. It is hard to see how actions performed with this sort of intention—I am really giving to Christ and not those in need—could be regarded as compassion for other people since they are effectively rendered invisible or reduced to instrumental value.

This appeal to show compassion to Christ rather than a person in need is different from the appeal that one should find Christ in all people since we are all made in the image of Christ, "When therefore you see a poor person, remember his words, by which he declared, that it is he himself who is fed. For though that which appears is not Christ, yet in this man's form Christ himself receives and begs."[174]

In sharing our common nature,[175] he is the source of our equality in honor as human beings. Christian compassionate affirmation of the fullness of humanity of others means that we are consciously oriented to others as living icons of Christ. We comport ourselves towards them in light of the sanctity and dignity they have as living icons of Christ made in his image. In being living icons of Christ, we embrace the compassion of his Incarnation for the sake of assisting others and for their salvation. After all, he calls all people to salvation: the fullness of life in communion with the Trinity, one another, and with creation. This fullness does not occur in this life, but in the life to come.

Along with hospitably inviting us to manifest compassion without borders to people for the sake of responding to suffering, vulnerability, and distress, Christ gives us the Church, the Body of Christ, for us to extend his compassionate and hospitable invitation to all people for a living, faithful relation with

---

[173]John Chrysostom, *Homilies on the First Epistle of St Paul to Timothy* 14 (NPNF[1] 13:454–55; PG 62:573).

[174]John Chrysostom, *Homilies on Matthew* 88 (NPNF[1] 10:523; PG 58:778–79).

[175]Christ is, after all, both one in essence (*homoousios*) with the Father and Holy Spirit and one in essence (*homoousios*) with us (Fourth Ecumenical Council of Chalcedon, AD 451).

him.[176] Orthodox Christians believe that the fullness of faith and truth are in the Church. But as Fr Georges Florovsky notes: "Pastors appeal to human freedom, to human will and call for decisions. This respect for freedom applies to all Christians and not just pastors. As Chrysostom used to say 'We have to accomplish the salvation of men by word, meekness, and exhortation.'"[177] This requires humility, acceptance of our own creaturely vulnerability and weakness, and full respect for human freedom. Moreover, in respecting human freedom and that the fullness of truth is found in Christ and the Church, we also must respect God's freedom in saving people. God will save those whom he wills since in the Orthodox Christian tradition the "Church has no monopoly on grace and truth and love . . . salvation depends upon the actual life of the person. . . . Only God is capable of judging how well a man lives according to the measure of grace, faith, understanding, and strength given to him."[178]

We recognize and affirm that the persons for whom we show compassion have the same human equality of honor with us that Christ has in his humanity. This means that we show compassion for others for their sake and not merely as a means to some end. But we also recognize that the vulnerability and suffering, which they endure, is borne by Christ in his incarnate solidarity with all humanity. "He is despised and rejected by men, a man of sorrows and acquainted with grief. Surely he has borne our griefs and carried our sorrows."[179]

In a compassionate orientation towards others, I am not moved by compassion to act for the sake of Christ instead of the person before me. Rather, I am moved by compassion to act for the sake of the other person and out of love for Christ. Christ himself indicates that the compassionate actions that I render to the person before me are accepted by him as if they were offered to him.[180] Indeed, Christ accepts all compassionate actions for others as offered to him even if people do not recognize that Christ is present in the other person.[181]

---

[176]"Go therefore and make disciples of all the nations, baptizing them in the name of the Father and of the Son and of the Holy Spirit, teaching them to observe all things that I have commanded you" (Mt 28.19–20).

[177]Georges Florovsky, "St John Chrysostom: The Prophet of Charity," *St Vladimir's Seminary Quarterly* 4.3–4 (1955): 37.

[178]Fr John Matusiak, "What about Other Christians," <https://oca.org/questions/otherconfessions/what-about-other-christians>, April 20, 2020. Cf. John Karmiris, "The Universality of Salvation in Christ," *Theologia* 52.1 (1981), 43–45 (in Greek), and George C. Papademetriou, "An Orthodox Christian Understanding of Non-Christian Religions," <https://www.goarch.org/-/an-orthodox-christian-view-of-non-christian-religions#_edn19>, April 20, 2020.

[179]Is 53.3–4. Read during Great and Holy Friday, Royal Hours, Sixth Hour.

[180]Mt 25.40.

[181]Mt 25.37–40.

Christian compassion is located in the immanent yet always transcendent economy of Kingdom of Heaven as described in the parable of the unmerciful servant.[182] This "economy" and its mode of interactions with others and with God is not oriented towards individual profit maximization or a kind of quid pro quo mode of exchange. The economy in the Kingdom of Heaven is a gift economy in which we are all invited to participate.[183] In this economy, we are to freely give of what we have received. When he compassionately forgave the debts of the servant, the king gave a gift of compassion and forgiveness to the servant and invited him to show that same gift to others as a way of giving thanks for the compassion and forgiveness that he received.[184]

Put in a slightly different manner: the compassion and mercy we receive from God during the Divine Liturgy is to be reflected in our liturgy after the Liturgy. The monastic reformer, Nikon of the Black Mountain, took express note of how the church and the hospice at the Monastery and Hospice of the Mother of God *tou Roidiou* provided the places where these two liturgies were linked. The church was the place where people observed the first and great commandment: "To love the Lord your God with all you heart and mind," while the hospice was the place where people observed the commandment to love our neighbor, "which means all humankind." Noting Christ's dictum that the Law and prophets depended on observing both of those commandments, Nikon wrote: "For these things the church and the hospice were provided."[185]

In the gift economy of the Kingdom of Heaven, our natural compassion takes on a fundamentally liturgical and eucharistic character in our liturgy after the Liturgy. In the Eucharist, we freely receive from the Father the great gift of Christ himself, his Body and Blood, in his love and compassion for us, in and through the Holy Spirit. To be sure, before the consecration and distribution of the Holy

---

[182]See Chapter 3, p. 116.

[183]Jones, "Opening the Doors of Compassion: Cultivating a Merciful Heart," 9. See Susan Holman, *The Hungry are Dying*, 32–34 for a discussion of the function of gift economies. The gift economy of compassion, in which we strive "to be compassionate as our Father is also compassionate" (Lk 6.37), however, is not what she describes as gift economies in the Roman Empire; namely, economies "in which reciprocal obligations maintained social stability between friends as well as benefactor and recipient" (32). Rather, it is patterned on Christ's injunction: "Freely you have received, freely give" (Mt 10.8), in which one hopes for nothing in return (Lk 6.36).

[184]Parable of the unmerciful servant (Mt 18.21–35).

[185]"Typikon of Nikon of the Black Mountain for the Monastery and Hospice of the Mother of God *tou Roidiou*," trans. Robert Allison, in *Byzantine Monastic Foundation Documents*, ed. John Philip Thomas, Angela C. Hero, and Giles Constable (Washington: Dumbarton Oaks, 2000), 1:430. This particular monastery, alas, was at a nadir point in its history when Nikon made this observation (425).

Gifts, we are enjoined to "lay aside all earthly cares that we may receive the King of All, who comes invisibly upborne by the angelic hosts."[186] Yet as we prepare to depart back into the world, we are enjoined once again in the final Prayer of Thanksgiving "to commend ourselves and one another and all our life to Christ our God." Commending or entrusting our entire life to Christ does just not mean passively accepting whatever happens in life. It means:

- To offer our entire life to Christ in thanksgiving;

- To be moved by a compassionate disposition or character to face the world with faith in the steadfastness of Christ's compassion and love for us: that he will not forsake those who trust in him; that he will be with us to the end of the world;[187]

- To embrace Christ's commands that provide the bridge connecting our reception of Christ's compassion in the Liturgy and our reflection of that compassion in our lives:
  - "Freely you have received, freely give."[188]
  - "Be compassionate as your Father also is compassionate."[189]
  - "Love one another as I have loved you."[190]

---

[186]From the *Cherubic Hymn* prior to the Great Entrance in the Divine Liturgy (*Divine Liturgy, Chrysostom*, 55).

[187]Mt 28.20.

[188]Mt 10.8.

[189]Lk 6.36.

[190]Jn 13.34.

CHAPTER 6

Limits to Compassion?

In the Orthodox Christian tradition, compassion is not reduced to a simple emotion that springs up periodically in people. It is, as we have seen, an embodied affective dispositional orientation to others in which we are holistically rooted in the heart as the locus of our life with the Trinity, Christ, and with creation. It is a foundational virtue in human life that is central to our striving to attain to a likeness to Christ and that is to be offered to all people without judgment. Are there times, however, when we should withhold compassion?

In the first section of this chapter, I will explore this question by considering the relation between compassion and justice. I will initially look at three main arguments that compassion and justice are fundamentally at odds with each other. They are at odds if 1) compassion is a simple, raw emotion; 2) compassion is expressed merely as supererogatory mercy or charity; and 3) compassion can be identified with a form of condescending pity that is compatible with denigrating and marginalizing people.

I will then turn to some arguments that compassion is linked with justice in certain key ways. First, since compassion is a way of "seeing" and affirming people in the fullness of their humanity, compassion plays a key affective role in affirming the dignity and value of people that is essential for obtaining justice whether retributive, distributive, or restorative. Next, I will argue that compassion can play a key role in the quest for social justice. By social justice I mean the establishment of social structures and institutions that promote human welfare free of the social stigmatization and delegitimation or denigration that "justifies" unjust social exclusion and oppression. In other words, compassion need not simply be expressed as charity or mercy to individuals or groups.

In the second part of the chapter, I will explore what appears to be the tension between compassion, as unbounded generosity towards others, and ethical requirements to resist evil as well as to set limits on people who engage in significant self-destructive actions or violent actions that aim to harm or kill others. I will follow the chapter with a brief Epilogue that sums up what I believe is the central role of compassion in Orthodox Christian spiritual life.

Compassion and Justice[1]

Compassion Unrelated to Justice

On the one hand, it would seem that compassion does not have much if any relation to justice. Here are three reasons why we might adopt this view.

The first reason: for Roger Crisp, compassion is essentially a non-cognitive feeling of pain or distress at another person's pain or distress. We saw an example of this type of compassion in Zebulun's paralyzing grief-stricken reaction to his brothers' plan to murder Joseph. Crisp even cites evidence that suggests infants are said to be capable of "feeling" compassion.[2] Compassion in this sense would seem to be a largely involuntary and inarticulate response to suffering. Even though this feeling may provide some emotional impetus for helping people, it is too unreliable to guide action by itself. Crisp even suggests that "because of its unreliability, I suspect that in the end the truly virtuous person will feel compassion not especially intensely and perhaps quite rarely" but rely on "rational considerations to most effectively help others."[3]

On this interpretation, compassion or a feeling of distress at another's suffering, which may prompt one to act, is wedded to an extreme form of particularism. It is directed to this particular person in this particular situation. It is devoid of any "resources" in itself to guide action in a general way or even in a prudential manner. Zebulun, you may recall, thought his weeping for Joseph influenced his brothers not to kill Joseph. But there was nothing particularly conscious or intentional about this weeping.[4]

Taken as a "mere feeling," compassion seems blind to justice, or at best a kind of undeveloped protest against injustice that is basically irrelevant for determining how people should be treated justly. Why? Justice, in a general sense, requires treating people as they deserve. Central to the claims of justice is that people deserve to be treated fairly, equally, and impartially. Even if we are primarily

---

[1] Justice, of course, takes many forms such as distributive justice, retributive justice, deterrence, restorative justice, and procedural justice.

[2] Roger Crisp, "Compassion and Beyond," 240. At this level, compassion, such as it is, and pity are probably interchangeable.

[3] Crisp, 245.

[4] See Chapter 5, p. 187.

concerned with what justice requires in a particular case—what justice requires for this particular person in this particular situation—we cannot avoid the universal demand either (1) that everyone else in any situation be treated in exactly the same way (justice as strict equality of treatment) or (2) that similar persons in similar situations be treated in the same way (proportionate justice).

If we adhere to strict equality or universality in administering justice, then we remove any discretion in deciding how people should be treated. In this case, our emotions or affective stances would seem to have no role in administering justice or treating people fairly. Three examples: First, if I announce on a syllabus that at least 500 points are necessary and sufficient to get an A and allow no room for discretion in assigning grades, then I cannot justly lower the grade of someone who gets 501 points whom I happen to loathe; I cannot justly raise the grade for someone who gets 499 points even though I have sympathy or compassion for the extenuating circumstances that have affected his or her performance in the class. Second, judges who must follow mandatory prison sentence guidelines cannot, as sworn officers of the court, depart from those guidelines regardless of their compassion for a particular person who has been found guilty of an offense and for whom the sentence would seem unusually harsh. Third, I may have an employee who does good work but for a variety of reasons—e.g., personal health, family responsibilities, transportation problems—simply cannot make it to work without frequent tardiness or time off. At some point, no matter how sympathetic I might be to this person's plight, if I cannot accommodate his situation in light of inflexible personnel regulation, I would have to discharge him assuming I could not successfully appeal the regulations to obtain an exception.

Proportional equality or universality does not require that everyone be treated identically but that similar people in similar circumstances be treated in the same way. We often use this sort of justice rather than strict equality. If I am distributing antibiotics to a group of people, I obviously would not give everyone the same amount or type of antibiotic. I would likely vary the amount and type according to medical need, the type of illness, financial need, and so forth. There is an array of criteria by which goods, services, burdens, and penalties can be legitimately distributed, such as merit, need, or social utility. If the non-cognitive accounts above are correct, compassion would effectively be useless in determining criteria for distributive justice or in equitably and fairly administering such justice in a particular situation. On these accounts, compassion seems to be a kind of subjective emotion that is unreliable. If I alter how I treat persons in a particular situation because I "feel compassion for them" but treat other persons or those same persons in a relevantly similar situation differently because I do not feel compassion for them, my treatment of them is unjust and arbitrary, however merciful it might seem.

The second reason: Certainly there are times when we express compassion for people with an intense, non-verbal focus on them. We may show compassion to a stranger whose family member has been killed in an automobile accident simply by silently comforting him. There is "nothing to say" in such situations. We simply must be present to him and bear with him as best we can in his suffering and grief. In that presence—a kind of compassionate co-presence—we may be intensely focused on that person and oblivious to others and even ourselves. On the other hand, as we saw in Chapter 5, compassion often involves a deliberate intentionality and understanding: moved by compassion, people can articulate the character of suffering or distress to which they are responding, the ways in which they are trying to assist, as well as reasons for acting.[5]

Even allowing for this, however, compassion is often linked with showing mercy (*eleos*), which seems to drive a wedge between compassion and justice. For example, the principle of retributive justice requires that people get exactly what they deserve. It is always unjust to punish innocent people. Strictly speaking, we are also required to punish people for what they do wrong. But there is a principle of permissive retribution that makes it morally permissible not to punish people, which can include showing mercy to people.[6] The principle of permissive retribution sets aside the principle of strict retribution. Rather than "right the balance" between the criminal and both the society and the victim that is demanded by retribution, compassion and mercy set aside the demands of a strict retributive justice in favor of forgiveness or lessened sanctions.[7]

For St Isaac the Syrian, the wedge between justice and compassion and mercy splits them apart:

> Compassion and justice in one soul are as a man adoring God and idols in one
> house. Everywhere compassion is the enemy of justice. Justice is the equality

[5]Crisp acknowledges this in more developed forms of compassion but does not give it any epistemic or normative weight; that is, for him even more developed forms of compassion fail to provide the understanding and moral guidance required for action (245).

[6]J. L. Mackie, "Morality and the Retributive Emotions," *Criminal Justice Ethics* 1.1 (1982): 4. Cf. Jacelyn Pollock, *Ethical Dilemmas and Decisions in Criminal Justice*, 9th edition (Boston: Cengage Learning, 2016), 332.

[7]Compassion, whether or not framed as showing mercy, is far more integral to restorative or community justice. But I will touch on that at the end of this section.

of the even scale which gives to every man as he deserves without deviation to any side and without any consideration of a reward for it[self]. Compassion is an affection which is stirred by bounty and which goes out to every one for their support. It repays him that has deserved evil. To him that has deserved good, it gives a double portion. If the former stands on the side of righteousness, then the latter is on the side of evil.[8]

The tension between justice and compassion is also expressed by the psalmist:

The Lord is compassionate and merciful, long-suffering and plenteous in mercy. His wrath will not endure until the end, neither will he be angry forever. He has not dealt with us according to our iniquities, nor rewarded us according to our sins. As high as heaven is above the earth, so the Lord has strengthened his mercy toward them that fear him.[9]

In other words, God is willing to suspend meting out retributive justice towards us in favor of showing mercy and compassion. God's compassionate response to human sinfulness that restores human beings to the fullness of life with him, one another, and the whole of creation is typically understood as an act of compassion and mercy on God's part and not a matter of justice.

As an aside, however, this seems to assume that God's justice is a matter only of retributive justice. But if the point of salvation and redemption is to heal people, repair the ruptures in relationships between people, nature, and God, and to restore the whole of creation to the fullness of life, then God's justice might be more fittingly framed as a kind of restorative justice and rehabilitation for which divine compassion plays an integral role.[10]

In any event, the parable of the good Samaritan[11] can be interpreted to suggest the same dis-relation between compassion or mercy and justice: the former sets aside or goes beyond what justice requires. In response to the question by a young man about who his neighbor is, Jesus tells the story of the good Samaritan. Finding a man beaten by the wayside, the Samaritan, moved by compassion, renders immediate aid and provides funds as well as lodging for the man's full recovery. This contrasts with the actions of a priest and a Levite who simply pass by the man.

---

[8]Isaac of Nineveh, *Mystic Treatises*, 50, 325. This translation is based on the Syriac text. It differs slightly from the translation based on the Greek text where it is found in *Homily* 51; Holy Transfiguration Monastery, *Ascetical Homilies*, 244. In the latter version, "mercy" replaces "compassion"; but the overall point is the same.

[9]Ps 102.8–11.

[10]See below, pp. 242–43 for a contrast between retributive and restorative justice.

[11]Lk 10.25–37.

Of the three men who encounter the man beaten by the road, Jesus observes and the young man agrees, that the Samaritan is the neighbor because he shows mercy (*eleos*) to the man who has been beaten.[12]

We might give the parable a libertarian reading. Libertarianism is a philosophical view that maintains people have no natural rights or moral claims to assistance from other people. People are entitled to assistance only from those persons or groups who have made some positive or conventional contract to assist them.[13] If so, then the man beaten by the road has no inherent just claim to be assisted. Since none of the men who pass by him have made any contract to assist him, he has no conventional or morally justified claim for assistance. Hence, just as God's forgiveness of our sins is a matter of mercy that sets aside retributive justice, so the good Samaritan's actions, within a context of libertarian justice, are a supererogatory or non-obligatory act of mercy independent of any moral obligation to render assistance. In any event, if showing compassion to others fundamentally means being merciful to them, then compassion is negatively related to justice in that compassionate or merciful actions set aside any inherent or moral as well as conventional claims of justice, through showing a generosity to people for which they have no just claim.

The third reason: Moreover, if compassion is confused with pity as I have characterized it, it may seem to function in environments that support social injustice and inequality. "Compassion patronage," or what I think is better called "pity patronage," likely characterizes at least some colonial manifestations of philanthropy. It is manifest in the ethno-centric "paternalism" of White Europeans and Americans who assisted people of color yet who viewed them as children, barbarians, primitives, and so forth. John Stuart Mill justified a paternalistic rule over people who were unable to care for themselves or protect themselves. But he also infamously justified such rule over "those backward states of society in which the race itself may be considered as in its nonage.... Despotism is a legitimate mode of government in dealing with barbarians, provided the end be their improvement."[14]

[12] Lk 10.36–7.

[13] See David T. Ozar, "Rights: What They Are and Where They Come From," in *Philosophical Issues in Human Rights: Theories and Applications*, ed. Patricia Werhane and A. R. Gini (New York: Random House, 1986), 20.

[14] John Stuart Mill, *On Liberty* (Kitchener, ON: Batoche Books, 2001), 14 (original text: 1859). Mill served as an administrator for the East India Company for many years. For his justification of "benevolent despotism" of the people of India by the British, see Abram L. Harris, "John Stuart Mill: Servant of the East India Company," *The Canadian Journal of Economics and Political Science / Revue canadienne d'Economique et de Science politique* 30.2 (1964): 191–93.

Philanthropy operating under such paternalism would be designed to "improve" people—that is, to "elevate" them to the sort of life that conformed with Western European conceptions of rationality or Christianity. Such philanthropy can also feed off economic inequality and exacerbate it.[15]

In recent times, Andy Baker has drawn on empirical evidence that shows white Americans are inclined to be more favorably disposed to provide aid to foreign people of African descent than those of East European descent. This inclination is not based on "perceived greater need" but on an "underlying racial paternalism that sees them as lacking in human agency."[16]

So far as this sort of philanthropy is motivated by pity, what people give with one hand through various forms of social and material assistance is taken away with the other hand, since the recipients of such assistance are still marked by invidious social categories that deny them any full "adult" participation and/or recognition in their own social world or globally. This sort of philanthropy runs counter to the demands of any form of social justice that opposes the unjust marginalization of people.

To briefly sum up: it seems that compassion and pity, at least in some manifestations:

(a) are indifferent to the claims of justice when viewed as a kind of immediate non-cognitive emotional "bonding" with someone in pain or distress; or

(b) set aside the claims of strict retributive justice or other forms of justice since compassionate action is viewed as supererogatory; or

(c) implicitly accept and legitimize paternalistic and inegalitarian social structures.

Compassion Linked with Justice

How then, on the other hand, might compassion be linked with justice? I want to emphasize that the distinction between compassion and pity that I developed in Chapter 2 and elsewhere is crucial to the following discussion. In particular, compassion for others involves not just certain actions for others or on their behalf

---

[15]For the latter point see the criticism of what Peter Buffet calls "Philanthropic Colonialism": Peter Buffet, "The Charitable-Industrial Complex," New York Times, July 26, 2013, <http://www.nytimes.com/2013/07/27/opinion/the-charitable-industrial-complex.html?_r=0>, April 20, 2020.

[16]Andy Baker, "Race, Paternalism, and Foreign Aid: Evidence from U.S. Public Opinion," *American Political Science Review* 109.1 (2015): 93–94.

but even more fundamentally how we view and regard them; namely, as a holistic affirmation of them "without accusation."

Justice, of course, requires fairness, equality, and impartiality. It demands that each person be treated with a basic respect and sense of dignity. Consequently, justice cannot be obtained when invidious distinctions of denigration and stigmatization hold sway either individually or collectively. They must be exposed and rooted out. So far as seeking justice is something that people and communities "live out," it cannot be reduced to rational norms, procedures, and rules. For example, a society may establish all sorts of rules, procedures, and norms as criteria for legal justice in criminal cases. This is called procedural justice and governs the entire criminal legal process from arrest, to charging, to prosecution, through sentencing.

Yet seeking and maintaining justice is fundamentally bound up with our lived interpersonal and social relationships to one another. Our lived experience of others is always embodied in character no matter how much we may try to live in our heads or follow rules or procedures in terms of reason alone. Seeking justice requires our lived embodied experience as well as a holistic affirmation of the full respect and equality of honor by nature that people deserve.

A society can promulgate all of its rules for the fair and just treatment of people. But if those who enforce the law under those rules are filled with animus towards a particular group, there is very likely to be discriminatory treatment of that group.[17] Compassion as I have argued in Chapter 5 is precisely the disposition, the orderliness of the heart and viscera (and mind!), that can "clear a space" to secure justice in this lived sense precisely because it constitutes an embodied, holistic orientation and openness towards others as "equal in honor." Compassion, properly linked with dispassion, pushes back on and actually frees us from the visceral and cognitive hardness by which we mistreat others.

If we turn to restorative justice, compassion becomes even more fundamental because compassion for those in broken relationships is aimed at reconciliation as far as possible. Restorative justice seeks to achieve reconciliation among people to repair the injuries that arise from unjust action. It aims to foster compassion, not pity, both towards and between victims and offenders.[18] The same is true of

[17] See Besiki Kutateladze, Vanessa Lynn, and Edward Liang, *Do Race and Ethnicity Matter in Prosecution? A Review of Empirical Studies* (New York: Vera Institute of Justice, 2012) for a literature review of racial bias in prosecution throughout the criminal justice process in the United States.

[18] For a discussion of the nature of and differences between retributive and restorative justice, see Michael Wenzel, Tyler G. Okimoto, et al., "Retributive and Restorative Justice," *Law and Human Behavior* 32 (2008):

rehabilitation, which is properly aimed at helping people overcome all of the passions and experiences that lead them to harm themselves and others.

Our natural capacity for compassion and mercy is the root of neighborliness, which is a fundamental good for any human community. Chrysostom observes that a "rule of the most perfect Christianity [is] . . . seeking those things that are for the common advantage [or, good]. . . . For nothing can so make a person an imitator of Christ as caring for his neighbor."[19] As the social philosopher, R. H. Tawney, also once observed: "There is no touchstone, except the treatment of childhood, which reveals the true character of a social philosophy more clearly than the spirit in which it regards the misfortunes of those of its members who fall by the way."[20] Compassionate neighborliness, however, should extend to everyone within a community or, more broadly, "to all" as Zebulun indicated when he exhorted his children to show compassion to all humans and to all animals.[21] This means that compassion, as I have characterized it, is oriented in principle to support and create the most inclusive communities and societies possible that are free both of the prejudicial distinctions by which people are marginalized as well as of social structures by which people dominate others based on these distinctions or for that matter by wealth, power, and status.

In what ways might compassion support the search for social justice as I have described it?[22] Very briefly, compassionate actions are often portrayed in strictly interpersonal terms: I show compassion for this particular individual. Given the apparent intentional focus of compassion as leading to actions for the sake of particular individuals, compassion would seem indifferent to questions of social and structural justice. Its concern seems to consist in "bringing charity to people" and not in addressing issues of institutional or structural injustice. But it seems to me that this view is simply wrong.[23] Surely, people can be moved by compassion

375–89. For an extended critique of restorative justice and the compassion it advocates, see Annalise Acorn, *Compulsory Compassion: A Critique of Restorative Justice* (Vancouver, BC: University of British Columbia, 2005). For a critical review of this work, see Bruce Archibald, "Why Restorative Justice is not Compulsory Compassion: Annalise Acorn's Labour of Love Lost," *Alberta Law Review* 42.3 (2005): 941–50.

[19]John Chrysostom, *Homilies on First Corinthians* 25 (NPNF¹ 12:146; PG 61:206).

[20]Richard Henry Tawney, *Religion and the Rise of Capitalism* (New York: New American Library, 1955), 268.

[21]*Testament of Zebulun* 5.1 (*Testaments* 263; Greek 123). Also, recall the point of the parable of the good Samaritan: the neighbor (*plēsion*) is the one who draws near (*pros elthōn*) to everyone, even those who are despised within society.

[22]For some helpful discussion, see Mary Collins, Kate Cooney, and Sarah Garlington, "Compassion in Contemporary Social Policy: Applications of Virtue Theory," *Journal of Social Policy 41.2 (2012): 251–69.*

[23]Recall that in the Old Testament, God's compassion is directed to the people of Israel and not just individuals. That is the entire point of God's manifestation of his glory and compassion to Moses on Mount Sinai:

to render assistance to many people in a refugee camp and not just one particular person for whom they express compassion at a particular moment. This is true of individuals and groups, e.g., many religious and secular organizations such as International Orthodox Christian Charities or Doctors without Borders. But even so, one might think that such compassionate action is not directed towards issues of justice but "mercy," whether in the sense of kindness or in the sense of what goes beyond what justice requires. But again, that is just not correct. I can be moved by compassion to bring water and food to people who are starving by endeavoring to rectify unjust conditions that deprive them of food and water.

Throughout history, personal and collective efforts driven by a sense of compassion to help people have often been directed at providing assistance to them but not with a concern to address issues of structural injustice and inequality. Acknowledging her life-long devotion to saints who had devoted their lives to caring for others, especially those who suffered from profound affliction and were often ostracized, such as lepers, Dorothy Day also noted two long-standing questions that persisted for her: "Why was so much done in remedying the evil instead of avoiding it in the first place? Where were the saints to try to change the social order, not just to minister to the slaves, but to do away with slavery?"[24]

Dorothy Day was challenging the sort of religiosity that divides the private sphere from the public sphere and restricts compassionate action to the "private" interrelations among individuals or various "charity" groups and other people. Fr Boris Bobrinskoy, however, once wrote that:

> There is, in the ultimate reality of things, no nonspiritual life that is closed off to the Holy Spirit. . . . The world that is called profane is in reality a profaned world and man is responsible for that. We have expelled God from this world: we do it every day. We chase him from public life by a Machiavellian form of separation between our private lives—pious and good—and the domains of politics, commerce, science, technology, love, culture and work, where everything is allowed. All these domains of human work depend upon the creative work of man, seized, modeled, and inspired by the Spirit of God.[25]

that he will remain faithful to the Israelites as a people and not just to Moses. So too, in the Christian tradition, the compassion that motivates the Incarnation of the Son of God is directed to the entire human race as well as to all of creation.

[24]Dorothy Day, *The Long Loneliness: The Autobiography of Dorothy Day* (New York: Harper Collins, 1958), 45.

[25]Bobrinskoy, *The Compassion of the Father*, 28. Quoted in the Introduction to the volume by Maxime Egger.

Why can we not be moved by compassion to address issues relevant to changing a social world that harmfully or unjustly affects human beings throughout their lifespan? Surely that would be vital for any properly comprehensive defense and promotion of the sanctity of life. While the Christian rulers of the Byzantine state, such as emperors, empresses, court dignitaries, and the Church did not systematically address or work to change serious economic equality or slavery, the rulers did enact legislation and create institutions intended to benefit those who were poor, sick, orphans, and so forth. [26] Moreover, *philanthrōpia* was considered to be a, if not the, prime virtue of the Byzantine emperor.[27] In fact the Emperor Justinian viewed his legislation as a manifestation of his *philanthrōpia*.[28]

The concern with social issues and social justice is just as important for the contemporary Orthodox Christian Church, as Demetrios Constantelos pointedly observed:

> Because of peculiar historical experiences—one might speak of vicissitudes—the Orthodox have often failed to respond to social problems such as racism, peace and war, social justice, and political oppression in a systematic manner. … [However] if some Orthodox fail to raise voices of protest against racism, injustice, and oppression, they betray the ethos of their Church. But when they concern themselves with contemporary social problems, they act in full agreement with the nature and character of their Church in history.[29]

If compassion is oriented towards helping to secure the welfare of people who are suffering or vulnerable, then surely, we ought to enquire into the causes of that suffering—personal and social—in order to address it. We deny the fundamental reality of our own sociality in this life if we ignore the social context, which is inherently structural and institutional, in which we live.[30] We also ignore that

---

[26]For a general survey, see Constantelos, *Byzantine Philanthropy*, 111–36. For slavery, see Constantelos, *Poverty, Society and Philanthropy*, 103–14; for hospitals, see Timothy Miller, *The Birth of the Hospital*, 103–105; and for orphans, see Timothy Miller, *The Orphans of Byzantium*, 69–77.

[27]Constantelos, *Byzantine Philanthropy*, 43–61.

[28]Constantelos, *Byzantine Philanthropy*, 47–48.

[29]Constantelos, "Origins of Christian Orthodox Diakonia," 33.

[30]For an excellent analysis of the social and structural or institutional character of human life, see Peter L. Berger and Thomas Luckmann, *The Social Construction of Reality: A Treatise in the Sociology of Knowledge* (New York: Penguin Books, 1991). Social and institutional structures and policies as well as social roles pertain not only to political, economic, or governmental entities; they extend also to the wide range of private or non-governmental organizations such as businesses, educational institutions, religious organizations, and so forth, as well as to smaller communities such as the family.

social context if we do not fully confront the ways in which it is created and sustained by collective human actions including our own support of such action. Hence, in addition to being moved by compassion to provide direct assistance to people who are victims of sex trafficking, one could, and should if able, work alone or with others to eliminate the unjust conditions that support and exacerbate their suffering. One could be moved by compassion to assist refugees by seeking to create "infrastructures" that would facilitate the efficient and just distribution of goods or, perhaps more importantly, by empowering refugees to creatively participate in shaping the social world in which they live—both within refugee camps and when they leave them.

We see a good illustration of the importance of compassionate awareness and action to address social and institutional justice by considering problematic institutional structures that inhibit the expression of compassionate health care. For example, if an organization expects health care workers to provide compassionate care, then the working conditions and institutional policies have to be supportive of such care. If healthcare organizations expect "front-line staff" to provide consistently compassionate health care yet do not create the conditions in which such health care can be delivered but rather tolerate conditions that undermine such care, the staff as well as the patients are effectively treated unjustly.[31]

Richard Mannion argues that "while it is tempting to blame poor practice and compassionless care on the individual doctor or nurse delivering care," problems can be traced to the "inadequate systems and unsupportive organisational environments" within which competent and well-intentioned staff interact. To rectify this, compassion is not just an issue for front-line staff. Rather, "it is something that [must be] accomplished and reproduced at all levels of the healthcare organization"[32] that will support front-line staff (first responders, to use a contemporary term) in delivering compassionate health care.

---

[31] See also Wendy Austin, "Against Compassion: Understanding Institutional Perfidy as Evil," *Interdiciplinary.net*, 1–11, now at <https://www.researchgate.net/publication/316613210_Re_Making_the_Procrustean_Bed_Standardization_and_Customization_as_Competing_Logics_in_Healthcare/fulltext/5909b36b0f7e9b1d08160fb7/316613210_Re_Making_the_Procrustean_Bed_Standardization_and_Customization_as_Competing_Logics_in_Healthcare.pdf?origin=publication_detail>, April 20, 2020.

[32] Russell Mannion, "Enabling Compassionate Healthcare: Perils, Prospects and Perspectives," *International Journal of Health Policy and Management* 2.3 (2014): 116, <doi: 10.15171/ijhpm.2014.34>, April 20, 2020. Of course, changing organization policies and procedures to support the compassionate work for front-line workers will likely fail or be impeded if the people who administer those policies and procedures are indifferent or hostile to offering compassionate support to those workers.

In other words, compassionate health care requires that policies and institutional structures exist for the sake of people. When the opposite takes place—people existing for the sake of policies and institutions and broader developmental goals—then as Johann Galtung eloquently writes: Such policies and institutions "become reified, and countless sacrifices are demanded in their name. . . . In the name of a human theory, considerable antihuman crime can be committed."[33] It seems clear, to me at least, that Mannion's observations and Galtung's warning would apply in a general way to institutional and social organizations and structures, whether private or public.

We obviously do not have compassion for policy and social structures. Still, social policies, institutions, and structures always serve human interests. The question is always: whose interests? Because it is especially "allergic," as it were, to the invidious distinctions by which some people dominate, marginalize, and exploit others, compassion—especially when collectively manifested—can open up a lived, neighborly space that makes possible a rejection of those distinctions and an insistence that oppressive social structures be reformed. Compassion for others does not by itself formulate the details of socially just policies and institutions. But the theological, rational, empirical, political, and other forms of analysis that work out the details of such policies should remain "linked" to the compassion that gives rise to them so that the formulation and implementation of policies remain connected to the very people it is meant to serve and "liberate."

Compassion and Resisting Evil

In this final section, I would like to offer some thoughts on the possible limitations of compassion in our daily and spiritual life by posing and responding to two questions. First question: does compassion require simply granting requests for assistance without setting any limits? Second question: does compassion for others who would harm us or other people require a kind of passive forbearance that would restrict us to prayerfully bearing the burden of the ways in which they treat us?

To the first question. In bearing with others in their struggles, compassion seems to be a kind of unhesitating and unqualified generosity and service to others, so that we attend to whatever they might "need." Compassion might appear

---

[33]Johan Galtung, "The Basic Needs Approach," in *Human Needs: A Contribution to the Current Debate*, ed. Katrin Lederer (Cambridge: Oelgeschlager, Gunn and Hain, Inc., 1980), 56. See Wendy Austin, "Against Compassion," 3–4 for an example of Galtung's warning in what she calls "rationalized health care."

to involve always "saying yes"—in words and in action—to whatever demands or requests people place on us. St John the Merciful purportedly never refused the request of those who sought his assistance.[34]

If unrestricted generosity and forbearance towards others marks love and compassion for them, then compassion for others would seem to have no "brakes" in acquiescing to the demands that others place on us or in pushing back on the ways in which they treat us or possibly others. Applying such "brakes"—resisting others or saying "no" to their demands and actions—would thus involve setting aside the compassion we might want to show them.

Compassion for others, however, aims to serve and assist others primarily for *their* sake. Despite our openness and generosity towards others, compassionate actions can go awry. With the best of intentions, we can do things for others that hinder or harm them, or enable them in self-destructive actions. While we may have been moved with compassionate intentions to help people, if our actions misfire and do not help them, presumably we would want to reconsider how we are trying to help them.

Consider people who suffer from drug addictions or engage in constantly manipulative behavior towards others. We do not help people in these cases simply by giving in to demands or by not holding them accountable for what they do within the limits of what they can reasonably manage cognitively, emotionally, physically, and so forth. At some point, out of concern for them, a "tough love" may be required that sets limits to our interactions with them and challenges in a loving way their behaviors and attitudes. This obviously does not mean that we do not continue to love them or bear with them in and through their struggles. It does not mean that we are not available to listen to people. Indeed, listening to others, to give them "their own voice," is vital to affirming the humanity of others.

The sad reality, however, is that if we simply give in to peoples' demands, we run the risk of enabling their behaviors. Rather than truly affirming them as not having to be locked into an addiction, for example, we can end up confirming them in their addiction by enabling behaviors that perpetuate the addictions. Moreover, enabling behaviors in this way can become dysfunctional for the "care giver," since it can create forms of codependency in which the caregiver becomes

---

[34]Life of St John the Merciful, Patriarch of Alexandria, <https://oca.org/saints/lives/2000/11/12/103286-st-john-the-merciful-patriarch-of-alexandria>, April 20, 2020 Cf. Dawes, *Three Byzantine Saints*, 198, 200, and 214. Both biographies of St John that are in this volume give vivid testimony to his extraordinary compassion.

entangled in an unhealthy relationship and is buoyed along by various second-ary gains or benefits to the caregiver that arise in giving care to someone. This misguided sense of compassion and forbearance begins to slide towards pity, when the secondary gains people get from co-dependent relationships motivate, whether consciously or unconsciously, their actions to assist others.[35]

There may seem, however, to be a bit of hypocrisy in this sort of tough love towards such people. If we engage in an honest assessment of our weaknesses and failures for the purposes of confession or simply for self-examination, we will most likely come up with a litany of the same sins over and over again, such as gossip, short temper, gluttony, and lust, which, as St John Chrysostom reminded us, does not count as a true form of repentance. Yet as an anonymous author confesses: "I realize that my constant sinning is the virtual absence in me of any struggle with evil. As soon as any excuse or suggestion appears, I plunge right into the abyss of sin, and only after my fall do I ask myself: What have I done? A fruitless question, because it does not help me grow better."[36]

We are, for all practical purposes, addicted to our ongoing sins or harmful passions that have us hooked. They control us and not vice versa. The editors of the English edition of the *Philokalia* give a very good summary description of the stages of temptation developed by the Greek Fathers: We initially face temptations from provocations that assault us. They are natural to us and do not constitute sins so long as we reject them. But there are various stages of getting "hooked" or assenting to temptations of which the last is "prepossession" that "results from repeated acts of sin which predispose a man to yield to particular temptations" and evil passions that "violently dominate the soul."[37]

We engage in all kinds of strategies to trivialize these passions, to justify them (e.g., the excuse: "Everyone else does this"), or to indulge them. How can we, in

[35] See Ingrid Bacon, Elizabeth McKay, Frances Reynolds, and Anne McIntyre, "The Lived Experience of Codependency: An Interpretative Phenomenological Analysis," *International Journal of Mental Health Addiction* (2018): 1–18, <https://doi.org/10.1007/s11469-018-9983-8>, April 20, 2020. for an extended discussion of the complex concept of codependency. Also, see Michael McGrath, "Codependency and Pathological Altruism," in *Pathological Altruism*, ed. Barbara Oaklet, Ariel Knafo, et al. (Oxford: Oxford University Press, 2011), 49–69 and Josephine Ferraro, "Psychotherapy Blog: Exploring the Secondary Gains of Codependency," <http://psychotherapist-nyc.blogspot.com/2010/02/psychotherapy-exploring-secondary-gains.html>, April 20, 2020.

[36] "Confession: From an Athonite Pamphlet by An Athonite," <https://stvladimirs.ca/confession-from-an-athonite-pamphlet-by-an-athonite/>, April 20, 2020. This is one of the very best models and guides for confession I have found to offer parishioners.

[37] See *Philokalia* (English edition) 4:435–37 for a good summary of the stages of temptation as developed by the Greek Fathers.

compassion for others who suffer addictions or other self-destructive behaviors and attitudes, practice a tough love towards them that we do not show to ourselves? Of course, if we genuinely loved ourselves—really accepted who we are as created in the image of Christ with the task of striving to become like him—we would double down on our own life of prayer, repentance, and remorse. A genuine self-love is just the opposite of an egoistic self-love that leads us away from God through indulging our harmful passions.

If our "tough love" for others is accompanied by our refusal to acknowledge the ways in which we are enslaved to our own passions, then that tough love does display a kind of hypocrisy.[38] Hence, compassion for others involves humility in the presence of others and this means coming to terms with our own vulnerability and our weakness in dealing with our own enslaving passions as we work with and for the sake of others.

As I mentioned earlier, tough love for others does not mean that we forsake them. Moreover, if we insist that people meet our expectations for change or that they stop sliding backwards (recidivism) as a condition for continuing a caring relationship with them, then we need to bear in mind our own stance before God. In repentance, we continually ask God to show us mercy, perhaps in large part, because of our ongoing enslavement to our own passions. If God is long-suffering with us,[39] how can we not in principle extend that support to others, especially with those who suffer from any number of experiences or impairments that seem to trap them into repeating cycles of behavior that we take to be self-destructive? On the other hand, when those self-destructive behaviors lead to the abuse and harm of other people, then out of compassion for both parties, physical and social relationships might have to be severed with the abusive person. Yet we can and should still pray earnestly for their healing.

There are simply no easy answers to these sorts of situations. The main point I want to make is that compassion in any robust sense of caring for others is something quite different from simply indulging or "giving in to" the demands those whom we try to assist. When we do this and form bonds of co-dependency in which we obtain pathological secondary gains from assisting others and these gains are what motivate our actions, then we are showing pity rather than compassion. This dynamic certainly played out in Lt Hofmiller's relation to Edith and her family.

[38]Lest we want to take the high ground and tout our own self-mastery over our passions, we might compare ourselves to any number of saints (e.g., St Mary of Egypt), known for the ruthless honesty about their own constant failure in conquering their passions.

[39]Ex 34.6; also recall the long penitential prayer from Zephaniah quoted in Chapter 3.

Second question: does compassion for others who would harm us or other people require a kind of passive forbearance that would restrict us simply to prayerfully bearing the burden of the ways in which they treat us? It might seem so: Christ instructs us

> not to resist an evil person. But whoever slaps you on your right cheek, turn the other to him also. If anyone wants to sue you and take away your tunic, let him have your cloak also. And whoever compels you to go one mile, go with him two.[40]

In commenting on this injunction and Matthew 5.44, "love your enemies, bless those who curse you, do good to those who hate you,"[41] St Maximus the Confessor argues that Christ intended to free us from all anger towards others so that we should simply correct them through "forbearance," so that we might be made worthy of perfect love.[42] Yet, immediately prior to these texts, St Maximus insists that we rebuke those who slander or gossip about others in our presence. For if we do not, we commit two sins: (1) we do not correct the persons who engage in slander and (2) we run the risk of succumbing to listening to it.[43]

Moreover, while St Maximus seems to view anger as something to be completely eliminated in seeking perfect love, St John Chrysostom remarks in his homily on this same gospel text that Christ does not

> altogether repudiate anger . . . because this passion is even useful if we know how to use it at the suitable time. . . . And what is the proper time for anger? Not when we avenge ourselves on others but when we check the unruliness [of their passions] and correct their negligence.[44]

Jesus begins his exhortation to "turn the other cheek" in contrast to the tendency to seek "an eye for an eye." The command to seek an eye for an eye does not justify vengeance; in fact, in forbids vengeance. Vengeance allows for unbridled retaliation against others (e.g., your life for my eye). The principle of an eye for an eye justifies punishment as strict retribution.[45] That is, retribution requires inflicting pain or other burdens on people that must be strictly proportionate to

[40]Mt 5.39–42.

[41]Mt 5.44.

[42]Maximus the Confessor, *Four Hundred Texts on Love* 1.61, 62 (*Philokalia* 2:59; Greek 2:9).

[43]Ibid., 1.60 (*Philokalia* 2:59; Greek 2:9).

[44]John Chrysostom, *Homilies on Matthew* 16 (NPNF[1] 10:110; PG 57:248).

[45]Mt 5.38 referring to Ex 21.24, Lev. 24.20, and Deut 19.21. See Walter Houston, "Exodus," in *The Oxford Bible Commentary*, ed. John Barton and John Muddiman (Oxford: Oxford University Press, 2001), 83.

the wrong committed in order to fairly right a wrong. Retribution, however, is not really concerned either with rehabilitating those who do wrong or for obtaining reconciliation between them and the people they have hurt. Jesus is not simply commanding people not to seek vengeance on others but to check—and perhaps even eliminate—the desire for retribution.

Jesus' injunction to turn the other cheek could be understood as St Maximus does—patient forbearance in the face of harm for the sake correcting someone. But it can also be understood as St John Chrysostom does: along with forbearance, showing appropriate assertiveness (to use a modern phrase) towards unjust actions and people that is fundamentally concerned with correction and reconciliation. This sort of assertiveness is legitimately an element of "doing good to those who hate you"[46] as a compassionate engagement with them.

Fr George Morelli provides an excellent example of this compassionate assertiveness in confronting bullying. Without at all minimizing the serious harms of bullying for people who are bullied as well as bullies, the compassionate response to bullying is not striking back at bullies but an assertiveness that rejects the bullying and responds to a bully with love.[47] Surely, when school children are bullied, besides working with those children, parents or school officials are also called to respond to bullying in a way that tries to understand what drives the bullying activities, which comes through talking or dialogue with people who bully, and to work firmly but *irenically* with them for the sake of healing—both for them and for those who are bullied—and reconciliation.[48] This does not mean that sanctions may not need to be imposed on bullies especially if they steadfastly refuse to work with efforts to help them move beyond bullying people.

[46]Mt 5.44.

[47]George Morelli, "Smart Parenting XXIII: Coping with Bullying," <http://ww1.antiochian.org/content/smart-parenting-xxiii-coping-bullying>, April 20, 2020. For a similar treatment from more secular perspective see Miki Kashtan, "Bullying through a Compassionate Lens," *Psychology Today*, May 18, 2012, <https://www.psychologytoday.com/us/blog/acquired-spontaneity/201205/bullying-through-compassionate-lens>, April 20, 2020.

[48]To illustrate this point in a different context of law enforcement see, Josh Bowers, "The Case for Compassionate Policing." <http://uvamagazine.org/articles/the_case_for_compassionate_policing>, April 20, 2020 and Michael D. Bush, "Police Officers as Peace Officers: A Philosophical and Theoretical Examination of Policing from a Peacemaking Approach," *Journal of Theoretical & Philosophical Criminology* 6.3 (2014): 194–205. For a perceptive personal observation by a professional police officer on the value of compassion in law enforcement, see Cheri Maples, "A Buddhist Cop's Approach to Justice," *Lions Roar: Buddhist Wisdom for our Time*, July 27, 2017, <https://www.lionsroar.com/a-buddhist-cops-approach-to-justice/>, April 20, 2020. For a discussion of the toxic effect of the loss or lack on compassion on people in law enforcement, see Robert Johnson, "Compassion in Command," *Law and Order*, Oct (2009), <http://www.hendonpub.com/resources/article_archive/results/details?id=2079>, April 20, 2020.

This last point is important: when we observe people being abused or harmed by others, we certainly should be moved by compassion and a sense of justice to assist victims of such abuse. We must act to protect them, to help extricate them from abusive or harmful situations and relationships, as well as to help them gain some stability outside of the relationship. We must, however, equally respond with compassion towards those who perpetrate such abuse with the offers of healing (rehabilitation) and reconciliation (what is called restorative justice).[49] Again, we may need to restrain those who perpetrate abuse or victimize others, or impose other sanctions on them. But the goal of such actions is never simply retribution, much less vengeance.[50]

"Love your enemies, bless them that curse you, do good to them that hate you, and pray for them which despitefully use you, and persecute you."[51] As difficult as it may be in the face of the aggressive and remorseless evil that human beings commit, Christian compassionate love for them never abandons seeing them as made in the image of Christ with the capacity to become like him. It always sees them in light of our shared humanity with Christ, including our mutual vulnerability and weakness. It is thus always oriented towards healing and inclusion in community. Compassion for others is bound to resist the evil that others may perpetrate for the sake of those on whom they inflict evil but also for the sake of those who inflict evil on people. But this resistance is fundamentally oriented towards non-violent means towards ending conflict and achieving reconciliation. Violence, including lethal force, may be regrettably necessary to defend innocent people. However, the Orthodox Church has typically seen taking human life, even in war, as an evil and not as something justifiable as good even if necessary to defend innocent life.[52]

---

[49]Keep in mind the adage: "Virtue is its own reward and vice is its own punishment." Evil and destructive passions and character traits harm those who have them by diminishing their own character and the realization of their humanity as we saw in Chapter 5, p. 220, regarding Chrysostom's description of the inhumanity of greed.

[50]For example, it is extremely helpful to contrast the focus on retribution and deterrence in the treatment of criminals in the United States criminal justice system with the fundamental focus on rehabilitation and reintegration of convicts into society in the Norwegian criminal justice system. See Emily Labutta, "The Prisoner as One of Us: Norwegian Wisdom for American Penal Practice," *Emory International Law Review* 31 (2017): 329–59; and Megan Fowler, "The Human Factor in Prison Design: Contrasting Prison Architecture in the United States and Scandinavia," ed. Lola Sheppard and David Roy, *103rd ACSA Annual Meeting Proceedings, The Expanding Periphery and the Migrating Center* (2015): 373–380, <http://apps.acsa-arch.org/resources/proceedings/indexsearch.aspx?txtKeyword1=126&ddField1=4>, April 20, 2020.

[51]Mt 5.44.

[52]Phillip LeMasters, "Orthodox Perspectives on Peace, War and Violence," *Ecumenical Review* 63.1 (2011): 55–56. See Stanley Harakas, "No Just War in the Fathers," *In Communion*, <https://incommunion.

The hardened passions, beliefs, and dispositions that may arise in killing people must be counterbalanced by continuous openness of the heart for repentance, as well as sorrow for violence and for forgiveness as well as reconciliation. Indeed, compassion must counter all of these hardened passions in order to prevent us from hating or demonizing those who would harm us.[53] These hardened dispositions lead not only to murder but also to oppression, manipulation, and exploitation. This repentance, as all repentance in the Orthodox Christian tradition, is aimed at healing. This repentance must be undertaken both by individuals and by communities: both by how I need to repent and how "we" collectively as communities need to repent.

In the case of war, as James Campbell notes, repentance is not simply to be undertaken by armed combatants but the nation as a whole and the religious communities in those countries since "the violence of warfare inevitably entangles all those who participate in these conflicts to some degree, whether voluntarily or involuntarily." This is reflected in a contemporary prayer for repentance during war as part of the Litany of Fervent Supplication:

> Also, we pray to you for a speedy end to the conflicts in Afghanistan and Iraq and that all who are entangled in their violence may embrace the riches of your kindness, forbearance, and patience, and enter into that godly grief which leads to repentance; grant that our hearts and theirs may turn to works of reconciliation, to mercy and compassion for all. . . .[54]

This prayer certainly could be offered as a petition for our collective as well as personal entanglement in a wide array of evils that plague the social world and institutions in which we live, e.g., racism, sexism, xenophobia, and greed. Repentance, it must be remembered, is not just a backwards-looking project of contrition for wrongdoing. It is, as St John Chrysostom said, the forward-looking

org/2005/08/02/no-just-war-in-the-fathers/>, April 20, 2020. For a counterpoint to these articles, see Alexander Webster, "Justifiable War as a 'Lesser Good' in Eastern Orthodox Moral Tradition" (*St Vladimir's Theological Quarterly*) 47.1 (2003): 3–57. Responses to Fr Webster's article in the same issue are provided by Joseph Woodhill (59–64), Jim Forest (65–7), Nikolas Gvosdev (69–75), Fr Philip LeMasters (77–82), David Pratt (83–95), and Fr John Breck (97–109).

[53]Lacking this compassion, if you recall, is what led Simeon, Gad, and Dan to plot the murder of their brother Joseph and, failing that, sell him into slavery. See Chapter 5, pp. 184–85.

[54]For the prayer and the immediately preceding quotation, see James Campbell, "A Prayer for Peace and Repentance," Nov. 24, 2010, <https://incommunion.org/2010/11/24/a-prayer-for-peace-and-repentance/>, April 20, 2020. The prayer is a contemporary petition for repentance during war as part of the Litany of Fervent Supplication. Originally developed by the Orthodox Peace Fellowship, the version in the quote was approved for parish use by the Holy Synod of the Orthodox Church in America in spring 2010.

project of not doing the same evil things over and over again. The cultivation of compassion both personally and collectively is vital to this forward-looking project both in countering the passions that lead to such evil and as a real commitment to the social justice that seeks to eradicate such evils.

Epilogue

I n the Prologue to this book, I indicated that a very practical question guided this project: "Why should we care about being compassionate as human beings and also as Orthodox Christians?" That question, of course, presupposed that we respond to the question: "What does it mean to be moved by compassion?" To respond to both of those questions, we traversed the remarkable expression and manifestation of compassion in the Divine Liturgy, Scripture, hymns, and the writings of many Church Fathers and other Orthodox Christian authors. We found that the profound manifestation of compassion that underlies and "drives" the entire event of Christ's Incarnation provided the key source for responding to these questions. This is because in his person, Christ unites divine compassion and human compassion to such a degree, that we ourselves, in striving to become living icons of Christ, are to embrace the compassion he shows to us in our own compassion for others.

The many indicators about the nature and role of compassion in human life that were drawn from Chapters 2 through 4 provided the basis for developing the nature of a compassionate disposition and virtue. It is a holistic orientation to others that is constituted by a genuine and thoroughgoing neighborliness that is open to others, and affirms them in their humanity and uniqueness as persons. It involves an alert sensitivity to suffering that bears with others in solidarity and community, and it is radically free from any judgment that stigmatizes or marginalizes others. In particular, compassion is fundamentally different from pity. We also saw that the challenge of perfecting this disposition and virtue required that we overcome our self-aggrandizing passions through striving to acquire dispassion and also radically come to terms with the vulnerability and weakness that belong to us simply as created beings.

It is clear, I hope, that there is nothing sentimental or naïve about compassion in the Orthodox Christian tradition and spiritual life. Our long penitential journey through Great Lent means coming to terms with the brokenness of the world; our personal brokenness; and, as communities, our collective brokenness. Christ bears all of this brokenness for us, and he subjected himself to it in his brutal suffering, humiliation, denigration, and the death that he endured for us on the cross. We must each accept our own responsibility for that death: "When we gaze at our own failings, we see such a swamp that nothing in another can equal it."[1]

Sober repentance lies at the core of Orthodox Christian spiritual life. "Now therefore, says the Lord your God, turn to me with all your heart, and with fasting, and with weeping, and with lamentation: and rend your hearts, and not your garments."[2] Hardened through our own sinfulness, we must repent in order to devote ourselves entirely to God both individually and collectively. Joel, for example, calls an entire people to repentance and not merely individuals: "Sound the trumpet in Zion, sanctify a fast, proclaim a solemn service: gather the people, sanctify the congregation, assemble the elders, gather the infants at the breast."[3]

Orthodox Christian repentance is accompanied by a wide range of ascetic practices, especially prayer. They aim, with God's help, at attaining dispassion: freedom from all of the self-aggrandizing and self-centered passions that separate us from God, from one another, and from ourselves. It is through this dispassion that we open our heart—our entire being—to the indwelling of the Father, Son, and Holy Spirit within us. Utterly dependent upon God's mercy, compassion, and the sanctifying grace of the Holy Spirit, it is within our heart that we discover ourselves as persons and can fully experience and manifest the reality of being moved by compassion. It is there that we discover ourselves as living icons of Christ and that we are called to be bearers of the divine love in the world as living icons of Christ.

The more we renounce ourselves and the world through seeking dispassion, the more we are united with God, who is perfect love. United with his love that never forsakes the world, we are sent forth *by his very divine love* to face and engage with the world compassionately and lovingly as does the Theotokos even in the everlasting blessedness with which she has been graced.[4] As St Maximus the Confessor writes: "The actualization and proof of perfect love for God is a genuine and willing attitude of goodwill towards one's neighbor."[5] This integrated love for God and neighbor is vital to our theosis or deification: "[He will be] God, who in imitation of God's love towards humanity (*philanthrôpia*),

---

[1] St Seraphim of Sarov. See above, p. 203 for the entire quotation.
[2] Joel 2.12–13.
[3] Joel 2.15–16.
[4] See Chapter 4, pp. 158–60.
[5] Maximus the Confessor, *Various Texts on Theology, the Divine Economy, and Virtue and Vice* 1.36 (*Philokalia* 2:172: Greek 2:97). He cites 1 John 4.20 in support: "For he who does not love his brother whom he has seen cannot love God whom he has not seen."

cures the sufferings of those who suffer through his own sufferings in a manner worthy of God . . ."[6]

In facing the world and reflecting—more precisely, struggling to reflect, since repentance is a lifelong endeavor—God's perfect and compassionate love, we embrace Christ's command "love one another as I have loved you."[7] That is, we take up our cross and follow Christ by imitating the self-sacrificial love by which he sacrificed himself for us. If we are mindful of Christ's own life and the many saints whose compassion we venerate, we will be mindful of the burdens that true compassion involves as best we are able to bear them.

In Chapter 6, we saw that compassion is not expressed simply as personal or corporate mercy and charity. It is fundamentally open to and supportive of seeking the social justice that supports structures and institutions promoting fully inclusive societies that affirm the equality of honor we have by nature and that are free of the denigration and stigmatization that result in marginalization and oppression. Orthodox Christian compassionate engagement with the world, however, is never reduced to a mere form of social activism. It is always a liturgy after the Liturgy: as we offer ourselves and the world to Christ and the Trinity in prayer and worship during the Liturgy, we offer ourselves and the world to Christ and the Trinity through our compassionate engagement with the world after the Liturgy.

Our engagement with the world undertaken *for the sake of the world* is thus offered to Christ, and for the sake of Christ, in response to and in thanksgiving for the mercy and compassion he bestows on us. In consequence, we are to commit ourselves to a "continuous liberation from the powers of the evil that are working inside us" and we are to engage with "efforts aimed at liberating human persons from all demonic structures of injustice, exploitation, agony, loneliness, and at creating real communion of persons in love."[8]

---

[6]Maximus the Confessor, *On the Ecclesiastical Mystagogy* [*Mystagogia*] 24, trans. Jonathan A. Armstrong, PPS 59 (Yonkers, NY: St Vladimir's Seminary Press, 2019), 95; PG 91:713. What St Maximus writes about *philanthrōpia* (which includes kindness in the broadest sense) equally extends to compassion (*eusplanchnia*).

[7]Jn 15.12.

[8]Archbishop Anastasios (Yannoulatos) of Albania, cited in Ion Bria, "The Liturgy after the Liturgy," *International Review of Missions* 67 (Jan. 1978): 86, 87.

Glossary for Hebrew Terms
Transliteration Guide for Greek Terms

I n this appendix, you will find some very brief definitions of the principal Hebrew terms I am using. For the Greek terms, I will provide the spelling in the Greek and in the transliterated form I am using. I will also provide the "Strong's Concordance Number" for each Greek (G . . .) and Hebrew (H . . .) word when available.

The concordance was developed in the nineteenth century by James Strong.[1] In addition to the print edition of his concordance, there are versions of the concordance on the internet. For example, if you go to Blue Letter Bible, https://www.blueletterbible.org/, you can enter a Strong's number into the search window and get information about the meaning of the term as well as all of the English translations of Old Testament texts related to the Hebrew words and English translations of New Testament texts related to the Greek words. There is no simple way online to coordinate Greek terms in the Septuagint with their Hebrew counterpart. But, at Blue Letter Bible, if you view an Old Testament verse in the Interlinear mode, the Septuagint Greek text will be displayed below the English and Hebrew text. The same is true if you view a New Testament translation in Interlinear mode.

If you are interested in how different English versions of the Bible render individual verses, you can go to Bible Hub at https://biblehub.com/, enter a particular verse into the search window and pull up a wide range of traditional and contemporary English translations.

---

[1]James Strong, *The Exhaustive Concordance of the Bible* (Peabody, MA: Hendrickson Publishers, 2004). His concordance does not extend to the Septuagint. For such a concordance, see Johan Lust, Erik Eynikel, and Katrin Hauspie, *A Greek-English Lexicon of the Septuagint* (Stuttgart: Deutsche Bibelgesellschart, 2015).

Hebrew terms

1. *Racham*, (H7355) and (H7356), and the related adjective *rachuwm*, (H7349), have a root sense of deep love and affection for someone and, thus, of concern and compassion or pity in a more traditional sense of that term. Ps 102.13 illustrates this: "As a father shows *racham* to his children, so God shows *racham* to those who fear [or revere] him." In texts such as Deuteronomy 13.17 or 2 Kings 13.23, God's *racham* takes on a sense of mercy since through his *racham* God indicates that he will turn away from his deserved anger towards the Israelites. Various English translations render this sense of *racham* as compassion or mercy. It is most often translated in Greek by *eleos* or *oiktirmos* and their related parts of speech. It is most often translated by "compassion," "pity," or "mercy." In some texts, the lack of *racham* indicates particular cruelty towards people, e.g., Isaiah 13.18 refers to the Medes who will show no *racham* even to unborn children. *Racham* is also related to the cognate term *rechem* (H7358), or womb.

2. Although my primary focus is on the term *racham*, I want to mention the term *chanan*, (H2603) and (H2604), and its related adjective *channum* (H2587). The root in the active sense has the meaning of being gracious, merciful, or stooping or bending and being kind or merciful to someone in need or who is an inferior. The term is paired with *racham* in Exodus 33.19 and Exodus 34.6 and elsewhere as part of the "compassion formula" in Exodus 34.6. It is most often translated in the active sense in Greek by *eleos* or *oiktirmos* and their related parts of speech. In the active sense it is often translated in English by "mercy" or "gracious" but not by "compassion" or "pity."

As I mentioned, the reader can consult the entries for the Strong's number for these terms at <https://www.blueletterbible.org/>. This site also provides information about these terms from other Hebrew dictionaries.

Greek terms

Here is a listing of the principal Greek terms used in this work together with their Strong's number.

1) ἐλεέω, *eleeō*: v.; G1653
2) ἐλεημοσύνη, *eleēmosynē*: n.; G1654
3) ἐλεήμων, *eleēmōn*: adj.; G1655

4) ἔλεος, *eleos*: n.; G1656

5) εὐσπλαγχνία, *eusplanchnia*: n.: NA, not used in the New Testament

6) οἰκτείρω, *oikteirō*: v.; G3627

7) οἰκτιρμός, *oiktirmos*:n.; G3628

8) οἰκτίρμων, *oiktirmōn*: adj.; G3629

9) σπλάγχνον/σπλάγχνα, *splanchnon/splanchna*: n.; G4698

10) σπλαγχνίζομαι, *splanchnizomai*: v.; G4697

11 συμπάθεια, *sympatheia*: n.: NA, not used in the New Testament

12 συμπαθέω, *sympatheō*: v.; G4834

13) συμπαθής, *sympathēs*: adj.; G4385

14) συμπάσχω, *sympaschō*: v.; G4841

15) φιλανθρωπία, *philanthrōpia*: n.; G5363

God: Essence, Persons, and Energies

The terms "energy/energies" (*energeia/energeiai*) in reference to God have a special significance in the Orthodox Christian tradition. I will devote this appendix to a very brief discussion of this notion and the broader distinction between essence (*ousia*), persons (*hypostases*), and energies (*energeiai*) in reference to God.[1] This will provide a basis for understanding God's compassion as a divine energy.

Orthodox Christian theology is a celebration (*hymnologia*) of God's paradoxical, wondrous hiddenness from and manifestation to creation, especially all the reason-endowed beings therein. We saw the to-and-fro of this celebration in many of the hymns about Christ's Incarnation.

H 11. He who dwells in the light that no man can approach and who upholds all things, in his ineffable compassion (*eusplanchnian*) is born of a Virgin ...[2]

So too, we celebrate the Trinity: the Father, Son, and Holy Spirit, who in their "essence" are utterly unknown and hidden from all of creation, yet are present to and shared with all of creation through their divine energies (*energeiai*). For readers who might not be familiar with this topic, let me provide a very brief selection of texts from the patristic and Byzantine tradition that give expression to this paradox—the mystery—of God's divine inaccessibility to creatures and divine accessibility to them.

Citing John 1.18, "No one has seen God at any time; the Only-begotten Son, which is in the bosom of the Father, He has declared Him," St John of Damascus writes: "After the first and blessed nature no one has ever known God, unless he himself has revealed himself to them, not only no human being, but also not even any of the supramundane powers themselves, by which I mean the cherubim and seraphim."[3] Yet he later writes: "Therefore the divine is infinite and incomprehensible, and this alone can be grasped about it, namely, infinity and

---

[1] For a general discussion of this distinction as it would apply to God and to created things, see John of Damascus, *On the Orthodox Faith* 59 (=3.15; PPS 62:198ff.; PG 94:1048).

[2] See Chapter 4, p. 137 for the complete text of this hymn.

[3] John of Damascus, *On the Orthodox Faith* 1 (=1.1; PPS 62:59; PG 94:789A).

incomprehensibility. Whatever we say about God kataphatically makes manifest not the nature but what is around the nature. Whether you talk about goodness, or justice, or wisdom, or anything else, you are talking not about God's nature but about what is around the nature (*ta peri tēn physin*),"[4] which as we will see momentarily are described as God's energies.

For St Dionysius the Areopagite, God is utterly beyond all being and essence, hidden, nameless, and utterly unknowable to any created being: Nothing "among beings, or anything known among beings, brings down the hiddenness, beyond all and beyond logos and intellect, of the divinity utterly beyond all and apart from all."[5] Yet God is manifest to us and knowable through his uncreated processions in which he is active in the world. Whatever names we can apply to God refer to "the powers—whether essence producing, life producing, wisdom producing [and so forth] which are brought forward out of God into us."[6] These powers are God and not creations or finite beings. So Dionysius writes: "Of God there is intellect, reason, knowledge, contact, sensation, opinion, imagination, name, and everything else. God is not known, not spoken, not named, not something among beings, and not known in something among beings."[7] Dionysius neatly summarizes this distinction without any division "in" God in this way: God "is cause of all; but himself: nothing (*ouden*) utterly beyond all essential determination (*hyperousiōs*) and apart from all."[8]

St Gregory of Palamas provides this concise summary: "For to God pertains both incomprehensibility and comprehensibility, though he himself is one. The same God is incomprehensible in his *essence*, but comprehensible from what he creates according to his divine energies," which include his pre-eternal will, providence, wisdom, and so forth.[9]

For St Gregory Palamas, as for the Orthodox Christian tradition more generally, there is a threefold distinction (*diakrisis*) without division (*diairesis*) in God: the nature/essence (*physis/ousia*), the divine persons (*hypostases*), and energies

[4]John of Damascus, *On the Orthodox Faith* 4 (=1.4; PPS 62:66; PG 94:800B).

[5]Dionysius the Areopagite, *Divine Names* 13.3; Pseudo-Dionysius the Areopagite, *The Divine Names and Mystical Theology*, trans. John D. Jones (Milwaukee, WI: Marquette University Press, 1980), 205 mod. (PG 3:961A).

[6]Dionysius, *Divine Names* 2.7 (Jones trans., 123; PG 3:645B–C).

[7]Dionysius, *Divine Names* 7.3 (Jones trans., 179; PG 3:872A). Cf. The divinity is cause of all; but itself: nothing (*ouden*) utterly beyond all essential determination (*hyperousiōs*) and apart from all.

[8]Dionysius, *Divine Names* 1.5 (Jones, 113 mod.; PG 3:593A).

[9]Gregory Palamas, *Topics of Natural and Theological Science and on the Moral and Ascetic Life: One Hundred and Fifty Texts* 81 (*Philokalia* 4:384; Greek 4:163–4).

(*energeiai*) of God the Trinity. The divine essence is common to the three persons of the Trinity (Father, Son, and Holy Spirit) and only them. They are all *homoousios* (of one essence) with each other. However, the divine *ousia* is utterly unknowable to created beings, who are incapable of participating in it. The energies, however, express the creative actions of the Trinity towards creation. Created beings participate in them and they are knowable by intelligent created beings. These real distinctions about God do not imply any division in God so as to make God composite. These distinctions do not simply reflect the ways in which created beings know God. The energies, while not simply identical to the divine essence, belong to God.[10] They are at times referred to as "around the essence or nature" (*peri tēn ousian/physin*).[11] However, the divine energies are fully divine; they are not created.

The distinction has its origins in early Greek patristic authors such as St Athanasius.[12] The most robust understanding of this distinction was developed in the fourteenth century by St Gregory Palamas, whose teaching is typically taken in the Orthodox Christian tradition to be the definitive view on this matter. The Orthodox Christian teaching on the distinction of the divine essence, persons, and energies contrasts rather sharply with conceptions of God as absolutely simple in various Western Christian traditions where the persons and the "attributes" of God are identical to the divine essence.[13]

In Chapter 5, I cited a text from St Gregory of Nyssa in which he acknowledges that mercy and *philanthrōpia* are energies of God, but that they arise only

[10]For an early but still very valuable study of Palamas and his understanding of the essence, person, energy distinction, see Basil Krivosheine, "The Ascetic and Theological Teaching of Gregory Palamas," *Eastern Churches Quarterly* 3 (1938): 138–56. See also M. Edmund Hussey, "The Persons-Energy Structure in the Theology of St Gregory Palamas," *St Vladimir's Theological Quarterly* 18.1 (1974): 22–43.

[11]Cf. Gregory of Nyssa, *On Not Three Gods* [*Ad Ablabium quod non sint tres dei*] (PG 45:121A); John of Damascus, *On the Orthodox Faith* 1.4 (PG 94:800); Gregory Palamas, *150 Chapters* 82 (*Philokalia* 4:385; Greek 4:164). Basil Krivosheine, "Simplicity of the Divine Nature and the Distinctions in God, According to St Gregory of Nyssa," *St Vladimir's Theological Quarterly* 21.2 (1977): 88–94 discusses this phrase in Gregory of Nyssa. Krivosheine notes that the English phrase "around the divine nature [or, essence]" translates the Greek only when "essence" (*ousia*) or "nature" (*physis*) are used in the accusative case (*peri tēn theias ousian/physin*) and not the genitive (*peri tēs theias ouias/physeōs*), which would mean "said of" or "pertains to" the divine essence or nature (88, n. 62).

[12]See Georges Florovsky, "St Athanasius's Concept of Creation," in *Studia Patristica*, Vol. 6, ed. F. L. Cross, Texte und Untersuchungen zur Geschichte der altchristlichen Literatur, vol. 81 (Berlin: *Akademie Verlag*, 1962), 36–57.

[13]For a general treatment of this issue and a comparison of the Western Christian (specifically scholastic), the Orthodox Christian, and the Neoplatonic conceptions of divine simplicity, the reader can consult John D. Jones, "An Absolutely Simple God: Frameworks for Reading Pseudo-Dionysius Areopagite," *The Thomist* 69 (2005): 371–406.

after and in response to the fall.[14] Palamas rejects any notion that a divine energy, which is a natural energy (*physikē energeia*), could be accidental (*symbebēkos*) in God—that is, a variable activity that does not belong to the nature of God.[15] For Palamas, the essence, persons, and the energies are all uncreated, eternal, and all are fully divine. It might seem, however, that for Gregory of Nyssa, mercy and compassion are created energies since they arise only after and in response to the fall. If so, it seems that Palamas would have difficulty with Nyssa's characterization of divine mercy as an energy that arises after sin.

In the *Triads*, however, St Gregory clearly acknowledges that "There are, however, energies of God which have a beginning and an end, as all the saints will confirm."[16] He does not provide a list of these energies. However, in his work *Contra Nicephorum Gregoram*, Palamas notes that Nicephorus uses the very text of St Gregory of Nyssa that I quoted to argue that the energies are created things. While Palamas does not exegete Nyssa's text here, he immediately rejects Nicephorus' interpretation. God's mercy may not appear and be recognized and named by humans until after the start of creation; but this does not entail that God's mercy (*eleos*), providence, and sanctification (*agiasmos*) do not belong "to the nature (*physin*) of God" even though God "shows mercy and sanctifies creatures when those who require it might be present." Palamas very clearly states that "the divine mercy (*eleos*) is uncreated."[17] There is no indication in this text that he thinks he is contradicting Nyssa on this point.[18]

[14]See Chapter 5, p. 206.

[15]Gregory Palamas, *150 Chapters* 135 (*Philokalia* 4:410; Greek 4:182).

[16]Palamas, *Triads* 3.2.8; Palamas, *Triads*, 77; *Défense des Saints Hésychastes*, trans. Jean Meyendorff, 2nd edn (Leuven: Spicilegium Sacrum Lovaniense, 1973), 659.

[17]Gregory Palamas, *Contra Nicephorum Gregoram, Oration* 2.60. In P. K. Chrestou, ed., Γρηγορίου τοῦ Παλαμᾶ συγγράμματα, vol. 4, (Thessaloniki, 1988): 231–377, retrieved from <http://stephanus.tlg.uci.edu/Iris/Cite?3254:018:161903>, April 20, 2020.

[18]For a detailed discussion of this distinction in St Gregory of Nyssa, see Basil Krivosheine, "Simplicity of the Divine Nature," 76–104. Whether the distinction as understood by St Gregory of Nyssa and other Cappadocian Fathers is fully identical with the Palamite distinction is a matter of some controversy: cf. Alexis Torrance, "Precedents for Palamas' Essence-Energies Theology in the Cappadocian Fathers," *Vigiliae Christianae* 63 (2009): 47–70.

Bibliography

A Monk of the Eastern Church (Lev Gillet). *The Year of the Grace of the Lord: A Scriptural and Liturgical Commentary on the Calendar of the Orthodox Church.* Translated by Deborah Cowan. Crestwood, NY: St Vladimir's Seminary Press, 1980.

Acorn, Annalise. *Compulsory Compassion: A Critique of Restorative Justice.* Vancouver, BC: University of British Columbia, 2005.

Allan, K. "Contextual Determinants on the Meaning of the N Word." *SpringerPlus* 5, 1141 (2016). <https://doi.org/10.1186/s40064-016-2813-1>.

Altman, Andrew. "Discrimination." *The Stanford Encyclopedia of Philosophy* (Winter 2016 Edition). Edited by Edward N. Zalta. <https://plato.stanford.edu/archives/win2016/entries/discrimination>.

Anargyroi, Agioi. "Synaxis of the Unmercenary Saints." *Full of Grace and Truth Blog.* Entry posted October 14, 2008. <http://full-of-grace-and-truth.blogspot.com/2008/10/synaxis-of-holy-unmercenaries.html>.

Argyle, A. W. "The Influence of the Testaments of the Twelve Patriarchs upon the New Testament." *Expository Times* 63.8 (May 1952): 256–58.

Aristotle. *The Rhetoric of Aristotle.* Translated by Richard C. Lebb. Cambridge: The University Press, 1909.

"The Apocalypse of Peter [*Apocalypsis Petri*]." In *The Apocryphal New Testament.* Translated by M. R. James, 505–24. Oxford: Clarendon Press, 1924.

Athanasius. *Arian History [Historia Arianorum ad Monachos].* Translated by M. Atkinson and Archibald Robertson. NPNF[2] 4:270–302.

———. *Contra Gentes.* Translated by Archibald Robertson. NPNF[2] 4:4–30.

Austin, Wendy. "Against Compassion: Understanding Institutional Perfidy as Evil." In *When Evil Met Magic: A Versatile Journey.* Interdisciplinary.net, 2013. <https://www.researchgate.net/publication/316613210_Re_Making_the_Procrustean_Bed_Standardization_and_Customization_as_Competing_Logics_in_Healthcare/fulltext/5909b36b0f7e9b1d08160fb7/316613210_Re_Making_the_Procrustean_Bed_Standardization_and_Customization_as_Competing_Logics_in_Healthcare.pdf?origin=publication_detail>.

Bacon, Ingrid, Elizabeth McKay, Frances Reynolds, and Anne McIntyre. "The Lived Experience of Codependency: An Interpretative Phenomenological Analysis." *International Journal of Mental Health Addiction* (2018): 1–18. <https://doi.org/10.1007/s11469-018-9983-8>.

Baker, Andy. "Race, Paternalism, and Foreign Aid: Evidence from U.S. Public Opinion." *American Political Science Review* 109.1 (2015): 93–109.

Bartholomew, Ecumenical Patriarch. *Speaking the Truth in Love.* New York: Fordham University Press, 2010.

Baynes, Leslie. *The Heavenly Book Motif in the Judeo-Christian Apocalypses 200 BCE–200 CE.* Leiden: Brill, 2012.

Ben-Zeév, Aaron. *The Subtlety of Emotions.* Cambridge, MA: MIT Press, 2000.

Berger, Peter L. and Thomas Luckmann. *The Social Construction of Reality: A Treatise in the Sociology of Knowledge.* New York: Penguin Books, 1991.

Bickerman, Elias. "The Date of the Testaments of the Twelve Patriarchs." *Journal of Biblical Literature* 69.3 (Sept. 1950): 245–260.

Bick, Ezra. *In His Mercy: Understanding the Thirteen Midot.* Jerusalem: Koren Publishers, 2011.

Bloom, Paul. "Against Empathy." *Boston Review: A Political and Literary Forum.* September 10, 2014. <http://bostonreview.net/forum/paul-bloom-against-empathy>.

_____. *Against Empathy: The Case for Rational Compassion.* New York: Harper Collins, 2016.

Blowers, Paul M. "2009 NAPS Presidential Address: Pity, Empathy, and the Tragic Spectacle of Human Suffering: Exploring the Emotional Culture of Compassion in Late Ancient Christianity." *Journal of Early Christian Studies* 18.1 (2010): 1–27.

Bobosch, Ted. "The Prodigal Son and Brother." Fr Ted's Blog: Meditations of An Orthodox Priest. Entry posted February 24, 2008. <https://frted.wordpress.com/2008/02/24/the-prodigal-son-brother/>.

Bobrinskoy, Boris. *The Compassion of the Father.* Translated by Anthony Gythiel with an introduction by Maxime Egger. Crestwood, NY: St Vladimir's Seminary Press, 2003.

Bowers, Josh. "The Case for Compassionate Policing." *UVA Magazine.* Entry posted 2015. <http://uvamagazine.org/articles/the_case_for_compassionate_policing>.

Berdyaev, Nicholas. "The Truth of Orthodoxy." Originally printed in *Vestnik Russkogo Zapadno-Evropeiskogo Ekzarkhata* 11 (July 1952): 4–10; translated by Alvian Smirensky. *The Wheel* 8 (2017): 47–8, <https://static1.squarespace.com/static/54d0df1ee4b036ef1e44b144/t/58efc8a6db29d67bb267dc42/1492109479567/Berdyaev.pdf>.

Brenton, Lancelot C. L. *The Septuagint LXX: Greek and English.* London: Samuel Bagster & Sons, Ltd., 1851. <https://www.ccel.org/bible/brenton/>.

Bria, Ion. "The Liturgy after the Liturgy." *International Review of Missions* 67.265 (1978): 86–90.

_____. *The Liturgy after the Liturgy: Mission and Witness from an Orthodox Perspective.* Geneva: WCC Publications, 1996.

Brown, Peter. *The Ransom of the Soul: Afterlife and Wealth in Early Christianity*. Cambridge, MA: Harvard University Press, 2015.

Bruce, Archibald. "Why Restorative Justice Is Not Compulsory Compassion: Annalise Acorn's Labour of Love Lost." *Alberta Law Review* 42.3 (2005): 941–50.

Bucur, Bogdan G. "'The Feet that Eve Heard in Paradise and Was Afraid': Observations on the Christology of Byzantine Hymns." *Philosophy and Theology* 18.1 (2006): 3–26.

————. "Foreordained from All Eternity: The Mystery of the Incarnation According to Some Early Christian and Byzantine Writers." *Dumbarton Oaks Papers* 62 (2008): 199–215.

Buffet, Peter. "The Charitable-Industrial Complex." *New York Times*. Entry posted July 26, 2013. <http://www.nytimes.com/2013/07/27/opinion/the-charitable-industrial-complex.html?_r=0>.

Burdett, Carolyn. "Post Darwin: Social Darwinism, Degeneration, Eugenics." *Discovering Literature: Romantics & Victorians* (The British Library). Entry posted May 15, 2014. <https://www.bl.uk/romantics-and-victorians/articles/post-darwin-social-darwinism-degeneration-eugenics>.

Bush, Michael D. "Police Officers as Peace Officers: A Philosophical and Theoretical Examination of Policing from a Peacemaking Approach." *Journal of Theoretical & Philosophical Criminology* 6.3 (2014): 194–205.

Butler, Joseph. *Fifteen Sermons Preached at Rolls Chapel: to which is added Six Sermons Preached on Publick Occasions*. London: Printed for J. and P. Knapton, 1749.

Campbell, Alan D. "The Monetary System, Taxation, and Publicans in the Time of Christ." *The Accounting Historians Journal* 13.2 (Fall 1986): 131–35.

Campbell, James. "A Prayer for Peace and Repentance." *In Communion*. Entry posted November 24, 2010. <https://incommunion.org/2010/11/24/a-prayer-for-peace-and-repentance/>.

Carnavos, Constantine. "Knowing God through Icons and Hymnody." *Greek Orthodox Theological Review* 23.3–4 (1978): 282–98.

Charles, Robert Henry. *The Greek Versions of the Testaments of the Twelve Patriarchs*. London: Adam and Charles Black, 1908.

Choniates, Michael. *Oration* 22. In Μιχαὴλ Ἀκομινάτου τοῦ χωνιάτου τὰ σωζόμενα [Michaēl Akominatou tou chōniatou ta sōzomena]. Translated and edited by S. P. Lampros, 2:358–68. Athens: 1879–1880.

Chryssavgis, John. "The Spiritual Way." In *The Cambridge Companion to Orthodox Christian Theology*. Edited by Mary Cunningham and Elizabeth Theokritoff. 150–63. Cambridge: Cambridge University Press, 2008.

Clement of Alexandria. *Who Is the Rich Man That Shall Be Saved? [Liber quis dives salvetur]*. Translated by William Wilson (ANF 2:589–605).

Cocker, Fiona, and Nerida Joss. "Compassion Fatigue among Healthcare, Emergency and Community Service Workers: A Systematic Review." *International Journal of Environmental Research and Public Health* 13.6 (2016): 618. <https://doi.org/10.3390/ijerph13060618>.

Collins, Mary, Kate Cooney, and Sarah Garlington. "Compassion in Contemporary Social Policy: Applications of Virtue Theory." *Journal of Social Policy* 41.2 (2012): 251–69.

"Confession: From an Athonite Pamphlet by An Athonite." St Vladimir's Parish, Alberta, Canada. Entry posted June 21, 2011. <https://stvladimirs.ca/confession-from-an-athonite-pamphlet-by-an-athonite/>.

Conomos, Dimitri. "Early Christian and Byzantine Music: History and Performance." Archdiocesan School of Byzantine Music. Entry posted November 15, 2012. <http://www.asbm.goarch.org/articles/early-christian-and-byzantine-music-history-and-performance/>.

_____. "Orthodox Byzantine Music." Archdiocesan School of Byzantine Music. Entry posted November 15, 2012. <http://www.asbm.goarch.org/articles/orthodox-byzantine-music/>.

Cook, James. "'Hear and Shudder!' John Chrysostom's Therapy of the Soul." In *Revisioning John Chrysostom: New Approaches, New Perspectives*. Edited by Chris L. de Wet and Wendy Mayer, 247–75. Leiden: Brill: 2019.

Constantelos, Demetrios J. *Byzantine Philanthropy and Social Welfare*. New Brunswick, NJ: Rutgers University Press, 1968.

_____. "Origins of Christian Orthodox Diakonia: Christian Orthodox Philanthropy in Church History." *Greek Orthodox Theological Review* 52.1–4 (2007): 1–36.

_____. *Poverty, Society and Philanthropy in the Late Mediaeval Greek World*. New Rochelle, NY: A. D. Caratzas, 1992.

Corrigan, Patrick W., ed. *The Stigma of Disease and Disability: Understanding Causes and Overcoming Injustices*. Washington: American Psychological Association, 2014.

Crenshaw, Kimberlé. "Demarginalizing the Intersection of Race and Sex: A Black Feminist Critique of Antidiscrimination Doctrine, Feminist Theory and Antiracist Politics." *The University of Chicago Legal Forum* 140 (1989): 139–67.

Crisp, Roger. "Compassion and Beyond." *Ethical Theory and Moral Practice* 11.3 (2008): 233–46.

Culbertson, Howard. "Poverty: Bible Verses on Caring for the Poor." Southern Nazarene University. <https://home.snu.edu/~hculbert/poor.htm>.

Cyril of Alexandria, *Commentary upon the Gospel according to S. Luke*. Translated by R. Payne Smith. Oxford: Oxford University Press, 1859.

_____. *Commentary on the Twelve Prophets*. Translated by Robert C. Hill. Washington: The Catholic University of America Press, 2008.

Cyril of Jerusalem. *Catechetical Lectures*. Translated by Edwin H. Gifford. NPNF²
7:1–157.

Day, Dorothy. *The Long Loneliness: The Autobiography of the Legendary Catholic Social
Activist*. New York: Harper Collins, 1958.

Dawes, Elizabeth and Norman H. Baynes, trans. *Three Byzantine Saints: Contemporary
Biographies of St Daniel the Stylite, St Theodore of Sykeon, and St John the Almsgiver*.
Crestwood, NY: St Vladimir's Seminary Press, 1996.

de Villiers, Henri. "The Sub Tuum Praesidium." *New Liturgical Movement*. Entry posted
February 3, 2011. <http://www.newliturgicalmovement.org/2011/02/sub-tuum-
praesidium.html#.XJP20i2ZPBI>.

De Vinne, Michael. "The Advocacy of Empty Bellies: Episcopal Representation of the
Poor in the Late Roman Empire." Ph.D. diss., Stanford University, 1995.

Divine Liturgy of St James the Holy Apostle and Brother of the Lord. Translated by William
Macdonald. ANF 7:527–551.

Drobner, H. R., and A. Viciano, eds. *Gregory of Nyssa: Homilies on the Beatitudes: An
English Version with Commentary and Supporting Studies, Proceedings of the Eighth
International Colloquium on Gregory of Nyssa (Paderborn, 14–18 Sept. 1998)*. Boston:
Brill Publishers, 2000.

Drillock, David. "Liturgical Song in the Worship of the Church." *St Vladimir's Theological Quarterly* 41.2–3 (1997): 183–218.

Eastern Orthodox Church. *The Great Octoechos*. 4 vols. West Roxbury, MA: Sophia Press,
2013.

Eisenberg, Ronald. "Thirteen Attributes of Mercy." Pages 180–182 in *Jewish Traditions:
JPS Guide*. Philadelphia: Jewish Publication Society, 2004. <https://www.myjewish-
learning.com/article/the-13-attributes-of-mercy/>.

El Shaddai Ministries. "The 13 Attributes of God-Exodus." <http://elshaddaiministries.
us/handouts/13_Attributes.pdf>.

Ellicott, Charles John. *A Bible Commentary for English Readers*. 8 vols. New York: Cassell
and Company Limited, 1905–6.

Ephrem Syrus, *Sermones paraenetici ad monachos Aegypti*, 26. Vol. 3 of Οσίου Εφραίμ τοῦ
Σύρου ἔργα. Edited by K. G. Phrantzoles, 36–294. Thessaloniki: To Perivoli tis Panagias, 1990.

Eusebius Pamphilius. *Church History*. Translated by Arthur C. McGiffert. NPNF²
1:81–387.

_____. *Eusebii Caesariensis Eclogae Propheticae*. Edited by T. Gaisford. Oxford: Typo-
grapheo Academico, 1842.

_____. *The Life of Constantine*. Translated by Ernest C. Richardson. NPNF²
1:481–559.

_____. *The Proof of the Gospel, being the Demonstratio evangelica of Eusebius of Caesarea.* Translated and edited by W. J. Ferrar. New York: Macmillan, 1920; reprint Eugene, OR: Wipf and Stock Publishers, 2001.

Evagrius of Pontus. *Expositio in Proverbia Salomonis.* Edited by C. Tischendorf, 76–122. *Notitia editionis codicis bibliorum Sinaitici.* Leipzig: F. A. Brockhaus, 1860.

_____. *Kephalaia gnostika: A New Translation of the Unreformed Text from the Syriac.* Translated with an introduction and commentary by Ilaria L. E. Ramelli. Atlanta: Society of Biblical Literature Press, 2015.

Evdokimov, Paul. *The Art of the Icon: A Theology of Beauty.* Translated by Steven Bigham. Redondo Beach, CA: Oakwood Publications, 1990.

Fanon, Franz. *Black Skin, White Masks.* Translated by Charles Lamm Markmann. London: Archway Press, 1986.

Farber, Zev. "Punishing Children for the Sins of their Parents." *The Torah.com: A Historical and Contextual Approach.* <http://thetorah.com/punishing-children-for-the-sins-of-their-parents/>.

Farley, Lawrence. *A Daily Calendar of Saints: A Synaxarion for Today's North American Church.* Chesterton, IN: Ancient Faith Publishing, 2018.

_____. "It Is Time for the Lord to Act: The Significance of Assembling." Orthodox Church in America. <https://oca.org/reflections/fr.-lawrence-farley/it-is-time-for-the-lord-to-act-the-significance-of-assembling>.

Feodorovna, Elizabeth (St Elizabeth the New Martyr). *The Martha-Mary Convent: and Rule of St Elizabeth the New Martyr.* Translated by St Elizabeth Convent. Jordanville, NY: The Printshop of St Job of Pochaev, 2005.

Ferguson, Everett. "Congregational Singing in the Early Church." *Acta Patristica et Byzantina* 15.1 (2004): 144–59.

Ferraro, Josephine. "Psychotherapy Blog: Exploring the Secondary Gains of Codependency." Psychotherapist-NYC Blog. Entry posted February 4, 2010. <http://psychotherapist-nyc.blogspot.com/2010/02/psychotherapy-exploring-secondary-gains.html>.

Florovsky, Georges. *The Byzantine Ascetic and Spiritual Fathers.* Translated by Raymond Miller. Belmont, MA: Notable & Academic Books, 1987.

_____. "Revelation, Philosophy and Theology." In *Creation and Redemption.* Translated by Richard Haugh, 21–42. Belmont, MA: Nordland Publishing Co., 1976.

_____. "St John Chrysostom: The Prophet of Charity." *St Vladimir's Seminary Quarterly* 4.3–4 (1955): 37–42.

Forest, Jim. *Praying with Icons.* Maryknoll, NY: Orbis Books, 2008.

Fowler, Megan. "The Human Factor in Prison Design: Contrasting Prison Architecture in the United States and Scandinavia." *103rd ACSA Annual Meeting Proceedings, The*

Expanding Periphery and the Migrating Center (2015): 373–380. <http://apps.acsa-arch.org/resources/proceedings/indexsearchaspx?txtKeyword1=126&ddField1=4>.

Galtung, Johan. "The Basic Needs Approach." In *Human Needs: A Contribution to the Current Debate*. Edited by Katrin Lederer, 55–125. Cambridge, MA: Oelgeschlager, Gunn, and Hain, Inc., 1980.

Gavrilyuk, Paul L. *The Suffering of the Impassible God*. New York: Oxford University Press, 2006.

Greek Orthodox Archdiocese of America. "The Divine Liturgy of St John Chrysostom." The Greek Orthodox Archdiocese of America. <https://www.goarch.org/-/the-divine-liturgy-of-saint-john-chrysostom>.

Greek Orthodox Metropolis of Denver. "Synaxis of the Forerunner, January 7." The Greek Orthodox Metropolis of Denver. <https://docplayer.gr/58132054-The-synaxis-of-the-honorable-glorious-prophet-forerunner-and-baptist-john-e-synaxis-tou-tiuioy-endoxoy-profitoy-prodrouoy-kai-vaptistou-ioannoy.html>.

Gregory of Nazianzus [Gregory the Theologian]. *Select Orations*. Translated by Martha Vinson. The Fathers of the Church, vol. 107. Washington: Catholic University of America Press: 2003.

Gregory of Nyssa. *Against Eunomius*. Translated by William Moore and Henry A. Wilson. NPNF² 5:33–248.

_____. *The Life of Moses*. Translated by Abraham Malherbe and Everett Ferguson. Mahwah, NJ: Paulist Press, 1978.

Gregory Palamas. *Contra Nicephorum Gregoram*. In Γρηγορίου τοῦ Παλαμᾶ συγγράμματα [Grēgoriou tou Palama syngrammata]. Edited by P. K. Chrestou. 4:231–377. Thessaloniki: Ekdotikos Oikos Kyromanos, 1988.

_____. *Défense des Saints Hésychastes*. Translated with an introduction, critical edition, and notes by Jean Meyendorff, 2nd edition. Leuven: Spicilegium Sacrum Lovaniense, 1973.

_____. *Gregory Palamas: The Triads*. Translated by Nicholas Gendle. Mahwah, NJ: Paulist Press, 1982.

_____. *Saint Gregory Palamas: The Homilies*. Translated by Christopher Veniamin. South Canaan, PA: Mount Thabor Publishing, 2009.

_____. *Topics of Natural and Theological Science and on the Moral and Ascetic Life: One Hundred and Fifty Texts*. Philokalia 4:346–417.

Grindenko, Anatoly. *Meditation: Chants for Great Lent*. Alliance. CD. 1999.

Gyatso, Tenzin. "Compassion and the Individual." The Office of His Holiness the Dalai Lama. <http://www.dalailama.com/messages/compassion>.

Haddad, Mimi. "Evidence for and Significance of Feminine God-Language from the Church Fathers to the Modern Era." *Priscilla Papers* 18.3 (2004): 3–11.

Hammer, Reuven, trans. *Sifre: A Tannaitic Commentary on the Book of Deuteronomy*. New Haven: Yale University Press, 1986.

Harakas, Stanley. "No Just War in the Fathers." *In Communion*. Entry posted August 2, 2005. <https://incommunion.org/2005/08/02/no-just-war-in-the-fathers/>.

Harris, Abram L. "John Stuart Mill: Servant of the East India Company." *The Canadian Journal of Economics and Political Science / Revue canadienne d'Economique et de Science politique* 30.2 (1964): 191–93. <doi:10.2307/139555. 185–202>.

Harrison, Nonna Verna. *God's Many Splendored Image: Theological Anthropology for Christian Formation*. Grand Rapids, MI: Baker Academic Publishing, 2010.

Heatherton, Todd, R. Kleck, et al. *The Social Psychology of Stigma*. New York: Guilford Press, 2000.

Hengel, Martin. *Crucifixion in the Ancient World and the Folly of the Message of the Cross*. Philadelphia: Fortress Press, 1977.

Hieromonk Makarios of Simonos Petra. *The Synaxarion: The Lives of Saints of the Orthodox Church*. Translated by Christopher Hookway. 7 vols. Ormylia, Greece: Holy Convent of the Annunciation of Our Lady, 1998.

Hierotheos of Nafpaktos. *Feasts of the Lord: An Introduction to the Twelve Feasts and Orthodox Christology*. Translated by Esther Williams. Levadia, Greece: Birth of the Theotokos Monastery, 2003.

Hobbes, Thomas. *Human Nature or the Fundamental Elements of Policy*. London: Printed for Matthew Gilliflower, Henry Rogers, and Tho. Fox, 1684.

Hollander, H. W., and M. de Jong. *The Testaments of the Twelve Patriarchs: A Commentary*. Leiden: Brill, 1985.

Holman, Susan. "The Entitled Poor: Human Rights Language in the Cappadocians." *Pro Ecclesia* 9.4 (2000): 476–89.

————. *God Knows There's Need: Christian Responses to Poverty*. Oxford: Oxford University Press, 2009.

————. *The Hungry are Dying*. Oxford: Oxford University Press, 2003.

Holy Transfiguration Monastery. *The Menaion*. 12 vols. Boston: Holy Transfiguration Monastery, 2005.

————. *The Pentecostarion*. 2nd edition. Boston: Holy Transfiguration Monastery, 2014.

Holy Trinity Monastery. *The Unabbreviated Horologion, or the Book of the Hours*. 2nd ed. Jordanville, NY: Printshop of St Job of Pochaev, 1997.

Hopko, Thomas. *The Orthodox Faith*, 4 vols. Yonkers, NY: St Vladimir's Seminary Press, 2016.

————. "On Stewardship and Philanthropy: Forty Sentences." In *Good and Faithful Servant: Stewardship in the Orthodox Church*. Edited by Anthony Scott, 133–53. Crestwood, NY: St Vladimir's Seminary Press, 2003.

Houston, Walter. "Exodus." In *The Oxford Bible Commentary*. Edited by John Barton and John Muddiman, 67–91. Oxford: Oxford University Press, 2001.

Hronas, Georgia, ed. and trans. *The Holy Unmercenary Doctors: The Saints Anargyroi: Physicians and Healers of the Orthodox Church, Translated from the Greek Great Synaxaristes of the Orthodox Church*. Minneapolis: Light and Life Publishing Company, 1999.

Hussey, M. Edmund. "The Persons-Energy Structure in the Theology of St Gregory Palamas." *St Vladimir's Theological Quarterly* 18.1 (1974): 22–43.

Isaac the Syrian/Isaac of Nineveh. *The Ascetical Homilies of St Isaac the Syrian [Orationes ascetici]*. Translated by Holy Transfiguration Monastery. Boston: Holy Transfiguration Monastery, 1984.

———. *Mystic Treatises by Isaac of Nineveh*. Translated by A. J. Wensinck. Amsterdam: De Akademie, 1923.

Jerome. *Commentary on Ezekiel*. Translated by W. H. Fremantle (NPNF² 6:500). Volume includes only prefaces to this commentary.

John Chrysostom. *Eight Sermons on the Book of Genesis*. Translated by Robert C. Hill. Boston: Holy Cross Orthodox Press, 2004.

———. *Homilies on 1 Corinthians*. NPNF¹ 12:1–269.

———. *Homilies on 2 Corinthians*. NPNF¹ 12:271–420.

———. *Homilies on Hebrews*. NPNF¹ 14:333–522.

———. *Homilies on John*. NPNF¹ 14:1–332.

———. *Homilies on Matthew*. NPNF¹ 10:1–534.

———. *Homilies on Philippians*. NPNF¹ 13:184–257.

———. *Homilies on 1 Thessalonians*. NPNF¹ 13:323–375.

———. *Homilies on 1 Timothy*. NPNF¹ 13:408–473.

John of Damascus. *On the Holy and Glorious Dormition and Transformation of our Lady Mary, Mother of God and Ever-Virgin*. In Brian Daley, trans. *On the Dormition of Mary: Early Patristic Homilies*. PPS 18. Crestwood, NY: St Vladimir's Seminary Press, 1998.

———. *On the Orthodox Faith: A New Translation of* An Exact Exposition of the Orthodox Faith. Introduction, Translation, and Notes by Norman Russell. PPS 62. Yonkers, NY: St Vladimir's Seminary Press, 2022.

———. *The Virtues and the Vices*. Philokalia 2:334–341.

Johnson, Robert. "Compassion in Command." Hendon Media Group. <http://www.hendonpub.com/resources/article_archive/results/details?id=2079>.

Johnson, Samuel. *A Dictionary of the English Language*, 3rd ed. Dublin: W. G. Jones, 1768.

Jones, Edward, Amerigo Farina, et al. *Social Stigma: The Psychology of Marked Relationships*. San Francisco: W. H. Freeman and Co., 1984.

Jones, John D. "Assessing Human Needs." *Philosophy and Theology* 5.1 (Fall 1990): 55–64.

———. "The Church as Neighbor: Corporately and Compassionately Engaged." *In Communion*. Entry posted April 26, 2013. <http://incommunion.org/2013/04/26/the-church-as-neighbor/>.

———. "Confronting Poverty and Stigmatization: An Eastern Orthodox Perspective." *Philosophy and Theology* 18.1 (2007): 169-94.

———. "How Basic Are Basic Needs?" *Journal for Peace and Justice Studies* 8.1 (1997): 37–56.

———. "Opening the Doors of Compassion: Cultivating a Merciful Heart." *In Communion* 64 (2012): 4–15.

———. *Poverty and the Human Condition*. New York: Edwin Mellen Press, 1900.

Karmiris, John. "The Universality of Salvation in Christ" (in Greek). *Theologia* 52.1 (1981): 14–45.

Kashtan, Miki. "Bullying through a Compassionate Lens." *Psychology Today*, May 18, 2012. <https://www.psychologytoday.com/us/blog/acquired-spontaneity/201205/bullying-through-compassionate-lens>.

Knorre, Boris K. "Icon of the Last Judgment: A Detailed Analysis." Museum of Russian Icons. <http://www.museumofrussianicons.org/wp-content/uploads/2016/09/KnorreLastJudgmentFinal.pdf>.

Kornfield, Jack. "Vulnerability and the Tender Heart" <https://jackkornfield.com/vulnerability-and-the-tender-heart>.

Kraut, Richard. "Altruism." *The Stanford Encyclopedia of Philosophy* (Fall 2020 edition), ed. Edward N. Zalta. <https://plato.stanford.edu/archives/fall2020/entries/altruism/>.

Krivosheine, Basil. "The Ascetic and Theological Teaching of Gregory Palamas." *Eastern Churches Quarterly* 3 (1938): 26–33, 71–84, 138–56, 193–214.

———. "Simplicity of the Divine Nature and the Distinctions in God, according to St Gregory of Nyssa." *St Vladimir's Theological Quarterly* 21. 2 (1977): 76–104.

Krstić, Danilo. *On Divine Philanthropia, from Plato to John Chrysostom*. Los Angeles: Sebastian Press, 2012.

Kutateladze, Besiki, Vanessa Lynn, and Edward Liang. "Do Race and Ethnicity Matter in Prosecution? A Review of Empirical Studies." New York: Vera Institute of Justice, 2012. <https://static.prisonpolicy.org/scans/vera/race-and-ethnicity-in-prosecution-first-edition.pdf>.

Labutta, Emily. "The Prisoner as One of Us: Norwegian Wisdom for American Penal Practice." *Emory International Law Review* 31 (2017): 329–59

Lamm, Claus, and Jasminka Majdandžić. "The Role of Shared Neural Activations, Mirror Neurons, and Morality in Empathy—A Critical Comment." *Neuroscience Research* 90 (2015): 15–24.

LeMasters, Phillip. "Orthodox Perspectives on Peace, War and Violence." *Ecumenical Review* 63.1 (2011): 54–61. <https://doi.org/10.1111/j.1758-6623.2010.00093.x>.

_____. "Philanthropia in Liturgy and Life: The Anaphora of Basil the Great and Eastern Orthodox Social Ethics." *St Vladimir's Theological Quarterly* 59.2 (2015): 187–211.

Liddell, Henry George, and Robert Scott. *A Greek-English Lexicon*. Revised and augmented by Sir Henry Stuart Jones and Roderick McKenzie. Oxford: Oxford University Press, 1996.

Littleton, Lynna Y., and Joan Engebretson. *Maternal, Neonatal, and Women's Health Nursing*. New York: Delmar Cengage Learning, 2002.

Longman III, Temper, and David Garland, eds. *The Expositor's Bible Commentary*. Grand Rapids, MI: Zondervan, 2009.

Lust, Johan, Erik Eynikel, and Katrin Hauspie. *A Greek-English Lexicon of the Septuagint*. Stuttgart: Deutsche Bibelgesellschart, 2015.

Mackie, J. L. "Morality and the Retributive Emotions." *Criminal Justice Ethics* 1.1 (1982): 3–10.

Mannion, Russell. "Enabling Compassionate Healthcare: Perils, Prospects and Perspectives." *International Journal of Health Policy and Management* 2.3 (2014): 115–17.

Maples, Cheri. "A Buddhist Cop's Approach to Justice." *Lions Roar: Buddhist Wisdom for our Time*. Entry posted July 27, 2017. <https://www.lionsroar.com/a-buddhist-cops-approach-to-justice/>.

Mary, Mother and Kallistos Ware, trans and eds. *The Festal Menaion*. South Canaan, PA: St Tikhon's Seminary Press, 1998.

_____. *The Lenten Triodion*. South Canaan, PA: St Tikhon's Seminary Press, 2002.

_____. *The Lenten Triodion: Supplementary Texts*. South Canaan, PA: St Tikhon's Seminary Press, 2007.

Maximus the Confessor. *On the Cosmic Mystery of Jesus Christ: Selected Writings from St Maximus the Confessor*. Translated by Paul Blowers and Robert Wilken. PPS 25. Crestwood, NY: St Vladimir's Seminary Press, 2003.

_____. *Four Hundred Texts on Love. Philokalia* 2:53–113.

_____. *On the Ecclesiastical Mystagogy [Mystagogia]* 24, Translated by Jonathan A. Armstrong. PPS 59. Yonkers, NY: St Vladimir's Seminary Press, 2019.

_____. *Various Texts on Theology, the Divine Economy, and Virtue and Vice. Philokalia* 2:164–184.

McGrath, Michael, "Codependency and Pathological Altruism." In *Pathological Altruism*. Edited by Barbara Oaklet, Ariel Knafo, et al., 49–69. Oxford: Oxford University Press, 2011.

McVey, Kathleen E. "Ephrem the Syrian's Use of Female Metaphors to Describe the Deity." *Zeitschrift für Antikes Christentum/Journal of Ancient Christianity* 5.2 (2006): 261–88.

Metzger, Bruce. *A Textual Commentary on the Greek New Testament.* 2nd Edition. New York: American Bible Society, 2002.

Meyendorff, John. *Byzantine Theology: Historical Trends and Doctrinal Themes.* New York: Fordham University Press, 1987.

Meyendorff, Paul. "The Sacrament of Hospitality: A Liturgical Understanding of Hospitality and Communion." *St Vladimir's Theological Quarterly* 62.1 (2018): 131–44.

Michopoulos, Tasos. S. "Mimisometha Nomon Theou: Gregory the Theologian's Ontology of Compassion." *Greek Orthodox Theological Review* 39 (1994): 109–21.

Mill, John Stuart. *On Liberty.* Kichener, ON: Batocke Books, 2001.

Miller, Timothy S. *The Birth of the Hospital in the Byzantine Empire.* Baltimore: The Johns Hopkins University Press, 1997.

_____. *The Orphans of Byzantium: Child Welfare in the Christian Empire.* Washington: The Catholic University of America Press, 2003.

Miller, Timothy S. and John W. Nesbitt. *Walking Corpses: Leprosy in Byzantium and the Medieval West.* Ithaca, NY: Cornell University Press, 2014.

Mirguet, Françoise. *An Early History of Compassion: Emotion and Imagination in Hellenistic Judaism.* New York: Cambridge University Press, 2017.

Monroe, Kristen. *Heart of Altruism: Perceptions of a Shared Humanity.* Princeton: Princeton University Press, 1996.

Morelli, George. "Smart Parenting XXIII: Coping with Bullying." Antiochian Orthodox Christian Archdiocese of North America. <http://ww1.antiochian.org/content/smart-parenting-xxiii-coping-bullying>.

National Forum of Greek Orthodox Church Musicians. "Prayers for Church Musicians." National Forum of Greek Orthodox Church Musicians. <http://churchmusic.goarch.org/events/churchmusicsunday/prayers/>.

Neil, Bronwen. "'The Blessed Passion of Holy Love': Maximus the Confessor's Spiritual Psychology." *Australian eJournal of Theology* 2 (2004): 1–8. <http://aejt.com.au/__data/assets/pdf_file/0005/395672/AEJT_2.8_Neil_Blessed_Passion.pdf>.

_____. "Models of Gift Giving in the Preaching of Leo the Great." *Journal of Early Christian Studies* 18.2 (2010): 225–59.

Nikodimos of the Holy Mountain and Makarios of Corinth, comp. *Philokalia tōn hierōn nēptikōn.* 5 vols. Athens: Astir Publishing Co, 1957–63.

_____. *The Philokalia: The Complete Text.* Translated and edited by G. E. H. Palmer, Philip Sherrard, and Kallistos Ware. 4 vols. London: Faber and Faber, 1981–95.

The Octoechos: The Hymns of the Cycle of the Eight Tones for Sundays and Weekdays. 4 vols. Translated by Isaac Lambertsen. Liberty, TN: St John of Kronstadt Press, 1999.

O'Gorman, Kevin D. "Dimensions of Hospitality: Exploring Ancient and Classical Origins." In *Hospitality: A Social Lens*. Edited by Conrad Lashley, Paul Lynch, and Allison Morrison, 17–32. Oxford: Elsevier, 2007.

Oden, Amy. *And You Welcomed Me: A Sourcebook on Hospitality in Early Christianity*. Nashville, TN: Abingdon Press, 2001.

Ozar, David T. "Rights: What They Are and Where They Come From." In *Philosophical Issues in Human Rights: Theories and Applications*. Edited by Patricia Werhane, A. R. Gini, 3–25. New York: Random House, 1986.

Papademetriou, George C. "An Orthodox Christian Understanding of Non-Christian Religions." <https://www.goarch.org/-/an-orthodox-christian-view-of-non-christian-religions#_edn19>.

Patton, Kimberly. "Can Evil Be Redeemed? Unorthodox Tensions in Eastern Orthodox Theology." In *Deliver us From Evil*. Edited by M. David Eckel and Bradely Herling, 186–206. London: Continuum International Publishing Group, 2008.

Pereira, Matthew J., ed. *Philanthropy and Social Compassion in Eastern Orthodox Tradition*. New York: Theotokos Press, 2010.

Peter of Damascus. *Twenty-Four Discourses*. Philokalia 3:211–281.

Philo of Alexandria. *On Virtues: Introduction, Translation, and Commentary*. Translated by Walter Wilson. Leiden: Brill, 2011.

Piper, John. "Prolegomena to Understanding Romans 9:14–15: An Interpretation of Exodus 33:19." *The Journal of the Evangelical Theological Society* 22.3 (1979): 203–216.

Prokurat, Michael, Alexander Golitzin, and Michael D. Peterson. *Historical Dictionary of the Orthodox Church*. Lanham, MD: Scarecrow Press, 1996.

Pseudo-Dionysius the Areopagite. *The Divine Names and Mystical Theology*. Translated with an introductory study by John D. Jones. Milwaukee: Marquette University Press, 1980.

Pseudo-Macarius. *The Fifty Spiritual Homilies and the Great Letter*. Translated by G. Maloney. Mahwah, NJ: Paulist Press, 1992.

Puhalo, Lazar. "The Moral Grief and Co-Suffering Love of Christ in Gethsemane." *Clarion: Journal of Spirituality and Justice*. Entry posted June 18, 2016. <http://www.clarion-journal.com/clarion_journal_of_spirit/2016/06/the-moral-grief-and-co-suffering-love-of-christ-in-gethsemane-lazar-puhalo.html>.

Ramelli, Ilaria. *The Christian Defense of Apokatastasis*. Leiden: Brill, 2019.

Roberts, Alexander and James Donaldson, eds. *The Ante-Nicene Fathers: Translations of the Writings of the Fathers Down to A.D. 325*. 10 vols. Grand Rapids, MI: Eerdmans, 1998. Online edition: Christian Ethereal Classics, <https://www.ccel.org/fathers.html>.

Rosan, Peter J. "The Varieties of Ethical Experience: A Phenomenology of Empathy, Sympathy, and Compassion." *Phänomenologische Forschungen* 1 (2014): 155–89.

Rosen, Rabbi David. "Moses in the Jewish Tradition." www.RabbiDavidRosen.net. <https://www.rabbidavidrosen.net/wp-content/uploads/2016/02/Moses-in-the-Jewish-Tradition.pdf>.

Rosenberg, Avroham Yoseif, ed. *The Complete Jewish Bible with Rashi Commentary.* <https://www.chabad.org/library/bible_cdo/aid/63255/jewish/The-Bible-with-Rashi.htm>.

Salaris, Steven C. "Preaching Christ Crucified at the Feast of the Transfiguration." Antiochian Orthodox Christian Archdiocese. <http://www.antiochian.org/node/21286>.

Sartre, Jean-Paul. *Anti-Semite and Jew.* Translated by George Becker. New York: Schocken Books, 1948.

Schaff, Philip and Henry Wace, eds. *A Select Library of Nicene and Post-Nicene Fathers of the Christian Church.* 28 vols. in 2 series. Grand Rapids, MI: Eerdmans, 1997. Online edition: Christian Ethereal Classics, <https://www.ccel.org/fathers.html>.

Schmemann, Alexander. *The Eucharist.* Crestwood, NY: St Vladimir's Seminary Press, 1987.

Schochet, Dovie. "What Are the 13 Attributes of Mercy?: Understanding the *Yud Gimel Midot Harachamim.*" Chabad-Lubavitch Media Center. <https://www.chabad.org/parshah/article_cdo/aid/3609722/jewish/What-Are-the-13-Attributes-of-Mercy.htm>.

Scholz, Robert. *Übergang zur Vaterschaft: Persönliche Nische, Belastung und protektive Faktoren.* Hamburg: Diplomica Verlag, 2002.

Severianus. *Homilia de lotione pedum 1.* In A. Wenger, "Une homélie inédite de Sévérien de Gabala sur le lavement des pieds." *Revue des Études Byzantines* 25 (1967): 225–29.

Shamah, Rabbi. "Parashat Yitro Part IV: Visiting Iniquity of Fathers upon Sons." *Sephardic Institute,* 2011.

Sherwood, Aaron. *The Word of God Has Not Failed: Paul's Use of the Old Testament in Romans 9.* Bellingham, WA: Lexham Press, 2015.

Sokolov, Dimitrii. *A Manual of the Orthodox Church's Divine Services.* New York: Wynkoop Hallenbeck Crawford, Co., 1899.

Spence, D. M., and Joseph S. Excell, eds. *The Pulpit Commentary.* Peabody, MA: Hendrickson Publishers, 1985.

St Athanasius Academy of Orthodox Theology. *The Orthodox Study Bible: Ancient Christianity Speaks to Today's World.* Nashville, TN: Thomas Nelson, 2008.

St Maxim the Greek Institute. "St Philothei of Athens 1522–1589." Pemptousia. Entry posted November 2, 2011. <http://pemptousia.com/2011/11/st-philothei-angelou-venizelou-athens-1522-1589-printed-pemptousia/>.

St Nicholas Russian Orthodox Church. "Divine Liturgy of St John Chrysostom English, with parts in Slavonic (in Russian letters)." <https://www.orthodox.net/services/sluzebnic-chrysostom-es.pdf>.

St Tikhon's Seminary Press. *The Divine Liturgy According to St John Chrysostom with Appendices*, 3rd ed. South Canaan, PA: St Tikhon's Seminary Press, 1994.

_____. *The Great Book of Needs: Expanded and Supplemented.* 4 vols. South Canaan, PA: St Tikhon's Seminary Press, 1999–2002.

_____. *Service Books of the Orthodox Church*. South Canaan, PA: St Tikhon's Seminary Press, 2010.

Stanford Medicine. "Pity." The Center for Compassion and Altruism Research and Education. <http://ccare.stanford.edu/research/sticher/compassion-definitions/pity/>.

Stăniloae, Dumitru. *Orthodox Spirituality: A Practical Guide for the Faithful and a Definitive Manual for the Scholar*. Translated by Archimandrite Jerome and Otilia Kloos. Waymart, PA: St Tikhon's Seminary Press: 2003.

Steenberg, Matthew C. "Children in Paradise: Adam and Eve as 'Infants' in Irenaeus of Lyons." *Journal of Early Christian Studies* 12.1 (2004): 1–35.

_____. *Of God and Man: Theology as Anthropology from Irenaeus to Athanasius*. New York: T&T Clark, 2009.

_____. "The Church." In *The Cambridge Companion to Orthodox Christian Theology*. Mary B. Cunningham and Elizabeth Theokritoff, eds., 121–35. Cambridge: Cambridge University Press, 2008.

Strong, James. *The Exhaustive Concordance of the Bible*. Peabody, MA: Hendrickson Publishers, 2004.

Stueber, Karsten. "Empathy." *The Stanford Encyclopedia of Philosophy* (Spring 2018 Edition), Edited by Edward N. Zalta. <https://plato.stanford.edu/archives/spr2018/entries/empathy.

Sulpitius (Suplicius) Severus. *Epistle II to Claudia on Virginity*. NPNF[2] 11:58–67.

Symeon the New Theologian. *The First Created Man*. Translated by Seraphim Rose. Platina, CA: St Herman of Alaska Brotherhood, 2001.

Taft, Robert, S.J. "Ecumenical Scholarship and the Catholic-Orthodox Epiclesis Dispute." Donohu Lecture 1996. *Ostkirchliche Studien* 45 (1996): 6–7.

Tawney, Richard Henry. *Religion and the Rise of Capitalism*. New York: New American Library, 1955.

Tertullian. *De Resurrectione Carnis*. Edited and translated by Ernest Evans. London, SPCK: 1960. <http://www.tertullian.org/articles/evans_res/evans_res_03latin.htm> and <http://www.tertullian.org/articles/evans_res/evans_res_04english.htm>.

Thayer, John. *A Greek-English Lexicon of the New Testament: being Grimm's Wilke's Clavis Novi Testamenti*. New York: Harper and Brothers, 1889.

Theodoros the Great Ascetic. *A Century of Spiritual Texts. Philokalia* 2:14–37.

Theokritoff, Elizabeth. "From Sacramental Life to Sacramental Living: Heeding the Message of the Environmental Crisis." *Greek Orthodox Theological Review* 44.1–4 (1999): 505–24.

Theophylact. *The Explanation by Blessed Theophylact of the Holy Gospel According to Luke.* Translated by Christopher Stade. House Springs, MO: Chrysostom Press, 2004.

_____. *The Explanation by Blessed Theophylact of the Holy Gospel According to Matthew.* Translated by Christopher Stade. House Springs, MO: Chrysostom Press, 2006.

Thomas Aquinas. *Summa Theologica.* Translated by Fathers of the English Dominican Province. New York: Benziger Brothers, 1947.

Thomas, John Philip, Angela C. Hero, and Giles Constable, eds. *Byzantine Monastic Foundation Documents.* Washington: Dumbarton Oaks Research Library and Collection, 2000.

Tudor, Steven. *Compassion and Remorse: Acknowledging the Suffering Other.* Leuven: Peeters Publishers, 2011.

TV Tropes. "Disabled Means Helpless." TV Tropes. Entry updated April 7, 2019. <https://tvtropes.org/pmwiki/pmwiki.php/Main/DisabledMeansHelpless>.

Van der Pool, Charles, ed.. *The Apostolic Bible Polyglot, Alpha Version, 2nd Edition.* Newport, OR: The Apostolic Press, 2013.

Von Arnim, Elizbeth, *The Princess Priscilla's Fortnight.* New York: Charles Scribner's Sons, 1914.

Ware, Kallistos. "How Do We Enter the Heart and What Do We Find When We Enter." In *Merton & Hesychasm: the Prayer of the Heart and the Eastern Church.* Fons Vitae Thomas Merton Series. Edited by Gray Henry, Bernadette Dieker, and Jonathan Montaldo, 3–16. Louisville, Kentucky. Fons Vitae, 2003.

_____. "The Mystery of the Human Person." *Sobornost incorporating Eastern Churches Review* 3.1 (1981): 62–69.

_____. "The Passions: Enemy or Friend?" *In Communion* 17 (Fall 1999). <https://incommunion.org/2004/10/18/the-passions-enemy-or-friend/>.

Weaver, David. "From Paul to Augustine: Romans 5.12 in Early Christian Exegesis." *St Vladimir's Theological Quarterly* 27.3 (1983): 187–206.

_____. "The Exegesis of Romans 5.12 among the Greek Fathers and Its Implication for the Doctrine of Original Sin: The 5th–12th Centuries, Pt 2." *St Vladimir's Theological Quarterly* 29.2 (1985): 133–59.

_____. "The Exegesis of Romans 5.12 among the Greek Fathers and Its Implication for the Doctrine of Original Sin: The 5th–12th Centuries, Pt 3." *St Vladimir's Theological Quarterly* 29.3 (1985): 231–57.

Webster, Alexander. "Justifiable War as a 'Lesser Good' in Eastern Orthodox Moral Tradition." *St Vladimir's Theological Quarterly* 47.1 (2003): 3–57.

Welch, John W. "The Good Samaritan: A Type and Shadow of the Plan of Salvation." *BYU Studies* 38.2 (1999): 51–115.

Wenzel, Michael, Tyler G. Okimoto, et al. "Retributive and Restorative Justice." *Law and Human Behavior* 32 (2008): 375–89.

Worrell, Tracy. *Disability in the Media, Examining Stigma and Identity*. Lanham, MD: Lexington Books, 2018.

Zacharias, Archimandrite. *The Hidden Man of the Heart: The Cultivation of the Heart in Orthodox Christian Anthropology*. Edited by Christopher Veniamin. Waymart, PA: Mount Thabor Publishing, 2008.

Zizioulas, John. *Being as Communion: Studies in Personhood and the Church*. Crestwood, NY: St Vladimir's Seminary Press, 2000.

Zweig, Stefan. *Beware of Pity*. Translated by Phyllis Blewitt and Trevor Blewitt. New York: The New York Review of Books, 2006.

_____. *La pitié dangereuse*. Translated by Alzir Hella. Paris: B. Garasset, 1939.

Scripture Index

OLD TESTAMENT

NEW TESTAMENT

Author Index

Subject Index[1]

[1]Page listings include material in text and footnotes. Terms include cognates (e.g., "compassion" includes "compassionate"). The texts of the hymns have not been systematically indexed.